Consciousness

Consciousness

A User's Guide

Adam Zeman

Yale University Press
New Haven and London

The author and publishers gratefully acknowledge A. P. Watt Ltd on behalf of Michael B. Yeats for permission to reprint lines from W. B. Yeats' 'The Circus Animals' Desertion'; Faber and Faber for permission to reprint lines from T. S. Eliot's 'East Coker', Sylvia Plath's 'The Manor Garden', Ted Hughes' 'Creation' and W. H. Auden's 'Shorts', 'Heavy Date' and 'The Sea and the Mirror'; the Society of Authors as the Literary Representative of the Estate of A. E. Housman for permission to reprint lines from Housman's 'A Shropshire Lad'; and Stainer & Bell Ltd, London, England for permission to reprint a line from Sydney Carter's 'Lord of the Dance'.

For information about this and other Yale University Press publications, please contact:
U.S. Office: sales.press@yale.edu   yalebooks.com
Europe Office: sales@yaleup.co.uk   www.yalebooks.co.uk

Set in FFScala by Northern Phototypesetting Co. Ltd, Bolton, Lancs.
Printed in the United States of America.

The Library of Congress has catalogued the hardcover edition as follows:

Zeman, Adam
    Consciousness : a user's guide / Adam Zeman.
        p. cm.
Includes bibliographical references and index.
    ISBN 0–300–09280–6
    1. Consciousness.   I. Title.
    QP411 .Z46 20002
    153—dc21   2002007032

A catalogue record for this book is available from the British Library.

ISBN 0–300–10497–9 (pbk.)

10 9 8 7 6 5 4 3 2

For Natalya, Flora and Ben:
three indisputable users of consciousness

The great regions of the mind correspond to the great regions of the brain.
Paul Broca, 1861

'You have always been a fervent proponent of the theory that when a man's head is cut off his life stops, he turns to dust and he ceases to exist. I am glad to be able to tell you in front of all my guests – despite the fact that their presence here is proof to the contrary – that your theory is intelligent and sound.'
Satan addressing one of his guests, in *The Master and Margarita*,
Mikhail Bulgakov

What is mind?
It doesn't matter.
What is matter?
Never mind.
Anon.

Contents

A note to the reader

I have written this book for anyone who is intrigued by experience, the brain, or the relationship between them. These interests can spring up in many ways: I have tried to make the book accessible to you, whatever your background. For the general reader who is curious to find out what science has to say about experience and the brain, I have taken pains to explain scientific terms and ideas as they crop up. Chapter 2, in particular, is a brief primer in neuroscience, which the expert might want to skip. For the student or practitioner of medicine, psychology or philosophy, who wants to know more about unfamiliar aspects of the science or philosophy of consciousness, I have attempted to give a sufficiently rich account of the subject to make the book worthwhile for you. There is a Glossary to remind readers, where necessary, of the meanings of unfamiliar words, unashamedly including ones which are very familiar to scientists. The Notes provide detailed references for factual claims, and occasionally amplify points where further discussion in the main text seemed out of place. The final section of each chapter recaps its main conclusions. I have included these summaries because I like to be given plenty of signposts when I read. A rapid raider who looked only at these sections would come away knowing what the book is about (and whether she wanted to read more), but would unfortunately miss all the fun. If you want a succinct description of the book's main ideas, turn to the closing section of the Introduction, or to the Epilogue. I have dealt with the tricky problem of gender by using the female and male personal pronouns more or less randomly.

Preface

Chains of smoking volcanoes mark out the fault lines in the earth's crust. The mounting eruption of interest in consciousness flows from a fault line in human thought. This rift runs, roughly speaking, between the sciences and the arts, the study of the body and the study of the mind. Clearly, what happens in our brains is connected with what passes through our minds, but how exactly are the two related? Over the past hundred years or so, the developing science of the brain has revealed this rift with increasing clarity – and hinted at some ways in which we might try to bridge it. The 'problem of consciousness', the 'mind–body' problem in modern disguise, lies in the fault line. This book aims to map out its depths.

I have been fascinated by this problem for over twenty years. I seem to keep colliding with it. At school I escaped the British tendency to keep hard science and literature in separate sealed compartments, but reading Shakespeare in the morning and Newton in the afternoon, so to speak, raises some questions in the teenage mind: in particular, how does the world described by mechanics relate to the realm of thought and experience to which Shakespeare gave 'a local habitation and a name'? I have never escaped from this teenage preoccupation. My puzzlement steered me towards philosophy, psychology and eventually medicine, but the puzzle only deepened. Working as a neurologist, seeing patients with a host of disorders of experience and behaviour from tingly feet to failing intellects, and trying to locate their source within the nervous system, I collide with the very same problem every day: how do events in our brains give rise to those in our minds? How do 100,000 million nerve cells give rise to consciousness? In brief, *why* are we conscious?

I wrote this book partly to satisfy my own curiosity about consciousness, partly because I felt a need for an introduction to the subject which would do justice both to the science and to the philosophy of consciousness, to 'mechanics' and to experience. Much of the recent writing about consciousness, some of it brilliant, has been polemical and partial: I have done my best to strike an equitable balance between the warring factions, to chart out the territory and draw a faithful map.

Several models have helped to guide me as I wrote, books with quite different subjects which share a wonderful compactness and lucidity. I shall be delighted if I have achieved a fraction of their clarity. They include Richard Gregory's *Eye and Brain*, Ernst Gombrich's *Art and Illusion*, Jeffrey Gray's *Psychology of Fear and Stress* and Dick Passingham's *The Human Primate*. I will refer often to Oliver Sacks, Stephen Gould and Daniel Dennett, who have written so well on subjects close to mine.

This book is necessarily eclectic. I have done my best to make it accurate but am all too well aware that it cannot be comprehensive. I have been helped by friends, teachers and colleagues who have looked over chapters, sometimes repeatedly. They include Rebecca Aylward, Peter Brown, Janet Carsten, Anthony Grayling, Andrew Glenerster, Sally Laird, Andy Lawrence, Andrew Lydiard, David Parkes, Dick Passingham, Matt Ridley, Ian Robertson, Timothy Sprigge, James Tickell, Alain Townsend, Sophie and Anthea Zeman. Specific advice on the vocabulary of consciousness around the world came from Charles Jedrej, Sally Laird, Judit Osman-Sagi and Yi-Bin Ni via Susan Whitfield. Professor Gareth Jones educated me about the assessment of awareness under anaesthesia, and Dr Colin Mumford about aviation medicine. A succession of mentors encouraged the interests which gave rise to this book: I thank Jim Cogan, John Field, Colin Harris, Jonathan Glover, Alan Cowey, John Oxbury, Ed Thompson, Anita Harding, John Hodges and Charles Warlow. Conversations over the years with Oliver Davies, Daniel Johnson, Oliver Letwin, David Mitchell, Charles Target, Crispin Tickell, Alex and Zbynek Zeman have fuelled my enthusiasm for consciousness. Librarians at the Norfolk and Norwich Hospital and the Western General Hospital in Edinburgh have been unfailingly helpful. The arbour at Four Corners and the sturdy walls of Acharonich have given me welcome shelter. I was lucky to find a sympathetic and imaginative editor in Robert Baldock at Yale University Press. Kevin Brown, Candida Brazil, Diana Yeh and Hazel Hutchison at Yale, and Elaine Lord in Edinburgh, have all given generous assistance. A special thank you is due to Anthony Grayling who has been the patient midwife of this book throughout its long labour, and to Rebecca, who has put up with a scribbling husband and is willing to read what he writes. Needless to say, the defects you will discover in the pages which follow are mine alone.

Introduction

The world . . . does not become manifest by its mere existence. Its becoming manifest is conditional on certain very special goings on in very special parts of this very world, namely on certain events that happen in a brain. That is an inordinately peculiar kind of implication . . .

Erwin Schrödinger[1]

Two sketches on a rainy day

While I write I can just make out the steady patter of the rain on the lawn. A grey light slants through the window. There is a fire rumbling in the grate, scenting the air with wood smoke. My chair is hard, and when my attention wanders from my work I feel the pressure of my elbows on its arms, the support from its straw seat, the resistance my feet encounter from the stone floor. I take a sip of coffee, warm, bitter, yet sweet from the milk. In spite of the fire, the English summer's day is chilly, and my skin is pricking slightly in the cold. Our child has been sleeping by the fire: I can hear her stirring, whimpering. Outside there is salt in the sea air, and the promise of a rainbow as the clouds break up.

What could be more real to us than such qualities of sight and sound, of taste and smell and touch? Sensations like these are as everyday and undeniable as anything we know. They crowd, they *are* our world.

Now consider a rival description of the same events. The description is incomplete, but its character is clear:

A variety of forms of energy impinge upon an organism. Invisible particles vibrate in the air, setting up a resonance in a membrane coiled, like a shell, within the ear. Once they have passed safely through the cornea and lens, quanta of radiation are absorbed by another sensitive membrane, in its eye. Air-borne molecules released by the burning wood drift into complementary molecules in its nose, which they fit like keys in locks. Forces acting at the surface of its skin deform microscopic structures just below the surface.

All these encounters produce a single common result. They change the electrical activity in nerves running back from its ears, eyes, nose and skin to brain. This in turn alters the release of chemicals at the terminals where these nerves communicate with others.

The nerves passing back into its brain are prodigiously numerous, and they branch, diverge and interweave in patterns of giddying complexity. Some pathways lead rapidly away again, down nerves which run to muscles or to glands, to trigger movement or secretion: secretion of saliva, for example, followed the arrival of some molecules of coffee in the nasal passages. But rapid journeys through this organism's nervous system are exceptional: circuitous routes which double back upon themselves are much more common.

These ensure that the activity set up within its brain by the impinging molecules and quanta has a complex fate. Some of the activity dies away to leave no trace after reverberating for a while. Some eventually influences action: it played a small part in the chain of events that led to the words you read in the first paragraph. Some leaves a lasting, though subtle, trace in the pathways it traverses, so that on a later occasion the same stimuli will excite a very slightly different set of paths.

This is the kind of account a scientist might provide of the same episode, arguably a more revealing one than the 'view from within' described in the first paragraph. Yet for all its penetrating vision it omits just the qualities of experience that struck us as so *real* in the first account. It leaves us wondering what kind of alchemy is needed to conjure the rich variety of experience, the wood smoke and the rainbow, from 'certain events that happen in a brain'.

The dilemma created by these two sketches is our point of departure. One describes what passes through our minds, the other what happens in our brains. Both seem to capture vital aspects of the truth about our lives, but the relationship between these two chains of events is deeply puzzling.

Can we dispense with one or the other type of description without any real loss? If we find that we need both of them to make sense of ourselves, can they be reconciled?

Déjà vu

The two sketches illustrate two ways of describing our experience: 'from within', in the first person, and 'from without', through the scientific study of the brain. The second, scientific, account is very general and abstract. It may suggest to you that even if there is some loose relationship between events in the brain and our experiences, the subtler nuances of feeling will never be shown to have a physical basis. The chapters that follow will call this into question. I offer a first example here to help to fix ideas.

Every few weeks a clinical neurologist will have a conversation with a new patient which goes something like this:

'Tell me what the attacks are like.'

'They're very difficult to describe. They can happen any time. I feel strange, rather as if I were dreaming. I feel that I don't belong where I am, as if I'm somehow not quite real. I have never felt anything like it before.'

'What else?'

'They scare me. It's such a weird feeling.'

'Do you know what's going on around you?'

'Pretty much. But I feel terribly removed from it.'

'Do you ever have the sense that just the same events have all happened before?'

'How did you know? Yes, I do, very much so, I should have told you. If someone is speaking to me I feel that I know just what they're about to say. If I'm watching television I know what the next picture will be. I don't know how I know. It's as if I'm remembering, but it's not an ordinary memory, it goes deeper somehow. I can't get hold of it. And everything seems familiar, when it's not.'

'What happens next?'

'I just come out of it, and then feel tired and blue for the rest of the day. Or I usually do. The time that made me go to see my doctor I must have passed out, I came round half on my chair, half on the floor. I must have been out for five minutes.'

In practice this description is almost diagnostic of epileptic seizures arising in the temporal lobe of the brain. The account of a recurring memory, only part-recalled but somehow touching a deep chord, combined with a sense of intense but inexplicable familiarity, are remarkably characteristic of this disorder. Such memories have the quality G.K. Chesterton described, in his recollection, many years later, of a scene glimpsed in early childhood, 'with a sort of aboriginal authenticity impossible to describe; something at the back of all my thoughts; like the very back scene of the theatre of things'.[2] Despite the elusive quality of these aboriginal experiences, sufferers describe them in surprisingly similar terms, allowing the neurologist his or her own *frisson* of recognition.

I choose this example because the experience is such a reliable pointer to an aberration in the function of a well-defined region of the brain, even though the disturbance of consciousness is complex and unusual. The cause of the seizure varies from case to case, from scarring caused by a 'feverish fit' in early childhood, to a tumour within the temporal lobe or one pressing on it from outside. The recurrent experience of *déjà vu* points to the site of the problem, not to its cause. But the example helps to make it clear that, however we conceive it, the relationship between brain events and experience is of the most intimate kind.

The view from nowhere[3]

What distinguishes a first-person account of events from a scientific description of them?

First-person descriptions report an individual's experience from an individual perspective: they tell us 'what it was like to be there'. They make no apologies for subjectivity, and should make none: if there were no subject there would be nothing to report.

Scientific description involves a meticulous effort to eliminate subjectivity, to achieve a reproducible, 'impersonal' description of the world, an account on which all disinterested observers can agree. The effort to achieve this leads away from the ordinary language of experience, into a technical vocabulary which is usually inaccessible to outsiders. This obscurity is justified by one astounding property of successful science: in making reliable predictions it provides control over the world. This kind of knowledge, in Francis Bacon's phrase, 'is power'.

Taking a generous view, one might conclude that there is no competition between these two forms of description. Their purposes are simply different. First-person accounts evoke a single point of view, while scientific accounts abstract features of the world common to all points of view. First-person accounts matter to us because we are interested in each other's thoughts and feelings; scientific accounts matter because we need to master our physical surroundings. But comparisons are inevitable, especially when the two descriptions appear to offer rival versions of the same events. Given its intrinsic interest and practical benefits, science may look like a clear winner: hard-won objectivity is surely preferable to effortless subjectivity.

This enthusiasm is understandable. There are two good reasons, though, for trying to hold it in check.

In the first place scientific knowledge is always provisional: it is uncertain which beliefs will stand and which will fall during the constant process of revision. As the Oxford physician Sir William Osler warned a group of newly qualified doctors at the turn of the century: 'Gentlemen, I must tell you that half of what you have been taught is wrong, and we don't know which half.'

The second reservation is more fundamental, and closer to the heart of this book: science may be impersonal, but it cannot transcend its human origins. It begins and ends with human observation and human thought. We will never quite arrive at a 'view from nowhere'. It is just as true of the highly disciplined form of description achieved by science as of the first-person account that if there were no subject there would be nothing to report.

Repetition in the finite mind

> The primary imagination I hold to be the living power and prime agent of all human perception, and as a repetition in the finite mind of the eternal act of creation in the infinite I AM.
>
> Samuel Coleridge[4]

You and I are able to report on events if and when we are conscious. The capacity for consciousness is fundamental to the value we place on our lives. Plato records Socrates' opinion that 'the unexamined life is not worth living'.[5] This might be disputed, but most of us would at least agree that an unconscious life is not worth living. The prolongation of human life, where one can be certain that consciousness is lost for ever, is generally regarded as a wasted effort.

The value we place on the lives of other creatures is also influenced by our views on their possession of consciousness, and its degree. This issue is at the centre of the debate on animal rights and it surfaces repeatedly in discussions of artificial intelligence. If we eventually encounter an alien life form the question of whether it does or does not enjoy consciousness is likely to be high on the agenda.

If the capacity for consciousness is fundamental, it is also personal: it requires a subject. The world goes on without us at our deaths, but a world of experience dies. This lies at the heart of the familiar paradox that life is cheap, but individual human lives are incomparably precious.

To be conscious is also to be engaged in an activity. This book will provide many illustrations, from the scientific study of the brain, of the dictum that 'what is felt is always action in an organism'.[6] It is clear from commonplace experience, as well, that consciousness involves an active contribution from its subject. Our dreams, for example, teach us that we can generate a vivid image of reality without any need for stimulation by the world around us.

Consciousness, then, is fundamental, personal and active. If all this is granted, the capacity for consciousness, celebrated in Coleridge's resounding phrases, seems to stand shoulder to shoulder with the existence of matter and life as one of the three great challenges for human understanding.

No one would claim that the scientific problems posed by matter and life have been definitively solved. But there was extraordinary progress in the twentieth century: we can extract power from the atom; more recently we have learned to alter the human genome, our inherited make-up. We cannot say as much for consciousness: the generation of experience by the brain remains deeply mysterious. There is heated disagreement about whether this problem can ever, in principle, be solved. Indeed, there is disagreement even about whether there is a problem to solve. This has the curious result that eminent scientists are currently offering theories of a phenomenon which other eminent thinkers assure them does not exist.

Introducing consciousness

The central question raised by neuroscience for our understanding of ourselves is easily stated: given that events in the brain provide the physical basis of consciousness, what is the relationship between our experience and the events in the brain that make it possible? The question raises other issues which go to the heart of philosophy: what kinds of things and properties does the world contain? How do we gain knowledge of them? What do we require of explanations? If our behaviour is determined by the activity of the nervous system what remains of human freedom and responsibility? These questions ramify into psychology, the scientific study of the mind, and into the large area of physiology that deals with the working of the brain. It is bound to touch on the traditional realm of religion.

The aims of this book are both modest and ambitious. It will present some of the central evidence that events in the brain do in fact provide the physical basis of consciousness, in tandem with an introduction to the philosophical debate which such evidence has fuelled. The questions raised are much too interesting to be left to specialists and I hope that I have made the book accessible to readers who have no previous acquaintance with these subjects. I hope also that it may help to mediate between those scientists and philosophers with an interest in consciousness who have had difficulty in seeing what disturbs the other party. I will not try to convince you of a new solution to the riddle: there are already plenty of ingenious and contradictory suggestions. But I mean to convince you that the riddle is real and absorbing.

Given this book's huge potential territory its focus must be sharp. Some definition of terms is needed at the outset. Chapter 1 examines the meanings of 'consciousness' and some related words, their history, and equivalent terms in other languages. Consciousness is a complex concept: a boxer regaining consciousness after his concussion, a teenager aching with self-consciousness, and a prime minister conscious that the nation has tired of him are in quite different, if distantly related, states of mind. This chapter will try to clarify these states, and establish which, if any of them, open up promising avenues of thought.

Chapter 2 provides a basic but wide-ranging introduction to the study of the nervous system. This sets the scene for the discussion of some areas of neuroscience relevant to consciousness in later chapters. Like the rest of the book, this chapter should be accessible to every interested reader: it assumes no previous knowledge of biology. Its recurring theme is that the 'prime agent of human perception', the human brain, really is a 'living power', a much more remarkable creation than any of the complex but lifeless systems so far engineered by man.

The central chapters (3–6) present the evidence from neuroscience that bears most directly on consciousness. The organisation of this part of the book takes heed of the broad distinction between the *capacity* for consciousness and its *content*. Listening to music, enjoying good food or a view involve quite different modes of sensation but all presupppose a certain common degree of alertness. Chapter 3 examines the neurological basis of this basic capacity for consciousness, Chapter 4 outlines some of its disorders. In Chapter 5, turning to the content of awareness, I discuss areas of the brain and processes within them which underlie one especially vivid kind of consciousness, the experience of sight. Chapter 6 describes some 'experiments of nature', and of man, which illuminate the relationship between consciousness and vision.

During our excursions into neuroscience, we will keep our philosophical interests in view. These chapters review a wealth of evidence that damage to the nervous system can damage and fragment awareness: this has implications for our understanding of the mind, for example for the conception of the mind as an immaterial and indivisible soul. We will review some exquisitely detailed correlations between experience and brain activity. But the very success of this line of research prompts one to ask how full an account of experience can *ever* be given by studying the anatomy and physiology of the brain.

Chapter 7 opens up another, complementary, approach to our central subject. The brain, and the states of consciousness to which it gives rise, are the products of evolution: an account of this process offers a historical answer to the question, 'Why are we conscious?' This chapter will sketch what is known about the evolution of nervous systems in general and the hominid brain in particular, stressing the part played by culture in the evolution of the latter. If consciousness is a product of evolution it was selected for good practical reasons: the chapter will consider the curious question of why consciousness is useful to us.

The final chapters take a step back to examine scientific theories of consciousness and philosophical accounts of the relationship between experience and activity in the brain. I decided that Chapter 8 had become necessary during the writing of the book, as a growing number of exciting but often incompatible ideas about the neural basis of awareness came on the scene. These are preliminary but interesting efforts to make scientific sense of consciousness.

Chapter 9 brings us full circle to review the dilemma posed by the two sketches of a rainy day, the puzzle of the relationship between what goes on in our brains and what passes through our minds, in the light of the evidence presented in the rest of the book. It examines the sharply conflicting views of a number of contemporary philosophers on three linked questions: what is the nature of the relation between conscious states and the neural activity associated with them? Is there any bar, in principle, to the construction of a conscious machine? What are the implications of the intimate relationship between consciousness and brain events for human freedom and responsibility?

Part I:
Introducing consciousness

1

As sweet by any other name? Consciousness, self-consciousness and conscience

There is no generally accepted definition of consciousness.

John Hodges[1]

'Eeh, doctor, the patient . . . she is somehow unconscious!'
(Words once used, in Kenya, to summon me to a bedside)

Introduction

Consciousness is in fashion, among scientists and philosophers on both sides of the Atlantic. It has been 'regained', 'rediscovered', 'reconsidered', and even 'explained'.[2] A *Journal of Consciousness Studies* carries forward the debate between students of psychology, physiology, anatomy, computation, artificial intelligence, religion and philosophy. The University of Arizona at Tucson plays host to a major biannual conference, 'Toward a Science of Consciousness';[3] the Association for the Scientific Study of Consciousness[4] promotes its investigation. Recently, interest has spread beyond the circle of learned journals and societies. The editors of magazines and daily papers, the producers of programmes on the sciences and the arts, all regard the nature of awareness and its basis in the brain as sufficiently sexy topics to warrant frequent bulletins.

You could be forgiven for assuming that the quest for consciousness must have an enticing quarry. Could so much intellectual effort be squandered on an imaginary prize? Well, perhaps it could. The pursuit of consciousness is unusual among scientific endeavours in that a powerful group of thinkers, including philosophers and scientists, has questioned the wisdom of setting off on the chase in the first place. They argue that the notion of consciousness is too deeply muddled to merit serious consideration.[5] It originates, so the argument runs, in everyday thinking about the mind, in 'folk psychology'. Its messy beginnings render it unsuited to scientific use. Philosophers should do their best to loosen the hold of this confusing notion on our thinking. Psychologists had better not bother themselves with it at all. If there are any 'problems of consciousness', they arise from our inconsistent and unsophisticated use of language.

In the face of these doubts we need to take stock before investing too much time and energy in pursuit of consciousness. We must try to be clearer about what we mean by the word, and by its close relations, 'self-consciousness' and 'conscience'. This enquiry into meaning is the main task of this chapter.

Language, the great enabler and disabler of our thinking, is thoroughly steeped in history. So before dissecting the senses of the family of consciousness words in English today, we should take a look at their origins. This chapter traces the history of 'consciousness' and its forebears from their beginnings into present-day use, before examining the contemporary senses of consciousness and self-consciousness. It also surveys the vocabulary which is used to express these ideas in some other contemporary languages. If consciousness is of real interest we should expect it to be a subject of discussion by busy human tongues across the world.

The history of 'conscience' – and her cousins

> It is well we should become aware of what we are doing when we speak, of the ancient, fragile, and immensely potent instruments words are.
>
> C. S. Lewis, *Studies in Words*[6]

Consciousness, self-consciousness and conscience bear close family resemblances. Over the centuries their shifting meanings have mingled and worked upon one another. In English, 'conscience' is the parent of the group, the begetter of 'consciousness'.

Conscience itself owes its origins to the combination of two Latin words, *scio*, meaning 'I know', and *cum*, meaning 'with' (which becomes 'con' when it is used as a prefix). *Conscius* is the adjective formed from the verb *conscio*, *conscientia* is the noun.

Conscio in Latin meant 'I know together with' in the sense of sharing knowledge. The knowledge in question was typically shared with another person, and was often of something secret or shameful: one would be 'conscius' with a co-conspirator. Writing in English in the seventeenth century, Thomas Hobbes drew on this sense: 'When two or more men know of one and the same fact [i.e. deed] they are said to be conscious of it one to another'.[7]

But if we can share knowledge with others, we can also share it with ourselves. This gives rise to the second sense of *conscius*. Bunyan had it in mind when he wrote: 'I am conscious to myself of many failings'.

These two senses, of knowledge shared with another and knowledge shared with oneself, have been called the 'strong' sense of *conscio*. Latin also allowed a weakened sense, which English would later echo, in which *conscio* meant little more than 'I know', or 'I know well', and in which *conscientia* meant knowledge, thought or mind.

All three senses entered English with 'conscience', the first equivalent of *conscientia* in our language. *Conscientia* in Latin was primarily a witness to the facts, whether reporting on external events – to which a pair of conspirators might be privy – or on the workings of a mind. But our knowledge of what has occurred and our views on its rights and wrongs are closely linked, making it understandable that the meaning of 'conscience' in English came to extend itself from witness to lawgiver, from the reporter at the scene of the crime to the legislator who outlaws or condemns it. Jeremy Taylor wrote, 'God rules in us by his substitute, our conscience'; Milton spoke of 'My umpire conscience'. Once this new usage was established a 'good conscience' could mean either a clear, unencumbered one, a witness with nothing discreditable to report, or a sound source of judgement on moral issues.

The words 'conscious' and 'consciousness' appear in English early in the seventeenth century. At first both were used in the strong sense, as later, by Pope, in 1744: 'An honest mind is not in the power of a dishonest: to break its peace there must be some guilt or consciousness'. But over the years their senses weakened, gradually losing the association with shared or guilty knowledge, and they came to refer first and foremost to the waking state: 'consciousness as opposed to dormancy, dreamless sleep, swoon, insensibility'.[8]

Yet the old senses live on, colouring the new: when we speak of 'human consciousness' one can still hear a distant echo of the 'sharing' implicit in the Latin *conscientia*; when John Locke wrote in the seventeenth century that the soul 'must necessarily be conscious of its own perceptions' he was using a word in which the connotation of knowledge shared with oneself or another was very much alive.

'Self-conscious' and 'self-consciousness' came on the scene in the seventeenth century soon after consciousness itself. The self reference seems to have had a rather variable influence on the word's meaning. It sometimes added little to its force: 'self-consciousness to the greatest villainy' (1675) was really no more than consciousness of it, with a hint of discreditable involvement. But other authors, including Locke, used the term to refer to consciousness of one's own identity, acts and thoughts. The most colloquial sense of self-consciousness, defined by the *Oxford English Dictionary* as 'so far self-centred as to suppose one is the object of observation by others', does not appear until the nineteenth century, nicely captured in a phrase by Carlyle: 'self-conscious, conscious of a world looking on'.

We should try to keep the history of these words in mind as we disentangle their uses in English today.

'What do you mean by . . . ?'

Consciousness

What do we mean by 'consciousness' in colloquial English? There is something forbidding about attempts to define abstract nouns. Rather than launch a direct assault on 'consciousness', let's start by tackling the more amiable adjective, and ask what we mean when we say someone is 'conscious'.

'Conscious' as 'awake'

When we say that someone is conscious, without further qualification, we generally mean that he or she is awake – rather, that is, than asleep or concussed, comatose, dead drunk, anaesthetised or in a hypnotic trance. We are referring to the individual's 'level' or 'state' of consciousness.

We speak, in this sense, of consciousness dwindling, waning, lapsing and recovering; it may be lost, depressed, regained. This sense of 'conscious' is used countless times each day in casualty departments and hospital wards throughout the English-speaking world. It is mostly captured by words like 'awake', 'aroused', 'alert' or 'vigilant'. The 'disorders of consciousness' treated and studied by neurologists, the 'fits, faints and funny turns' discussed in Chapter 4, appeal to this sense of the word.

This use of 'consciousness' is unmysterious and relatively uncontroversial. We are generally good judges of whether others are or are not conscious, in this sense. We bring objective criteria to bear: Can he speak, preferably sensibly? Is he oriented in place and time? Are his eyes open? If not, do they open when we speak to him? Is he moving, with spontaneity and purpose, or at least on request? If the answer to all these questions is affirmative, we would be in no doubt that our companion is conscious, capable of a making a well-integrated response to his surroundings. We often equate wakefulness, judged by criteria like these, with the capacity for experience. But if we do so, we will sometimes be wrong.

Useful as they are, these criteria do not always tell us what we really want to know about someone's state of consciousness. People may be conscious even if none of them is satisfied; and we will at least contemplate the possibility that someone might *not* be conscious even if all the criteria are satisfied. Patients who are paralysed by muscle relaxants during surgery occasionally provide a disturbing example of the former state of affairs. If the anaesthetic is inadequate to obliterate consciousness, they will be able to give a detailed account of their experiences afterwards, even though at the time they gave – could give – no indication of awareness. We shall return to such alarming states in Chapter 4. Philosophers have recently been intrigued by the latter possibility, that despite all appearances to the contrary – despite the ability, for example, to engage you in lively conversation – your companion might be *unconscious*: we shall encounter these remarkable 'zombies' in Chapter 9. Such examples point us towards the second, more difficult, and much more controversial sense of 'consciousness'.

'Conscious' as 'aware of'

When we say that someone is conscious in this second sense, we imply that he or she is enjoying some experience. We imply that there is 'something it feels like to be' this person at this very moment, in a sense in which there is nothing it feels like to be a stone, or to be lost in dreamless sleep.[9] In this use, we generally add the word 'of' to enable us to specify the content of consciousness. I, for instance, over the last few moments, have been *conscious of* the sound of a tractor chugging in the distance, of someone reading a story aloud to a child downstairs, of the tapping sound made by my fingers on the keyboard as I write, of the sentence which is forming itself on the screen of my laptop, of a slight twinge of backache as I lean forward from my chair.

The 'contents' of consciousness in this sense of the word are sensory or perceptual. They include the family of bodily sensations, tingles, tickles, itches, aches and pains and the deliverances of the five traditional senses: all that we see, hear, taste, smell, touch. The contents of consciousness usually have a rich texture. Our experience from moment to moment, like the brief segment of the 'stream of consciousness' which I have just described, is alive with meaning and feeling, supplied without effort by processes which are themselves unconscious. Experience arrives classified and interpreted by memory, imbued with emotion, integrated in a course of action. Some component of my memory, for instance, without needing to be asked, informed me that the husky chug I could hear outside belonged to a certain farm vehicle; the sound of the tractor in the lane, evocative – for me – of holidays and country walks, reinforced my sense of leisure; tempered by the twinge of backache, this sense became a part of my experience as I worked, providing the background to the partly frustrating, partly agreeable effort to put my thoughts into words. The interplay of sensation, memory, emotion and action is the foundation of ordinary experience. We live, the apt phrase of the American biologist Gerald Edelman, in a 'remembered present'[10] – with half an eye on the future.

Several writers have agreed with William James that we can make some useful generalisations about consciousness in its second sense (which we might define as 'the current content of perceptual experience').[11] It is stable for short periods, of up to a few seconds, but characteristically changeful over time; it is selective, with a foreground and a background, and a limited capacity, but we are able to make the most of its limited resources by directing attention to this or that target, shifting the focus of consciousness from an item in the foreground to an item in the background of our thoughts; it ranges over innumerable contents, with potential contributions from each of our senses, and from all our major psychological processes, including thought, emotion, memory, imagination, language and the planning of action; its contents are unified at one time, and continuous over time in the sense that memory allows us to connect consciousness of the present with consciousness of the past; it is generally 'intentional' in the philosophical sense that it is consciousness *of* things in the world, directed *at* this or that;

it is personal, involving a subject with a necessarily limited point of view, and 'aspectual', conditioned by the perspective which our viewpoint affords.

The changeful, personal, aspectual nature of consciousness means that we are much less confident that we can share what others are 'conscious of' than that we can judge whether they are conscious at all. Although we normally assume that others perceive the world in ways broadly akin to our own, we accept that differences of age, of sex, of culture, of personal and educational history all influence the quality of their experience. Changes in our own perspective, as we grow up, or get to know a neighbourhood, become acquainted with a job or learn a language, give us some insight into the way experience of a static situation can be transformed by changes taking place in *us*.

Knowing something of these everyday transformations suggests that there may be forms of human experience which we cannot recapture or share in full: the consciousness, for example, of a child of 18 months, on the threshold of language, or of someone blind and deaf, like Helen Keller. If human experience of these kinds lies at the limits of our imaginative powers, what can we know of the perceptual worlds inhabited by animals with senses we do not possess at all?

Bats, for example, are mammals, with brains resembling – although very much smaller than – ours. Most of us intuitively suppose that mammals other than ourselves enjoy some kind of consciousness. (We will give thought to whether this supposition can be justified later.) If we are right about this, bats, like other mammals, have some perceptual experience of the world around them. But their impression of their surroundings is not created visually, like ours, but by echolocation, the use of reflected sound to build up an 'auditory image'. What is it like, then, to be a bat? It strikes most people, on first encountering this question, that these animals probably do have an experience of the world, but that it must be remarkably – perhaps unfathomably – dissimilar to ours.[12]

You may want to protest that this second sense of 'conscious' is not really colloquial at all. The first sense – 'conscious' as awake – is all very well. Nurses and doctors, friends and relations really do take an interest in whether the patient is conscious in this sense, but how often do we speak, in ordinary conversation, of consciousness in the sense of the 'current content of perceptual experience'? Perhaps I am smuggling in a dubious technical term under cover of 'ordinary language'.

There is some justice in this, but we do in fact make use of this second sense, although usually in less practical contexts than the first. I have already used the term 'stream of consciousness', linked with the attempt to convey the natural flow of thought and experience in literary narrative, in the manner of Virginia Woolf or William Faulkner. We can speak of 'human consciousness', referring to the sum of human experience, and alluding to its distinctive features. George Eliot wrote of 'the transition from a happy to an unhappy consciousness'. And we still speak colloquially of 'being conscious of' perceptual experiences ('as I woke I became conscious of a strange low roaring sound . . .') – although when we do so it is often, as Gilbert Ryle observed, 'to indicate a certain noteworthy nebulousness and consequent inarticulateness of the apprehension'[13] – a disturbing stage in the process of perception at which an experience is salient but still lacks a clear identity.

The fact that we use a term in colloquial speech does not, however, guarantee that it can survive philosophical scrutiny. As we shall see, there are circumstances created by psychological experiment or neurological disease – as well as some occurring in everyday life – in which we find it difficult, or impossible, to say whether a certain item was or was not consciously experienced. Such examples strain our ordinary concept of consciousness. And it may well be that some of our naïve beliefs about consciousness, particularly in our second sense, are confused in ways that create spurious philosophical problems.

But this sense of the word ('the current content of perceptual experience' or 'the way things currently seem to me, what they are like') is sufficiently familiar and robust to serve as a signpost to the second of this book's chief concerns. Its main aims are to explore the science and philosophy bearing on consciousness in the senses so far outlined: consciousness in the sense, first, of the waking state and second, of the perceptual experience the waking state permits.

'Consciousness' as 'mind'

This sense of 'conscious' is the most wide-ranging, the most inclusive, of the three. It encompasses all that we can know, think, mean, intend, all that we can hope, wish, remember or believe. 'To be conscious of' in this sense is to acknowledge this or that to be the case. While the first two senses of the word concern our current behaviour and experience, 'conscious' in this third sense can be used to report our acquaintance with any state of affairs whatsoever: I can be conscious 'of your plan to leave tomorrow', 'that the government's popularity has sunk to a new low', 'that you didn't really mean what you said'. By emphasising our 'consciousness' in such sentences we often intend to emphasise that the matter in question has been considered carefully, turned over in our minds – that we have, so to speak, shared the knowledge of it fully with ourselves.

In this third sense the realm of consciousness is simply the realm of the mind: we can describe ourselves as being conscious of anything that might pass through our minds. This use of the word is in keeping with its history, but provides too large a target for scientific study. Doing algebra, looking at a cat, framing an intention to leave soon are such disparate activities that a search for common features on the grounds that all can be 'conscious' – in this third sense – might prove unrewarding. The excitement about 'consciousness' among scientists and philosophers in recent years has relatively little to do with this meaning of the word: it arises from our growing understanding of the neural basis of the waking state and the contents of our experience.

In passing, though, we might note that one of the most frequent and natural uses of 'conscious' in this sense concerns our intentions and purposes: we speak of 'a conscious attempt to influence the proceedings', a 'conscious aim to explore further than we had gone before', a 'conscious desire to improve matters'. This natural usage points to an important link between consciousness and volition, the act of willing, or its outcome, deliberate action. Willed or voluntary acts are those with aims of which we are conscious and are – usually – prepared to acknowledge. Thus the third sense of consciousness bridges perception and action, the events we perceive and the ones we bring about. Their intimate relationship will be one of this book's recurring themes.

Self-consciousness

> I hit myself; I hate myself; I'm self-sufficient; I feel like my old self; I'm selfish; my humiliation was self-inflicted; I couldn't contain myself. . . . Self . . . means my body, personality, my actions, my competence, my continuity, my needs, my agency and my subjective space . . . self is a way of pointing . . .[14]
>
> R. Schafer, *Self-Awareness in Animals and Humans*[14]

There is a natural temptation to suppose that being 'self-conscious' is a matter of being conscious of a 'self', a shadowy familiar, part substance and part ghost. In fact, like 'conscious', we use 'self-conscious' in a variety of ways. Some of these have been the focus of recent scientific work, examining self-consciousness among our primate cousins, with implications for its evolutionary history, and its emergence in the course of human childhood. This research has yielded fascinating insights, and helped to clarify the concept of self-consciousness, achieving some real progress in our knowledge of self-knowledge.

'Self-conscious' as 'awkward, embarrassment-prone'

> Some nymphs there are too conscious of their face . . .
>
> Alexander Pope, *The Rape of the Lock*[15]

To call someone 'self-conscious' in this most idiomatic sense of the word is to say that they are awkward in the company of others: 'I felt so self-conscious when she was watching me that I couldn't do anything naturally . . .'. Interestingly, this awkwardness results from excessive sensitivity about the attention of others when it is directed towards us. In other words, we are self-conscious when we are excessively aware of others' awareness of ourselves! This humdrum sense of 'self-conscious' thus turns out to be rather sophisticated, hinting at a link between consciousness of self and consciousness of others, which, as we shall see, is right up to date.

'Self-conscious' as 'self-detecting'

This second sense is much less idiomatic, but it tends to suggest itself after a little reflection on what we *might* mean by self-consciousness. Certain sensations arise in or on us. My sensations as a ladybird walks across my hand involve a certain sort of 'self-consciousness': consciousness of a sensation impinging on me. Similarly I am aware of my own actions, and can sometimes learn to modify them on the basis of punishments and rewards: consciousness of actions that I myself perform also involves a certain kind of 'self-awareness'.

This is, however, a minimal sense. It amounts to little more than the second sense of consciousness, our current perceptual awareness, but emphasises that this is directed towards events brought about by, or ones which directly impinge upon, the creature in question.

There is evidence that animals, even quite humble ones, share this kind of self-consciousness. Rats, for example, can be trained to respond to a signal in a way that depends upon what they were doing last: they are capable of learning, for instance, that if they were washing their face when a signal was given they should press one lever, whereas if they were rearing they should press another.[16] The animals appear able to register and recall their recent behaviour. There is no doubt that they can also register and recall recent sensations occurring at close quarters.

These abilities are indispensable for human and animal alike, but while they imply self-consciousness of a limited kind they do not require what has been described as an 'idea of me'. The third sense of self-consciousness implies the dawning of a concept of self.

'Self-conscious' as 'self-recognising'

Once I recognise myself in a mirror I . . . refer myself constantly to the ideal, fictitious or imaginary me.

Merleau-Ponty[17]

'No daddy – *myself do it.*'

Flora, aged two, whenever I try to help

In 1970 an American psychologist, Gordon Gallup, published a paper which caught the imagination of students of both human psychology and animal behaviour.[18] Gallup works with primates, the mammalian 'order' comprising prosimians (such as lemurs), monkeys, apes and man. He became interested in what primates understood, or could learn, about reflections. He noticed that if chimpanzees were allowed to see themselves in a mirror they started by treating their reflection as an intruder in the cage. Despite this initial misunderstanding, chimps rapidly learned that the reflection was, in fact, their own image. Their perceptiveness should not surprise us too much: chimps belong to the same 'superfamily' of the primate order as we do, and are our closest living relatives. But the capacity for self-recognition is not possessed by every primate: Gallup also observed that monkeys, possessors of much smaller brains than chimps, were unable to learn that mirrors showed them their own reflections, even after periods of exposure numbering thousands of hours.

Gallup followed up these observations with a simple but powerful experiment. After administering a general anaesthetic, he painted marks on the chimps and monkeys in positions in which they could only be seen with the aid of a mirror. Great care was taken to ensure that the paint was non-irritant and odourless. When the animals had recovered from the anaesthetic they were exposed to a mirror, in the absence of companions who might have drawn their attention to the marks. Chimps rapidly noticed the marks with the aid of their mirror, and then examined them in great detail: the monkeys never did so, despite paying close attention to similar marks if they were visible without need of mirrors.

This result has been confirmed repeatedly since, and extended to a range of other animals. Orang-utans certainly, and gorillas probably, share our human ability to recognise our mirror image as our own reflection. Monkeys seem to be unable to learn that they are looking at themselves, although they are able to learn that mirrors can be used to see things which are otherwise out of view.

This spectrum of 'mirror behaviours' has been nicely illustrated by two American psychologists with the help of Walt Disney.[19] Tigger, in Disney's 1958 version of *Winnie the Pooh*, announces proudly to Pooh Bear that: 'I'm the only one!' Pooh points to the mirror, and asks Tigger to account for his reflection. Tigger decides that the reflection must be an impostor, but frightens himself so much in his attempts to drive the impostor off that he has to take refuge under a bed. Pooh has a clearer grasp of the nature of mirror images. He uses his reflection to guide his efforts to repair some untidy sewing on his back. The extent of his understanding is thrown into question, though, when he turns to the mirror, after mending himself, and thanks his reflection. The Ugly Duckling has advanced a step further: catching sight of himself in the still water of a lake he 'turns towards the viewer with a look of abject despair, and points at himself as if to say "c'est moi"'. Tigger and Pooh, on this analogy, illustrate two aspects of the monkey's understanding of mirrors: they can make use of them, as Pooh does, but, like Tigger, regard their reflections as independent agents, suitable recipients of threats and thanks. The Ugly Duckling, by contrast, shares the chimp's awareness that when he examines the mirror he is examining himself.

'Mirror self-recognition' has provided an immensely fruitful subject for comparative psychologists, but does the ability to recognise themselves in mirrors imply that chimps possess the full extent of human self-awareness? This is open to question: 'Is what the animal sees in the mirror a self with a sense of its own continuity, of its enduring yet finite existence . . . of what makes it unique compared to other selves and, at the same time, of its psychological commonality with those other selves?' – or does it simply 'recognise its body in the mirror . . . with little conception of its own mental life?'[20]

At the very least, we can be confident that a chimp, unlike a monkey, has a mental world large enough to include 'itself' – its body – in its conception of reality. This self-representation may be limited, but, as we shall see, it is a significant step on the road to a distinctively human variety of self-awareness. Monkeys, by contrast, although they are no doubt 'self-conscious' in our second sense, do not appear to include themselves in their inventory of the world's contents.

The clearest indication of the significance of self-recognition in mirrors comes from the study of children. Chimps show signs of mirror self-recognition from between the ages of two and three years. Human children are quicker off the mark, achieving success in tests akin to Gallup's marks experiment at around 18 months.

This achievement has some interesting precursors.[21] From the age of just under one year infants show signs of embarrassment on catching a glimpse of their own reflection. At about the same age they begin to show fragments of pretend play, rather suggesting that they are aware of themselves as the objects of others' attention (my one-year-old daughter once imitated my cough with a grin that seemed to say that she knew I knew it was done for fun: in 'recognising simulation as such' her behaviour went beyond simple imitation). By 15 months children appear to recognise when another person is imitating them.

Soon after the emergence of full self-recognition in mirrors at around 18 months a cluster of other achievements indicate the first flowering of an 'idea of me': children master the first-person pronoun, begin to engage in more elaborate pretence and to exchange roles in their play. An interest in self-adornment makes its first appearance. It is presumably no coincidence that the remarkable discovery of bloody-mindedness by the two-year-old child, technically described as 'negativism', coincides with these other, more welcome, advances.

Acquiring an idea of me has additional implications for emotions and relationships. It facilitates what have been described as second-order – or self-evaluative – emotions.[22] First-order emotions, such as joy, anger, sadness, interest, disgust and fear, do not presuppose any self-representation, or self-evaluation. By contrast, embarrassment, envy, pride, guilt and shame all require a sense of the self – as an object of others' attention, a competitor with others for limited rewards, or a moral agent, subject to praise and blame.

As well as sophisticating our emotions, possessing an idea of self deepens relationships. It is telling that children first try to comfort distressed companions around the age of 18 months: empathy requires the realisation that others resemble oneself, a realisation that in turn requires some notion of 'self'. Mutual awareness of self and other is an automatic expectation in all but the most one-sided human relations.

If successful self-recognition in mirrors is something of a psychological Rubicon in children, does it indicate a comparable degree of psychological sophistication in chimps? The answer is a guarded 'yes'. Chimps engage in pretend play, and enjoy reversing roles; chimps involved in experimental attempts to teach them language have grasped the use of the personal pronouns. It is reasonable to attribute an 'idea of me' comparable to the two-year-old human's to the chimp, other apes and possibly the dolphin.

Thus the child who recognises herself in a mirror at the age of 18 months soon becomes able to refer to herself with the first-person pronoun, to experiment with her identity in play, to admire others and to envy them, to share some of their sorrows and their joys and, in a small way, to criticise herself. She is self-conscious in our third sense: she has come to recognise herself. There is accumulating evidence, though, that another major stride of understanding is needed before a child possesses 'self-consciousness' in its final and most sophisticated sense – a stride the chimp, unlike the child, may never make.

'Self-conscious' as 'aware of awareness'

In our ordinary everyday thought and talk we constantly attribute mental states to one another, and to ourselves. I have just eaten a giant peanut bar because I was *hungry, know* that I *like* the *taste* of the variety stashed away in my desk, and *thought* that it would stave off further *pangs* until dinner. The words I have underlined refer to mental states of one kind or another. If we were deprived of such notions we would be at a loss to explain the bulk of what matters most to most of us: human behaviour.

The knowledge that underpins our use of mental terms has come to be described, in recent years, as a 'theory of mind'.[23] Two- and three-year-old children – and, probably, chimps – have the makings of such a theory. Two-year-olds know and use words for perception: 'see', 'hear', 'smell', 'touch', 'taste', and words for desire such as 'want', 'like' and 'need'. Their ability to recognise that they have captured another's attention allows them to use these terms with some psychological sophistication, expressing such thoughts as 'I see Mummy sees me'. We have already encountered their abilities to recognise themselves, and to engage in 'pretend' play. Three-year-olds reliably distinguish between physical items which are open to public inspection, and mental items, like dreams, which are not.

Yet their understanding of mental states is, by adult standards, incomplete. In particular, they tend to fail on tests which require an understanding of how beliefs are formed – and of the effects of having false ones. For example, it is only at the grand age of four that children become able to predict how deceptive appearances will mislead. Shown a packet of sweets that turns out – to their surprise – to be full of pencils, three-year-old children, after making this disappointing discovery, consistently say that a newcomer will think the box is full of pencils. Shown two objects that can be distinguished only by touch, and two others that can be distinguished only by sight, three-year-olds are unable to predict which pair a newcomer will be able to differentiate using one or other sense.

Views differ on how best to describe the transition to an understanding of the nature of belief which occurs between the ages of three and five – an understanding of the beliefs which experience affords us, and which, true or false, guide us through life. But there is general agreement that by the age of five a child is equipped with a vocabulary of mental terms which can handle states of belief as well as states of perception and desire.

Their ability to use this sophisticated weaponry of psychological explanation suggests that by the age of five, if not earlier, children are self-conscious in the fourth and most exacting sense of the word: they have become 'aware of awareness', conceiving of themselves as subjects of experience. They assume, without hesitation, that others share the same capacity: indeed there is some evidence that their self-understanding and their understanding of others are strictly parallel developments. The emergence of self-consciousness, in this peculiarly human sense, from the kind of self-recognition exhibited by two-year-olds and chimps, is gradual rather than sudden, but by the time children arrive at their primary schools it is usually well under way. Can we imagine ourselves without this variety of self-consciousness, which is often cited, with some justification, as the distinguishing mark of humanity?

Lacking the notion that one is a subject of experience would block much of our everyday thinking about ourselves and others. The notion allows us to appreciate that we, and others, glimpse the world from eccentric points of view, and are prey to deception and misapprehension. This knowledge is indispensable when we 'read' each other's words and actions. Understanding that we all share the predicament of a limited point of view, and a broadly similar set of desires and emotions, allows the flowering of empathy. Lacking these fundamental insights would condemn us to a devastating psychological blindness.

We may not need to try to *imagine* this state of affairs. A tragic experiment of nature may show us how we would function if we failed to develop these distinctively human varieties of self-consciousnesss.[24] 'Autism' encompasses a wide spectrum of childhood disorders which manifest themselves in more or less severely impaired social relationships, abnormalities of language and impoverished imaginative play. Most students of these conditions agree that children suffering from autism have damaged or disordered brains, but the condition is compatible with high intelligence, and the underlying 'lesion' must be a selective one. Simon Baron-Cohen and others have suggested that the key psychological problem in sufferers from these conditions is an inability to 'read minds' with the ease displayed by the average – or even the backward – four-year-old.

The autistic children studied by Baron-Cohen often develop a concept of the simpler mental states, like 'wanting' and 'seeing'. But notions of belief and pretence, of sources of knowledge and the means of concealment, of the distinctions between appearance and reality, between dream objects and solid ones, baffle them. Temple Grandin, a highly able, successful and articulate 'autist', described herself to Oliver Sacks as feeling 'like an anthropologist on Mars' in her social relationships: 'Children . . . by the age of three or four', she told him, 'already "understand" human beings in a way [I] can never hope to'.[25]

This penultimate sense of self-consciousness, in which it means the 'awareness of awareness', brings us full circle to the first. For the teenager who is hamstrung by 'self-consciousness' in its first colloquial usage, is excessively sensitive to the attention turned on him by others. He is displaying just the kind of sensitivity that seems to be *lacking* in autism. Although we tend to regard 'self-consciousness' as a social disadvantage, we would not really wish to be without it. Only a nuance separates the poise of 'self-awareness' – which eases our social exchanges by keeping us posted about the impression we are making on others – from the encumbrance of 'self-consciousness'.

'Self-consciousness' as 'self-knowledge'

'When I make a word do a lot of work like that,' said Humpty Dumpty, 'I always pay it extra'.

Lewis Carroll, *Alice Through the Looking Glass*[26]

In the discussion of consciousness I pointed out its tendency – in its final, most general sense – to extend its range to encompass all the activities of mind. 'Self-consciousness' shares this extravagant inclination: it can be used to refer to our knowledge of the entire psychological and social context in which we come to know ourselves. Thus my 'idea of me' takes in not just a body and a mind, but also membership of a cultural community, a profession, a family group, the use of a particular language and so on.

In this extended sense, self-consciousness continues to develop and mature, throughout our individual lives – as it has done through the course of history. Consider the contrast between the 'self-consciousness' of an Egyptian priest, dedicated to the service of the sun, a medieval Christian monk, wedded to poverty, chastity and obedience, and a contemporary scientist, pursuing objective truths in a secular age; or compare our understanding of ourselves at the ages of six, 16 and 60.

Self-consciousness in this final sense finds its richest human expression in self-depiction: in self-portraiture and autobiography, a far cry from the dawning self-recognition of the chimp. Children, interestingly, are enthusiastic amateur practitioners of both activities. Professional self-description continues to occupy many, if not most, authors and artists throughout their lives.

Human self-knowledge, our consciousness of our shared fragility and transience, of our incomplete insight and partial fulfilment, is one of our greatest gifts but also one of our deepest sources of sorrow: it lifts us up, in an old-fashioned turn of phrase, into the company of angels, and, as it does so, casts us into intellectual exile from most, indeed probably from all, of our animal cousins.

Is 'self-consciousness' presupposed by 'consciousness'?

Before leaving the subject of self-consciousness, we should touch on one other issue: its relationship to 'consciousness' unqualified. Does consciousness – as has been argued from time to time – *presuppose* self-consciousness?

It should be clear from our circuitous journey around the senses of these two words that this question can only be answered intelligently in relation to specified senses of the two words. Ask yourself, for example, whether self-consciousness in the sense of having an 'idea of me' is a prerequisite for awakening, or for enjoying the taste of a cheese or the lilt of a tune, or for believing that home is just round the corner. This exercise suggests to me that self-consciousness is a sophistication of simple 'consciousness' rather than its precondition.

One train of thought which might lead one to the opposite conclusion runs something like this. If I am aware of my surroundings, I am thereby aware that I am aware of them. Awareness of my awareness is a species of self-awareness: thus awareness presupposes self-awareness.

The first premise of this argument is, however, open to question, on logical, experiential and experimental grounds. The logical criticism is that while being aware of one's surroundings presupposes awareness, it does not presuppose the further, 'second-order', ability to reflect on our awareness.

The 'experiential' argument is that when we attend most intensely to objects around us, or to our own thoughts, we speak of 'losing ourselves' in our concentration. This suggests, accurately I believe, that the awareness of awareness is an optional, derivative activity – which is not to say that it does not confer the advantages we have touched on.

Finally, the empirical study of consciousness is beginning to shed light on these distinctions. We have seen that monkeys, unlike apes, persistently fail to recognise themselves in mirrors, suggesting that they have at best a restricted concept of self. However, in work which I discuss in detail in Chapter 6, Alan Cowey, an experimental psychologist at the University of Oxford, has shown that macaque monkeys distinguish what they see consciously from visual information which enables them to perform simple tasks, but which is not available to consciousness.[27] On this evidence, having an 'idea of me' is not a precondition for being able to contrast conscious vision to reflex response.

All this suggests – rather in accordance with common sense – that self-consciousness is not a precondition for simple consciousness. The visual awareness of the macaque, the capacity for self-recognition in chimp and two-year-old child, and the concept of experience which we deploy beyond the age of four are related but distinct achievements.

Conscience

So when the woman saw that the tree . . . was to be desired to make one wise, she took of its fruit and ate . . . Then the eyes of both were opened, and they knew that they were naked; and they sewed fig leaves together and made themselves aprons.

The Book of Genesis[28]

. . . any animal whatever, endowed with well-marked social instincts, would inevitably acquire a moral sense or conscience, as soon as its intellectual powers had become as well developed, or anything like as well developed, as in man.

Charles Darwin, *The Descent of Man*[29]

Consciousness and self-consciousness no longer have overt moral connotations, although both can have a bearing on the moral sphere: if I am conscious that I treated you badly when we last met I will be particularly self-conscious when we meet next. Conscience, by contrast, is now exclusively associated with the moral dimension of life.

In contemporary English we speak of conscience reminding us of what we have done – when we should not have – and of nagging us about what we have left undone – when we should have. In these familiar circumstances we say that something or someone is on our conscience: if we manage to make good our sins and omissions, the reward is a clear conscience. As well as reminding us of our misbehaviour, conscience rules on what is right: 'what does your conscience tell you?' we sometimes ask. Different 'consciences' can, of course, come up with different answers.

Despite its historical primacy, and its importance in our everyday lives, conscience is not a key focus of the current interest in consciousness, nor a central concern of this book. But as both Darwin and the author of Genesis imply, there is a significant link between human self-consciousness and human morality. Both seem to imply that the price of self-knowledge is conscience.

On the biblical account it was through disobedience to God that we acquired knowledge of ourselves, discovered shame, and were cast out from the paradise of innocence, mortal and painfully human. The story of the expulsion from Eden is an evocative allegory of the journey we all make from the self-forgetfulness of childhood to the self-knowledge which illuminates and dogs our adult lives.

Darwin offers a more charitable, but related, view of the human condition. He argues that in combination with our sociability, our evolving intelligence was bound to lead 'to the Golden rule, "As ye would that men should do unto you, do ye to them likewise", and this lies at the foundation of morality'.[30]

A note on awareness

With its mixed beginnings in both the Southern and the Northern European tongues, our language has a rich store of synonyms: 'conscious' and 'aware' are good examples. 'Awareness', like 'beware', has a Germanic origin, although the word may share its roots with the Latin *verere*, meaning fear. I shall use both 'consciousness' and 'awareness' in this book – but not quite interchangeably. Synonyms are seldom if ever exact, and 'conscious' and 'aware' are distinguished by a few delicate shades of meaning.

We don't, on the whole, use 'aware' in the first sense of conscious, to mean, simply, 'awake'. Awareness implies consciousness *of* this or that. This implication makes it natural for doctors to describe patients in the persistent vegetative state as 'awake but not aware'.[31] 'Aware' can be used with equal ease in the second or third senses of 'conscious': I am aware of the pangs in my stomach, and that it is time for lunch.

'Self-aware' also has a slightly less extensive set of uses than 'self-conscious'. Self-consciousness can be an impediment: self-awarenesss seldom, if ever, is. If we describe someone as 'self-aware' we tend to imply a compliment: she knows what effect she'll have on others and will act accordingly, with tact. With this one reservation 'self-aware' is used in all the senses we discovered for 'self-conscious'.

Consciousness in other tongues

If consciousness matters, we should expect to find words expressing its various senses in every human language. It would be a surprise, though, if their meanings exactly matched the complex senses of consciousness words in English. For example, 'conscious' in the sense of awake might well be expressed by a different word to 'conscious' in the sense of knowing this or that. On the other hand, if other languages altogether lack a vocabulary of consciousness we might reasonably wonder whether our language is tricking us into a fascination with a mirage.

There are around 30 major groups of languages across the world. Our linguistic neighbours, whose languages share with ours an Indo-European origin in the ancient Indian Sanskrit, should have little difficulty in translating 'consciousness'. So it proves.[32]

In Russian, *soznanie* – derived from *so*, meaning 'with', and *znat*, meaning 'know' – can be used to translate 'consciousness' in all three senses we distinguished. *Sovest* – from *so* combined with *vest*, an archaic verb for 'to know' – corresponds to 'conscience'. The groups of senses we have come across in English do not match up precisely to their Rusian counterparts: for example, my Russian-speaking friend can't come up with a word for 'self-conscious' in the sense of awkward from the *soznat* family.

She wondered at first whether the Russians were immune to this English disease, but, on reflection, other unrelated words, to do with embarrassment and ineptness, were able to capture the sense.

In Danish *bevidsthed* makes use of the intensifying prefix *be* and another word for knowledge, *vide*. *Bevidsthed* can be used to translate 'conscious' in the sense of awake and of our awareness of our surroundings. It can also be used in the context of 'deliberate' acts – ones which are performed with conscious intent. The word for 'conscience' in Danish, *samvittighed*, is a distant relation of *bevidsthed*; *sam*, once again, implies something shared, while *vittig*, the modern word for 'witty', specifies knowledge. The group of words to which *vide* and *vittig* belong has an ancient history, stemming from the Sanskritic *veda* meaning 'knowledge, sacred knowledge, sacred book', surviving in the English 'wit', 'vision' and 'idea'.

Do languages outside the Indo-European family have more trouble with 'consciousness' than our near relations? Hungarian has its origins elsewhere, in the Finno-Ugric language group, but manages perfectly well to translate the consciousness words. *Tudatos*, from *tud*, 'to know', translates 'consciousness' in all three senses we distinguished; *ontudat* is 'self-esteem', *entudat* means 'having a concept of oneself'. 'Conscience' in Hungarian, like Russian, belongs to a different word family: *lelkiismeret* literally translates as 'soul-knowledge'.

Hungarians have an unusual language, but their culture is European. We need to range further afield if we're to provide a stringent test for the hypothesis that every human language has the means to discuss consciousness. How about Chinese?

Reading a glossary of terms for 'conscious' in Chinese gives the English-speaker the sense of moving from prose into poetry. This may be an illusion, but it is a pleasing one. 'Conscious' as 'awake' is translated by *qing xing*: *qing* means 'blue' or 'as clear as the sky or water'; *xing* shares its origins with *jiu*, the word for alcohol. The implication is that consciousness is a state of transparent clarity, in contrast to the murky gloom of drowsiness and sleep.

To be conscious *of* something can be translated by *gan jue* or *yi shi*: *gan* is related to the word for heart, regarded in ancient Chinese thought as the thinking organ; *jue* means enlightenment. *Yi* and *shi* are rather similar: *yi* is related to heart, *shi* to speech and knowledge.

Self-consciousness in the sense of awkwardness can be translated by *niu ni*, words which are also related to 'heart', implying that the sufferer is burdened by an excess of heart – or, we might say, of thought. Self-consciousness in the sense of having an 'idea of me' is *zi jue*, literally 'self-enlightenment'.

Let us try another continent. Ingessana is the language spoken by the subsistence farmers of the Ingessana hills in the Sudan, between the White and the Blue Niles. The verb *den* is a transitive verb, used in the sense of 'gazing at something in particular'. 'Young men gazing at girls' translates as 'bungurk den nyulge'. But *den* can also be used in a more general sense to refer to the waking state or alertness. When used in this way the object of attention is *ok*, a highly abstract word meaning 'place' and/or 'time'. So, to say 'he was conscious', the Ingessana say *ii den ok*, which can be literally translated as 'he was gazing at the situation in general as it unfolded all around'.

Translating consciousness in its second sense, of experience, into Ingessana is more difficult – but not impossible. A hunter who has stopped moving and is listening, looking and possibly even sniffing for prey might be asked *u faden nyii?*: 'what are you sensing?' Knowledge of something or other, the third sense of consciousness, is translated by the verb *nyil*. 'Self' in Ingessana is expressed, very reasonably, by their word for 'body', *iing*.

So far we have encountered no exceptions to the rule that human languages are capable of expressing the senses of 'consciousness' I distinguished. After all, the distinction between sleep and waking, the idea of having experience, the concept of self, are basic ingredients of everyday thought. One would expect other tongues to be able to express them – unless the distinctions enshrined in our language are much more parochial and arbitrary than they appear to us.

The idea that our thought, language and behaviour are indeed parochial and arbitrary gained a large following in anthropology in the middle years of the twentieth century. Reassessment of the evidence has challenged this view. There is a growing consensus that despite the manifest variety of human cultures there are many true 'universals' in human behaviour. Some, perhaps most, of these have a biological, evolutionary, explanation. In Chapter 6 we will come across the evidence, for example, that there is a universal language of facial expression, allowing individuals from all over the world to communicate such states as happiness, sadness, anger and disgust. In a similar vein, every culture seems to possess a set of basic concepts describing our psychology.

Donald Brown, an American anthropologist, offers the following account of the basic psychological beliefs discernible in 'all societies, all cultures and all languages'.[33] He numbers these among the basic notions of the 'universal people', his shorthand for the characteristics common to human groups around the world:

> The universal people have a concept of the person in the psychological sense. They distinguish self from others, and they can see the self both as subject and object. They do not see the person as a wholly passive recipient of external action, nor do they see the self as wholly autonomous. To some degree, they see the person as responsible for his or her actions. They distinguish actions that are under control from those that are not. They understand the concept of intention. They know that people have a private inner life, have memories, make plans, choose between alternatives and otherwise make decisions (not without ambivalent feelings sometimes). They know that people can feel pain and other emotions. They distinguish normal from abnormal mental states. Their personality theory allows them to think of individuals departing from the pattern of behaviour associated with whatever status they occupy, and they can explain these departures in terms of the individual's character. They are spontaneously and intuitively able to, so to say, get in the minds of others to imagine how they are thinking and feeling.

If Brown is right it is no surprise that we should have found the means to express the basic concepts of consciousness in all the languages we have examined. We have not found exact equivalents to our own words: we did not expect to. The subtleties of the vocabulary used to express the various senses of consciousness at a given place and time will reflect the history of the language and local systems of thought. Nor does the widespread use of these concepts demonstrate that they can stand up to the rigours of philosophy or science. But it is reassuring to discover that everyone everywhere has felt the need to discuss awareness.

Consciousness in prospect

'Consciousness', 'self-consciousness' and 'conscience' have a long and complex past. Undoubtedly, part of the 'problem of consciousness' lies in the tangled web of their meanings. But *only* part of the problem – for once we have teased out the senses of these words, difficult and fascinating questions remain for both science and philosophy.

To recap: we have seen, in a number of languages, that words for consciousness stem from a root referring to 'knowledge'. This makes a good deal of sense. Being awake – our first sense of consciousness – is a pre-condition for acquiring knowledge of all kinds. Once awake, we usually come by knowledge through experience – the second sense of consciousness. The knowledge we gain is then 'conscious' in the third sense we distinguished.

We ourselves are numbered among the things of which we can have knowledge: such knowledge is the fruit of 'self-consciousness'. When we learn to recognise our bodies we come to know ourselves as objects; but human beings also gradually come to realise that they are subjects – of experience. Our knowledge of ourselves is bound up with our knowledge of others, and with the question of how we should treat them. This leads us into the realm of conscience.

We have now marked out the territory of this book. The science of waking and sleeping, consciousness in its first sense, is the subject of Chapters 3 and 4. In Chapters 5 and 6 we shall explore the science of vision, an especially vivid ingredient of our consciousness in the second sense of the word. But before we plunge headlong into the science of consciousness I need to prepare the ground for you a little: in the next chapter I shall introduce you to the brain.

2

'The nerves in the brain, oh damn 'em': a sketch of the human nervous system

Well imagine: the nerves in the brain – oh, damn 'em – have sort of little tails . . .

Fyodor Dostoevsky[1]

Introduction

We need two sets of introductions if we are to get a hold on the relationship between consciousness and events in the brain. Chapter 1 has introduced you to the senses of consciousness. The aim of this chapter is to introduce you to the brain.

I shall assume that you know nothing about biology or science. I sympathise if you do not, as I emerged from 12 years of otherwise perfectly good British schooling without ever being taught a syllable of biology. I got to grips with it years later, awkwardly dissecting my first frog in a handsome Victorian university museum. My neighbours were more seasoned workers – palaeontologists, carefully prising dinosaurs from their fragile beds of rock.

It is scarcely possible to convey the sum of current knowledge of the nervous system – the brain, the spinal cord and the nerves that run to muscle and sense organs – in the space of 30-odd pages. I shall do my best, though, to equip you with a basic, wide-ranging outline of neuroscience, to pave the way for the more detailed account of the anatomy and physiology of consciousness and vision at the heart of the book.

The insights into the workings of nerve and brain gained over the past hundred years reflect a huge – and very productive – intellectual effort. Sheer curiosity about the nervous system has been one driving force behind this effort; a wish to do something to help those afflicted by the disorders of the nervous system has also played a part; but many scientists have had another, rather personal, motive: the belief that by understanding the brain they come closer to understanding themselves.

From one perspective, the nervous system is outlandishly complex, but from another its essentials are quite simple. Let's start with the simple view.

The simple nervous system

The simple nervous system consists of *cells* which are *interconnected*: their function is to transmit signals, enabling animals to respond to events with appropriate actions. To understand the cells of the nervous system you need to know a little about cells in general.

Cells[2]

Large living things like us are extraordinary cooperative ventures, great communities of independent parts. This is readily apparent on the large scale: we all know that our health depends upon a collaboration between our heart and our lungs, liver and kidneys, bowels and bone. Transplant surgery illustrates their potential autonomy: my heart could beat in place of yours; with gentle handling, it would survive a journey of a few hundred miles between us.

It is less apparent that our organs themselves are communities of parts. This discovery required the invention of the light microscope which first suggested, about 150 years ago, that the tissues from which we are formed, like coral reefs, are colonies of microscopic cells.

Cells are the smallest potentially independent living units of the body, the 'atoms' of biology. Each contains a full complement of genetic material, consumes energy, generates waste and constantly repairs and refashions itself. Given the right conditions and sufficient care, most human cell types can now be teased apart from their owner, and grown in the laboratory.

Cells are small, but not fantastically so: the 'red cells' of the blood, for example, which carry oxygen around the body, are smaller than most. They are about $^1/_{100}$th of a millimetre across, a distance you cannot quite read off your ruler but which doesn't strain the imagination too severely. It is, nonetheless, possible to pack a quite prodigious number of them into us: there are a million million red cells in a litre of blood, of which about 5 litres are coursing through your veins.

We have been able to examine the detail that lies *within* the cell only relatively recently, for about fifty years, since the invention of the more powerful electron microscope. With the help of this tool it became apparent that cells have their own internal architecture. They are bounded, and protected, by a 'membrane', a surrounding double layer of fat and protein. This is of particular importance to nerves, as we shall see. Within the cell, a 'cytoskeleton' of minute fibres helps to organise its various residents, known as its 'organelles': the work of the cell is divided among them (see Figures 2.1 and 2.2).

The 'nucleus' of the cell is the chief of the organelles. It contains our genes, the inherited instructions, coded in our chromosomes, which are required to build and to maintain the human body. These are an identical copy of the instructions contained in the fertilised egg, from which the newborn babe and all its cells are formed over the 40 weeks of gestation. Because these instructions are present in every cell, it should in principle

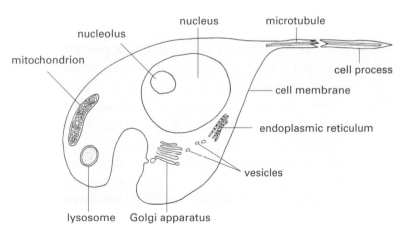

Figure 2.1 The architecture of a cell Microscopy reveals a world within the cell. The nucleus and mitochondria are discussed in the text. The other organelles shown are involved in the manufacture of proteins (nucleolus, endoplasmic reticulum); in packaging and transporting materials within the cell (Golgi apparatus, vesicles); in waste disposal (lysosomes); or in controlling the cell's structure and its movements (microtubule, process).

Proteins embedded in the membrane allow signal conduction
and communication between the cell and the world beyond

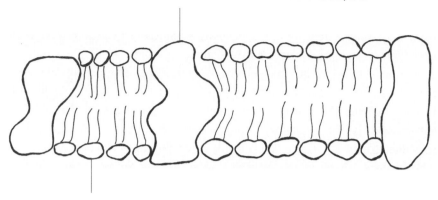

The main constituent of the cell membrane is a double layer
of fat which seals the cell from its watery surroundings

Figure 2.2 The cell membrane This double-layered coat of fat, studded with proteins,
is at the interface between the cell and its surroundings. It plays a vital
role in neurons: proteins embedded in the neural membrane make it possible for
neurons to conduct signals and communicate with one another.

be possible to grow you – more accurately, to clone your identical twin –
from any single cell among your many millions. Since I wrote the first draft
of this chapter, a celebrated sheep named Dolly has been successfully
cloned from a single cell. There is every prospect that genetic technology
will soon allow us to reproduce by similar means, if we so wish.

The instructions which spell out our nature are written in a chemical
code, known as DNA, to which we will return later in the book. These
instructions are recipes for the production of a great many different kinds
of protein – several tens of thousands of them. Proteins are large molecules. They consist of strings of smaller ones called amino acids, which
themselves come in about 25 varieties. A set of organelles beside the
nucleus, equipped with an elaborate chemical machinery, use the instructions issued by the nucleus to string together amino acids in the order specified by the genes.

The proteins that result differ widely in size and shape and serve a myriad
functions: some are 'structural', contributing to the architecture of the cell;
others, 'enzymes', regulate the host of chemical reactions on which the life
of the cell depends; others are inserted in the membrane, yet others are
exported from the cell. This protein factory is particularly productive during
growth, when cells are rapidly reproducing themselves, but it continues to
operate as long as we live, maintaining the fabric and function of the cell.

The synthesis of proteins, like many of the other activities of the cell, consumes energy and requires fuel. Unicellular organisms, such as amoebae, are much occupied by the pursuit of fuel. Human cells are largely spared this job, as blood penetrates our tissues, bringing with it oxygen, sugars, fats, amino acids and the other essentials of life.

The organelles which have the job of extracting energy from the fuels that reach the cell are known as mitochondria. They have a remarkable history: they are thought to have originated as bacteria which entered into a symbiotic relationship with an early ancestor of our cells about 1,500 million years ago, almost half the age of the earth. In keeping with their independent origins they retain a small complement of their own genes, unique in this respect among the organelles. A rare group of human diseases is transmitted by mutant mitochondrial DNA: these disorders can be inherited only from one's mother as all our mitochondria originate in the maternal egg, none from paternal sperm.

All this may give you a sense of vanishing horizons: bodies contain organs, organs contain cells, cells are nests of organelles – is there no end to this succession of living worlds within worlds? Happily, there is. As we focus within the cell on to its component parts we begin to leave behind the world of living things, which breathe, ingest, excrete, and pursue food and mates, and to enter the world of chemical reactions. There is an intermediate realm, studied by biochemists, the realm of molecules, like proteins and DNA, which have been shaped in the course of evolution for the sustenance of life, but chemistry itself belongs to a different order of creation, and we will not follow it further.

The cells of the human body all conform more or less to the idealised description I have just given. But I have been guilty of one major simplification: human cells are by no means all identical (see Figure 2.3). As the body takes shape in the womb, populations of cells enter different streams of development: one, for example, is destined to give rise to the lungs, another to muscle, a third to the kidneys and bladder. The resulting cell types in the various tissues look and behave very differently: the delicate cells of the lung permit the passage of gases to and fro; cells in muscle, packed with sliding fibres, contract and move our parts; cells of the kidney form blood-filtration units and looping pipes which distil urine. These differences come about because only some of the total complement of genetic recipes is expressed in each cell type: others are rendered silent as development proceeds. There is no need for every cell in a large 'multicellular' creature like us to perform every function. In the economy of the

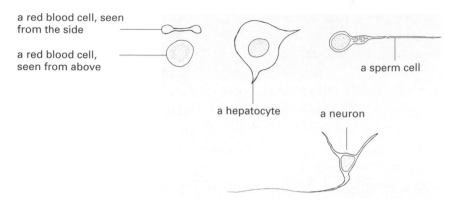

Figure 2.3 Cell types A red blood cell, a 'hepatocyte', the major cell type of the liver, a sperm cell and a neuron illustrate the diversity of human cells.

body, as in the economy of human society, specialisation makes for a comfortable life.

The chief specialist cell in the nervous system is known as the neuron. Its peculiarities reflect its primary function, as a signalling device. It is time for us to get to know it better.

Neurons[3]

All the minute elements of a cell, the nucleus and its companion organelles, are present in neurons: they are in fact exceptionally busy cells, with a high demand for nourishment, a brisk expenditure of energy and rapid turnover of protein.

The most striking superficial difference between neuronal cells and others, for instance the red cells of the blood, is their shape, but, given that their business is to convey signals from one place to another, it is no surprise that neurons are elongated beasts. They tend to resemble trees, with branching roots to receive incoming messages, a smooth trunk to transmit them and a bushy crown through which they send their message on. Accordingly, the vocabulary with which we describe the parts of a neuron originates in the forest: the neuron's branching roots are its 'dendrites', from the Greek *dendron*, a 'tree'; its trunk is an axon, from the Greek for axle and its crown is an 'arborisation' (see Figure 2.4).

The message the axon transmits is electrical. To explain this requires a brief digression. Among their other remarkable properties, all the cells of the body are minute batteries: that is to say, they concentrate a small amount of electrical charge. Specifically, the inside of the cell contains an

branched dendrites receive
signals from other neurons

the neuron's cell body
contains the nucleus
and sustains the cell

the axon conveys
an all-or-nothing
electrical signal away
from the cell body
to communicate with
other neurons via
the synapses it makes
with them

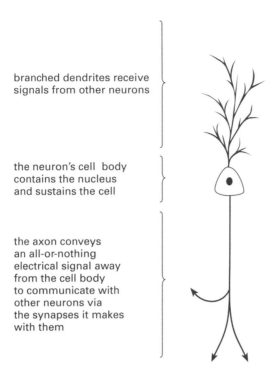

Figure 2.4 The neuron and its parts Neurons are often reminiscent of plants and trees, with branching roots and ramifying crowns. The vocabulary used to describe them echoes these similarities. 'Dendrites', branching out from the cell body, receive contacts from the termini of other neurons; the cell body houses the nucleus and chemical machinery required to sustain the cell; an 'axon' conveys the neuron's electrical signal away from the cell body: it may branch into a terminal 'arborisation' where it makes contact with other cells.

excess of negative charge when compared with the outside. This state of affairs creates an opportunity which the cells of nerve and muscle have exploited to the full. A momentary reversal of the electrical difference can be transmitted down the cell – to send a message. This binary 'all or nothing' signal is known as the *action potential*: it succinctly expresses the moment-to-moment results of the neuron's key decision in life, whether or not to fire. Many neurons in fact fire spontaneously at a steady rate: if so, they can convey information either by increasing or by decreasing the rate of their action potentials, just as a hush in the sound from a crowd conveys as much as a roar.

Because neurons crackle with electricity it is tempting to think of them as wires, simply transmitting pulses of current around the nervous system. The analogy is apt but incomplete: they are not merely 'live', but living.

Besides the electrical traffic pulsing down them, there is a constant movement of materials: a process of 'axonal transport' slowly conveys a stream of molecules up and down the neuron at a rate varying from less than 1 millimetre to around 4 centimetres a day, enabling the cell body to supply its distant processes and keeping it informed about their needs. If this flow is stemmed, the neuron swells visibly at the obstruction, just as a branch of a tree will bulge at a ligature. Neurons can be deceived into transporting substances which are of no use to them, or which impair their function. Neuroanatomists, who chart the pathways of the nervous system, exploit this weakness by injecting tracers in one part of the brain which they can later visualise in another – with the implication that the two areas communicate; some toxins, like the one responsible for tetanus, smuggle themselves into neurons and hitch a ride to the spot where they work their mischief.

Despite their otherwise energetic lifestyle, neurons have the peculiarity that they seldom reproduce themselves after our birth.[4] There is, as we shall discover, a very good reason for this, but it means that the nervous system is less able to repair itself than most of our other organs, if it is damaged by accident or disease.

Neuronal neighbours

No cell is an island. All the tissues of the body, from liver to brain, contain a variety of cell types, and neurons, therefore, have their neighbours. 'Glial' cells are the most abundant, as numerous as neurons; they come in three principal varieties.

Oligodendrocytes manufacture a form of insulation for most of the axons of neurons in the central nervous system. They do so by wrapping their own membrane repeatedly around the axon to create a fatty sheath, known as 'myelin': this greatly increases the speed with which the axon can transmit its action potential, from a few metres/second to as much as 100 metres/second. Damage to myelin, disrupting electrical transmission down the axon, lies at the root of a number of human diseases, including multiple sclerosis.

Astrocytes are fibrous glial cells, which provide structural support for adult neurons, and guidance for the growing tips of foetal neurons when they are finding their way in the brain. They help to maintain the right chemical conditions for electrical signalling by taking up potassium – a substance which neurons extrude when they are electrically active – and releasing it elsewhere. Their processes contribute to the 'blood–brain barrier' which normally excludes the cells of the blood and most of its proteins from the immediate surroundings of the rather fastidious neuron.

The third glial type, the microglia, are the scavengers of the brain, tidying up damaged cells and their debris. Unlike neurons, some glial cells continue to multiply in life: the downside of their fecundity is that they give rise to the majority of brain tumours.

Other cells rub shoulders with neurons and glia. The busy metabolism of the nervous system requires a rich circulation. Blood vessels therefore abound in the brain. At the fringes of the nervous system, the cells of the 'meninges' and 'ependyma' line the brain and spinal cord. Together with the choroid plexus, a tufty tissue dedicated to secretion, they produce the 'cerebrospinal fluid', in which the brain and spinal cord are bathed, and which helps to insulate them from the jolts of life: half a litre of this transparent liquid is produced and reabsorbed each day. The meninges are the site of infection in meningitis, a condition in which the otherwise clear waters of the spinal fluid become clouded with bacteria.

These are the cells of the nervous system, the neurons and their various neighbours. Their most fundamental job is the faithful transmission of signals. But what triggers neurons into electrical action? The answer lies with the second element of our 'simple nervous system', at the junctions between cells.

Interconnections

By a celebrated irony the great nineteenth-century Italian neuro-microscopist, Camillo Golgi, who discovered the method for highlighting individual neurons with a silver stain which anatomists still use today, was never convinced that neurons were truly separate from one another. The gap that separates them is too small to be resolved by the light microscope, and in Golgi's day there remained a distinct possibility that the nervous system would prove to be a 'syncitium', a continuous network of cells. The work of his Spanish collaborator and eventual rival, Ramon y Cajal, and later of the electron microscopists, showed beyond any doubt that, although neurons are tightly packed, they are separate from one another, meeting at junctions known as *synapses*, tiny clefts between one cell and the next. As a rule, the terminal 'arborisation' of the axon makes a number of synapses with the dendrites, and sometimes with the cell bodies, of the cells to which it signals.

This raises an obvious question. Electrical signals manage to make their way down living axons, but how can they bridge the gulf between one cell and the next? They do not need to. At the synapse the currency of neural signalling changes. In place of an electrical impulse, a chemical messenger floats across the cleft. Its effect, on arrival, is to make it more or less likely that the cell on which it impinges will discharge an electrical impulse.

An early experiment demonstrating that transmission at synapses has a chemical basis is notable partly because it came to its inventor, the German pharmacologist Otto Loewi, in a dream. Loewi knew that electrical stimulation of the vagus nerve, which runs to the heart, slowed its beating. His dream suggested to him that he should try the effect of injecting the fluid bathing a stimulated heart into the fluid surrounding an unstimulated one: as he had hoped, this injection slowed the second heart, indicating that the stimulated nerve releases a chemical which leaked into the fluid bathing it. We shall encounter this important chemical, the neurotransmitter acetylcholine, later.

The synapse, and the chemicals which cross it, complete our picture of a simple nervous system. Its function is to enable an animal to respond to events it senses in its environs with appropriate actions: a *signalling* system of some kind is required to detect the events and orchestrate apt responses. The nervous system meets this need. Neuron, synapse and neurotransmitter, the components of this elegant device for electrochemical signalling, are the simple essence of the human nervous system (see Figure 2.5).

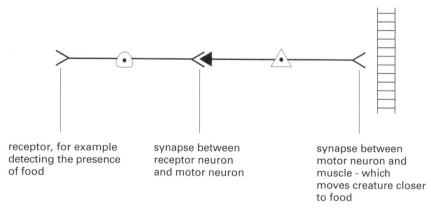

receptor, for example detecting the presence of food

synapse between receptor neuron and motor neuron

synapse between motor neuron and muscle - which moves creature closer to food

Figure 2.5 A simple signalling system The simplest neuronal signalling system, similar to the system which controls some human reflexes, consists of two neurons and a muscle. In this example, a sensory neuron detects the presence of food, signals this to a 'motor neuron', and activates a muscle so placed that it moves the creature closer to its food source.

Simplicity embodied

Before we move on to the undeniable complexities of the human brain, it is worth pausing to admire a genuinely simple and much-studied nervous system. *Caenorhabditis elegans* is a roundworm with a distinguished record in science. Work by Sidney Brenner, originally in Cambridge, and others, over the last 30 years has provided an amazingly detailed description of this reliable animal's make-up.[5]

C. elegans in maturity contains exactly 959 cells, 302 of which are are neurons. These are to be found in the same locations and fulfil the same roles in every normal member of the species. The 302 cells make about 8,000 connections; these have also been mapped, and appear just as invariant as the cells themselves.

C. elegans' genes require about 1/500th as much DNA as ours. These genes in turn have been comprehensively mapped, making it possible to explore the detailed relationships between the animal's genetic make-up, the course of its development and its mature anatomy and behaviour.

Another relatively simple animal has won great fame in neuroscience. The sea snail *Aplysia californica*, with 20,000 neurons, makes *C. elegans* look something of a dunce. Nevertheless its repertoire of behaviour remains quite limited. It has some capacity to adapt its behaviour to circumstance, for example toning down its defensive withdrawal response after repeated stimulation.[6] These modifications have been intensively studied by the American neuroscientist, Eric Kandel, whose work has begun to reveal the details of the neuronal basis for simple forms of learning. But the nervous systems which interest us most are of a rather different kind.

The complex nervous system

The essentials of the nervous system may be simple, but a change of focus reveals dizzying complexity. A complex nervous system – such as ours – consists of astounding numbers of neurons, of widely varying types, organised into intricate local and long-range networks; these cells communicate with one another across several kinds of synapse using any of a large array of chemical messengers with a variety of effects. To help us find our way around I will once again discuss the cells themselves and their interconnections in turn.

Neurons – and their networks

Neuronal numbers and types

There are approximately 100,000 million neurons in the human nervous system. This is a goodly number: there are around 20 times as many neurons in your brain as there are human beings on earth. The number is the more remarkable if one recalls that there is a sense in which each of them enjoys an independent life.

Unlike the red cells of the blood which are packed into our circulation in even greater numbers, neurons are highly diverse. Neuronal types differ in size and in shape, in their chemistry and in the design of the networks to which they contribute.

Large neurons are among the largest cells in the body. The axon that activates a small muscle in your foot runs to it from the cell body of a neuron located in the spinal cord, at a level just below your umbilicus. This cell can be as much as a metre in length. It is an excellent example of a 'projection' neuron, which conveys a message to a site remote from its source. At the other extreme of neuronal size, an 'interneuron' in the brain or spinal cord, a cell which engages only in short-range communication with its immediate neighbours, might have an extent of less than a millimetre.

Shape is partly dictated by size: the appearance of the 3-footer is bound to be predominantly long and thin. But under the microscope variety abounds, giving rise to a wealth of descriptive terms (see Figures 2.7 and 2.11): 'stellate', 'basket', 'granule' and 'chandelier' cells are among the smaller interneurons of the brain; projection neurons are often 'pyramidal', named after the shape of their cell bodies, with a tall apical dendrite, basal dendrites encrusted with spines, and an inconspicuous axon heading out; 'Purkinje' cells, named after a nineteenth-century Czech microscopist, the projection neurons of a part of the brain called the cerebellum, have elegant dendrites splayed out in a single plane which would pass muster in the most disciplined town park. Size, shape and chemistry go hand in hand, but I will defer more talk of the chemical differences between neurons until we return to interconnections, where chemistry comes into its own.

Neuronal networks

By emphasising the variety within the nervous system I may be conveying an impression of disorder, as if the brain were a random thicket of cells. Far from it: the various cell types find their place within orderly networks, in which small structured units of interconnecting cells are stacked up side by side.

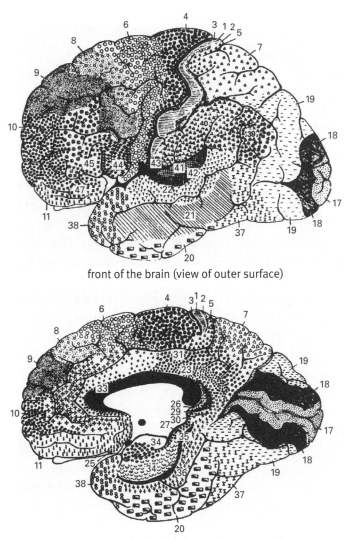

front of the brain (view of outer surface)

front of the brain (view of inner surface)

Figure 2.6 Brodmann's map of the human brain Korbinian Brodmann's map of cortical areas was drawn almost a century ago on the basis of microscopic differences of cortical structure. The distinctions Brodmann drew for anatomical reasons have turned out to correspond to functional boundaries, and his map remains in common use today.

The cerebral cortex, for instance, is the wrinkled outer mantle of the brain. It is only 2–4 millimetres thick, but its area, increased by its infoldings, is a little over a square metre in each hemisphere, comparable to a fair-sized tablecloth. Its detailed structure varies considerably as one travels over its surface. Indeed, at the start of the twentieth century, the German anatomist Korbinian Brodmann distinguished more than 50 areas, but most of these share a broad organisational plan (see Figure 2.6).

The repeating unit in the cortex is a column of cells, about a tenth of a millimetre across, extending throughout the thickness of the cortex. Six layers of cells are traditionally distinguished within each cortical column (see Figure 2.7). Small interneurons in layer IV receive most of the incoming signals, the 'afference', to the column; these communicate directly and indirectly with two tiers of projection neurons: superficial pyramidal cells in layers II and III transmit the column's output, its 'efference', to other regions of cortex; deep pyramidal cells in layers V and VI report to more remote targets in the nervous system, beyond the cortex itself.

Cells both large and small within each column share a common purpose: the computation of a certain pattern of output from a given pattern of inputs. They communicate intensely with one another, more sparingly with cells in neighbouring columns. Numerous columns within a single region of cortex can be active simultaneously, in parallel. They are the modules of cortical anatomy, exemplifying the order which underlies variety within every part of the nervous system.

We will encounter several other examples of modular design in our travels round the brain, and discover that local networks, such as cortical columns, are invariably part of larger, long-range, networks. Some of these are our best candidates for the neural basis of experience. The networks which subserve vision are the main subject of Chapter 5.

Neuronal beginnings

Given the cellular diversity and anatomical intricacy of the nervous system, it should be no surprise that its growth and upkeep make heavy demands on our genes. In fact, between two and three times as many of the instructions encoded in the genome are expressed in the nervous system as in any other organ. Much of this inheritance is on show well before birth.

One can discern the earliest beginnings of the nervous system in a human embryo in the third week after conception, when one of the three sheets of cells of which the disc-like embryo then consists folds in upon itself to form a hollow tube (see Figure 2.8). This resembles the nervous system of some of our more distant ancestors, and these humble origins leave their traces in the hollow spaces at the centre of the adult nervous system: the ventricles of the brain and the central canal of the spinal cord.

Spina bifida, exposure of part of the spinal cord, results if the canal fails to close, with drastic consequences for the normal functioning of the cord.

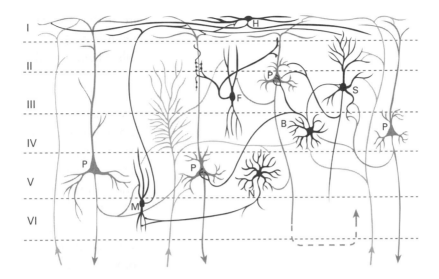

Figure 2.7 The layers of the cortex The six-layered structures of the cerebral cortex and the types of neuron found within them. It gives an impression of the way inputs to and outputs from the cortex are organised: the incoming axons at the left and right are from other areas of the cortex, while the central incoming axon is conveying specific sensory information. Cell types: P = pyramidal, M = Martinotti, F = fusiform, H = horizontal, N = neurogliaform, B = basket, S = stellate.

As it normally closes about a week after the canal first begins to form, advice *before* conception is much more effective than antenatal counselling in the prevention of this disorder. If, instead, the hollow spaces within the nervous system close normally but later enlarge abnormally, other mischief ensues. Syringomyelia is an expansion of the central canal of the spinal cord, squeezing the cells and axons it impinges on to cause numb arms, weak hands and stiff legs; hydrocephalus, 'water on the brain', is an expansion of the ventricles within the brain, which presses it against the inside of the skull, potentially disabling all its functions.

Within two weeks of its formation the neural tube begins to flex and swell, foreshadowing its future growth: a 'forebrain' expansion will give rise to the hemispheres of the brain; midbrain and hindbrain expansions prefigure the stem of the brain, which links the hemispheres to the spinal cord. Over the next eight months of prenatal life this swelling tube lengthens, thickens, bends and folds (see Figure 2.9). Successive waves of cells are generated by the division of progenitors which hug the central spaces of the nervous system. These cells migrate into position, and start to form orderly connections with targets near and far.

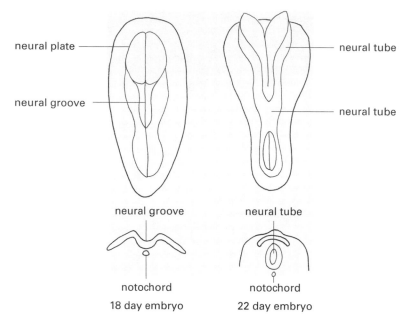

neural plate — neural tube

neural groove — neural tube

neural groove — neural tube

notochord — notochord

18 day embryo — 22 day embryo

Figure 2.8 The nervous system in the embryo The left-hand drawing shows the view from above a human embryo at about 18 days after conception: a slipper-shaped region, the neural plate, contains the cells which will go on to form the nervous system; by 22 days (right-hand drawing) the neural folds, which arise from the neural plate, have begun to fuse, creating a neural tube, the hollow forerunner of the brain and spinal cord. The small drawings below show end-on views of the middle of the embryo at the same stages of development as the sketches above them.

The near-miraculous ability of the nervous system to organise its own intricate structure as it grows is one of the several features that distinguishes it from the human technology to which it is often compared. It culminates, eventually, in the fully fledged nervous system. Allow me to show you around it.

A tour of the human nervous system

The scale of individual neurons is microscopic, but they congregate in macroscopic – visible to the naked eye – chunks of neural tissue. Our tour of the nervous system will navigate regions which you could see and touch if they were laid bare for your inspection, although I will say a little more about them than simple inspection would reveal. It seems sensible to begin with the most familiar part of the nervous system, which lies just under the skin.

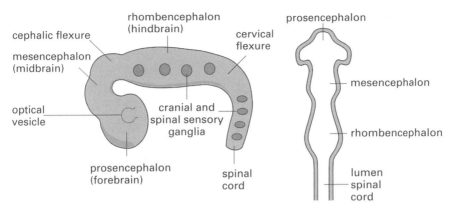

Figure 2.9 The divisions of the embryonic brain at four weeks A side view and schematic top view of the four-week-old embryo. The beginnings of the nerves which will grow out to the head and body are already apparent. The tubular structure of the nervous system is in evidence.

PERIPHERAL NERVES

Straighten your left arm and place two fingers of your right hand on the bony outcrop which forms the inner margin of your elbow. Roll your fingers just beyond and above the outcrop and you will find a sensitive mobile cord, the 'ulnar nerve'. A nerve is a bundle of thousands of axons running to and from neuronal cell bodies in – or very close to – the spinal cord. It conveys a two-way traffic, incoming from sense organs, outgoing to muscles. When you deal the ulnar nerve a glancing blow you have hit the 'funny bone'; as you recover, you may notice some tingling in the ring and little fingers to which this nerve supplies sensation. Repeated blows can cause the muscles of the hand to waste away, as most of them are controlled by axons in the ulnar nerve.

The ulnar is one of three principal nerves which serve the arm. The others are better concealed. The axons within the nerve differ in size and in the presence or absence of a myelin sheath. Large myelinated axons are the quickies, conducting signals at up to 100 metres/second. They are responsible for functions in which speed is of the essence, like the rapid dance of a pianist's fingers over the keys. The myelin ensheathing peripheral axons is manufactured by Schwann cells, rather than the oligodendrocytes of the central nervous system. These are named after Theodor Schwann, a nineteenth-century German biologist who established the 'cell theory' for human tissues generally. Small unmyelinated fibres are at work, for example, in pain sensation: their slow signalling helps to explain the unpleasant 'after-pain' which sometimes follows the first sharp shock of a skin wound.

Each of the axons within the nerve can do no more or less than convey a pattern of electrical activity. The *significance* of its activity depends upon its source and destination.

The incoming fibres in the ulnar nerve originate in microscopic sense organs in skin, muscle and tendon. These organs serve to convert local physical perturbations – the proximity of warmth or cold, a dimpling of the skin by gentle pressure, a vibration at a fingertip, the movement of a muscle as it shortens – into a discharge travelling down an axon. Sight, hearing, taste and smell are similarly served by the more conspicuous sense organs in eye, ear, tongue and nose, and by their own 'afferent' nerves. In every case the bald principle is the same: a sense organ transforms a physical stimulus into the common electrical currency of neural signalling.

Outgoing fibres activate muscles. They do so across a modified synapse known as the neuromuscular junction, by releasing the neurotransmitter acetylcholine, which we encountered earlier in the context of Otto Loewi's dream. The muscles themselves respond by producing an action potential, which leads eventually to their contraction. Just as all sensation depends on electrical signals conveyed from sense organs by afferent nerves, so all our actions depend on electrical signals conveyed to muscles in efferent nerves. Every item of human behaviour, our speech and our writing, our gesture and dance, is achieved by a patterned contraction of muscles.

Peripheral nerves, like the ulnar, collectively comprise the 'peripheral nervous system' – as against the 'central nervous system' consisting of the brain and spinal cord (see Figure 2.10). Before we press into the interior from this crucial outpost of the nervous system, we should notice one further distinction.

The 'motor' functions of peripheral nerves which we have touched on – subserving gesture and speech for instance – are the preserve of the 'voluntary nervous system', and the 'striated' muscle which it commands, so called because of its stripy appearance under the microscope. A minority of the axons within a peripheral nerve belong to the 'autonomic' division of the nervous system. This concerns itself with the almost entirely unconscious regulation of our internal organs and their 'smooth muscle': contraction of the gut, racing of the heart, erection of the penis, for example, all depend on signalling within the autonomic nervous system – and can all notoriously defy our conscious plans. Our blood vessels also have smooth muscle in their walls: when we blush, the autonomic nervous system is giving us away.

The autonomic nervous system has two principal divisions, with broadly opposing actions, the 'sympathetic' and the 'parasympathetic'. The

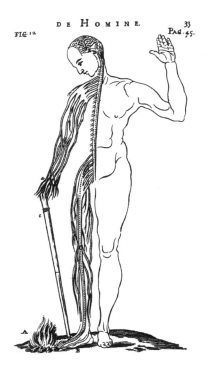

Figure 2.10 The nervous system This seventeenth-century illustration shows the nervous system in its entirety: the brain and spinal cord comprise the central nervous system. The spinal roots can be seen emerging from the spinal cord. They are shown running into the nerves of the arms and legs; in the trunk, where they have been cut short in this figure, they course into nerves running around the body to supply the skin and muscles. These nerves, of limbs and trunk, together with the cranial nerves of the head, make up the peripheral nervous system. The figure was drawn to illustrate the nervous pathways which allow us to withdraw from a painful stimulus, and is deliberately diagrammatic.

sympathetic, for example, speeds the heart and dilates the pupils, while the parasympathetic slows the heart and constricts the pupils. The cell bodies of autonomic neurons reside outside the spinal cord, either close beside it, in the case of the 'sympathetic chain', or close to the targets of the autonomic nerves, in the 'ganglia' of the parasympathetic nervous system. There are said to be as many autonomic neurons in the gut, for example, as there are neurons in the entire length of the spinal cord. We are as a rule serenely unaware of the continuous neural activity in this vital system. This implies that perceptual consciousness is not an inevitable accompaniment of the operation of large neuronal networks, a point we shall return to.

THE SPINAL CORD

The peripheral nerves of the limbs run to and from the spinal cord. They enter it by way of a series of 27 paired 'spinal roots', nerve bundles which penetrate between the bony 'vertebrae' whose protruding spines you feel if you run your fingers down your back.

The structure of the embryonic nervous system is still on show in the cord. It has a tiny 'central canal', the remnant of the hollow tube which gives rise to nervous tissue. This is surrounded by the 'grey matter' of the spinal cord, a nest of neuronal cell bodies; if you slice across the cord and look down on the cut surface, the grey matter is butterfly shaped. This, in turn, is surrounded by the cord's 'white matter', a thick rim of ascending and descending axons through which the brain and cord communicate.

The parent cell bodies of the axons running to muscle reside within the cord, in its 'anterior horn', the forward sections of the two butterfly wings. These are the cells which relentlessly degenerate in 'motor neuron disease': deprived of their nerve supply, the muscles of sufferers from this sad condition gradually waste away. Of the incoming sensory fibres, some make their first synapse in the 'dorsal horns', the back sections of the wings; others travel in the 'dorsal columns' of the white matter to reach the brain directly.

The spinal cord is an indispensable conduit for neural signalling to and from the body. Serious injury to it, common enough at work and play, causes paralysis and loss of sensation below the level of damage. This is usually irreparable: severed peripheral nerves can grow slowly back to their targets, at about one millimetre a day, but self-repair after injuries to axons in the central nervous system, including the spinal cord, is very limited.

But the cord is not *just* an information highway. The grey matter of the cord transforms the signals reaching it. Many reflexes are organised there. When a neurologist taps below the kneecap to elicit a jerk of the leg, he is testing a spinal 'reflex loop': sensory input, from organs in tendon and muscle which detect the tap, travels back to the cord; it excites a group of motor neurones in the anterior horn; these signal back to the muscle stretched by the tap, which contracts, causing the jerk.

BRAINSTEM AND CEREBELLUM

Where the spine meets the skull, the spinal cord passes through a large opening, the 'foramen magnum', and merges with the brain. The brain itself has three clearly separable major parts: the *brainstem* emerges from the spinal cord, a curved shaft of nervous tissue, which is surrounded at its top end by the paired *cerebral hemispheres*, their surface formed by the convolutions of the cortex. At the back of the brainstem, tucked in beneath the hemispheres, sits the rounded *cerebellum*.

Broadly speaking, the brainstem has three functions: first, it serves the head much as the spinal cord serves the limbs and trunk, controlling the movements of the eyes, the muscles of the face, speech and swallowing, and receiving signals which mediate facial sensation, taste and hearing. Second, it transmits all the signals by which the brain, the cord and the brainstem communicate. Third, and most importantly for us, it contains interconnected clusters of neurons which govern both the heart and lungs below and the hemispheres above: these cells of the 'reticular formation' control the most fundamental rhythms of our conscious lives, our waking, dreaming, sleeping. The genesis of these rhythms, and their disorders, are the subjects of Chapters 3 and 4. So vital is the brainstem to life and consciousness that 'brain death' is often defined as death of the *brainstem*. As it is reliably followed within hours to days by death pure and simple, British law permits organs to be removed for donation once brainstem death is established beyond doubt.

The cerebellum fits snugly behind the brainstem, above the base of the skull. It comprises only 10 per cent of the volume of the brain but contains more than half of its total complement of neurons. Its appearance superficially suggests that it is a second brain, nestling beneath the cerebrum, and this suggestion is not far wrong. Its microscopic anatomy reveals a distinctive and highly repetitive modular design, quite unlike the columnar structure of the cortex (see Figure 2.11).

This design is repeated throughout the cerebellum, but the function of its three main subdivisions depends on the site of their input and output. Its most ancient region, the 'vestibulocerebellum', helps to maintain our balance and to coordinate the movements of our head and eyes; the 'spino-cerebellum' contributes to balance, and to the smooth execution of trunk and limb movements; the 'cerebrocerebellum' participates in their initiation, planning and timing. Damage to the cerebellum can be the result of an inherited predisposition, or may follow the interruption of its blood supply in stroke, or the patchy inflammation – a kind of 'brain rash' – seen in multiple sclerosis. The damage manifests itself in slurring of speech, clumsiness of fine movements, tremor and unsteadiness.

The cerebellum has traditionally been regarded as a 'neuronal machine', an on-board computer coordinating movement, but evidence is accumulating to suggest that the cerebellum coordinates thought and emotion in much the way that it coordinates movement. This idea is a reminder that

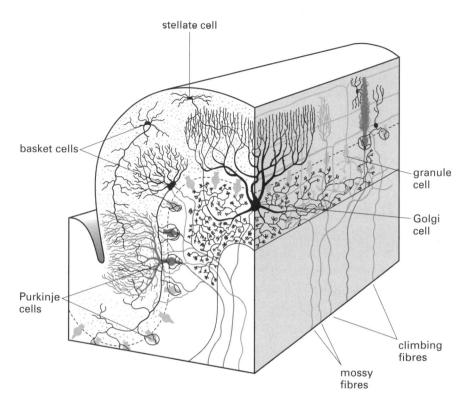

stellate cell

basket cells

granule cell

Golgi cell

Purkinje cells

climbing fibres

mossy fibres

Figure 2.11 The architecture of the cerebellum This beautiful figure illustrates the cell types and organisation of the cortex of the cerebellum, a brain region mainly involved in programming smooth and accurate movements.

distinctions like those between movement and experience, which we like to draw in our compartmentalised thinking, are not always respected by the brain.

WITHIN THE HEMISPHERES

Imagine that you were travelling up from the central canal of the spinal cord, into the central fluid-filled spaces of the brain. Your journey through the brainstem would take you from the tented expanse of the fourth ventricle, overarched by the cerebellum, into the claustrophobic confines of the aqueduct of Sylvius within the midbrain. You would emerge from this canal in a tall cave at the heart of the cerebrum proper, known as the third ventricle. In the distance you might catch a glimpse of the foraminae of Monro, the openings of the third ventricle into the more spacious lateral ventricles. But linger a little before you sail on. The floor and walls of the third ventricle contain the first major structures of the forebrain (see Figure 2.12).

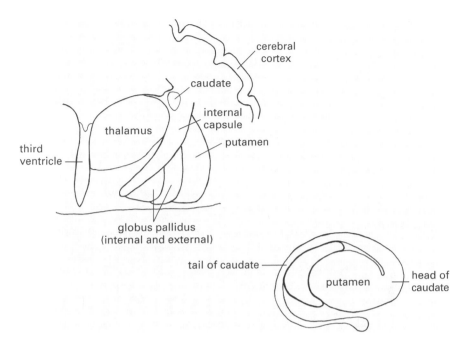

Figure 2.12 The thalami and basal ganglia These figures show the positions of the thalamus, which contains a microcosm of cerebral activity, and the basal ganglia, a brain system best recognised for its role in programming movement, but which also has wide-ranging effects on thought and behaviour. The upper drawing shows the brain as if cut from above, 'from ear to ear': the text describes the structures one would encounter if one were to travel outward from the third ventricle to the cortex. The lower drawing shows that the putamen and caudate, seen from the side, are really parts of a single structure, the 'striatum', partly divided by the fibres of the internal capsule; the globus pallidus is nestling out of sight, hidden behind the putamen.

In the walls of the third ventricle, to each side, lie the thalami, twin nests of neuronal cell bodies. The *thalamus* is a relay station for signals to and from the cortex, but this description understates its importance. Fifteen or more distinct aggregrations of neurons – known rather confusingly as 'nuclei' – can be discerned within the thalamus. One, for example, receives much of the neural input from the eyes, another much of the afference from the cerebellum. This input is sent on to appropriate cortical regions and these send fibres back in return, so that the thalamic nuclei are equipped for a dialogue with their targets. All cortical regions communicate with the thalamus, and it also receives important input from the regions of the brainstem which regulate wakefulness and arousal. Activity in the nuclei of the thalamus is therefore a microcosm of hemispheric function, and the thalamus is well placed both to regulate alertness generally and to focus selective attention. Small volumes of damage to the thalamus can be devastating. Figure 2.13 shows a scan from a patient who suffered a stroke, due to a blocked blood vessel, affecting both sides of the thalamus. At the time of the stroke he was unrousable, and he remains, several years later, drowsy and inattentive. Widespread damage to the thalamus sometimes underlies the condition of permanent 'wakefulness without awareness' which is known as the 'persistent vegetative state'. Understandably several neuroscientists have suggested that the thalamus plays a key role in consciousness: we shall return to it later.

In the floor of the third ventricle lies the *hypothalamus*, with the pituitary gland suspended from its belly. This comprises less than 1 per cent of the volume of the human brain, but has an importance out of all proportion to its size. It samples the body's internal environment, monitoring parameters such as blood sugar, temperature, and the blood's concentration of salts; it draws on this information to regulate the autonomic nervous system and the pituitary gland, through which it controls the secretion of thyroid, adrenal,[7] growth and sex hormones; it kindles and douses our appetites for such things as food, drink and sex; it underlies circadian

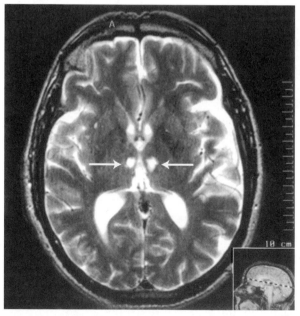

Figure 2.13 An MRI scan showing a stroke causing coma The stroke – affecting both sides of the thalamus – caused coma at the time, and left persisting drowsiness and difficulty in concentrating some years on. The relevant areas of damage are arrowed. the adjacent 'bright' areas, deep in the brain, are the ventricles.

rhythms and influences arousal; it contributes to the neural circuitry which allows us to acquire new memories.

The hypothalamus operates at the boundary between the biological and the physical environment, between the 'internal milieu' of the body and the surroundings on which we depend to sustain the internal milieu. For example, if you become dehydrated after a brisk walk on a hot day, the hypothalamus will detect a rise in the concentration of your blood, release a hormone which reduces urine production, and at the same time call into play behaviour calculated to quench the feeling the hypothalamus incites – the feeling of thirst. Should you become amorous or frightened, the hypothalamus will similarly orchestrate the internal preparations for sex or flight. It is the neural crux of all our simpler urges. If the function of the hypothalamus is disturbed, the resulting symptoms include excessive thirst and hunger, or loss of appetite; drowsiness; ups and downs in body temperature, and hormonal mayhem.

If you were to disembark in the third ventricle and travel from the thalamus, out towards the surface of the brain, you would first encounter a zone of white matter, *the internal capsule,* connecting the cortex with other parts of the brain and spinal cord. Passing beyond this you run up against the last major structures before reaching the cortex itself. These are the nuclear masses of the *basal ganglia,* the *caudate, putamen* and *globus pallidus.*

The caudate and putamen are really a single nucleus, divided by the internal capsule. They receive afference from widespread areas of cortex; this is processed and then transmitted to the globus pallidus; from the globus pallidus, the output of the basal ganglia returns to the cortex by way of the thalamus, completing a complex loop. This loop, from cortex to basal ganglia and back to cortex via the thalamus, is rather similar to the route taken by signals passing to and from the cerebellum. But the basal ganglia have their own distinctive internal architecture and functions and cause distinctive forms of mischief when they go wrong.

Like the cerebellum, they are traditionally regarded as structures governing movement. Certainly, many of their disorders affect movement. A deficiency of the neurotransmitter dopamine, which is conveyed to the basal ganglia by axons travelling from the brainstem, causes the tremor, slowing, stiffness and unsteadiness which characterise Parkinson's disease; the 'dancing' fidgets of 'chorea' represent the opposite extreme of basal ganglia dysfunction. Chorea was once common as a complication of infections by the streptococci which can cause sore throats; it now occurs more often in patients overtreated for Parkinson's disease,[8] or suffering from the inherited basal ganglia disorder of Huntington's disease. But as we have seen, the brain does not always respect our distinctions between movement, thought and emotion. Parts of the basal ganglia are closely linked to brain regions concerned with emotion, the limbic system (of which more soon) and damage to the basal ganglia can have major effects on personality and behaviour. 'Neuroleptic' drugs, which greatly ameliorate the symptoms of schizophrenia, act in these areas of the basal ganglia to oppose the effects of dopamine.

THE CEREBRAL CORTEX

Beyond the basal ganglia, and another rim of white matter, we reach the brain's infolded surface, the cerebral cortex. Its steep hills and deep valleys – its gyri and sulci – provide a host of landmarks to anyone exploring the surface of the brain. Before we survey this uneven terrain, three generalisations are helpful in understanding its functions.

First, each of our hemispheres receives sensory information from the opposite side of space, and controls the opposite side of the body. Second, to a greater degree in man than in any other animal, the two hemispheres have distinct specialised capacities: the left, controlling the usually dominant right hand, is the seat of our ability to use language and to peform skilled actions, while the right plays a leading part in, for example, the perception of three-dimensional space and music. In health the two hemispheres remain in close touch by way of several commissures: much the largest of these is the *corpus callosum*, which arches above the third ventricle.[9] Third, it is now accepted that small regions of cortex – sometimes coinciding with the regions Brodmann's map distinguished – perform specialised functions. For example, damage to a certain small area of the cortex subserving vision, known as area V4, can strip the visual world of colour, sparing only a palette of greys. V4 is therefore described as a 'colour area', without the implication that this area functioning *in isolation* could give rise to colour vision: it is necessary, not sufficient.[10] At all times, in a waking brain, a host of small cortical regions are at work 'in parallel' on their specialised tasks.[11]

Each cerebral hemisphere is roughly divided into four lobes (see Figure 2.14). The *frontal lobes* extend from the forward tip of the brain, which rests on the bone above the eyes, back to the 'central sulcus'. As it happens, this sulcus is also an important functional boundary, between areas which have a mainly motor function in front, and those with a mainly sensory function behind. Behind the central sulcus lies the *parietal lobe*, particularly associated with bodily sensation and our appreciation of spatial relationships. It runs back to its boundary with the hindmost *occipital lobe,* which is largely devoted to vision. The *temporal lobes* occupy the curved lateral extension of the hemispheres which rest above the ears, separated from the frontal and parietal lobes above by the 'Sylvian fissures'. The lateral

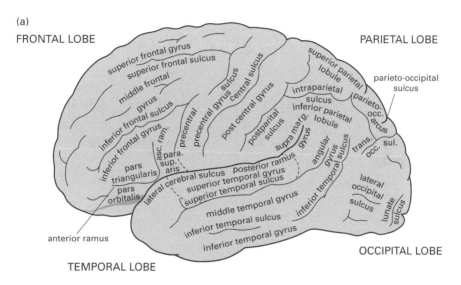

(a)

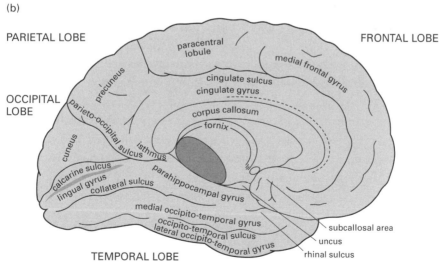

(b)

Figure 2.14 A side view of the brain Two views of a cerebral hemisphere: the side view, and a view of the concealed surface of the same hemisphere, which is pressed against the corresponding surface of the opposite hemisphere in life. The figure shows the positions of the four lobes of the brain, and their major subdivisions.

ventricles course within the lobes so that if we had continued our journey within the cerebrospinal fluid we could eventually have reached the deep interior of each.

The frontal lobes contain the 'primary motor area', a strip of cortex running down the hemisphere just in front of the central sulcus. This area is a 'motor map' of the body: stimulation of a given area of the map gives rise to movement in a given body part. The leg, for example, is represented by the lip of cortex extending on to the inner aspect of the hemisphere. A tumour here might come to light by causing seizures which consist in the involuntary tapping of a foot. 'Maps' of many kinds, representing features of our movements and of the perceptual world, are ubiquitous in the cortex.

The primary motor area accounts for only a fraction of the frontal lobes, which are particularly expanded in man, but the flavour of frontal lobe function as a whole is 'motor', if we allow this term to encompass the *organisation* of thought and behaviour in general – 'executive function' in psychologists' jargon. Injuries to the frontal lobes tend to impair problem solving, planning and conduct: they disturb the balance of the personality, tipping it either towards lethargic indifference or disinhibited exuberance. The victims of frontal lobe injury are usually blithely unaware of their predicament: the ability to monitor and adjust their own behaviour – 'insight' – is precisely what they have lost. This predicament is famously illustrated by the case of Phineas Gage, probably the most celebrated in the history of behavioural neurology.[12] Gage was the foreman of a team of railroad constructors in the 1860s. A premature detonation sent a metal rod into an eye from below and up through his frontal lobes. Astonishingly he survived without any obvious major handicap, but his previously conscientious and industrious nature was transformed by the injury. He became 'fitful, irreverent . . . capricious' and died a few years later from natural causes. His skull was preserved: the focus of damage was to the undersurface of the frontal lobes, an area which is now recognised to play an important part in the regulation of social behaviour. The frontal lobes play a similar role in the sequencing of fluent speech to their role in the control of movement and behaviour: following damage to Broca's area, named after the French neurologist who described it in 1861, speech becomes halting and effortful, although the ability to understand what others say is generally intact.

The temporal lobes are associated particularly with memory. The hippocampus, a structure named because of its vague resemblance to a seahorse, tucked into the inner surface of the temporal lobe, is essential for the acquisition of lasting 'declarative' memories ('declarative' in the sense that they are accessible to report, in contrast to 'procedural' memories, like our knowledge of how to ride a bike, which reside elsewhere in the brain). The second most famous case in behavioural neuropsychology illustrates this point. HM was a man of 27, with disabling epilepsy, when the Canadian neurosurgeon, Walter Scoville, removed the hippocampi from both sides of his brain in 1953.[13] His epilepsy responded well to this treatment and HM was superficially unscathed. But he paid a high price for the amelioration of his seizures: following surgery, HM was unable to acquire new conscious memories. Locked into a changeless present, he could no longer add to the cumulative record of personal experience – episodic memory – through which we make sense of our lives. He remained, for example, unable to recognise psychologists who tested him virtually daily throughout several decades.

In retrospect HM's predicament was almost as remarkable for the abilities which survived his surgery as for those which the surgeon's knife excised. In particular, HM did not lose his database of knowledge about things: the stock of concepts and vocabulary through which we interpret the world.[14] Rarely these abilities *are* selectively eroded in patients with progressive but selective cell loss in the brain.[15] In these cases the damage is centred on the *outer* surface of the temporal lobes, suggesting that these are the home of our well-established stock of 'semantic' memories.

The divisions between the lobes of the brain are arbitrary, and any account of their functions is bound to be untidy. While the temporal lobes are especially involved with varieties of memory, they also contain the primary cortical areas for smell and hearing, and an area, Wernicke's, which complements Broca's 'motor' speech area by decoding the meaning of speech sounds.

The occipital lobes are very largely concerned with vision and we shall hear much more of them later. The parietal lobes contain the 'primary sensory cortex', a series of sensory maps of the body, arrayed alongside the motor map in the adjacent frontal lobe. The appreciation of both bodily and external space, and the preparation for movement in space, are major functions of the parietal lobes. An inability to dress, often associated with difficulty in finding one's way around, is a characteristic symptom of disorders of the right parietal lobe: it sometimes develops abruptly, following a stroke. The left parietal lobe is particularly implicated in the skilled use of tools.

One further anatomical concept is useful, although it cuts across the lobar boundaries I have been drawing. The *limbic system* occupies the 'limbus', or edge of the hemispheres. It consists of a number of structures, some in the cortex, some in the thalamus and hypothalamus, which are densely interconnected (see Figure 2.15). The cortical parts of the limbic system have a relatively primitive microscopic structure, hinting at their ancient evolutionary origins: this type of cortex dominates the brain of 'lower' vertebrates. The limbic structures are collectively involved in the experience and expression of emotion and the acquisition and retrieval of memories. The link between memory and emotion makes a good deal of sense: it is in our interests to remember what excites us, whether with pleasure or pain, while what bores us is safely forgotten. There is a large overlap between the limbic system and the cortical areas concerned with smell, which probably explains the directness with which a scent can sometimes evoke long-buried memories.

As signals enter the brain from the senses they disperse in countless directions. To understand this complexity it is helpful to know that the information flowing through the brain tends to follow a characteristic course.[16] It streams first through areas which are dedicated to analysing input from the sense in question, like the primary auditory areas in the temporal lobe. From these 'unimodal' areas it passes on to 'heteromodal' areas which combine the information from the senses, allowing us to create the coherent world of our experience. From the heteromodal sensory cortex, it passes into limbic regions which assign significance to the events we sense – and memorise them, if need be. At several stages information passes from these cortical structures to 'subcortical' ones, the thalamus,

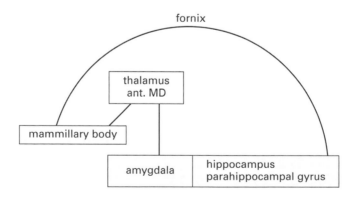

Figure 2.15 The limbic system A schematic diagram of the structures in the limbic system which are required to form new conscious memories. A look back to Figure 2.14 shows the positions of the parahippocampal gyrus and the fornix in the inner aspect of the hemisphere. The amygdala, thalamus and mamillary bodies are deep structures, hidden in Figure 2.14.

basal ganglia and cerebellum, returning in a modified form to the cortex. By all these routes, the heteromodal and limbic cortices influence the frontal lobes, where actions are prepared, released and monitored (see Figure 2.16).

This guide to cortical localisation is distinctly rough and ready. Any complicated function, such as sight, involves activity in networks of cortical areas, in parts of all four lobes. Some of this activity will be difficult to characterise, neither strictly motor nor strictly sensory – as one might expect in an organ which is constantly *transforming* sensory stimulation into a motor output.

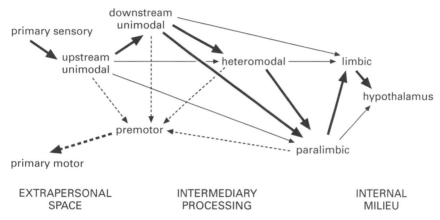

Figure 2.16 Pathways of information flow through the human brain The fate of information entering the brain: signals from the senses enter regions of cortex devoted to them (first 'upstream' and then 'downstream' unimodal cortex); in processed form, they may then enter 'heteromodal' sensory cortex, where signals from different senses are brought together; both unimodal and heteromodal cortices communicate with the limbic system which is closely linked to memory and to the internal state of the body; sensory and limbic cortices communicate with motor and 'premotor' regions in the frontal lobe which governs action.

Interconnections redrawn

We have seen how the humble nerve cell provides the foundation for a system of great complexity, by virtue of neuronal numbers, cellular diversity and an intricate organisation. The points of contact at which neurons communicate also look simple enough at first blush, but if we inspect them more closely a host of synaptic subtleties come into view.

Synaptic numbers and types

The number of synapses, intercellular connections, in the nervous system, puts the number of neurons into the shade. A single neuron, for example a cerebellar Purkinje cell, may receive 200,000 connections from the parallel fibres which synapse on its dendrites: this allows signals from 200,000 other cells to influence its activity. Conversely, a single cell, for example a sensory neuron in the spinal cord, may signal to as many as 1,000 target neurons, by way of its axonal arborisation. If we recall that there are something like 100,000 million nerve cells in the nervous system, it becomes clear that the permutations of activity permitted by the number of cells and their interconnections are quite prodigious.

The great majority of synapses in the human nervous system conform to the general description I gave earlier: they are points of contact between neurons at which a chemical is released by one cell and detected by another, with consequences for the activity of the latter (see Figure 2.17). But some synapses are more equal than others. The purchase of a presynaptic neuron on the activity of the postsynaptic cell depends on the location of its synapse: those remote from the cell body of the postsynaptic cell exert a less powerful effect than synapses close to the 'axon hillock' from which the action potential is released. Synapses can indeed be made with almost any part of the postsynaptic cell: one variety of connection, the axo-axonal synapse, allows the presynaptic cell to influence transmitter release by another terminal.

As an aside, it has turned out that Golgi was not entirely mistaken in his belief that the nervous system is a seamless 'syncitium', a network in which

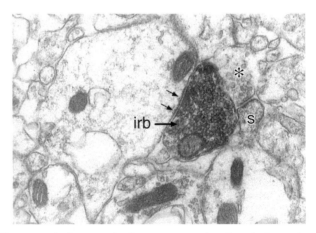

Figure 2.17 Synapses A photograph of a synapse made using electron microscopy (the magnification is times 50,000). The dark area marked irb (a synaptic terminal or 'bouton') containing just visible spheres of membrane ('vesicles' full of neurotransmitter) is separated from the cell to its left, with which it is making a synapse, by a tiny synaptic cleft (indicated by small arrows). The dark area is dark because the neurotransmitter within it has been chemically 'labelled'. The area marked with a star contains unlabelled vesicles making contact with another dendrite, marked s.

the cells flow one into another. Some neurons – a small minority in the human nervous system – communicate via 'gap junctions' which allow the electrical activity to pass unimpeded between cells, without need of a chemical messenger.

Synapses then are exceedingly numerous, and their effect depends on their position. A second major dimension of synaptic complexity is supplied by the variety of chemical substances released at the synapse, which are known as neurotransmitters.

Neurotransmitters

The experiment that came to Otto Loewi in the night, enabling him to prove that the vagus nerve releases a chemical at its synapses with the heart, led eventually to the isolation of a ubiquitous neurochemical: acetylcholine. Besides its role in the autonomic nervous system, which Loewi investigated, acetylcholine is released by axons at their junctions with striated muscles – those over which we can normally exert voluntary control. Its effect there is blocked by 'curare', a plant-derived toxin used by South American Indians on arrow tips to paralyse their prey. During the twentieth century curare became an important anaesthetic drug, allowing the anaesthetist to paralyse her prey – with the advantage to the surgeon of a completely relaxed subject.

Acetylcholine is found in the brain as well: it is, for instance, released widely in the cerebral cortex by fibres which originate from the brainstem or deep in the hemispheres. Drugs opposing its activity in the cortex tend to cause confusion and amnesia; permanent depletion of acetylcholine is one of the hallmarks of Alzheimer's disease, and drugs which promote its activity have recently been licensed for the treatment of this condition. It helps to control movement as well as memory: the very drugs which can give rise to confusion by blocking its action are sometimes used to good effect in Parkinson's disease, rectifying an imbalance caused by the lack of another neurotransmitter, dopamine.

Identifying the neurotransmitters of the central nervous system, and understanding in detail how they work, occupied the working lives of many pharmacologists over the past century. The brain, of course, contains innumerable chemicals which are *not* involved in neurotransmission. To show that a chemical really is a messenger requires that several criteria be satisfied: it must be manufactured by the presynaptic neuron, released in amounts sufficient to account for its effect, act convincingly on the postsynaptic cell, and make a graceful exit after doing so.

Two broad classes of chemicals have been shown to fulfil these criteria. A group of around 10 'small molecules', relatively simple substances, includes all the 'classical' neurotransmitters, among them acetylcholine. Most of these small messengers either are, or are derived from, amino acids, which we encountered earlier as the building blocks of proteins. Dopamine, adrenaline, serotonin and histamine are derivatives; glutamate, glycine and GABA are themselves amino acids.

The members of the second large and growing group of messengers are essentially small proteins. The most celebrated of these transmitters, the endorphins, act to modulate pain perception: opium and its derivatives, such as heroin, mimic the actions of the endorphins in the brain. Indeed substances that mimic, oppose, boost or otherwise modify the actions of neurotransmitters are among the most widely used drugs in medicine, brought to bear on conditions as diverse as epilepsy, schizophrenia, depression and Parkinson's disease.

A single neuron releases the same chemicals at all its synapses. Until recently, it was thought that each neuron released only a single transmitter. It is now clear that 'co-transmission', the simultaneous release of a protein and a 'classical' transmitter at the same synapse, is quite common: but the same combination of substances is released consistently by a given cell.

A messenger must have an audience, and the audience determines the reaction. News of an election victory or an Olympic gold evokes quite different responses in different quarters. The chemical messages delivered by neurotransmitters have highly attuned targets, known as 'receptors': these determine the response to the arrival of the transmitter, and their variety creates a third source of complexity at the synapse.

Receptors and channels

When acetylcholine is released from the axon terminal of a motor neuron and drifts across the synapse, its target is a specialised region of the muscle membrane, known as the motor end plate. This region is rich in a protein into which molecules of acetylcholine fit like keys into locks: the protein is known as the acetylcholine 'receptor'.

The analogy with key and lock is apt: the binding of acetylcholine by the receptor opens a channel which allows the passage of sodium, a substance present in much higher concentration outside the cell than in. Sodium carries a positive electrical charge, and its entry into the cell alters the difference in charge between its interior and its exterior. Once the influx of positive charge passses a critical 'threshold', it releases the muscle's own 'action potential', which eventually leads to muscular contraction. The sodium channel closes rapidly as acetylcholine detaches itself from its receptor and is broken down by an enzyme designed to terminate its action.

The acetylcholine receptors of the motor end plate are relatively accessible to study, and very well understood. The broad principles of chemical transmission gleaned from this 'neuromuscular junction' are applicable elsewhere, but a great diversity of receptor types has been discovered at the synapses made by nerve on nerve.

The channels in muscle which bind acetylcholine and admit sodium belong to the first of the two great families of receptors, known technically as 'transmitter-gated ion channels' (ions are charged particles like sodium). Other members of this family admit other ions: channels which open to admit calcium tend to excite the cell; channels which open to potassium or chloride tend to inhibit its firing. As the receptor, rather than the messenger itself, determines the meaning of the message, there is no reason why a given transmitter should not have very different effects at different receptors: indeed, as we shall see, this commonly occurs. There are, though, some useful rules of thumb: receptors for glutamate consistently excite, while receptors for GABA consistently inhibit, neuronal firing.

Gated ion channels are designed for rapid effect: binding of transmitter leads directly and rapidly to a change in the electrical conditions in the target cell. The second family of receptors has a somewhat more leisurely action: when a member of this family is activated by the arrival of the neurotransmitter to which it is receptive, it releases a 'second messenger' into the interior of the cell.

Second messengers set in train a process of chemical reaction in the cell. This may result in the opening or closure of a class of ion channels: second messengers can therefore alter the cell's electrical balance, albeit by roundabout means. But the effects of second messengers are not restricted to the cell membrane: they are in position to modulate the functions of a wide range of proteins within the cell; most fundamentally, they can influence the synthesis of proteins by altering the 'read-out' from DNA. Thus action at the synapse is not always a matter of lightning speed: it can exert a persisting and subtle effect on the life of its target cell.

The crude division of receptors into two large groups, those gating ion channels and those activating second messengers, conceals further diversity.[17] Acetylcholine acts both on gated ion channels, and on receptors elsewhere which activate second messengers. There are at least four types of glutamate receptor, and six different types of dopamine receptor. Designing drugs which act specifically on certain receptor subtypes has become a major industry. For example, the drugs used traditionally by psychiatrists to calm the disturbances of perception, thought and behaviour occurring in psychosis, had the undesirable side-effect of causing a state of immobility resembling Parkinson's disease. By targeting the appropriate dopamine receptor subtypes (D3 and 4) it has become possible to avoid such a pronounced effect on movement.

Taken together, synaptic numbers, the variety of the transmitters they release and the diversity of the receptors to which transmitters bind allow a complexity of chemical signalling to match the intricacy of neuronal organisation. There is one final but vital synaptic subtlety.

Synaptic plasticity

The ability to adapt to circumstances is one of the hallmarks of life. A bodybuilder's bulging biceps, an athlete's slow pulse, a sunbather's well-tanned form all testify to the capacity of our tissues to react to recent demands. Even our bones are shaped by use, and wither with disuse. The ubiquitous 'plasticity' of living things is the biological backdrop to our ability to learn. Throughout our long lives our experience shapes our behaviour. It is very likely that the neural plasticity which makes this possible is centred at the synapse, creating a fourth dimension of synaptic plasticity.

At birth our brains possess more or less their final complement of neurons, but synapse formation continues briskly for some time. We know that synaptic numbers in the brains of young animals are influenced by their environment: 'enrichment' of the surroundings of neonatal rats, providing additional sensory and motor stimulation, leads to a measurable increase in synaptic contacts.[18] Work with young animals and with children deprived of vision in one eye suggests that active neurons expand the territory over which they form synapses, at the expense of inactive ones.[19] In the developing brain, activity, in general, boosts synaptic numbers and strengthens synaptic links.

The thought that a somewhat similar process might underlie memory throughout our lives struck a Canadian psychologist in the 1940s. Donald Hebb suspected that our experience from moment to moment depends upon the activity of networks or 'assemblies' of cells. If this were so, and if there were a mechanism which automatically strengthened the connections between simultaneously active cells, 'memory' might emerge as a natural result of their activity. 'Hebb's rule' turned out to have been a farsighted proposal.

The shaping of synaptic transmission by activity has now been described in several contexts. One of the most interesting phenomena is known as 'long-term potentiation' (LTP), which occurs in the hippocampus, the region of the brain required for the formation of new conscious memories. LTP depends upon the successful activation of a postsynaptic cell by incoming signals. Once this activation is achieved, future signals in the same pathway evoke a stronger response than before – and this effect persists for some time.

The idea that the brain consists of neural networks, in which activity arriving in parallel channels determines connection strengths, has had major repercussions for efforts to design intelligent computers. These machines may prove useful both in themselves and as a powerful means of modelling processes in the brain: we shall encounter them again.[20]

Conclusion: the nerves in the brain

This chapter has taken you on a quick tour of a landscape with which it takes years to become really familiar. I hope that it was helpful to identify the features of the landscape before homing in on elaborate detail. In simple terms, the nervous system is a network of nerve cells which communicate at synapses; its task is to transform patterns of sensory input into patterns of motor output, allowing its owner to adapt behaviour to experience, present and past.

In some 'lower' animals it is now possible to trace the flow of information through the nervous system, cell by cell. We do not have such a God-like view of events in the human nervous system because of several dimensions of complexity. Its cells are fantastically numerous, diverse and intricately organised; their interconnections are more numerous still, employ an army of chemical messengers, a host of membrane receptors and are constantly remodelled by their use and disuse.

Occasionally I wonder whether anything so improbable can possibly be true. If you have been dogged by a similar doubt, one consideration helps a little to make all the complexity plausible. A complex nervous system contains the same elements and performs the same general functions as a simple one. With the aid of molecular biology – which makes it possible to analyse proteins and genes – it is becoming clear that much of the complexity of the human brain depends upon the endless elaboration of simple elements. For instance, all the protein 'channels' I have described belong to just a few families. There are close resemblances between family members, in shape, in function and in the genes which 'code' for them: all the receptors which trigger second messengers belong to one 'gene' family, all the receptors which gate ionic channels to another. Gene duplication is a quite common chance occurrence in reproduction. Over the immense periods of our evolutionary past this created the opportunity for an extraordinary series of variations on a theme to be produced.

Do we know a little or a lot about the brain? There has certainly been a huge accumulation of information over the last hundred years. Some of what we think we know will turn out to be false or misconceived, and our most secure knowledge often fails to answer the questions we most want answers to. It is quite possible, at this early stage in the investigation of such a complex entity, that some fundamental principles of the brain's operation have yet to emerge. If and when they do, all that we know at present will appear in a new light.

I hope, especially, that I have conveyed some of the biological splendour of the brain. It is often depicted as an ingenious microcomputer. So it is. But this analogy fails to do justice to the brain's teeming activity. It pulsates with the rhythm of its rich circulation; it constantly burns fuel – at the rate of a 20 watt bulb – and constantly generates waste, borne away by the bloodstream that conveys its energy supply; it is bathed in cerebrospinal fluid which is always forming, circulating, re-entering the blood; every neuron is conveying material up and down its processes to nourish its extremities – and all are signalling. If it is a humming computer, it is also bursting with life.

Part II:
The capacity for consciousness

3

The springs of awareness: the structural basis of consciousness (i)

Oblivion is a kind of annihilation.

Sir Thomas Browne, *Christian Morals*[1]

. . . as a dream doth flatter,
In sleep a king, but waking no such matter.

William Shakespeare, Sonnet LXXXVII

Introduction

In the course of a lifetime we spend about 20 years asleep. As we wake, each day, we must create our world of experience anew. The regular annihilation and renewal of awareness is one of the ordinary miracles of life: we take it entirely for granted, until a night or two of insomnia reminds us how essential, yet how elusive, sleep can be.

The regular alternation of waking and sleep seems a natural place to start trying to understand the biology of awareness. It is also a rewarding point of departure, as a succession of remarkable discoveries over the past hundred years has illuminated the neural basis of this fundamental rhythm of consciousness.

Two interlacing threads of enquiry have proved especially informative. The first concerns the dynamic function of the nervous system, the rapid play of electricity in muscle, nerve and brain. It runs from the demonstration by the Italian physiologist Galvani, at the end of the eighteenth century, that 'animal electricity' could bring about the contraction of muscles, through the discovery, 50 years later, that signalling in nerves has an electrical basis, to the work of a secretive German psychiatrist who announced in 1929 that he had recorded the 'electroencephalogram of man'. This might, in retrospect, be regarded as the triumphant and logical culmination of a series of discoveries: it did not appear so at the time, and, like all important work in science, it posed as many questions as it solved. Many of these have been answered since, with major gains in our understanding of conscious states, and, in particular, of sleep.

The second thread concerns structure, especially the structure of the brainstem. This might appear a much less exciting subject for study, the anatomy of gloomy backrooms in the great mansion of the brain. On the contrary, the brainstem is fascinating, and indisputably does the business: activity within its varied parts regulates consciousness, determines mood and sustains life. Like the electricity of the brain, its secrets have been unearthed with painful slowness. Many, no doubt, are buried still.

The electricity of the brain

'On the electroencephalogram of man'

> I . . . believe that I have discovered the electroencephalogram of man.
>
> Hans Berger, 1929[2]

Electricity has been used to stimulate the nerves of man since Roman times. Electric eels and torpedo fish – which stun their prey with the help of a hefty current – were called into service to deliver shocks which were, presumably, considered therapeutic. As it became possible to generate small amounts of electricity using 'friction machines' in the eighteenth century, its medical applications were extended. Robert Whytt, an English physician of the period, described

> A man aged 25, who, from a palsy (paralysis) of twelve years continuance, had lost all power of motion in his left arm, after trying other remedies in vain, at last had recourse to electricity; by every shock of which the muscles of his arm were made to contract; and the member itself, which was very much withered, after having been electrified for some weeks, became plumper.[3]

In 1791 Galvani, the Professor of Anatomy in Bologna, published the results of his experiments.[4] He had shown definitively that electricity, produced in various ways, could excite both nerve and muscle. He argued that 'animal electricity', rather than the 'animal spirits' of earlier medical theory, was the substance 'secreted by the brain and distributed by the nerves'. Galvani's nephew, Giovanni Aldini, had to defend his case vigorously against the scepticism of Alessandro Volta, his compatriot and inventor of the electric battery, but Galvani's 'beautiful and divine discovery'[5] proved to be the foundation of a new science. Within a few years Aldini had shown that stimulation of the exposed brains of oxen 'could produce movements of the eyelids, lips and eyes', confirming Galvani's view that electricity plays its part in the brain, as well as in nerve and muscle.

Delivering an electric shock to some part of the nervous system is a relatively crude manoeuvre: detecting the system's own intrinsic electrical activity is much more of a challenge. A physiologist working in Berlin, Emil Du Bois-Reymond, achieved this in 1848 when he recorded the passage of an electrical impulse along a nerve. He wrote, modestly enough, that he had realised 'in full actuality . . . the hundred years' dream of physicists and physiologists, to wit, the identification of the nervous principle with electricity'.[6]

These electrical discoveries are a crucial part of the background to the discovery of our 'brain waves', or, more properly, of the 'electroencephalogram of man'. Another aspect of the scientific landscape of the mid-nineteenth century deserves a mention alongside the growing evidence that electricity was the key to the 'excitability' of living things.

While Galvani was investigating the effects of electricity on the legs of frogs, Franz Joseph Gall, a Viennese physician, was pursuing his conviction that human moral and intellectual faculties were localised in the cerebral cortex. He believed, moreover, that the contours of the overlying skull reflected the special abilities and deficiencies of the brain beneath. The 'pseudo-science' of phrenology which Gall developed may seem laughable now, and was certainly much mocked. As we shall see, Gall was not entirely on the wrong track, but many of his claims, and especially those of his more extravagant followers, were unsustainable.

The issue of 'cortical localisation' was taken up by several more sober experimentalists and physicians during the nineteenth century. On the basis of experiments in which he damaged the brains of a variety of animals, the French physiologist Marie-Jean-Pierre Flourens concluded in 1824 that 'all sensations, all perceptions and all volition occupy concurrently the same seat' in the cortex.[7] This was a comprehensive rejection of the idea of localisation. But the evidence for some degree of localisation gradually accumulated.

The observations made by the French physician and anatomist Paul Broca in 1861, on his patient Monsieur Leborgne, were a turning point in the debate.[8] The unfortunate Leborgne, aged only 51, had been hospitalised for 21 years before his death because of a slow but relentless illness which had robbed him first of speech and then of the use of his right arm and leg: he had acquired the nickname 'Tan' from the sound which he usually uttered when he tried to speak.

Broca had been party to recent discussions at the Société d'Anthropologie in Paris at which his colleagues had debated the issue of localisation: Simon Aubertin had produced some evidence that the faculty of speech depended on the function of the frontal lobes. Broca invited Aubertin to examine 'Tan' and to predict the site responsible for his inability to speak. Monsieur Leborgne, who was by then gravely ill, died six days later. Broca brought his brain on the following day to the Société d'Anthropologie. Simon Aubertin's prediction was vindicated. The brain was in fact damaged in several regions, but the most conspicuous site was on the 'convexity', the curved outer surface, of the left frontal lobe. Over the following years Broca was able to show that this area of cortex – known now as Broca's area – was consistently damaged in patients with dysphasias, disorders of language, resembling Tan's, and that the damaged area was usually on the left side of the brain.

While tragic 'experiments of nature', such as Monsieur Leborgne, were studied closely by physicians like Broca and Aubertin, certain experiments of man also began to lend support to the 'localisationist's' cause. In 1870 Gustav Fritsch, an anatomist, and Eduard Hitzig, a psychiatrist, both in their early thirties, explored the effects of stimulating the exposed brains of dogs with weak electric currents, 'just enough to be felt when applied to the tip of the tongue'. The experiments were performed on a dressing table in a bedroom in Hitzig's house in Berlin. They located an area of the cortical surface over which weak currents evoked the contraction of muscles on the opposite side of the body. As they moved their stimulator around this region different muscles successively came into play. They had discovered the motor cortex and shown that it contains a map of possible movements.[9]

This approach was taken up by David Ferrier in England. Working at the West Riding Lunatic Asylum, and later in London, he explored the cortex with stimulation, and investigated the effects of well-circumscribed 'lesions', showing, for example, that the sense of smell depends on the 'uncinate gyrus', at the tip of the temporal lobe. This bore out the observations of the contemporary neurologist, John Hughlings-Jackson, that hallucinations of smell were a common accompaniment of epileptic fits arising from tumours in this part of the brain.

The knowledge that electricity plays a key part in the activity of the brain, and the hypothesis, increasingly well attested, that the various functions of the brain are localised within it, were the starting points for a young scientist in Liverpool in the 1870s. Richard Caton was the son of a Yorkshire physician. He also trained as a doctor, in Edinburgh, then worked for a while as a cardiologist at the Liverpool Children's Infirmary. But his inclinations were academic, and by 1872 he had been appointed a Lecturer in Physiology. After some initial research on electrical currents in muscle and nerve, he set himself the task of detecting the electrical correlates of sensation in the brain.

By 1875, in experiments performed on rabbits, he had discovered that when 'a bright light was thrown upon the retina' 'variation of the current' could often be recorded in the posterior part of the brain. This discovery – that currents in the brain can be evoked by natural stimulation of the senses – was the focus of Caton's interest. These are known nowadays as 'evoked potentials', and are recorded many times a day in every neurology department in the world. But, in retrospect, some of Caton's other observations were even more remarkable. He noticed that 'feeble currents of varying direction' were 'in constant fluctuation' in the brain of unstimulated animals, and that more marked fluctuations coincided with a 'change in the animal's mental condition': on awaking from sleep, when anaesthesia was induced and at death, when the current fell to zero. This was the first description of the constant spontaneous electrical activity of the living brain.

The story of Caton's subsequent career rather refreshingly conjures up a less specialised age than ours. Caton published several papers on the currents of the brain, presenting his work as far afield as Moscow and Washington. Appointed to the Chair of Physiology in Liverpool in 1884, he resigned from it in 1891, at the age of 49. His interests were returning to clinical medicine: he wrote to the *British Medical Journal* in that year on 'Typhoid and salads', and two years later published a report on 'Two cases of lead poisoning'. He also published on 'The temples, hospital and medical school of Cos'. Lord Mayor of Liverpool in 1907, he died 'a figure much revered in the many fields to which his energy and versatility had contributed'. This late Victorian career had a far happier ending than the life of the scientist who took up Caton's work and extended it to man, on the more troubled continent of Europe.

As often happens, a number of others working independently came to conclusions similar to Caton's at much the same time. Austrian, Polish and Russian physiologists all recorded evoked potentials in the 1870s and '80s.[10] Several of Caton's colleagues abroad had also noticed the spontaneous activity which he had stumbled across. Beck reported an 'active independent current . . . a spontaneous excitation of the nerve centres'; some of this activity was rhythmic, and Beck noticed that 'every kind of stimulation' could, intriguingly, abolish it. Danilevsky, in Russia, described 'spontaneous oscillations of the brain current or a peculiar rhythm'. Nikolai Wedensky, a physiologist in St Petersburg, had devised a telephone with which he could 'listen' to the electrical discharge in muscles. When he connected his telephone to a hemisphere of the brains of cats and dogs, in 1889, he heard 'the oscillations of the nerve currents', although the sounds were 'very faint, almost imperceptible'.

While they might be feeble and faint, these currents and sounds were tremendously exciting. The possibility that they represented the objective correlate of awareness was not lost on the physiologists who first recorded them. The hope that they would reveal 'the physical bases of consciousness' energised the work of the German psychiatrist who published his famous paper 'On the electroencephalogram of man' in 1929.

Hans Berger was the son of a Bavarian doctor. His mother was the daughter of a German poet who had an interest in oriental philosophy. Berger's intellectual interests were correspondingly broad, and at first he planned to become an astronomer. An experience during his military service, at the age of 20, changed his course in life. He and his horse slipped in a ravine and came close to falling beneath a gun battery. When Berger returned to his barracks he found a telegram awaiting him from his father, enquiring whether all was well. His sister had announced to his parents earlier that day 'that she knew with certainty that he had suffered an accident'. Although Berger never explored the possibility of telepathy in his scientific work, he explained later that this curious train of events had turned him from astronomy to a lifelong interest in the relationship between physical and psychological events.

He was appointed to the Chair of Psychiatry in Jena, where he had worked since the 1890s, at the end of the First World War. He was the father of four children; Klaus, his only son, born in 1912, was one of the experimental subjects described in the 1929 paper, which reported work performed on and off over 17 years, largely in secret. Berger's days were timetabled with obsessional precision, and he made his recordings between five and eight in the evening, wisely waiting until all the electrical equipment in his clinic had been switched off.

Curiously, although the early students of the brain currents in animals had noticed that it was sometimes possible to record them from the scalp, no one before Berger appears to have tried consistently to record electrical events from the brain – or scalp – of man. His initial experiments involved patients who had undergone neurosurgery, and had been left with defects in the bones of the skull which offered Berger an advantageous electrical window on to the brain. He moved on to record from healthy subjects with intact skulls, for example a medical student 'who had lost almost all his hair', and his long-suffering – and close-cropped – son Klaus, from whom he made 73 tracings over 14 sessions.

His recordings confirmed that it was possible to detect a variety of rhythmic electrical oscillations over the scalp. They were tiny, fractions of a thousandth of a volt. Berger was highly self-critical and considered a whole series of alternative explanations for his findings to the one he hoped to prove: that these oscillations reflected the native electrical activity of the human brain. Carefully he entertained the possibilities that electrical short circuits, wobbling contacts, the pulsation of blood in the brain, movements created by breathing, the electrical activity of the heart, contraction of scalp muscles, eye movements or the skin of the scalp itself might be the source of the currents, and performed experiments enabling him to reject them all. There is a note of triumph in his conclusion, muted by the caution of his scholarship: 'I therefore, indeed, believe that I have discovered the electroencephalogram of man and that I have published it here for the first time' (see Figure 3.1).

As I hinted, the closing pages in the story of Berger's life are sad ones. Unsympathetic to the Nazis, Berger was removed from his post as Professor of Psychiatry in September 1938. His laboratory was dismantled. He retired

Figure 3.1 Hans Berger's record of alpha rhythm from Klaus' head One of the illustrations from Berger's first paper, the recording was made from his close-shaven son, Klaus. The lower trace represents time in tenths of a second. Berger described these prominent regular oscillations, best recorded from a relaxed subject with the eyes closed, as 'alpha' waves in his second paper.

to a small country town and sank into depression. Failing to recognise his own condition, he took his own life, in hospital, in May 1941. Another of the European pioneers, Adolf Beck, who had been imprisoned by the Russians in Kiev during the First World War, suffered a similar fate. An elderly Polish Jew, he swallowed a capsule of potassium cyanide supplied by his doctor son rather than travel to the camps.

Berger's first classic paper on the EEG closes with a series of questions which have fuelled almost a century of research. What is the effect of sensory stimulation on the EEG? What happens in sleep, or under the influence of drugs which alter mental state? Most intriguingly of all, what is the effect of intellectual activity? The Austrian physiologist, Ernst Fleischl, had speculated in 1883: 'Perhaps it will even be possible to observe, by recording from the scalp, currents evoked by various psychological acts of one's own brain'.[11] This was Berger's keenest ambition. What became of his great discovery after his death, once the chaos of war had abated?

The EEG today

Berger himself had noticed the occurrence of two contrasting rhythms in his earliest recordings from the human brain. In his second paper, published in 1930, he chose names for these which are used to this day.[12] 'Alpha' rhythm comprises prominent and remarkably regular waves at a frequency of 8–13 cycles/second. These are particularly well seen over the back of the head, when the subject's eyes are closed. Alpha is the signature of relaxed wakefulness, the hallmark – in Berger's words – of the 'passive EEG'. Opening the eyes, novel sensory events and any mental exertion – such as performing mental arithmetic – tend to reduce or abolish alpha, which is largely replaced by 'beta', Berger's second rhythm. This consists of faster, less regular and smaller waves with a frequency greater than 13 cycles/second: these are the denizens of the 'active EEG' (see Figure 3.2).

Berger's work was at first viewed with scepticism, particularly by experimental physiologists, who felt that such regular oscillations were unlikely to originate from the complex electrical workings of the human brain. By 1934, however, the distinguished Cambridge physiologist Lord Adrian had been convinced of the reality of the 'Berger rhythm', and a number of other waveforms were soon described.

Slow rhythms were recognised as the electroencephalographic correlates of sleep and of coma. The slowest of all, occurring at a frequency of under 4 cycles/second or less, were termed 'delta'; waves intermediate between

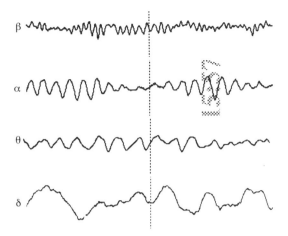

Figure 3.2 Rhythms of brain activity These four recordings, from different subjects, show the four rhythms commonly encountered in the EEG: beta rhythm at 14–25 cycles/second is characteristic of the active wakeful brain; alpha, at 8–13 cycles/second, is seen during relaxed wakefulness with the eyes closed; slower rhythms, theta (4–7 cycles/second) and delta (less than 4 cycles/second), are seen during normal sleep and in states of depressed consciousness, such as coma. The dotted line divides a 2-second period in two.

delta and alpha, occurring at 4–8 cycles/second, became known as 'theta'. These waves are not entirely restricted to states of lowered consciousness: the EEG of young children is dominated by slow activity, and foci of slow waves often occur at sites of injury in the adult brain, for example over areas damaged by stroke. Some brain areas normally generate slow waves during waking: theta rhythms can be recorded over the waking hippocampi, the 'sea-horses' tucked into the temporal lobes which allow us to acquire new memories.[13]

Most EEGs consist of a mixture of these wave types, and look dauntingly complex (see Figure 4.1, p.118). An experienced eye, or a mathematical analysis, can resolve the pattern recorded into its constituent waveforms. These are typically a blend of alpha and beta rhythms in the healthy waking adult brain. The possible relevance of gamma waves – a subtype of beta rhythm, occurring at a frequency of 25–100 cycles/second – to consciousness has attracted great interest recently: they will resurface later in this book.

Our knowledge of the physiology of the brain has grown hugely since these various waveforms were first described. Berger could only speculate about the brain mechanisms which might generate such unexpectedly regular electrical events. What have we learned since?

The most remarkable implication of the EEG is that the numerous cells of the cerebral cortex – which lie beneath the electrodes used to record the

EEG – have a tendency to work in synchrony. Only synchronised activity in substantial numbers of cortical cells could generate currents large enough to be detected over the scalp. It is generally agreed nowadays that the specific source of these currents is activity in the dendrites of cortical neurons.[14]

Why should these currents be synchronous and rhythmic? We still have a sketchy understanding of many of the rhythms of the EEG, but two familiar features of neural design are at work: the behaviour of individual neurons and their organisation in networks. As I mentioned in the last chapter, many neurons are spontaneously active: this activity is often rhythmic. If neurons are suitably interconnected, intrinsically rhythmic patterns of discharge in a subset of cells in the network can generate widespread synchronous patterns like those of the EEG. The neurons whose spontaneous rhythms contribute to the EEG lie in two regions: in the expanse of the cerebral cortex and within the striatened confines of the thalamus.[15] This structure, the gateway to the cortex, is especially well placed to synchronise rhythms throughout the brain.

On a first encounter one might easily suppose that the EEG is the true physical embodiment of consciousness, slowing to near standstill in deep sleep, coasting comfortably in waking repose, surging ahead as attention is focused, erupting into angry paroxysms in an epileptic seizure. The parallels are remarkable. Closer acquaintance sows a few doubts: the correlation between the EEG and our behaviour and experience occasionally breaks down. The EEG, after all, only allows us a glimpse of the activity from moment to moment in some parts of the cerebral cortex – not a panoramic view of the whole brain and its functions. But the most frustrating limitations of the EEG are practical: as Berger realised from the start, contraction of muscles, the activity of the heart and the movements of the eyes can all easily drown out the small voice of the electricity of the brain.

Interpreting the EEG makes two conflicting and simultaneous demands: one must disregard all the sources of the 'noise' which flicker in the background, but at the same time remain watchful for subtle significant detail. As the EEG is nowadays usually recorded on 16 parallel channels which range across the scalp this skill can be hard won, and given such a mass of information, in a recording which can run to hundreds of pages, there is a real risk of misinterpretation.

In neurology, as a result, the 'diagnostic' EEG has sometimes fallen into disrepute. One revered but mild-mannered professor wrote, in words which were damning from him, that 'although it is possible to conduct an extensive practice without recourse to the EEG its use is now almost obligatory for social reasons'.[16] I was once greatly impressed, and surprised, when an expert colleague continued to flick through the pages of an EEG he was reporting as he chatted to me, with his head turned over his shoulder. When I queried the wisdom of this approach, he told me that any abnormality present on only a few pages is not worth bothering with.

Despite its limitations the EEG is a useful tool, especially in diagnosing and understanding the disorders of awareness, like epilepsy, described in the following chapter. But practical uses aside, the EEG has been immensely important for our theoretical understanding of consciousness. Berger had, as he claimed, found a 'concomitant phenomenon of the continuous nerve processes which take place in the brain' – one which could be detected easily by recording from the scalp, and which provided a means of tracking conscious states. When careful attention was turned in the 1950s to the behaviour of the EEG during the rhythm of waking and sleep a host of new discoveries tumbled out.

The patterning of conscious states

After a few minutes of vigorous protest at finding himself in his cot, our baby falls asleep, abruptly, as if a switch has turned. When I look at him a few moments later, I am alarmed by what I see. He is relaxed, but occasionally one of his hands jerks unexpectedly. His breathing is irregular, snatched in tiny gasps. His eyes are only half closed; every few seconds they dart here and there, as if in pursuit of invisible targets. What can have happened to him? Is he having a fit? But when I look again he is calm: his breaths are regular, eyes still, arms raised above his head with palms placidly upturned.

We tend to see rather little of each other's sleep until we have children. Parents, infinitely grateful for their offspring's naps, have plenty of opportunity to observe them: they must have known since time began that sleep is a complex state. At times small sleeping children are virtually unrousable, as conveniently portable as a sack of potatoes; at others, like my son, they seem to be in the grip of an alien force, gasping and twitching, searching for unseen sights.

It is odd that the regular occurrence of these variations through the night, and their significance, went more or less unrecognised until the work of two successive graduate students of a Chicago physiologist, Nathaniel Kleitman, in the 1950s. In 1955 one of these students, E. Aserinsky, published the first detailed account of the patterning of sleep.[17] He had noticed that at intervals through the night, quiet sleep, during which the eyes were still, gave way to periods of rapid eye movements. This was interesting, but humdrum in comparison to his second discovery: sleepers woken at these times are very likely to report a dream – much more likely than during 'quiet' sleep.

Aserinsky's colleague in Kleitman's laboratory, William Dement, picked up the the threads of his work. He showed first that the sleeper's estimate of the duration of his dream correlates with the time spent in 'rapid eye movement' sleep, known as REM, reinforcing the link Aserinsky had discovered between dreaming and REM. Next, he found that the large rhythmic slow waves which dominate the EEG during quiet sleep were replaced during REM by a fast low-voltage pattern almost indistinguishable from the EEG of the ordinary waking consciousness.

In 1957 he and Kleitman published the results of a study which must have been exhausting as well as exhaustive: they had recorded eye movements, body movements and the EEG continuously during 126 nights of undisturbed sleep in 33 subjects. Their study showed clearly that sleep is not the straightforward descent into oblivion it might appear: on the contrary, it is actively organised, an orderly succession of physiological – and subjective – states (see Figure 3.3).[18]

To describe their observations Dement and Kleitman introduced a classification of sleep stages which is, in essence, still used today.[19] The lightest sleep occurs in stage 1. This is the stage one can sometimes observe in

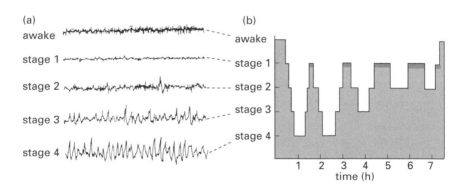

Figure 3.3 The architecture of sleep The EEG recordings on the left show the gradual transition from the rapid rhythms of the waking stage (Berger's beta rhythm) to the theta and delta frequencies of the sleeping EEG. The right-hand figure shows the cyclical patterning of sleep, with alternating periods of slow wave and rapid eye movement sleep (indicated by the darker bars), the latter lengthening as the night goes on.

a tired colleague during a dull meeting in a warm room: the head nods, and the eyes roll up as the lids drop down – sometimes repeatedly. At the same time alpha rhythm becomes less prominent, to be replaced by a mixture of slow and fast frequencies. Slow rolling eye movements – quite unlike the rapid eye movements of REM – set in, once stage 1 is established. This stage of sleep occupies no more than 5 per cent of the night.

About 45 per cent of the night's sleep is spent in stage 2. At this stage sleep is properly under way, the sleeper pretty motionless and eye movements are infrequent. The EEG contains a good deal of slow activity, theta and delta, but stage 2 is also the occasion for an electrical firework display: 'sleep spindles', 'K-complexes' and 'vertex sharp waves', cavort around the cortex. We shall track these electrical beasts back to their lair in a while.

In stages 3 and 4 sleep deepens. Our muscles relax, our eyes are still, and the EEG slows even further. In stage 3, by definition, high amplitude delta waves are present 20–50 per cent of the time, and in stage 4 for the majority of the time. Accordingly stages 3 and 4 are sometimes referred to as 'slow wave sleep'.

Dement and Kleitman watched a descent through these stages during the first hour or so of the night. Stage 4 began rapidly, within half an hour of sleep onset, and continued for about half an hour. But then, remarkably, their sleepers reascended the ladder of sleep stages, all the way back to stage 1 – or, rather, to something that misleadingly resembled it. For now, about 90 minutes into the night, Dement and Kleitman could detect the rapid eye movements of dreaming sleep. They made another unexpected but pregnant observation: despite the energetic activity of their eyes, the sleepers moved their bodies rather little during REM, less in fact than in the adjacent periods of sleep. The EEG might resemble the waking state, but REM proved to be a stage of deep muscular relaxation. The dissociation between the active appearance of the EEG and the passivity of the sleeper gives rise to the other name for REM: paradoxical sleep.

After a few minutes of REM, Dement's closely observed sleepers dropped down the ladder once again, into a second spell of slow wave sleep – and so on throughout the night. This cyclical succession of sleep stages was an extraordinary discovery. But it was apparent from the start that the cycle was a complex one, evolving as the hours pass.

In the first cycle or two, deep slow wave sleep predominates, and spells of REM are quite brief, lasting just a few minutes. As the night passes these trends reverse, with less deep and less protracted slow wave sleep and more extended REM. This explains the quite high likelihood that we will wake in the morning with a dream in our minds. Woken at 2 a.m., we are more likely to have to drag ourselves up from stage 3 or 4, an effort we rather dislike.

What of my son's darting eyes? Why did he jump straight into REM, omitting the usual measured descent into sleep? He was, in fact, obeying the rules appropriate to his age. Adults spend about one-fifth of their seven hours of sleep in REM, whereas infants are in REM for more than half their 17 sleeping hours. Given this preponderance, it is not too surprising that 'sleep-onset REM' should be a common event in babes. Why small children should require so much REM sleep is an interesting question, to which we shall return.

A new technology has recently added a fascinating footnote to these observations. Electric currents generate magnetic fields, so that it should in principle be possible to detect fluctuations in the the magnetic fields surrounding an active brain. So it has proved, but achieving this requires much more formidable equipment than the humble EEG. The subject must sit in a specially shielded room to screen out 'magnetic noise' from the environment; 'superconducting quantum interference devices' (probably equally mysterious to both you and me) are used to detect the magnetic signal.

This formidable device has yet to prove its real worth, but in 1990 Rudolfo Llinas, an American neuroscientist, reported that he had recorded a rapid oscillation in the gamma frequency in waking subjects, which was also present during REM but absent from slow wave sleep (see Figure 3.4).[20] This similarity between REM sleep and waking was qualified by a telling contrast: tones played to waking subjects 'reset' their gamma rhythm, but had no effect on the fast oscillation in the brains of subjects in REM. Llinas' findings corroborate the well-established similarity between the waking and dreaming EEG. They hint at a role for fast oscillations, around 40 waves/second, in the genesis of consciousness, another theme we will return to. Finally, they nicely illustrate the contrast between the responsive state of waking consciousness and the brain's introspective attitude during paradoxical sleep.

The rhythm of descent into slow wave sleep and ascent back to REM which recurs throughout the night is, of course, a component of the more extended rhythm familiar to us all, of sleeping and waking, rest and activity, night and day. A variety of 'circadian rhythms' is normally synchronised by the fundamental solar rhythm of light and darkness: for example, our body temperature and the secretion of many of our hormones, like our sleeping and waking, follow a 24-hour cycle. Experiments isolating volunteers from daylight and other artificial clues to time of day have shown that

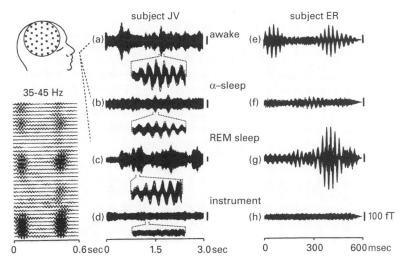

Figure 3.4 40 Hz oscillations in sleep and wakefulness Recordings made using MEG reveal prominent high frequency oscillations at 35–45 cycles/second, synchronised across the head, in the waking state and during dreaming (REM) sleep. The diagram at top left shows the position of the sensors over the head; recordings from the sensors in the 35–45 cycle/second range are shown at bottom left; the right-hand traces show superpositions of the traces in two subjects in the waking state, during slow wave (delta) sleep, and during REM sleep; the bottom trace shows the 'noise' from the instrument.

the cycle regulating temperature and hormones persists in these circumstances, and can dissociate from the cycle of waking and sleep.[21] Left to themselves, body temperature and hormone secretion oscillate every 24–25 hours; the cycle of sleep and waking can break free from these, establishing a more eccentric rhythm.

The past 40 years of research have revealed an elaborate and unsuspected order in the depths of sleep. While the students of sleep kept themselves up through the small hours, others pursued the tantalising possibility of 'perceiving the currents generated in our own brain by various mental acts'.[22]

Cognitive potentials

The early work on the electrical activity of animals' brains had established that it was possible to record a cerebral response to sensory stimulation. This was usually detected in regions which were already suspected of serving the senses: visual stimuli, for example, reliably excited the occipital lobes, the hindmost reach of the cortex, known from other evidence to play a role in vision. Similarly, in 1899, Vladimir Larionov reported his discovery that tones of different pitch excite adjacent but distinct locations in the temporal cortex of dogs.

Since then 'evoked potentials' have become one of the standard laboratory tests in clinical neurology, a useful means of probing the 'sensory pathways' in neurological disorders. The response to a single stimulus is quite weak in comparison to the spontaneous background of the EEG: responses to numerous stimuli are therefore 'averaged' to extract the sensory signal from the surrounding electrical noise.

Provided your senses are healthy, an evoked response of some kind can be recorded whether or not you are paying attention to the stimulus, and even in sleep. An audible click, for example, gives rise to a characteristic series of scalp potentials as the response ascends through the brainstem from the point at which the auditory nerve enters the brain. The five robust peaks of the 'brainstem auditory evoked potential' (see Figure 3.5) flag a series of neuronal landmarks traversed by the auditory signals in the first ten thousandths of a second of their journey.

By the time 300 thousandths of a second have elapsed things are rather different. The 'P300' is the most salient of a family of responses which are related not to the occurrence of the stimulus but to its significance.[23] If you are asked to listen to a monotonous succession of 'beeps' punctuated every so often by a refreshing 'boop', the boop but not the beep will be greeted by an electrical signal. A missing 'beep' also gives rise to a P300, emphasising that this response springs not from the stimulus but from our expectations. If the same series of tones is played when you are absorbed by a book the brainstem auditory evoked potential persists, but the 'attentional' P300 disappears altogether. Unlike the earlier sensory components of the auditory evoked response, the P300 is not specific to hearing: a rare attended visual or tactile stimulus excites the same response. Here then is the first fulfilment of Fleischl's dream, the electrical correlate of a 'mental act', if of a rather specific kind: the act of noting the occurrence of an anticipated but exceptional event.

The precise neuronal source of the P300 remains controversial, highlighting a common problem with the EEG. An electrical potential detected at the scalp could have a variety of sources in the brain: a weak source close to the electrode or a strong one at a distance. 'Localisation' is not the forte of electrical recording. Its great virtue is precision of timing: the EEG can faithfully track changes in potentials at the scalp as they occur. Studies of potentials like the P300 indicate, for example, that attention can influence the neural response to sensory stimuli as early as 20–50 thousandths of a second after the stimulus occurs.

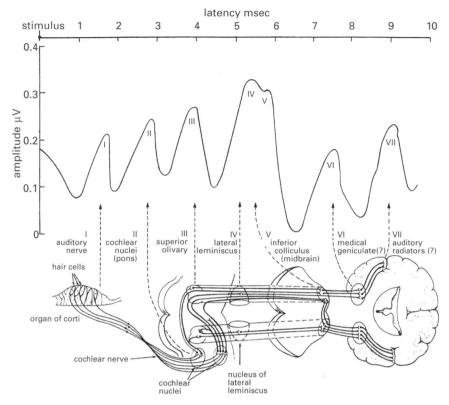

Figure 3.5 The brainstem auditory evoked response The five waves which can be recorded from the scalp during the first ten thousandths of a second after a sound reaches the ear. These correspond to successive bursts of neuronal activity as the 'auditory' signal travels from the inner ear (the hair cells in the Organ of Corti) into and through the brainstem. The source of waves VI and VII is less certain. The medial geniculate nucleus lies in the thalamus. The auditory radiations are the pathways taken by auditory signals throughout the cerebral hemispheres.

Where other lines of evidence indicate the likely locations of neural activity when we perform a given task, electrical studies can help sketch the sequence of events. We know, for example, that if you are asked to come up with a related verb in response to a given noun – say, tea – Broca's area comes into play. This is not the case when you simply repeat the same noun. Detailed EEG detects activity over the vicinity of Broca's area within half of a second of the stimulus in the verb generation task, occurring ahead of excitation in other language areas. This approach to the EEG, using large numbers of electrical contacts with the scalp and powerful computers to process the results, is sophisticated, novel and in its early days, but it promises to shed new light on the dynamics of 'thought' in the human brain.

We have now encountered evidence that the electricity of the brain, recorded from the scalp, mirrors our level of consciousness, our sensations, our expectations and our intellectual activity. Thirty years ago two German scientists discovered that it also manifests our intention to move.

If the EEG before a voluntary movement is examined by averaging techniques similar to those used to record evoked potentials, an electrical disturbance, the *Bereitschaftspotential*, is apparent for about a second before the movement is made (see Figure 3.6). It is thought to reflect the 'planning' of movement in brain regions which surround the motor cortex. It is absent in the moments preceding an involuntary movement, like the 'jump' of startled surprise. If sensory evoked potentials reflect the neural background of perception, the 'pre-movement potential' is the electrical correlate of the will.

Reflect on this for a moment. Raise one of your fingers, or wriggle a toe. For a second before you did so your brain was planning the movement, and this could have been recorded from your scalp. A second is a long time in the brain, underlining the remarkable truth that every mental event, from sensation to action, depends on a long-drawn-out chain of neural events. Thought may be quick, but it has a measurable speed: Berger's scientific descendants are in a position to time it.

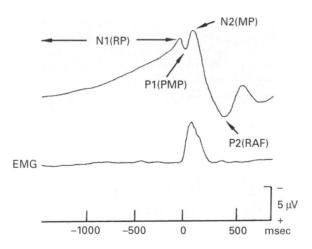

Figure 3.6 The readiness potential The bottom of the figure shows the time scale in thousandths of a second; time 0 corresponds to a hand movement, indicated by the deflection on the EMG trace (this is the 'electromyogram' which monitors the movements of muscles electrically); the top trace shows electrical activity recorded from the top of the head prior to, during and after the movement: the RP is the 'readiness potential', which precedes voluntary movements by up to a second; PMP is the pre-motion potential, MP the motor potential and RAF the reafference potential.

We have run ahead of the central subject of this chapter – the raw capacity for consciousness – into the realms of thought and action. To recap, in a sentence, the insight of key importance to us from the past century's work on the EEG is that patterns of electrical activity in the brain correlate with states of consciousness. Let's pursue this activity now, from the EEG at the scalp, into the core of the nervous system, where the neural controllers of our states of consciousness reside.

Controlling consciousness

Epidemic stupor

> . . . down where all the ladders start,
> In the foul rag-and-bone shop of the heart
> W.B. Yeats, 'The Circus Animals' Desertion'[24]

Plague prospers in the wake of war. A plague which first swept across Europe towards the end of the First World War, vanishing ten years later almost as abruptly as it arrived, remains to this day a deeply mysterious affliction. But even as it laid waste innumerable lives, it quietly helped to open a new chapter in our understanding of the neurology of consciousness.

This unusual brain disorder attracted the notice of Constantin von Economo, a Viennese neurologist and psychiatrist, towards the end of 1916. He gave it the name it still bears, 'encephalitis lethargica'.[25] An encephalitis is an infection or inflammation of the brain; the symptoms it causes depend on which parts of the brain it invades. The patients arriving at the Vienna Psychiatric Clinic had 'a strange variety of symptoms', but the most striking of these were disordered states of arousal.

Some drifted into a somnolent torpor over the course of a few days; others were 'catatonic', inaccessibly frozen into unnatural postures which they maintained for hours or days on end; yet others were seized with uncontrollable excitement, punctuated by 'crises' of involuntary movement. Sleep – or something like it – either overwhelmed or cruelly eluded them. Just as the illness confounded the usual rhythm of waking and rest, its galaxy of symptoms, physical and psychological, confounded the tenuous distinction between neurology and psychiatry.

Sufferers from the somnolent variety fell 'asleep in the act of sitting and standing, and even while walking, or during meals, with all signs of yawning and tiredness'; severely affected cases might enter a state 'of more or less permanent sleep', lasting for weeks or months. By contrast, the patient with 'hyperkinetic' disease 'tosses about in bed, pushes the blankets back, pulls them up again, sits up, throws himself back again in wild sort of haste, jumps out of bed, strikes out aimlessly, talks incoherently, clucks his tongue, and whistles – this unrest lasting for days and nights without a stop'.

Many succumbed to this strange disorder; some recovered, a few were left for decades in a twilight state of impaired arousal and immobility, memorably described in Oliver Sacks' *Awakenings*.[26] At the time, there was little that could be done for the victims of the sickness except to record their fate, and to seek its explanation in their damaged brains.

The damage was centred in the brainstem and the 'diencephalon', the structures of thalamus and hypothalamus which bridge the brainstem and the hemispheres. 'Experiments of nature' are never as precise as the human scientist might wish, but it was possible for von Economo, who published the classic study of the disease in 1929, to make a rough correlation between sites of damage in the brainstem and their effects on awareness.

Somnolence was particularly associated with injuries of the midbrain, at the top of the brainstem; insomnia followed damage to areas of the hypothalamus. These observations suggested that while the cerebral cortex might be the key to our intellectual abilities, the brainstem was the source of arousal. Given that von Economo's patients often developed abnormalities of mood and movement as well, it seemed likely to him that the brainstem also influences these.

All the capitals of Europe saw their share of the 'epidemic stupor'. In France many were treated in the hospital which has as strong a claim as any to be the birthplace of neurology. Near the Jardin des Plantes and the Seine, close to the centre of Paris, the Pitié-Salpêtrière was once Louis XIII's gunpowder store. Jean-Martin Charcot practised and taught here in the later years of the nineteenth century, establishing the foundations of the new science of nervous diseases. In 1918, 25 years after Charcot's death, a Belgian doctor in his mid-twenties, Frederic Bremer, made his professional pilgrimage to the Salpêtrière, working as a foreign 'assistant' on the neurology service. While he was there, the epidemic of encephalitis lethargica was at its peak.

This experience engendered Bremer's interest in the physiology of sleep, but other lines of research on the brainstem took up his time, first in Boston, and then at home in Brussels. It was seventeen years after his encounter with the 'sleepy sickness', in 1935, that Bremer published a paper which lent the precision of human experiment to von Economo's conclusions. Bremer had discovered – through a mixture of educated insight and sheer chance – that surgical separation of a cat's brain from its spinal cord, leaving the brainstem intact, had no effect on the normal sequence of sleep and waking or on the cat's capacity for arousal. In complete contrast, separation of the forebrain from the brainstem, by making a cut through the midbrain, brought about a state resembling deep sleep – both in terms of the cat's behaviour and of its EEG.[27]

Bremer concluded that the brainstem normally activated the hemispheres above it by transmitting information from the senses: signals mediating touch, joint position and hearing were all interrupted by his surgery. He later confessed that he had not been 'anatomically minded' at the time he drew this conclusion. Indeed, the anatomically rather obvious fact that the surgery would not have affected signals relating to vision, taste and smell should perhaps have made him question his hypothesis.

Fertile scientists like Frederic Bremer train students who are quick to spot the weak points of their mentors' work. Giuseppe Moruzzi spent time with Bremer as a young scientist. In 1949, with Horace Magoun, Moruzzi published a paper which acknowledged Bremer's 'fundamental discovery', but threw it into a wholly new light.

A wonderful net

Moruzzi and Magoun's own discovery sounds technical but proved momentous.[28] They found that electrical stimulation of areas close to the centre of the brainstem desynchronises or 'activates' the slow rhythmic EEG of cats in natural drowsiness or under light anaesthesia. The region from which this response could be elicited was quite extensive, running through the brainstem core into the diencephalon. The areas in question were *not* concerned with transmitting specific sensory information, as Bremer had supposed; indeed later work showed that interrupting the sensory pathways, selectively, failed to prevent the activation of the hemispheres by stimulation of the brainstem core. Moruzzi suspected that there was an 'activating system' in the brainstem, and that it achieved its alerting effect on the hemispheres by way of the thalamus, into which the brainstem core projects.

The part of the brainstem in question coincided with a region long recognised by anatomists for its 'primitive' pattern of ramifying, interconnecting cells, the 'reticular formation', named after the Latin *reticulum* meaning 'net'. Like many another tangled wood, this neuronal territory has proved treacherous to explorers, but full of surprising rewards.

The anatomy of the brainstem is fairly baffling, but as you may recall it contains three main elements. First, there are numerous 'fibres of passage', bundles of axons running through from the hemispheres to the spinal cord and vice versa. Second, there are 'nuclei', tightly packed groups of cells, most of which have a clear-cut function: the axons which run to the muscles of facial expression, for example, originate in one of the nuclei in the pons; cells which receive sensory signals from the face comprise another long nucleus which runs much of the length of the brainstem. Third, there is a region of interconnecting cells, which hugs the centre of the brainstem along most of its extent: the reticular formation.

The structure of the reticular formation initially appears quite straight-forward. Small cells on the edge comprise its 'parvicellular' regions; large cells towards its core make up the 'magnocellular' regions. But while the connections of cells in most areas of the brain appear exquisitely specific, the organisation of the reticular formation seems designed to cause maximum confusion.

All the senses signal to it, mostly into the 'parvicellular' periphery. Whereas sensory signals are usually segregated initially in the brain, in the reticular formation they muddle together. But, on reflection, this is what you might expect of an 'activating system'. It doesn't matter whether a touch from a hand, a knock on the door or a flash of lightning startles you from your reverie: what matters is that *something* has happened – and you had better take notice.

The parvicellular periphery, receiving sensory signals, excites the magnocellular core. This in turn – Moruzzi and Magoun were right – communicates with the thalamus, which 'gates' signalling to the cortex. In the sleeping brain cortex and thalamus engage in rhythmical pillow talk: stimulation of the reticular formation interrupts this drowsy dialogue, and a crackle of faster rhythms replaces the slow waves of sleep.

Here then was an explanation for the somnolence of von Economo's patients and of Bremer's brain-injured cats: normal arousal requires the 'activating' input of the reticular formation in the brainstem. But from the start it was clear that behavioural arousal was not the only function of the reticular system – and that, despite its tangled anatomy, it is a structured system, whose parts serve distinct functions.

Whereas the upper brainstem is crucial for arousal, the lower reaches of the reticular formation, in the medulla and pons, are concerned more with keeping us alive than with keeping us awake. They regulate the rhythm of our breathing, and the behaviour of the heart and circulation. A disorder fancifully named 'Ondine's curse', in memory of the dangers of betraying a Scandinavian water sprite, occasionally follows damage here: sufferers breathe more or less adequately while awake, so long as the muscles of breathing are under voluntary control. They risk death on falling asleep, as the brainstem no longer reliably triggers automatic breaths.

An entirely new line of evidence has recently confirmed Moruzzi's theory. It has become possible to inspect changes in the activity of the *human* brain during sleep and waking more directly than ever before. As neuronal activity increases in an area of the brain, blood flow and the rate of consumption of oxygen and glucose in that area also increase. These changes can be revealed using one of several techniques, known collectively as 'functional imaging', which allow the experimenter to identify brain regions active in a particular state or during the performance of a task. Evidence obtained using these powerful techniques will crop up repeatedly in the following chapters. In the context of sleep, functional imaging has shown that in slow wave sleep brain activity decreases particularly in the upper brainstem and thalamus, as well as in areas of prefrontal and limbic cortex. During REM sleep the upper brainstem and thalamus are reactivated.[29] Correspondingly, during slow wave sleep, global energy consumption by the brain falls by about 20 per cent, rising back to waking levels in dream sleep.

The fundamental importance of the upper reticular formation to arousal, and of its lower parts to our breathing and circulation, has been clear now for almost 50 years. An explanation of its influence on mood, suspected by von Economo, and a new appreciation of its complexity, had to wait for another technical advance. This was the creation of a 'wet physiology' to complement the 'dry' variety practised by Bremer, Moruzzi and Magoun.

The chemistry of consciousness

The gains are mainly in the stain.

Floyd Bloom[30]

When I first read about the brainstem's 'ascending reticular activating sytem' as a student it was usually illustrated by bold and very simple diagrams (see Figure 3.7). These are accurately described, in a recent review of the subject, as 'depicting pathways of unknown origin acting diffusely by means of unknown transmitters on unknown targets'. All this has changed. New techniques, combining microscopy with carefully tailored

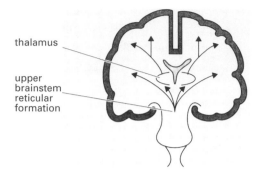

thalamus

upper
brainstem
reticular
formation

Figure 3.7 The reticular activating system The highly schematic figure emphasises
the importance of the upper brainstem and thalamus in activating the cerebral
hemispheres.

stains, have made it possible to highlight groups of cells producing specific
transmitters and to trace their 'projections' through the brain. These have
revealed a series of neuronal systems within the broad territory of the reticular system which differ in their chemistry, their anatomical connections
and in the relationship of their activity to our states of awareness.

We briefly encountered the chemicals concerned in the last chapter.
Much of the brain's noradrenaline, dopamine, serotonin, acetylcholine and
histamine originates in or close to the brainstem in a series of named and
numbered nuclei, which project extensively to the hemispheres. Noradrenaline is particularly associated with the locus ceruleus, the 'blue
nucleus' in the pons; dopamine with the substantia nigra, in the midbrain,
which perishes in Parkinson's disease; serotonin with the 'raphe nuclei'
which hug the centre of the brainstem, the site of action of many antidepressants, including Prozac; acetylcholine with nuclei in the pons
involved with REM sleep, and with the basal nucleus of Meynert, in the
forebrain, a target of injury in Alzheimer's disease (see Figure 3.8). Histamine is released in the thalamus by fibres which originate below it, in the
headquarters of the autonomic nervous system, the hypothalamus.

These transmitters pervade the cerebral cortex. Axons conveying acetylcholine, noradrenaline and histamine also penetrate the thalamus. The
extensive pathways which convey them allow the neurons of the brainstem
to exert a powerful influence on the activity of the circuits of thalamus
and cortex.

Why should there be so many chemical systems? Are they distinctive
ingredients in the brain's recipe for consciousness? They evidently are,
although we are only just beginning to glimpse their various contributions.

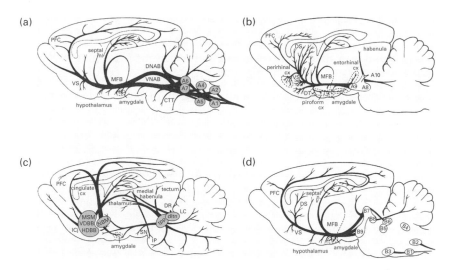

Figure 3.8 The chemistry of wakefulness The 'gain from the stain': several chemically distinct parts of the activating system have now been identified: (a) shows the pathways which transmit noradrenaline, (b) the pathways using dopamine, (c) acetylcholine and (d) serotonin (illustrated here in the rat's brain).

The influence of acetylcholine on conscious states is potent and relatively well understood.[31] Activity in 'cholinergic' (acetylcholine-producing) neurons tends to desynchronise the EEG, a key feature of waking and REM sleep. Infusion of low doses of a drug which mimics the effect of acetylcholine during human slow wave sleep induces REM sleep; higher doses cause wakefulness. The cells of the pedunculopontine and laterodorsal tegmental nuclei in the pons,[32] which are particularly active during REM sleep, are cholinergic (acetylcholine-producing). Locally applied to the targets of these nuclei, acetylcholine reproduces the phenomena of REM sleep. Drugs which oppose the action of acetylcholine, like some antidepressants, make us sleepy.

While acetylcholine is implicated in both of the 'EEG-desynchronised' states, wakefulness and REM sleep, the activity of noradrenergic (noradrenaline-producing) cells is greatest during wakefulness, subsides during slow wave sleep and reaches its nadir in REM sleep. A popular current model of the rhythmic succession of slow wave and REM sleep proposes that there is a 'reciprocal interaction' between cholinergic 'REM-on neurons' and noradrenergic and serotonergic 'REM-off neurons' in and around the brainstem reticular formation.

One might expect these chemicals to be involved in some way in causing sleepiness, but the chemistry of this all too familiar state is a confusing topic. Serotonin has been regarded as a sleep promoter. Rapid depletion of brain serotonin certainly causes severe, if temporary, insomnia, but its role in the normal inception of sleep is unclear. Accumulation of a substance called adenosine during wakefulness may be important, reducing the activity in the cholinergic nuclei which help to maintain wakefulness. A host of other natural 'somnogens' has been described: some of these probably help to put us to bed but their relative importance is not yet clear.[33]

In the light of our new knowledge of the chemistry of awareness, has Moruzzi's idea that the brainstem contains an 'ascending reticular activating system' outgrown its usefulness? Every element of the concept can be called into question. 'Activation' is only one of the functions of this network of structures; the widely projecting brainstem systems shown in Figure 3.8 look sure to play a crucial part in the control of other functions, like attention, mood, motivation and movement, creating the background for all our experience and behaviour.[34] The activating structures aren't confined to the brainstem: they extend up into the thalamus and hemispheres; only some of them have a 'reticular' structure; and activation descends to the spinal cord as well as ascending to the brain. Nevertheless the concept captures important truths: the brainstem is crucial to arousal, reticular anatomy contributes, and an important component of the activation which is vital to awareness ascends from deep down upwards. Like many good ideas, the concept of the ascending reticular activating system may some day deserve a decent burial. For the time being, it remains an enlightening simplification.

The place where consciousness dwells

> There is no room or place where consciousness dwells.
>
> Wilder Penfield[35]

I hope that two ideas stand proud from this chapter's profusion of detail. The first is that our states of awareness are mirrored by the electrical activity of the brain; the second that both are profoundly affected by an 'activating system' located in or close to the brainstem. But it would be misleading to regard the brainstem as the elusive 'place where consciousness dwells'. Rather than providing the one true home for consciousness, the activating system contributes a number of key centres or 'nodes' to a widely distributed network. Even in isolation from the cortex these are capable of generating a cycle of rest and arousal.[36] Some of the nodes in this neural network have been studied in detail in recent years. I shall sketch one or two of the resulting discoveries which illustrate what vital but specialised roles these centres serve.

A tiny cluster of cells in the hypothalamus lies just above a junction made by the optic nerves, which run back from the eye. This junction is called the optic chiasm, and the cell cluster is known as the 'suprachiasmatic nucleus'. The hypothalamus, you will recall, is concerned with monitoring and meeting our more basic needs. It comes as a surprise to learn that it receives a share of axons directly from the retina. These terminate in the suprachiasmatic nucleus. What is the nucleus hoping to see? The answer is, simply, light.

The suprachiasmatic nucleus turns out to be intrinsically rhythmic, with a cycle of activity close to 24 hours. The rhythm persists in 'tissue explants', nests of tissue which have been surgically removed and cultured in the laboratory, suggesting that the nucleus may be the pacemaker for the body's circadian rhythms of activity, temperature and hormonal secretion. The function of the pathway from the retina is to 'entrain' the natural circadian rhythm of the suprachiasmatic nucleus to the rhythm of day and night. It takes a while to reset the nucleus when we change time zone – hence the disconcerting experience of jet lag.

An ingenious experiment demonstrates the key influence of the nucleus on our cycles of activity.[37] It depended on the discovery of a mutant hamster with a disordered brain clock. The hamster in question inherits a suprachiasmatic nucleus with a circadian rhythm of only 20 hours. This has the result that the unfortunate hamster's rhythm of rest and activity is almost always out of kilter with the day–night cycle. Martin Ralphs and his colleagues exploited this quirk of hamster genetics by transplanting mutant nuclei into animals whose own circadian rhythms had been abolished by removal of the suprachiasmatic nucleus prior to the transplant. Transplantation reinstated the circadian rhythm, but with a difference: the recipients of the transplants now exhibited the unusual 20-hour rhythm of the donors.

Damage to the suprachiasmatic nucleus does not affect awareness. It is not the place where consciousness dwells – but it may be its chief timekeeper. If it fails, sleep and waking become randomly distributed throughout the day.

The thalamus is home to a second cell group with a well-defined role in the process of arousal, the 'reticular nucleus'. As we have seen, the thalamus is a way-station for sensory signals *en route* to the cortex and a hub for communication between regions of the hemispheres. Most of its nuclei receive from and transmit to other areas of the brain. The 'reticular nucleus' is an exception. It receives collaterals, side branches, from axons arriving at the thalamus from the cortex and from axons departing from the thalamus to the cortex. Its own output flows into the other nuclei of the thalamus. It is now known to be the source of the signature of light sleep, the 'sleep spindle'.[38]

These and other similar synchronous oscillations express the behaviour of the thalamus in its sleeping state, known to physiologists as its 'burst mode': its cells burst rhythmically in a three-cornered exchange between the thalamus proper, its reticular nucleus and the cortex. While this exchange continues the brain is largely closed to external stimuli: the thalamus acts as a partial barrier to the incoming sensory signals. Activation of the thalamus by the brainstem switches it back to 'spike mode', allowing its neurons to resume their role as faithful messengers, conveying news of every kind to and from the cortex. This shift, from burst mode to spike mode in the thalamus, opens the gates of awareness.

By now we have encountered most of the more fully explored nodes in the network controlling sleep and waking: the cholinergic nuclei which help to switch the thalamus from its resting oscillatory state to the responsive mode required for consciousness; noradrenergic and serotonergic nuclei, which are particularly active in the waking state and bring to an end REM sleep; the suprachiasmatic nucleus which keeps body time in step with solar time; the reticular nucleus of the thalamus which inscribes the signature of early sleep. Granted that there is no single place where consciousness dwells, is there a centre for sleep, a neural on-switch for rest?

This is unfortunately a murky area in a controversial field. Several brain regions have been proposed as 'hypnogenic' centres. One lies in the lower brainstem. Its existence was first suspected following experiments by Moruzzi, the architect of the concept of the ascending reticular activating system. Anaesthetising this area selectively *wakes* a sleeping cat. Stimulation of a sensory nucleus in this region, the nucleus of the solitary tract, tended to synchronise the EEG. Stimulation of a second area, the 'preoptic' region of the hypothalamus, induces slow wave sleep; damage here can cause insomnia. This area, intriguingly, helps to regulate heat loss – we know that body temperature falls during sleep, and that elevation of body temperature during the day increases sleep duration. There may be other hypnogenic areas in the basal forebrain and the thalamus. But it seems certain that slow wave sleep, like waking consciousness, will prove to be the outcome of an interaction between numerous specialised nodes in a neural network, rather than the result of throwing a single switch in the brain.

All that we have learned about the biological basis of sleep and waking prompts an intriguing – and deeply puzzling – question. Why should we sleep at all?

Why do we sleep?

A child aged three: 'Because it's night.'

Her sister, aged six: 'If we didn't we'd get really tired and stuff, and we wouldn't be able to do anything.'

No one knows why we sleep. When I asked my young daughters for their views on the matter I was delighted that each produced a version of the two most popular current explanations: that sleep evolved to keep us out of harm's way when it's dark, and that it somehow makes good the wear and tear we suffer in the day.

There is little doubt that, like other mammals, we do need sleep. Total sleep deprivation is lethal for the rat in about 21 days. The effect appears to be specific to sleep loss, rather than a non-specific effect of the stress of sleep deprivation. Such aggressive sleep deprivation experiments have not been performed in humans, but numerous studies over the last hundred years have documented the disruptive effects of sleep deprivation on thought and behaviour.[39]

In 1964 Randy Gardner, a schoolboy from San Diego, set the world record for sustained wakefulness at 264 hours. He was studied closely in the later parts of his vigil by scientists from a nearby naval sleep laboratory. The longest period of sleep deprivation achieved in a study of a group of subjects is 205 hours, also an impressive total, more than eight full days.

Such studies have found little in the way of general physical decline. A minor fall in body temperature is common, along with an increase in appetite. But thought and behaviour suffer considerably: it becomes progressively more difficult to maintain attention or a train of thought, to find words, to learn new material and to judge the passage of time. By 205 hours the subjects of an experiment conducted in Los Angeles in 1966 were approaching the ceiling of custom-built scales for 'visual misperception', 'temporal disorientation' and 'cognitive disorganisation' (see Figure 3.9 and Table 3.1). Although psychotic behaviour is unusual in previously balanced subjects, a degree of 'irritability, aggression and suspiciousness' often emerges, as I can confirm from experience as a junior hospital doctor in the bad old days.

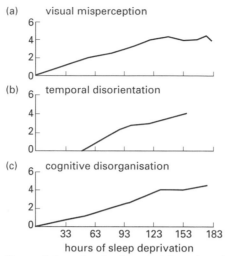

Figure 3.9 The effects of sleep deprivation on vision, thought and orientation in time
A week of sleep deprivation has major effects on perception and thought. See Table 3.1 for details of the scales used to assess the subjects.

Table 3.1 Scales for visual misperception, temporal disorientation and cognitive disorganisation used to study the effects of sleep deprivation

(a)
1. Eye itching, burning or tired; difficulty seeing, blurred vision or diplopia.
2. Visual illusions; changes in or loss of shape, size, movement, colour or texture constancies; disturbed depth perception.
   Examples: 'The floor seems wavy.'
   'The light seems to flicker.'
   'The size and colour of the chairs seem to change'.
3. Labelling of illusions, but with no doubt concerning their illusory character.
   Examples: 'Looks like fog around the light.'
   'That black mark looked like it was changing into different rock formations.'
4. Labelling of illusions with some doubt concerning their reality.
   Examples: 'I thought there was fuzz around the bottle.'
   'I thought steam was rising from the floor, so I tested my eyes to check whether it was real.'
5. Labelling of illusions (hallucinations) with, for a time at least, belief in their reality.
   Examples: 'I saw hair in my milk. The others said there wasn't any, but I still felt there was and would not drink it.'
   'That (Rorshach card) looked like an envelope, I turned it over to check, and it had my name and address on it.'

(b)
1. Time seems to pass slowly, or to be 'different' in duration.
2. Occasional mistakes in thinking about time with spontaneous correction.
3. Occasional mistakes as above, but does not recognise error until questioned.
4. More frequent mistakes which subject believes to be correct. Uncertain when confronted.
5. Gross disorientation in time, or unshaken belief in mistaken concept of time.

(c)
1. Slowing of mental processes, some difficulty thinking of words (no undue interference with normal communication).
2. Occasional mistakes or failures in thinking and speech which can be corrected easily.
3. Loses train of thought, forgetting what he was thinking or talking about, leaving statements incomplete, etc. Sudden unexplained shifts in trend of thought or speech; can correct with effort if challenged.
4. Some thoughts or statements become completely incoherent. Clarification is not altogether possible. Some confusion of fantasies, dreams, or intrusive thoughts, with reality.
5. Rambling, incoherent speech for brief periods, with failure to recognise errors. Unable to straighten out jumble of incoherent thoughts when challenged.

Normality is rapidly restored by sleep. There is no need to repay the whole 'sleep debt'. Randy Gardner had largely recovered after 15 hours of sleep on the first night after his vigil. He slept in on the following two days, 'repaying' in all 24 per cent of his debt. After deprivation, the structure of sleep changes: less time is spent in the lighter stages, more in deep slow wave sleep and REM. Over the course of a few nights, sleepers recovering from a period of deprivation make good the greater part of their lost stage 4 sleep and one-third to one-half of the lost REM.

This has led to the proposal by James Horne and others that our sleep can be divided into 'core' and 'optional' components: core sleep is supposedly required for cerebral repair and lasts for about five hours: much of this must be made up after sleep deprivation. Optional sleep is a luxury which we can, with some complaining, do without.

This all seems very plausible. Why should there be any doubt that we need sleep – core sleep, at least – to 'knit up the ravell'd sleave of care', as my six-year-old suggested? Doubt springs from several sources.

The first is that we just don't know what kind of 'cerebral repair', if any, sleep accomplishes. The next few decades of sleep research may resolve this problem. The second is that there are some well-documented studies of very short sleepers, who can get by with 2–4 hours per night and possibly even less. This perhaps shouldn't come as too much of a surprise: most biological 'variables', like height, weight and intelligence, spread out along a continuum with a few individuals at each extreme. Why should this not also be true of sleep? There are no well-documented reports of healthy individuals who have managed without any sleep at all. The third source of doubt is more difficult to dispel.

Imagine that my three-year-old was right, and that we sleep 'because it's night', when there's not much else to do. On this theory sleep is a relatively safe, energy-efficient time filler. Imagine that to ensure that we spend the night in this harmless way we evolved sleepiness. Perhaps this is all there is to sleepiness: after a while it overwhelms us, not because we need sleep to repair the damage done by the day, but because we are the slaves of a 'sleep instinct'.

There is plenty of evidence that the pattern and duration of an animal's sleep is related to its ecology. Grazing ungulates, like sheep, gazelle and deer, need to spend a lot of time chewing the cud and are at risk from predators: both factors militate against extended sleep and these species indeed sleep relatively little, between two and four hours a night. The most dramatic instances of sleep shaped in response to the conditions of life are the annual orgies of sleep – or something like it – indulged in by some animals at unpromising times of year: hibernation, shallow torpor and seasonal sleep.

In normal sleep, small mammals drop their body temperature by around 2°C. Shallow torpor is a state usually induced by food shortage in autumn and spring, in which body temperature falls by 10°C. The brain activity of shallow torpor resembles normal sleep, with less REM than usual, and a lower amplitude of EEG activity, reflecting the lowered brain temperature. For some animals, such as squirrels, shallow torpor is the route of entry into hibernation, which is associated with a further sharp fall in body temperature from the waking norm of around 40°C right down to single figures. Hibernation goes beyond sleep and the EEG flattens altogether. Seasonal sleep is an alternative state of prolonged 'sleep-cum-shallow-torpor' adopted by a number of species including the grizzly bear in response to the winter's monotonous darkness and cold.

Could it be that all sleep, like shallow torpor, is an adaptation to unpropitious times, and sleepiness no more than a trick played on us by our natures to keep us in a safe place when there's nothing better to do? There are some circumstantial arguments against this rather depressing view.

We have seen that after sleep deprivation, we repay a part of the sleep debt. Unfortunately this does not advance the argument much: it may reflect the need for some repair work but it could be that we are making an empty payment, merely appeasing our whetted appetite for sleep. A more powerful argument is advanced by James Horne in his excellent book on the functions of sleep. Mammals continue to sleep in circumstances which make it pretty inconvenient. Some ingenious adaptations have occurred to make this possible. In the bottlenose dolphin and porpoise, for example, with occasional brief exceptions, sleep is restricted to one hemisphere of the brain at any one time. Deep sleep never occurs in both hemispheres at once. If one hemisphere is deprived of sleep, recovery sleep occurs selectively on that side. The unusual phenomenon of 'uni-hemispheric sleep' is probably an adaptation to the dolphin's need to make frequent trips to the surface of the water to breathe. If sleep is induced in both hemispheres at once the dolphin drowns. The survival of sleep here suggests that it does a necessary job.

One further argument can be advanced. If sleepiness is merely a device to get us out of harm's way at night one might predict that strong incentives would allow us to overcome its effects. This is true to some extent, but both laboratory experiments and anecdotes of disasters caused by sleepiness show that, beyond the second night of sleep deprivation, its effects on our performance become insuperable. This suggests that lack of sleep affects more than motivation, but does not prove the case: it could just be that the sleep instinct is very powerful.

It strikes me that both explanations of the need for sleep are likely to contain a grain of truth. Seasonal sleep is self-evidently an adaptation to prevailing conditions, but it would be rather surprising if ordinary sleep, occupying a third of our lives, did not serve some genuine restorative function, besides keeping us tucked up in bed.

I have discussed sleep so far rather as if it were a uniform state. It is not, of course. Slow wave sleep and REM may well have different functions. Certainly, the balance between them changes greatly with age. REM is preponderant in the growing brain: we have seen that while an adult spends only one-fifth of her seven hours of sleep in REM, a neonate devotes half of her 17 hours to the sport. This suggests that REM has something to do with brain growth and 'plasticity', and perhaps therefore with memory in later life: but the function of REM, like the function of slow wave sleep, remains a subject of speculation rather than confident knowledge.

The debate on the function of sleep reminds me of another equally fascinating and equally frustrating subject of grand theories: the origin of language. This topic occasioned so much fruitless controversy that further communications on the matter were banned by the Société de Linguistique de Paris in 1866.[40] I fear that we will remain forever ignorant about the details of the early evolution of human language, but the chances are excellent that we will one day understand the functions of sleep in the human brain.

Conclusion: the conditions for awareness

This chapter has explored the biology of consciousness in the first of the senses we distinguished in Chapter 1, consciousness as 'the waking state', the precondition for experience. It has told the tale of two linked series of discoveries.

The first began in earnest with the demonstration, at the end of the nineteenth century, that the brains of animals are always electrically active. Hans Berger reported the first recordings of the 'electroencephalogram of man' in 1929. Within a few years it was clear that electrical activity in the human brain varied with states of arousal: fast 'beta' rhythms abound in the active brain, 'alpha' rhythm resonates during wakeful relaxation and the slowest activity of all, 'theta' and 'delta' rhythms, appeared to dominate sleep. In the 1950s, work from Nathaniel Kleitman's laboratory revealed an unsuspected patterning of sleep, a cyclical alternation of descent into slow wave slumber with ascent into the paradoxical sleep in which we dream. Techniques allowing the 'averaging' of repeated signals in the EEG forced another line of advance: it became possible to detect the human brain's activity during sensation, attention and movement, realising Berger's ambition to identify the electrical correlates of thought. The most fundamental implication of all these electrical discoveries is that large assemblies of neurons have a propensity to act in synchrony: the dancing rhythms of consciousness may be more complex than the slow waves of sleep but concerted neuronal activity lies at the heart of both.

We traced the second series of discoveries from their origins in a plague. Constantin von Economo's study of encephalitis lethargica, shortly after the First World War, suggested to him that the brainstem and diencephalon must contain centres which regulate states of consciousness – as well as movement and mood. Experiments with animals by Bremer, Moruzzi and Magoun supported von Economo's idea, indicating the existence of an independent activating system in the 'reticular' core of the brainstem. Subsequent work by Jouvet and others showed that the patterning of sleep, like the maintenance of arousal, depends on the brainstem core and diencephalon. Over the past 20 years more sophisticated anatomical techniques have revealed great chemical complexity within the reticular formation, which turns out to be the home of a whole family of interacting activating centres. Meanwhile contemporary physiologists have begun to unearth the cellular basis of the rhythms which Berger first described in man, and to explore the mechanisms, centred on the thalamus, which open and close the gates of consciousness.

The integrity of the activating system, its rhythmic regulation of arousal, underpins our waking consciousness – and makes experience possible. The brain structures which supply the *content* of experience are the subject of Chapter 5. But before we turn to these I shall sketch what we know of some of the substances and afflictions which can cloud or abolish arousal. These have taught us a great deal about consciousness, and they illustrate its intimate dependence on the unencumbered workings of the brain.

4

The brothers of death: pathologies of consciousness

Half our dayes we passe in the shadowe of the earth, and the brother of death exacteth a third part of our lives.

Sir Thomas Browne[1]

Introduction

Consciousness is a vulnerable biological achievement. It has a host of pre-conditions besides the patterning of arousal which we explored in the last chapter. The brain is constantly in need of oxygen and glucose, ferried in by the bloodstream, propelled headwards by the heart: any interruption to supply makes itself known within seconds, and consciousness rapidly fades. The less precipitous failure of our other organs, such as the liver or kidneys, creates an unfavourable chemical milieu for the nervous system, leading, untreated, to coma. Coma also results from careless use of the many drugs with which we enjoy upsetting our bodies' delicate chemistry. Mischief within or without the brain can trigger epilepsy, in which the healthy ebb and flow of neural signals is overwhelmed by paroxysms of electricity. Sleep can erupt at inappropriate moments, exhaust us by its absence and lure the sleepwalker into perilous expeditions in the night.

Rather than try to catalogue every known disorder of consciousness in this chapter, I shall concentrate on a few of these experiments of nature, and one or two of man, which reveal the mechanisms of awareness with particular clarity. They teach one inescapable lesson: consciousness, as we understand and enjoy it, is a thoroughly physical business.

The study of these disorders has helped to tease apart the threads of awareness, and forced physicians and anaesthetists to look for ways of detecting its presence and charting its course. Towards the end of the chapter we shall turn to the measurement of consciousness, which remains an imperfect science. The reasons for its imperfection provoke some important questions at the frontier between philosophy and science.

Faints, fits and funny turns

Faints

> Andromache, with palpitating heart . . . saw them dragging her husband in front of the town . . . hauling him along at an easy canter towards the Achaean ships. The world went black as night before her eyes . . .
>
> Homer, *Iliad*, Book XXII

> Strain silently and strain hard.
>
> (from a training video for fighter pilots)[2]

A faint is the most familiar form of 'syncope'. *Synkoptein*, the Greek origin of 'syncope', means to 'cut' or 'break'. Syncope refers to a transient interruption of consciousness, caused by lack of oxygen and usually due to a widespread but temporary failure of the blood supply to the brain. Fainting is very common: around half of us succumb at some time, making it likely that you have either fainted yourself or seen someone else do so. Why does it happen? The explanation requires a small digression.

The brain is constantly active, and neurons are hungry cells. Pound for pound, the brain consumes more energy than any other organ. When we are sitting quietly, one-fifth of the blood leaving the heart, one-fifth of the oxygen we breathe and most of the circulating glucose in the bloodstream are destined for the brain. Its metabolism resembles a slow-burning stove, combusting sugar in a stream of oxygen, thereby obtaining energy and exhaling carbon dioxide. Its own fuel reserves are small, making it reliant on regular deliveries. These depend on one critical factor: blood pressure. At the risk of stating the obvious I will remind you what this is.

The regular contraction of the heart pumps blood into large arteries, under pressure, just like water travelling from a tap through a garden hose.

From large arteries the blood passes into small, its cells eventually squeezing themselves into microscopic 'capillaries', with walls only one cell thick: here the blood gives up its riches, such as oxygen, and takes up the by-products of metabolism, like carbon dioxide. From the capillaries the blood, darker now that it has surrendered its oxygen, is collected into veins, and returns to the right side of the heart. Thence it is sent to the lungs, to replenish its oxygen supply and discharge its carbon dioxide, speeds on back to the left side of the heart, and out again to the arteries. The pressure in the system depends upon both the heart's muscular contraction *and* on the tension in the muscular walls of blood vessels. If the heart slows or the arteries suddenly relax, especially in someone who is standing up, blood pressure falls abruptly and the bloodstream may find itself unable to conquer gravity and refresh the part that needs it most: the brain.

This is what happens when we faint. For a variety of reasons blood pressure becomes unequal to its uphill task and the brain loses its blood supply. Because the brain has a constant need for oxygen, consciousness fails, the sufferer falls, and the brain's blood supply is restored by gravity. What triggers this slightly alarming train of events? Let me tell you an illustrative story.

The first daunting practical challenge in the life of a medical student is the need to learn to take blood. I made my début with the help of a friendly phlebotomist – a professional blood-letter – in her room on the edge of an out-patient clinic in Oxford. We chose a victim in his early thirties, who looked burly and vigorous enough as I recall. By sheer chance, but fortunately as it turned out, we decided that the most comfortable procedure would be to sit him on a couch. With beginner's luck my needle entered straight in the vein, and I began to draw back on the syringe, glad to see a flush of blood. As I did so my patient, who had been watching the proceedings with intent concentration, went deathly pale and subsided on to the pillow, his eyes rolling up in their sockets. I hadn't bargained on this dramatic reaction, and was extremely relieved when he came round some seconds later. He told me afterwards that he always fainted at the sight of blood but hadn't liked to say.

Pain, emotion and the sight of blood and gore are all potent triggers of faints. For obscure reasons, susceptible individuals respond to these with an involuntary slowing of the heart and relaxation of their arteries, particularly in muscle. Their blood pressure disappears, blood vessels in the skin constrict, causing pallor, and a faint ensues. Horizontal posture is then required to put things right. Well-intentioned efforts to prevent someone who is fainting from slipping to the ground are distinctly counterproductive.

Several other circumstances raise the risk of fainting. Most of them coincide at rock concerts. Thomas Lempert and Martin Bauer, whose research we shall encounter in a moment, joined first aid workers during a concert by New Kids on the Block.[3] Lempert and Bauer interviewed 40 of the 400 girls who fainted in the course of the show. They usually reported a combination of precipitants: sleep deprivation, hunger, prolonged standing, overbreathing and a strain on the chest brought about by a mixture of screaming and pressure from the crowd. The neurologists realised that their best advice would do no good: 'sleep, eat, sit, keep cool and stay out of the crowd. But what teenage fan will do that?'

Neurologists are often asked whether a patient's 'blackout' might have been due to a faint. We like to say that it was. Faints are usually innocuous events, both in terms of their medical prognosis and of their social impact: they have no implications for a patient's right to drive or or for his employment prospects. Epilepsy, which is often the rival diagnosis, unfortunately threatens both. The neurological fraternity was therefore keenly interested by Lempert and his colleagues' highly detailed analysis of 56 episodes of syncope.

Although most of us faint, or witness a faint, at some stage, it is scarcely an everyday occurrence. Rather than lurking at pop concerts in the hope of spotting a swoon in progress, Lempert and Bauer invited 59 healthy medical students to engage in a well-known prank, the 'fainting lark', a close relation of the 'mess trick'.[4] I hesitate to describe this in detail, lest I am held responsible for a fainting epidemic. Suffice it to say that the trick involves a combination of squatting, panting, rising to one's feet and bearing down. If you are curious about the details you can consult Lempert's paper. With the help of this manoeuvre 42 of their 59 subjects experienced 'complete syncope': they became unresponsive, and fell, with no subsequent recollection of the event. As the subjects came round they were continually asked to count aloud. The authors reviewed a video recording of each faint 'approximately 100 times'. Their account of what happened makes compelling, and surprising, reading.

Consciousness was lost for around 12 seconds, in the sense that about 12 seconds elapsed between the fall and the subject's first attempt to count. About 3 seconds after the fall, the great majority of subjects made a few convulsive movements. These lasted 7 seconds, occasionally persisting until just after consciousness had returned. The eyes usually remained open and generally rolled up. Five seconds into the faint other involuntary movements tended to occur, like turns of the head, eye movements or 'repetitive purposeless movements such as lip-licking, chewing or fumbling'. About half the subjects made a 'righting movement', raising their head, sitting up or standing while silent and amnesic. Most reported some kind of visual or auditory hallucination during the faint. These often involved no more than a rushing sound or the sight of a coloured patch, but some experienced a pleasant sense of 'weightlessness, detachment and peace'. Four had the feeling that they had left their bodies. Individuals whose syncope was incomplete were particularly interesting: 13 subjects remembered their falls, but 'described a state of impaired external awareness, disorientation and loss of voluntary motor control': as well as falling, they were at first unable to count. Another subject, by contrast, remained upright throughout, staring straight ahead, but failed to count for 10 seconds and proved to have no memory of the episode. A study of the EEG during syncope in nine subjects, who were asked back for a second go, revealed a slowing of cerebral rhythms into the theta and delta range at the time when consciousness was lost.

This research has several implications. First, for the physician it sounds a warning note. Many of the events which Lempert recorded during these episodes, such as convulsive movements, eye rolling, lip licking, fumbling and hallucinations, occur in epilepsy. If they can *also* occur in syncope one should use them very cautiously in diagnosis. Second, the ease with which these blackouts were induced reminds us that consciousness is a delicate creation. Finally, these detailed observations hint at a conclusion of great interest to us: the process of fainting and recovery appears to dissociate a number of abilities which we tend to assume are all part and parcel of the waking state. 'Righting' movements like sitting up or standing, which we would normally regard as voluntary, occurred before subjects could speak or lay down a memory of events; memory returned before speech became possible; complex dream-like experience occurred, apparently, in the midst of 'unconsciousness'. We shall return to this theme.

The meticulous care with which Lempert and his colleagues studied the 'mess trick' has been matched by some other research on syncope with a military flavour. Aerial combat in the age of jet aircraft takes place at dizzying speeds and fighter pilots are exposed to sickening accelerations. At times, for example when the aircraft points its nose towards the sky and begins a backward loop, or banks steeply to turn, the acceleration is 'head-to-foot', and opposes the acceleration of the bloodstream by the heart. If the plane's acceleration is sufficiently rapid, blood flow to the brain is interrupted and syncope occurs. As this is something of a catastrophe in the circumstances, the American and British Air Forces have both found it worth their while to construct 'centrifuges' which can reproduce the forces inflicted on pilots in combat while they remain safely on the ground.

The American study of 'G-LOC' – loss of consciousness induced by this accelerative, gravity-like 'G' force – has been running for over 10 years and has recorded more than 500 episodes of syncope.[5] A G-force which abruptly impairs blood flow to the brain – around seven times the normal force of gravity – causes loss of consciousness in about 7 seconds, a figure supported by other evidence. In these experiments the reduction of blood flow continued for a further 5–7 seconds. Complete syncope lasted for about 12 seconds, with convulsive jerks occurring in most subjects towards the end of this period, apparently as blood flow to the brain was re-established. A further 12 seconds of confusion ensued before the pilots became able to extinguish a warning light and a tone, triggered by their syncope, as they had been trained to. As in Lempert's study, many subjects reported 'dream events'. It is hard to dissent from the naval physician's conclusion that 24 seconds is 'a very long period indeed for a fighter pilot not to be in control of a multimillion dollar aircraft should G-loc occur'. Those 24 seconds of oblivion have been responsible for a number of disasters, costly in both human life and in 'materiel'. Anti-gravity suits and straining manoeuvres (the subject of the epigraph at the head of this section) provide some protection from G-LOC.

The critical deficiency in the brain giving rise to syncope is lack of oxygen. One final example of experimental syncope, also taken from aviation medicine, results directly from oxygen deprivation, without any alteration of blood flow to the brain. The air we breathe normally contains 21 per cent oxygen, 78 per cent nitrogen, with a few other constituents in trace amounts. At 18,000 feet, almost two-thirds of the way up Everest, the atmospheric pressure is around half its value at sea level. This is just above the level of the highest permanent human habitations: if you and I were abruptly lifted to this altitude we would feel extremely ill. This is in essence what occurs if a plane flying at altitude loses its cabin air pressure. As this does occasionally occur, it has also merited close study in air force labs.[6]

When rapid decompression occurs at 21,000 feet the 'time of useful consciousness' – unless pressurised oxygen is made available – is about 10 minutes. At 30,000 feet this falls to one minute. At 40,000 feet, the cruising height of long-distance passenger jets, it is a mere 30 seconds. These results have been established in experiments using decompression chambers, on the ground, to reduce the oxygen pressure to the levels found at these altitudes. This research has also documented the symptoms of approaching syncope: a sense of malaise and detachment, dizziness, giddiness, ringing in the ears, mounting difficulty in maintaining concentration, tingling in the limbs and a gradual fading of vision herald the eventual loss of consciousness.

I have not given you a comprehensive tour of the landscape of syncope. The blood flow to the brain can be imperilled in a wide variety of ways, not least when the heart stops beating altogether. But I hope you have sensed the vulnerability of consciousness, which is pathetically dependent on a steady stream of an invisible gas. You will also have picked up a hint that the abilities we associate with waking consciousness can fragment when the brain is in trouble. Movement, memory, speech and imagination may fail and recover independently. Which of these constitutes 'consciousness'? Is our first sense of consciousness, the 'waking state', more complex than we thought? Let us gather some more evidence before we try to solve these puzzles. The study of epilepsy has a good deal to teach us about them.

Fits

No better neurological work can be done than the precise investigation of epileptic paroxysms.

John Hughlings-Jackson, 1889[7]

Machine not working.

(words spoken by a seven-year-old child at the onset of his seizure)

The living brain hums with electricity. The 'faint, almost imperceptible oscillations of the nerve currents' in the brains of cats and dogs which the physiologist Nikolai Wedensky strained to hear over his 'telephone' in 1889 (see p. 82 above), like the 40/second oscillations Rudolfo Llinas detected a century later with the daunting apparatus of modern physics, reflect the brain's incessant rhythmical activity. Epilepsy is a state of electrical rebellion, in which the brain's electricity escapes from its normal checks and balances and takes on a life of its own. It is the most common serious disorder encountered by neurologists, the quintessential pathology of consciousness.

Epileptic seizures have many causes and come in many shapes and sizes. Their causes include most of the disorders which can affect the cortex of the brain – from subtle disturbances of brain growth *in utero*, to infection, tumour and stroke. 'Systemic' illnesses which disturb the chemistry of the blood can also be to blame, ranging from failure of organs – like the kidneys – to a deficiency of an element like calcium or an excess of a drug as familiar and innocuous as penicillin. Some epilepsies are inherited, in ways we are just beginning to understand.

The common denominator of epileptic seizures is that part or all of the brain enters a state of synchronised electrical activity: the complex rhythms of the waking EEG are replaced by a montonous pattern of 'paroxysmal' discharge (see Figure 4.1). What happens next depends on whether all or part of the brain is involved. This distinction, between generalised and partial attacks, provides the basis on which seizures are classified.

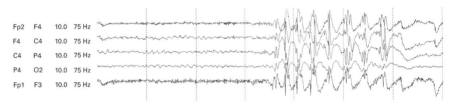

Fp2	F4	10.0	75 Hz
F4	C4	10.0	75 Hz
C4	P4	10.0	75 Hz
P4	O2	10.0	75 Hz
Fp1	F3	10.0	75 Hz

Figure 4.1 The EEG in epilepsy A brain wave recording (EEG) of electrical activity across the brain in a teenager with epilepsy. Each line of the trace examines the electrical activity over a different region of the scalp. During the (normal) first four seconds of the recording the predominant frequencies are rapid, in the alpha and beta ranges. Towards the end of the fourth second this activity is abruptly replaced by 'spike and wave' activity occurring at 3 cycles/second: this corresponds to a brief 'absence seizure' in which consciousness is briefly interrupted, without any limb jerking as a rule.

Primary generalised seizures involve the whole brain from the start – or very near the start – of the attack. Let me introduce you to an imaginary friend, whom I feel I know very well.

Joe is 15 now, and fed up. Two years ago Joe and his parents, especially his parents, began to be disconcerted by his clumsiness at breakfast. Without warning he would tip his cereal over the kitchen floor, or catapult a piece of toast across the table. This didn't happen all that often. It was attributed to the after-effects of late nights. At around the same time, his friends noticed that he occasionally 'blanked out' during conversation, just for a second or two, picking up the thread more or less where he'd left off. They teased him; he was puzzled. Then one morning, getting up early to go fishing after dancing late at a party, Joe had a really bad breakfast. He spilt his cereal, then his tea, went stiff, slipped to the ground and shook all over for a minute that seemed like an hour to his brother and sister. He was astonished to wake up on the kitchen floor a few minutes later, aching all over, with several anxious faces peering down and an ambulance man preparing to load him on to a stretcher.

This story ends happily. Joe has a syndrome – juvenile myoclonic epilepsy – which generally responds well to antiepileptic drugs. Three kinds of generalised seizure are buried in Joe's story.

His mishaps over breakfast result from brief 'myoclonic' attacks, sudden unheralded contractions of a group of muscles. You have almost certainly experienced myoclonus of a different kind, when you 'miss a step' and come to with a start, just as you drop off to sleep. Joe's friends had noticed his second variety of attack: he lost the thread of conversations when epileptic 'absences' extinguished his awareness.

The myoclonus and the absence attacks were easy to laugh off. The third type of seizure seemed altogether more ominous: on the morning after the party, a series of momentary myoclonic seizures culminated in a major 'tonic-clonic' attack, giving rise to the stereotype of an epileptic fit, with loss of consciousness, stiffening and then shaking, an embarrassing tendency for the bladder to empty and a painful tendency for the teeth to clamp down on the tongue. These attacks are very frightening. It is not surprising that onlookers so often think that they are witnessing a death.

All three types of seizure involved a generalised disturbance of electrical activity in the brain, rather like the one shown in Figure 4.1. Brief generalised seizures, like Joe's myoclonus, often leave awareness intact. Absences and tonic-clonic seizures generally suppress it.

In contrast, 'focal' or 'partial' seizures arise, as their name suggests, from electrical activity localised to a discharging focus somewhere in the brain. Their effects depend upon their location: *every* function of the cortex is potentially vulnerable.

Seizures in the occipital lobe give rise to visual experience – typically 'unformed' hallucinations of flashing lights. Discharges in the temporal lobe generate a wealth of unusual symptoms: a queasy feeling that rises from the stomach to the head, and sensations of eerie familiarity or strangeness – *déjà* and *jamais vu* – are especially common: we encountered a typical example in the introduction. Distortions of vision, like a sudden magnification of the view, complex visual or auditory hallucinations, intense but elusive tastes and smells, disabling giddiness, sensations of abject terror and of sexual pleasure are less common but all well-recognised expressions of epilepsy arising from the temporal lobes. Parietal lobe seizures tend to distort or embellish sensations arising from our body. Frontal lobe attacks cause 'motor seizures', classically 'marching' along a limb over a matter of seconds in the manner first described by Hughlings-Jackson. The child who called out to his parents, 'Machine not working' had noticed the beginning of such an attack. All these are known as 'simple' partial seizures. If one compares the brain to a musical instrument whose melodies are our experiences and actions, these seizures are like a mischievous wind playing over the strings, plucking a memory here, an emotion here, in one victim a burning smell, in another a twitch of the mouth.[8]

During partial seizures which affect the content of experience giving rise to an epileptic 'aura', a strange state of affairs obtains. Hughlings-Jackson, the 'father of British neurology', referred to this as a 'double consciousness', combining our ordinary critical awareness of events and the subjective awareness induced by the attack. These coexist during the seizure – and sometimes interact, giving rise to poignant encounters between the ordinary realm of experience and action and the alien realm of mechanism and disease.

These encounters are the defining feature of 'reflex epilepsy', in which seizures are evoked by stimulation. This occurs most commonly in patients with 'photosensitive' epilepsy, whose attacks are triggered by flickering light. But some sufferers are sensitive to much more subtly defined triggers. These can be related to perceptual experience, to mood or to thought. The contemplation of a difficult chess move, writing symbols (but not drawing figures), performing mental arithmetic (multiplication and division but not addition and subtraction), listening to music with a certain emotional tone and reading are among the stimuli described as potent and consistent triggers in individual patients.[9] A colleague encountered a jogger who found that turning a particular corner on a familiar route evoked his attacks. Most of us accept that a seizure is a 'physical' event without reluctance; we are less sure about ordinary experience. These examples of reflex epilepsy are a vivid demonstration of the physicality of experience itself.

Here is an account of a 'musicogenic' epilepsy, taken from a classic description of several such cases published in 1937:[10] a woman, FC, aged 25, had

> since the age of 17 . . . been subject to attacks of 'faintness' on hearing certain types of music – particularly that produced by piano or organ . . . On her admission to hospital gramophone records were played . . . at first a dance tune was tried, but she soon remarked that such music would not produce the desired effect. An orchestral record was then chosen [*Valse des Fleurs*, by Tchaikovsky]. After about fifteen seconds her

face took on a restless and pained expression, and the respiration became laboured. The eyelids opened and shut rapidly, and then began to flutter. She appeared distressed, her fingers clutching the bedclothes, and her lips performing rapid 'smacking' movements as if she were tasting something unpleasant. Then a fixed and vacant expression became noticeable followed at once by generalised clonic convulsions. . . . Three minutes after the cessation of convulsive movements the patient opened her eyes, but seemed still oblivious of her surroundings and did not reply to questions. . . . Despite treatment . . . she continued to be afflicted with similar attacks, almost every one of which was precipitated by music.

While specific experiences sometimes engender seizures, attacks can also sometimes be resisted by an act of will. This is quite common. Sufferers learn psychological tricks which enable them to avert a fit. A patient whose aura consisted of the sense that she was 'unreal' was often able to abort the episode by 'asking someone to speak to her and . . . listening intently'.[11] Listening closely to music had the same effect. Here again ordinary thought and experience, the desire to avoid the fit and the effort to resist it, are plainly doing business with a rebellious brain.

We have seen by now that epilepsy can rob us altogether of awareness, when it spreads throughout the brain, or colour the content of awareness, when it plays over eloquent regions of cortex. Our thoughts and experience can evoke or suppress its attacks, if a 'double consciousness' allows the ordered and disordered regions of the brain to interact. One other aspect of this extraordinary disorder is of particular interest to us: like syncope, it sometimes carves 'awareness' at its seams, separating abilities, like speech and memory, which normally operate together. We can turn again to Hughlings-Jackson for a wonderful example.

John Hughlings-Jackson came to London at the age of 24 in 1859. With interests ranging into philosophy and psychology, Hughlings-Jackson came close to giving up medicine, but was persuaded by friends to remain a doctor. In 1863 he took up an appointment at the National Hospital for Neurology in Queen Square, where his handwritten casebooks still line one of the rooms in the out-patients department. He wrote extensively on epilepsy, and on its lessons for the localisation of function in the brain.

In 1888, in the pages of *Brain*, which remains neurology's most august journal, Hughlings-Jackson published a paper, 'On a particular variety of epilepsy', which ended with an account of a 'very important case'.[12] This was penned by the patient himself, a 'highly educated medical man', known as Dr Z. This is the final episode from Dr Z's account:

> A fourth occasion is perhaps worth record. I was attending a young patient whom his mother had brought me with some history of lung symptoms. I wished to examine the chest and asked him to undress on a couch. I thought he looked ill, but have no recollection of any intention to recommend him to take to his bed at once or of any diagnosis. While he was undressing I felt the onset of a petit-mal [a minor attack]. I remember taking out my stethoscope and turning away a little to avoid conversation. The next thing I recollect is that I was sitting at a writing table in the same room, speaking to another person, and as my consciousness became more complete, recollected my patient, but saw he was not in the room. I was interested to ascertain what had happened, and had an opportunity an hour later of seeing him in bed, with the note of a diagnosis I had made of 'pneumonia of the left base' [the left lung]. I gathered indirectly from conversation that I had made a physical examination, written these words, and advised him to take to bed at once. I re-examined him with some curiosity, and found that my conscious diagnosis was the same as my unconscious – or perhaps I should say, unremembered – diagnosis had been. I was a good deal surprised, but not so unpleasantly as I should have thought probable.

What had happened to Dr Z? Earlier in his account he suggests that his behaviour during the unremembered process of diagnosis was an 'automatism'. One might question whether he can really have functioned automatically during his examination of the child, and Dr Z himself indicates his uncertainty in the passage I have quoted: perhaps he was 'conscious', but his seizure prevented him from laying down a memory of the event. This idea would be in keeping with the nature of his 'petit mal', which he describes with characteristic eloquence:

> the central feature has been mental . . . a feeling of Recollection ie of realising that what is occupying the attention is what has occupied it before, and indeed has been familiar, but has been for a time forgotten, and now is recovered with a slight sense of satisfaction, as if it had been sought for . . . at the same time . . . I am dimly aware that the recollection is fictitious and my state abnormal.

A focal seizure often leaves focal brain dysfunction in its wake: an aura of recollection might well result in a period of amnesia. There is indeed now plenty of evidence that transient amnesia is occasionally the sole expression of an epileptic seizure.[13]

Dr Z's variety of epilepsy teases apart two of the central strands of our ordinary understanding of consciousness: the ability to perform demanding intellectual tasks, like making a diagnosis of pneumonia, and the ability to recall doing so afterwards. Most of us would assume that someone capable of the former was conscious at the time, in the sense both of being awake and of enjoying experience – even if unable to recall the events later.

Other varieties of seizure selectively disable other psychological abilities we usually possess when we're awake.[14] A seizure may render its subject 'unresponsive' because he is unable to understand speech or unable to produce it, unable to move, or just disinclined to do so because of intense preoccupation with hallucinatory experience. In these circumstances it may be difficult or impossible to know what, if anything, a sufferer is experiencing. But it is clear that the abilities which we effortlessly integrate in our waking lives – memory, speech, movement, attention, imagination – can fall prey individually to the whimsical play of rebellious electricity in the brain.

Funny turns

Faints and fits are by far the most common causes of a short spell of unwished-for unconsciousness. Other neurological disorders occasionally have the same effect: a 'transient ischaemic attack' – or 'mini-stroke' – which briefly deprives the brainstem activating system of its blood supply can cause unconsciousness. This is almost always accompanied by other symptoms of mischief in this area of the brain, like double vision or slurring of speech. Rarely migraine affects the same structures with the same result.

One other disorder is notoriously shy of diagnosis, and comes, once in a while, to haunt all doctors who puzzle over 'funny turns'. Although the brain is dependent on glucose to fuel its metabolism, its stores of sugar are small. If the steady supply of sugar in the bloodstream fails, confusion rapidly sets in, giving way within minutes to unconsciousness unless the sugar supply is restored. Moderate reduction of the blood glucose causes odd behaviour which is sometimes mistaken for 'hysteria' or psychiatric illness.

'Hypoglycaemia', low blood sugar, is most commonly due to an overdose of insulin, occasionally to a tumour which secretes this hormone. There are some very rare causes. A few years ago the *British Medical Journal* described a successful self-diagnosis by a man who had avoided 'fruit, sugar and confectionery' all his life, as he thought he 'did not enjoy the taste'.[15] A series of blackouts in his twenties led to a diagnosis of epilepsy, with advice to give up foreign travelling, something he and his wife particularly enjoyed, and to surrender his driving licence. A few months later he noticed that sugary drinks made him feel dizzy. At much the same time, by chance, he read a newspaper account of 'hereditary fructose intolerance'. In this disorder fructose, the principal sugar in many fruits, and sucrose, which we shovel into our tea, interfere with the work of the liver, and cause a precipitous fall in blood glucose. He showed the paper to his doctor, who took him seriously. Genetic testing, which had recently become available, revealed that the patient's parents each carried a gene for the disorder: a double dose in their son gave rise to the disease.

The disorders we have been touring so far in this chapter illustrate the brain's dependence on oxygen, glucose and good electrical order. These requirements expose consciousness to a fair range of natural perils. We like to add to these by poisoning ourselves. Let's take a look at a few of our favourite choices.

Opium, alcohol and other anaesthetics

Opium

Amongst the remedies which it has pleased Almighty God to give to man to relieve his suffering, none is so universal and so efficiacious as opium.

Thomas Sydenham, 1680[16]

Ah'm off tae Johnny Swan's for ONE hit, just ONE FUCKIN HIT tae get us ower this long, hard day.

Irvine Welsh, *Trainspotting*[17]

The arrival of a patient who is unconscious for reasons that are initially mysterious is an everyday event in Accident and Emergency departments up and down the land. The most common single explanation is self-poisoning.

A great variety of drugs act upon the brain. In broad terms drugs acquire their powers from their *shape* – the shape of their constituent molecules. The surface of neurons is studded with a panoply of proteins and other complex compounds, into which drugs can enter as keys enter locks. Some turn the lock, triggering the protein into its natural activity; others get stuck in the lock, ensuring the door stays closed. This analogy, of course, oversimplifies drug action, but the general principle – that most drugs interact with specific targets in ways that depend on the physical fit between the two – is sound.

The word 'opium' is derived from the Greek for 'juice'. Opium, the drug, is obtained from the juice of the poppy, *Papaver somniferum*, and its remarkable properties have been known since at least the third century BC. Opium and the 'opiate' drugs purified from it are supremely powerful painkillers. Their ability to give pleasure and to slay suffering as well as pain, at least for an hour or two, has led to their widespread social use, often with tragic results. Doses larger than those required to deal with pain, or to generate pleasure, lead to coma. As this deepens, the drive to breathe is lost. Death is then waiting in the wings.

Evidence began to accumulate in the 1960 and 1970s that there was a family of synaptic receptors within the brain which avidly 'bound' the opiates. As it is unlikely that we have evolved a group of receptors solely to take advantage of the poppy, this suggested that there might be natural substances within the brain which act through the same receptors. So it proved.

In 1973 John Hughes and Hans Kosterlitz, pharmacologists working in Aberdeen, reported the first isolation of endogenous 'opioids' from the brain.[18] Since then the biology of the opioids has become an immensely complex field, but one can glimpse a few key findings through the haze of work in progress.

The endogenous opioids are 'peptides', short strings of amino acids snipped from longer protein precursors (the term 'opioid' is used to refer to both endogenous and exogenous substances with effects resembling opium). They belong to three related families, the enkephalins, endorphins and dynorphins; each has its own precursor. The opioids are neurotransmitters. Their predominant effect is to inhibit their targets, an effect they achieve through the help of second messengers.

The receptors to which they bind also come in three flavours, known by the Greek letters mu, delta and kappa. Thus even within this single class of peptide neurotransmitters there is rich scope for subtleties of interaction, with variety both in the chemistry of the peptide and in the structure of its receptors.

The effect of opioids on the awareness of pain is explained by the presence of receptors at several levels of the nervous system. Their activation within the spinal cord reduces the release of neurotransmitters by axons bearing news of injury; if the news gets through to the cord despite this, opioids reduce the chances that it will be broadcast on to the brain, by inhibiting the activity of the messenger neurons.

In the brainstem opioids activate a second, 'descending', system: instilling drugs like morphine into the 'periaqueductal grey' matter of the midbrain relieves pain by a circuitous series of steps, involving other transmitters, which ultimately reduces pain signalling from the spinal cord.

Finally the opioids induce euphoria and tranquillity by yet another mechanism, soothing the troubled response to pain. This is thought to occur at least in part through an enhanced release of dopamine from cells in the midbrain. These send their axons to the 'nucleus accumbens', a part of the basal ganglia with intimate connections to the limbic system which, you will recall, regulates emotion.

These discoveries shed light on addiction. There's no doubt that a rush of opiate to the brain gives quite a kick, not unlike the thrill of orgasm. The desire to repeat this experience is understandable. But once the brain becomes accustomed to an external supply, it adapts, reducing its own release of opioids or the sensitivity of its receptors. Pain then chases pleasure, creating a powerful need to feed the habit.

Opioids suffuse our consciousness. In a high enough dose they suppress it altogether. We have the beginnings of a detailed explanation of their effects. It is intriguing that a single chemical system should influence pleasure and pain in such a variety of ways. This observation suggests that, besides deciphering the logic of the brain's anatomy and physiology, we will need to crack a chemical code if we are to understand the neural basis of experience.

Alcohol and other anaesthetics

> Gentlemen, this is no humbug.
>> (words spoken by Dr Warren, after performing the first public operation under ether anaesthesia supplied by Dr Morton in Boston, 1846)[19]

> The thick, sweet mystery of chloroform,
> The drunken dark, the little death-in-life . . .
>> W.E. Henley, 'Before'[20]

The shelves of the average off-licence, groaning with wines, beers, lagers, spirits, liqueurs, are an amazing testament to human ingenuity. The thirst is simple, but we quench it in a thousand ways. Although connoisseurs would dispute this, the really essential ingredient is the same in every bottle. Alcohol is a simple molecule, with a profound and familiar effect on consciousness. It troubles most of us little, as we lift our glass to our lips, that we have such a poor understanding of its actions in the brain.

It came as a surprise to me that its best established action is as a general anaesthetic – although alcohol is not, in practice, a very useful member of this family of drugs, with little margin between the dose required for satisfactory anaesthesia and the dose which stops us breathing.

The first really serviceable general anaesthetic, nitrous oxide, was synthesised, unknowingly, by the chemist Joseph Priestley in 1776.[21] At the end of the century, while investigating the 'respirability' of a variety of gases, another chemist, working at the Institute of Pneumatic Medicine in Bristol, discovered its 'extraordinary effects'. A bad toothache gave the chemist Humphry Davy an opportunity to test it against pain: 'on the day when the inflammation was most troublesome I breathed three large doses . . . the thrilling came on as usual, and uneasiness was for a few minutes swallowed up in pleasure'.

Davy foresaw that nitrous oxide might be used 'with advantage during surgical operations'. Twenty years later, the physicist Michael Faraday discovered that diethyl ether had similar properties. But until the 1840s these substances were put to use mainly in travelling circuses and at 'frolic parties'. In 1845 Horace Wells, an American dentist who had seen nitrous oxide used in a stage-show, allowed a colleague to draw one of his teeth while he breathed the gas, and suffered no pain. Wells embarrassingly failed to convince a critical audience in a demonstration at the Massachusetts General Hospital, when his patient cried out, the 'gas-bag being removed too soon'. The following year a colleague of Wells, William Morton, succeeded where Wells had failed, using ether.

The story is famous, but warrants retelling. Dr Warren, the surgeon, attended the operating dome in morning dress. A number of assistants were available to restrain the patient, should Morton fail. Morton was late. After 15 minutes Dr Warren became impatient, taking up his scalpel with the words, 'As Dr Morton has not arrived I assume he is otherwise engaged.' In the nick of time, Morton entered. Dr Warren indicated the man strapped to the table, and said expectantly to Morton, 'Well, Sir, your patient is ready.' After a few minute of ether inhalation, Gilbert Abbott was unconscious, giving Morton his chance to reply: 'Dr Warren, *your* patient is ready.' The operation proceeded without pain or incident. At the close Dr Warren turned to the astonished audience, announcing 'Gentlemen, this is no humbug.' Dr Bigelow, a surgeon attending the demonstration, said afterwards 'I have seen something today that will go around the world.'

The anaesthetic possibilities of chloroform were discovered in the following year in Edinburgh, by the obstetrician, Sir James Simpson, who continued Humphry Davy's practice of self-experimentation: 'a small bottle of chloroform was searched for, and recovered from beneath a heap of waste paper. . . . On awaking, Dr Simpson's first perception was mental – "This is far stronger and better than ether" said he to himself. His second was to note that he was prostrate on the floor and that among his friends about him there was both confusion and alarm. Dr Duncan was unconscious beneath a chair and Dr Keith was struggling'[22].

Over the century and a half since these first anaesthetic adventures, a number of other gases have come into use. Anaesthesia has become a precise and exacting science. This makes it all the more remarkable that we have, at best, a shaky understanding of how anaesthetics work, and that establishing whether an anaesthetic has achieved its prime goal – of removing awareness – is sometimes problematic.

Anaesthetics suppress the activities of worm, newt and mouse just as efficiently as human consciousness. Somehow or other, anaesthetics must attack the bedrock of nervous tissue. Where and how do they act?

There is consensus, but not certainty, that at the concentrations which are relevant to their use in medicine anaesthetics act at synapses, reducing excitation. At higher concentrations they can paralyse the neuron altogether, blocking both the transmission of electrical signals and the transport of materials down the axon. What confers the ability of anaesthetics to depress neuronal function for an hour or two, without any long-term harm? The first hint of an answer came at the turn of the century when two scientists working independently, Meyer and Overton, came up with similar observations, with a distinctly culinary flavour. The anaesthetic powers of anaesthetic gases appeared to be closely related to their solubility in olive oil: the more readily they dissolved, the more potently they acted (see Figure 4.2).

For a long while the natural interpretation of this result was that all anaesthetics acted at a common site, which in some way resembled olive oil. The obvious candidate was the fatty neuronal membrane, which charged particles stream across when the neuron signals. If anaesthetics disrupted the membrane's functions as they dissolved in its fats, one might predict just the relationship between solubility and potency which Meyer and Overton had discovered.

Although the Meyer–Overton rule has on the whole held up well to scrutiny, recent discoveries suggest that anaesthetics make a more selective

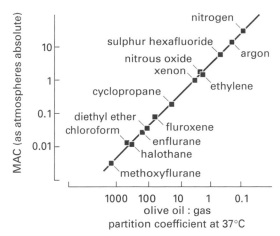

Figure 4.2 The relationship between the potency of anaesthetics and their solubility in olive oil Anaesthetics which are highly fat soluble exert an anaesthetic effect at low concentrations (the MAC is a measure of the concentration of the anaesthetic in the lung which is required for anaesthesia).

assault on our neurons than used to be envisaged. One important piece of evidence originates from the firefly. 'Luciferase' is a protein made by the firefly which emits light in the presence of oxygen, magnesium, a source of energy and its chemical partner, 'luciferin'. Franks and Lieb, British scientists working at Imperial College in London, established that anaesthetics black out luciferase, apparently by preventing its interaction with luciferin.[23] Their ability to do this correlates closely with their anaesthetic potency in man: direct interactions with proteins in the neuronal membrane are very likely to be relevant to the effects of anaesthetics in the brain.

But do anaesthetics depress the activity of the brain diffusely, without fear or favour, or do they pick out specific parts of the nervous system in their assault on consciousness? Techniques which image the living brain are beginning to suggest answers to this question.[24] Brain activity is globally reduced during anaesthesia, but thalamic function is particularly depressed, hinting at similarities between anaesthesia and sleep.[25] The reduction in energy consumption within the brain goes hand in hand with a slowing of cerebral rhythms and a loss of synchronisation between activity in distant cortical regions.[26]

But however anaesthetics work exactly, at least they reliably put us to sleep. Or do they?

Awareness under anaesthesia

> I did not know who or where I was, or what on earth was happening. . . .
> This relatively happy state was interrupted by a voice in the space above
> me (some remark about my bladder) and I instantly understood my
> predicament: that I was lying . . . covered in green towels, my abdomen
> split open . . . I remained in this state of mind . . . continuously filled
> with fear, listening to every word, every sound in the theatre, quite
> compos mentis and fully appreciating my position. . . . The pain . . . was
> bad from the onset and it increased in severity. . . . The nearest compar-
> ison would be the pain of a tooth drilled without local anaesthetic – when
> the drill hits a nerve. *Multiply* this pain. . . . I can even feel the breath of
> it now as I am writing all this down.[27]

These words are taken from the 'unedited recollections of a medically qualified lady' who had the misfortune to regain awareness during a Caesarean.
Her description of her experience was published, as a salutary tale, in the
British Journal of Anaesthesia. Consciousness with pain and subsequent recall
during supposed anaesthesia is, mercifully, very rare. How is it possible?

Much of modern surgery depends on the use of paralysing drugs. By
relaxing our muscles, these allow surgeons to operate on internal organs
which would otherwise be inaccessible. The paralysis usually makes it necessary for the anaesthetist to take over the patient's breathing. Once under
the sway of these drugs, a patient who regains awareness during anaesthesia has no means of making her predicament known.

Professor J.G. Jones, now at Cambridge University, has studied perception and memory during anaesthesia for many years.[28] He estimates that full
awareness of the kind described by the 'medically qualified lady' occurs in
about one in every 10,000 'anaesthetics'. It usually indicates that the anaesthetic (unlike the paralysing agent) has failed to reach the patient altogether.

Other varieties of consciousness under supposed anaesthesia occur
more commonly. They provide further illustration of the ways in which
'ordinary' awareness can fragment in unusual circumstances.

Some degree of awareness with subsequent recall of the experience, but
without pain, is estimated to occur in between two and four anaesthetics in
every 1,000. This is explained by the tendency for anaesthetics to provide
analgesia – relief from pain – at doses which are not high enough to
suppress awareness altogether.

This is a relatively benign shortcoming in an anaesthetic. More perturb-
ing is the possibility that some anaesthetics allow both awareness and pain

to occur during surgery – but prevent their subsequent recall. Evidence that this occurs has been obtained using the alarmingly named 'isolated forearm technique'.

By inflating a blood pressure cuff around one arm of a patient undergoing surgery it is possible to block the influx of muscle relaxant and preserve voluntary movement in the hand. Hand movements can then be used to communicate with the anaesthetist – if the patient is conscious of events. Ian Russel, an anaesthetist working in Hull, has used this technique to investigate the 'depth' of anaesthesia produced by a number of drugs, and to establish whether 'autonomic' signs of arousal – such as increases in pulse and blood pressure – reliably reflect the patient's degree of awareness.[29]

In one such study – of an anaesthetic technique of which Dr Russel seems to have had justified suspicions – 23 of 32 patients were able to communicate with him at some time during surgery. He asked 20 of them whether they were in pain: all gave an affirmative response. He concluded that these drugs may ensure 'general amnesia' – only three patients had any recall of events during surgery and this was vague – but they certainly failed to ensure general anaesthesia. A secondary finding was that 'autonomic' responses, which included sweating and tears, were unreliable signs of awareness, predicting fewer than half of the occasions on which the patients proved able to communicate.

This work shows that it is possible to be conscious during 'anaesthesia', but free of pain, with subsequent recall; and possible to be conscious, and in pain, without subsequent recall. Other studies show that events occurring during anaesthesia can influence subsequent behaviour despite the lack of any conscious recall of them. Such influences are taken as evidence of 'implicit memory' of the events: memory, that is, which may not be available to consciousness but which is nonetheless ingrained in the brain.

A group of German scientists investigated this issue by playing a recording of *Robinson Crusoe* to patients for 10 minutes during cardiac surgery.[30] A control group underwent surgery without hearing the story. None of the subjects had any conscious recall of the story at an interview following surgery. But as well as seeking conscious recollections, the investigators asked the subjects for their associations with the word 'Friday'. The control patients came up with such things as 'fish for dinner'. In contrast, five of the ten patients in one experimental group linked Friday with *Robinson Crusoe*. Overall there was a highly significant difference between the associations of the control group and the patients who had heard the story. In case you are wondering, the experimenters had wisely ensured that the post-operative assessments were made by a researcher who did not know which group the subject belonged to, to avoid suggesting associations to the patients inadvertently. The German group also used a technique during surgery which enabled them to predict accurately which of their patients would acquire implicit memories. We shall return to this aspect of the study later.

The possibility of consciousness during 'anaesthesia' is clearly disturbing for patients and anaesthetists alike. Professor Jones compares the anaesthetist's predicament to a pilot flying without an altimeter. The pilot's prime objective is to avoid unintended contact with the ground: his altimeter is a pretty basic aid in this endeavour. The anaesthetist's prime aim – besides preserving life – is to suppress consciousness of the surgical proceedings. But in the paralysed patient she lacks an altimeter for awareness, and has to rely on rules of thumb. There is a danger of flying too low, and permitting pain. There is also a risk of flying needlessly high, which may have its own cost, such as a slow recovery from the anaesthetic. Anaesthetists are therefore keenly interested in finding ways of measuring awareness which don't rely on the patient's overt protestation. As we shall see, they have had some success.

Varieties of coma

The patient in coma . . . is neither awake nor asleep.

Antonio Culebras[31]

Like all the major functions of the body, consciousness is usually under delicate control. Sleep and waking oscillate through our nights and days. As we have seen, sleep itself has an organised structure. Although both our bodies and our brains enjoy some rest when we slumber, the fall in the brain's energy consumption is quite modest, about 25 per cent during slow wave sleep. When we dream the brain works at least as hard as during our waking hours.

Coma is a disruption of this nicely balanced state of affairs, an unscheduled depression of consciousness. Like epilepsy, coma is a baggy category, ranging in severity from a state resembling sleep to one resembling death. It has a multitude of causes.[32] These belong to three broad groups: small areas of damage in the brainstem, large areas of damage in the hemispheres, and processes involving the brain diffusely, such as poisoning by drugs and infections.

The damage responsible for coma in the first and second groups is usually caused by such things as a bang on the head, a stroke or a tumour. In the brainstem these directly disturb the activating system we toured in the last chapter; in the hemispheres, they cause the brain to swell, squeezing the brainstem as a secondary effect. We have already encountered a number of specific causes in the third group. In the wake of a long-drawn-out seizure, a short spell of coma is common. A fall of the blood glucose is a dramatically treatable cause (because an injection of glucose swiftly reverses the problem): doctors should never forget it. Opiates and anaesthetics give rise to a drug-induced coma.

Coma is usually a staging post *en route* to some other destination. This may be a full recovery. A patient etched on my memory, because I discovered that his plight was the result of low blood glucose 20 minutes later than I would have wished, was none the worse for his experience. The other outcomes of coma are less happy: two of these have occasioned plenty of controversy in recent years.

Coma due to extensive damage to the hemispheres or to the thalamus, with relative preservation of the brainstem, sometimes gives way to a state which superficially resembles ordinary consciousness. Sleep alternates with waking, presumably because the structures which regulate sleep and waking in the brainstem are intact. While awake, the sufferer's eyes are open. Smiles may pass across his face; he may shed tears or moan. There is no doubt in such a case that wakefulness is present: but what of awareness?

This condition, the persistent vegetative state, is sometimes described as a condition of 'wakeful unconsciousness' or 'wakefulness without awareness'.[33] Despite the recovery of the sleep–wake cycle, sufferers appear to be unaware of their surroundings and their bodies, make no purposeful response to stimulation, and neither understand nor produce speech (see Figure 4.3).

It is impossible to be absolutely sure that another human being, especially one who appears to be awake, is utterly unaware. Indeed, a recent report from a centre which specialises in the care of such cases claims that the vegetative state is diagnosed in error about half the time. Nevertheless, there is general agreement that this state – of wakefulness without awareness – sometimes genuinely occurs. Confidence in the diagnosis grows when brain scans show damage in all the brain areas which are thought to supply the content of consciousness, or when studies of the brain's energy consumption show that it has fallen profoundly. In the persistent vegetative

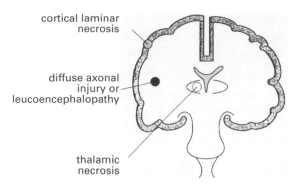

cortical laminar
necrosis

diffuse axonal
injury or
leucoencephalopathy

thalamic
necrosis

Figure 4.3 The pathology of the persistent vegetative state The vegetative state can be caused by damage to the thalamus, widespread damage to the white matter of the brain, or damage to the cortex. 'Laminar necrosis' is cell death which particularly affects certain cortical layers.

state it may drop to around one-third of its normal value, well below the levels recorded in sleep or even in general anaesthesia.

Studies of large groups of patients in this state indicate that after a certain duration – from six months to one year, varying with the cause – the persistent vegetative state is very likely to be permanent. Many believe that further medical support is then inappropriate, a view upheld by British courts.

In the vegetative state the brainstem survives while the hemispheres perish. In the state of 'brain death' the hemispheres may be perfectly healthy, but the brainstem has succumbed.[34] We diagnose this unhappy outcome of coma when brainstem functions are all unequivocally absent: these range from the control of breathing to the reflex movement of the eyes. Remediable causes of this state of affairs – such as an overdose of certain drugs – must have been excluded before brain death is diagnosed. The implications of this diagnosis are of course profound. Once it has been made, assuming the family gives consent, it is regarded as legitimate – in the United Kingdom – to remove a patient's organs for transplantation.

It may seem curious that the brainstem is the crux of life: the hemispheres, surely, are the key to our humanity and intellect. So they may be, but intellect ain't everything. We can survive the loss of our hemispheres, albeit much diminished, but even if life is given its best chance by artificial ventilation the loss of the brainstem appears to lead inexorably to death. A recent study from Taiwan[35] followed 73 patients who satisfied criteria for brainstem death: the heart stopped beating in all 73 within seven days despite full-scale life support.

One last condition which can mimic coma deserves a mention here. Partial damage to the brainstem occasionally spares the activating system, while disabling the fibre tracts and nuclei which enable us to move our face and limbs. In these circumstances awareness may survive while almost all means of expressing it are lost, an unhappy state of affairs known as the 'locked-in syndrome'. Sufferers from this disorder usually retain the ability to make voluntary up and down movements of their eyes, and can use these to communicate. This was the fate of Jean-Dominique Bauby, the author of the bestseller *The Diving-Bell and the Butterfly*.[36] It is difficult to rule out the disturbing possibility that individuals like Bauby are not the only sufferers from the syndrome – but rather the only ones we can readily recognise.

Hysteria and trance

We have been travelling in this chapter, so far, through the heartland of neurology. Even in this central territory much remains to be described, but the outlines of a map are now in place. We need to make a foray into less certain country now, where neurologists feel nervous, because we are not even sure what *kind* of account to try to give of what we see and hear.

Let me give an example. A girl in her late teens called Sarah is sent to a neurology clinic because of her 'seizures'. These tend to occur at home, in the evening. Without warning she drops to the ground and convulses, sometimes for as long as 10 minutes. She tells me that she knows nothing at all about these episodes, until she comes round on the floor with a headache, feeling sick. This has happened once or twice a month during the preceding year. Her mother has witnessed several attacks. Anxiety runs high.

Her family doctor quite understandably thinks she has epilepsy, and has started an anticonvulsant drug, so far without effect. Her mother's description of the attacks also suggests epilepsy to me. I find no particular reason why she should have this condition, and no abnormalities of her nervous system when I check her over, but both these negatives are common enough. Tests including an EEG are also unhelpful, but a single EEG between attacks will be normal in about 60 per cent of undoubted sufferers from epilepsy. We try two or three different drugs, at reasonable doses – but the attacks continue.

A few months into our consultations I begin to question my diagnosis. The attacks sounded right – but perhaps they are not epileptic after all. I enquire further, along different lines. The attacks began a few months after

Sarah's father left home, and then left the country. The separation was acrimonious, and he has not kept in touch. I put out feelers when we meet next, explaining that 'seizures' are not always epileptic, that the stresses of life can sometimes trigger these kinds of things: Sarah says that she doesn't know what I'm talking about. If they aren't fits she can't think what they are. Her boyfriend says they are, anyway. So there.

We fall back, eventually, on the last diagnostic resort. Sarah is admitted to hospital and filmed continuously for a week with simultaneous recording of her EEG. Her drugs are reduced sharply during the admission. Obligingly, Sarah has three typical attacks. Apart from the electrical 'noise' produced by her energetic gyrations the EEG remains normal throughout. A doctor who examines her during the attack has the impression that she resists his efforts. The movements in the attack do not look wholly involuntary. One can't help noticing that they are sexually suggestive.

I know from past experience that challenging Sarah with an accusation of simulating these attacks would be counterproductive. We offer her good news: although her case has been puzzling, we are sure she doesn't have epilepsy, and her unpleasant drugs can be stopped. We think the attacks are stress related and that it will be helpful for her to speak to a counsellor. I explain this rather nervously, but Sarah takes it surprisingly well. She wants to learn to drive: one year after her attacks have stopped,[37] which I'm sure they will, she can. Sarah is lucky: in her case the neurological story ends here. Life is not always so easy.

What is one to make of Sarah's claim that she was unaware of her attacks? Perhaps she was simply lying. Undoubtedly patients sometimes do. But many observers of 'hysterical' symptoms like Sarah's seizures have taken a more complex and sympathetic view, suggesting that they are, in some sense, unconscious and involuntary simulations of disease. The idea that a *simulation* – which one would normally suppose to require a conscious act of will – may, after all, be 'unconscious' seems to imply that consciousness can 'dissociate' or split.

This possibility has fascinated a number of neurologists and psychiatrists, notably including Jean Martin Charcot and Sigmund Freud. Although inescapable in clinical neurology, and extremely interesting, this subject is an intellectual minefield.[38] I am so far from knowing how to avoid self-detonation that I will follow it no further, except to point to a possible analogy, which was also of great interest to Charcot and to Freud.

Hypnosis is out of fashion currently. I have had first-hand experience of it only once, when I was allowed to watch a colleague using hypnosis as an aid in the treatment of asthma and needle phobia in two patients one evening. She was a delightful woman, attractive but motherly, with a deep and musical voice. Her patients were asked to make themselves comfortable on a low couch in a warm, lamplit room. So relaxing and caressing was the monologue which followed that I could quite understand Freud's view that it is 'only a short step' from hypnosis to falling in love: as an observer, let alone a patient, I found myself inclining towards the 'same humble subjection, the same compliance, the same absence of criticism towards the hypnotist as towards a loved object'.[39]

I don't know whether the treatment worked. There have been many claims, and there is some evidence, for the therapeutic powers of the hypnotic trance, a state induced by sustained concentration on a soothing, repetitive stimulus. It has been used to provide surgical anaesthesia, to allow the recovery of buried memories and to modify later behaviour, through post-hypnotic suggestion.

The scenario in which a suggestion made under hypnosis is inaccessible on recovery, but enacted later, at the appropriate moment, once again summons up an image of consciousness splitting – into a mainstream, which is suspended in the trance, and a side-stream which is susceptible to hypnotic suggestion and ensures that the suggestion is seen through.

As things stand, hypnotic trance and hysterical dissociation are both mysterious. One line of thought may help us to understand Sarah.

This book provides many illustrations of the maxim that the brain is the organ of experience and behaviour. If this is so one would expect that disorders of the brain will express themselves in derangements of experience and behaviour. 'Derangement of behaviour' is a roundabout way of describing a 'curious way to act'. We can act in curious ways because we can't help it, if we are ill – or because, for some reason, we feel like doing so. Neurological disorders are generally quite easy to enact deliberately, precisely because they are disorders of action. We all act out roles in our everyday lives, sometimes self-consciously, sometimes without giving them too much thought. Might Sarah somehow have got into the habit of acting out her attacks – perhaps because something suggested to her that she had epilepsy?

The sceptical idea that suggestibility and role-playing underlie hysteria and hypnotism is an old one. But whether hysteria and hypnosis really belong among the dramatic arts, or among the family of altered states of consciousness, remains a subject of heated dispute.

Did you have a good night?

> If sleep it was, of what nature, we can scarcely refrain from asking, are
> such sleeps as these?
>
> Virginia Woolf, *Orlando*[40]

Our sleep is prey to a thousand ills, but these all belong to three main kinds:
too little sleep, too much and some strange perturbations of slumber.
These are known more technically as insomnias, hypersomnias and parasomnias. The science of sleep has become a large and fascinating branch
of medicine. I shall be selective, concentrating on a few examples which
illustrate the mechanisms governing sleep.

Insomnia

None of us can have escaped the occasional sleepless night when we're
worried or upset, overexcited or have overdone the caffeine or booze. If
nothing else, this experience brings home to us the importance of sleep,
and its close interrelationship with mood. More persistent insomnia can
result from a host of physical and psychological afflictions. I shall mention
a couple of these which pick up themes from the previous chapter.

The alternation of sleep and waking is normally one component of a
group of rhythms, which also control our temperature cycle and the secretion of hormones. These rhythms are orchestrated in the hypothalamus,
where the suprachiasmatic nucleus is itself kept in step by the fundamental
alternation of night and day.

Most of us adjust our habits, more or less readily, to the conventional
timing of sleep. Some of us, owlish in our preferences, like to talk late and
sleep in; others are larks who go to bed early and want to rise at dawn.[41]
These preferences are sometimes extreme, and give rise to real difficulties
in adapting to conventional hours, forcing a choice between sleepy con-
formity and adequate rest at the price of eccentric schedules. 'Delayed
sleep phase syndrome' is the technical description of the state of the
extreme owl, who is happy enough with seven hours' sleep but wants to
take them when most of us are up and about.[42] Quite why the owl's timing
goes awry is still unclear, but help – if desired, for owls are proud birds –
is at hand. 'Phototherapy', exposure to bright artificial light for an hour in
the morning, 'chronotherapy', a process of gradual resetting of the clock,
and treatment with melatonin in the evening, a hormone which normally

surges when the lights go out, can all go some way towards reconciling owl and lark.

Whatever their difficulties with conventional bedtimes, at least the owl and the lark run on a 24-hour clock. 'Non-24-hour-sleep-wake-disorder', while rare, is more of a problem.[43] It occurs quite commonly in the blind, in whom the suprachiasmatic nucleus is free to run at its intrinsic rate, with a cycle approaching 25 hours. In these circumstances the preferred bedtime often marches through day and night, an hour later every time, coinciding more or less with conventional timings for just two or three days each month.

These troubles are substantial nuisances but perfectly survivable. Occasionally insomnia is a harbinger of more serious disease. The onset of encephalitis lethargica sometimes announced itself with a chaotic 'unrest lasting for days and nights without stop'. This disorder is now largely a historical curiosity, although rare cases continue to crop up. But our biology is forever producing new and strange disorders.

One grave and currently topical cause of insomnia was described for the first time from Italy in 1985.[44] 'Fatal familial insomnia' belongs to the same family of disorders as the bovine spongiform encephalopathy, or BSE, which has been epidemic among British cattle for the last few decades, and Creutzfeldt-Jakob disease, its human counterpart. These are all caused by the accumulation of 'prion protein' in the brain. This protein is present in the healthy brain in small amounts, but in the 'prion disorders' the protein is altered in some way, rendering it 'indigestible' by the waste disposal system which normally turns over our ageing cellular constituents. It then accumulates, with disastrous results. These diseases have the odd property that they can be acquired either by infection or inheritance. Disease can result from infection, because the altered protein has the capacity to convert the normal variety into the altered form. Heritability is thought to be due to the existence of inherited variations in the structure of the prion protein, some of which render it liable to spontaneous transformation into the indigestible form.

Insomnia was invariably the first symptom of the 'peculiar fatal disorder of sleep' described in 14 members of a large Italian family in 1985. Over the months following the onset of insomnia, normal sleep and its associated EEG patterns virtually disappeared. As this occurred, episodes of 'stupor' became increasingly common, accompanied by dream-like experience and behaviour appropriate to the content of the dreams. A 53-year-old sufferer 'was frequently disturbed by vivid dreams, during which he would rise from his bed, stand and give a military salute. When he was awakened by his relatives, he would report dreaming of attending a coronation'. These disorders of consciousness went hand in hand with autonomic distur-bances, such as a mild fever, and a loss of the usual circadian rhythm of hormonal secretion. The condition progressed relentlessly to death.

The brunt of the damage in the brain was borne by nuclei in the thala-mus – the anterior and dorsomedial – which communicate primarily with the limbic system. This chimes with the evidence we encountered in the last chapter, pointing to the importance of the thalamus in the control of conscious states.

Hypersomnia

Insomnia and hypersomnia, the two 'dyssomnias', are intimately linked: the commonest reason for being sleepy in the day is sleeping poorly in the night. One remarkable condition, narcolepsy, combines elements of every kind of sleep disorder.

Patients with narcolepsy are subject to an irresistible urge to nap by day.[45] Given a sufficiently cosy corner, we can all drop off, if we're tired enough. Sufferers from narcolepsy do without the cosy corner: they fall asleep during meals, on the loo and, to their partners' dismay, even while making love. A second symptom is particularly suggestive of the diagnosis: brief paralysis – cataplexy – sets in at moments of emotional arousal. Laughter is the commonest precipitant, but other emotions will do. The paralysis may be total, or may amount to no more than a sagging of the jaw or a weakening of the knees. A patient described to me her lifelong ten-dency to slip helplessly to the floor whenever she realised she was in pos-session of some news which would interest her companion, or at the moment of playing a winning card. Two other symptoms occur at the threshold between sleep and waking: vivid hallucinations in the first moments of slumber and 'sleep paralysis', an alarming inability to move for a minute or two while dropping off to sleep or on awakening. To add insult to injury, sufferers often sleep poorly at night.

The idea that the basic problem in narcolepsy lies with the regulation of REM sleep makes sense of these puzzling symptoms. While most of us drop down gradually through the orderly stages of slow wave sleep after we switch off the light, people with narcolepsy enter REM almost at once. Their hallucinations result from this abrupt juxtaposition of waking and dreaming sleep; sleep paralysis occurs when the 'motor inhibition', which prevents us from enacting our dreams, comes into, or remains in, play while the brain is half-awake; the same mechanism, triggered by emotion, gives rise to cataplexy.

Narcolepsy has been recognised for over a hundred years,[46] but its underlying cause has been mysterious. Very recent research may have pinpointed this. 'Orexins' are a newly discovered class of peptide neurotransmitter, manufactured in cells in the hypothalamus and then transported to be released at synapses at several sites in the brainstem. The name 'orexin' – the opposite of an 'anorexin' – was chosen because the substance stimulates appetite in rats. Dogs with a condition very similar to human narcolepsy turn out to have an inherited abnormality in the orexin receptor. People with narcolepsy appear to be markedly deficient in orexin in the brain.[47] This explanation may or may not stand the test of time: but it is plausible, linking the human disorder with a disturbance in the brainstem regions which regulate REM sleep, and with its animal equivalent.

Sufferers from narcolepsy are liable to one other troublesome symptom, which can have threatening legal consequences, as they did for this patient described in 1979: 'While shopping for groceries, she had once filled her market cart with many jars of pickles, had pushed the cart out of the store and then become aware of her actions; she was able to return the cart and pickles without notice . . . more recently she had been apprehended after taking some tools from a hardware store'. After being placed on probation, 'she was again shopping for groceries and was caught in the act of stuffing her purse with packages of meat of a sort that she would not ordinarily choose. . . . In all the cases of shoplifting, the patient claimed to be unaware of her actions; she did little to hide them and took items for which she had little use'.[48]

This maladroit shoplifter suffered from narcolepsy. She was displaying the 'automatic behaviour' which is now recognised as a feature of the condition. It is usually ushered in by a feeling of drowsiness which the sufferer tries to fight off, followed by a 'blank' period for which the sufferer has no subsequent recall. Behaviour during the 'blank' may appear purposeful, but is 'typically repetitive and stereotyped'. This behaviour probably belongs in the third category of sleep disorder, the parasomnias.

Parasomnia

A professor is a man who talks in other people's sleep.

Anon.

. . . those who 'commit any crime whilst they sleep, are compared to infants . . . and therefore are not punisht'.

Mackenzie, *Discourse Upon the Laws of Scotland*[49]

Parasomnias are intermittent abnormalities of behaviour or experience during sleep. I shall briefly mention five which are relevant to our interests: sleepwalking, sleep terrors and their close relative 'sleep drunkenness', nightmares, and the recently recognised 'REM sleep behaviour disorder'.

Sleepwalking, somnambulism, can be decidedly bad for your health. I was alarmed by the tale told me by a patient who, during her Mediterranean holiday, left her first-floor flat by the window, waking up on the concrete below. Sleepwalkers may look purposeful, but, on the whole, they are not: like my patient, they run a real risk of accidental injury. During their walk they are taciturn; once woken, confused and amnesic about their adventure. One might imagine that sleepwalkers are caught up in a dream: recording of their EEG shows that they are, instead, incompletely aroused from deep slow wave sleep.

Such partial arousal is also the basis of sleep terrors, 'pavor nocturnus'. Some parents will instantly recognise the description of a child waking unexpectedly in the first few hours of sleep, with a piercing scream, wide eyes and panting breaths: inconsolable at first, the child will slowly settle back to sleep. 'L'ivresse du sommeil', sleep drunkenness, is a related condition, a state of confusion lasting from minutes to hours, following sudden arousal from deep sleep. Occasionally aggression accompanies the confusion: sleep drunkenness has been accepted as a defence for homicide under a number of legal systems: 'a man was aroused early at night by his wife, who was shouting a false alarm of "there are robbers, burglars in the backyard". In a confused state the husband impulsively grabbed a gun from his night table, ran to the front window and killed a night watchman in the street'.[50]

Sleepwalking, sleep terrors and sleep drunkenness are first cousins: all occur on waking from slow wave sleep, typically in the first part of the night when our sleep is deepest. They can be induced deliberately, by disturbing sufferers at this time. They may occur in various combinations within a single family. These disorders are not too uncommon: around 15 per cent of children aged 5–12 sleepwalk at least once; 3–6 per cent make a habit of it.[51]

Nightmares, however, are universal. They occur in REM sleep and are also a common cause of awakening in young people, although I suspect my children now invent them as an acceptable excuse for a visit in the night. During a nightmare, as in any other kind of dream, we are, as a rule, extremely floppy. An exception to this rule has recently come to light.

'"I was on a motorcycle going down the highway when another motor-cyclist comes up alongside me and tries to ram me with his motorcycle. Well, I decided I'm going to kick his motorcycle away and at that point my wife woke up and said 'What in heavens are you doing to me?', because I was kicking the hell out of her". In the dream he saw clearly, heard nothing and felt fear of being rammed.' These are the words of a 'dapper, pleasant, well-adjusted man aged 67 enjoying retirement', who had always been a rather restless sleeper, but who began to act out his dreams at the age of 63, at considerable risk to his own health and his wife's.[52] Another patient described by the same researchers once 'grabbed his wife's neck with both hands while dreaming that he had just staggered a deer with a blow to its head and was going to break its neck. . . . Since then his wife has generally slept apart from him.'

Detailed study of these subjects' sleep revealed that their activities began at the onset of REM sleep and were appropriate to the content of their dreams. In cases in which this disorder is associated with neurological disease this tends to be centred in the brainstem.

It is very likely that this disorder is the human equivalent of a syndrome which has been explored in work with animals over the last two decades. Small precisely targeted areas of damage in the pons abolish the muscular relaxation which normally occurs in dreaming sleep, and allow the release of 'oneiric' dream behaviour. This behaviour often includes stereotyped aggression, which may well be akin to the dangerous manoeuvres of human sufferers from 'REM sleep behaviour disorder'.

Many of the phenomena we have encountered in this chapter illustrate the possibility of dissociating aspects of ordinary consciousness: movement, language, memory, pain all come apart in certain circumstances. The disorders of sleep illustrate another kind of dissociation, the occurrence of mixtures of the three main states of arousal. Figure 4.4 indicates how several of the disorders I have mentioned fall into areas of overlap between wakefulness, dreaming and slow wave sleep.

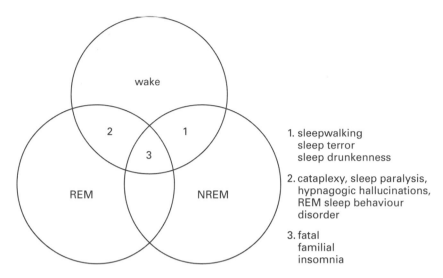

1. sleepwalking
   sleep terror
   sleep drunkenness

2. cataplexy, sleep paralysis,
   hypnagogic hallucinations,
   REM sleep behaviour
   disorder

3. fatal
   familial
   insomnia

Figure 4.4 Overlaps between states of consciousness An illustration of the overlaps which can arise between the three major states of consciousness. Overlaps between wakefulness and NREM (zone 1) occur in sleepwalking, sleep terrors and confusional arousals; overlaps between wakefulness and REM (zone 2) occur in narcolepsy (in cataplexy, sleep paralysis and hypnagogic hallucinations), REM sleep behaviour disorders and lucid dreaming; overlaps between all three conscious states (zone 3) have been described occasionally.

The measurement of awareness

Disorders of consciousness are common and important. It is vital for medics to have some way of quantifying consciousness, so that we can judge whether a patient unconscious from a bang on the head is improving or deteriorating, or whether someone undergoing anaesthesia is in need of a top-up to prevent awareness breaking through.

The example of the 'lucid interval' illustrates the point. The following sequence of events can result from a blow to the head: a few moments of unconsciousness follow the impact, say a fall to the ground from a horse. The victim then recovers, realises what has happened, and complains of a headache. This is her lucid interval. Ten minutes later confusion sets in; 20 minutes later the victim is drowsy. Half an hour later the end may be nigh, unless someone has been alerted – by the declining level of consciousness – to the likelihood that a blood clot is accumulating alongside the brain, squeezing the brainstem and requiring rapid removal.

The large vocabulary of diminished consciousness – drowsiness, stupor, obtundation, semi-coma – is so vague as to be next to useless in defining a patient's state of awareness. The introduction of 'coma scales' was therefore an important step forwards, providing a tool for the 'objective' description of levels of consciousness.

The most widely used coma scale originates in Glasgow, a city with something of a reputation for the mixture of alcohol and exuberance which is prone to injure heads.[53] The Glasgow Coma Scale is a simple measure of awareness following brain injury. Three parameters – eye opening, best 'motor response' (that is the patient's most purposeful movement) and best 'verbal response' – are scored using the scheme reproduced in Figure 4.5: the composite 'coma score', with a maximum of 15 and a minimum of 3, is the sum of the three components. Our unlucky rider, for example, would have plunged from her horse to a transient low of 3, recovered rapidly to 15 and then gradually slipped down the scale, point by point, as she lapsed into coma.

C O M A	Eyes Open	Spontaneously	4		Eyes closed by swelling = C
		To Speech	3		
		To Pain	2		
		None	1		
A S C	Best Verbal Response	Orientated	5		Endotracheal tube or tracheostomy = T
		Confused	4		
		Inappropriate Words	3		
		Incomprehensible Sounds	2		
		None	1		
A L E	Best Motor Response	Obey Commands	6		Record the best arm response
		Localise Pain	5		
		Flexion to Pain	4		
		Abnormal Flexion	3		
		Extension to Pain	2		
		None	1		
	G.C.S. Total				

Figure 4.5 The Glasgow Coma Scale This widely used scale enables doctors to make an objective assessment of patients' level of consciousness by careful observation of eye opening, speech and movement (as a rule: see the text for exceptions).

The coma score correlates roughly with the gravity of the injury to the brain. It has proved to be a useful basis for decisions about treatment, such as when to operate, when to take measures to reduce the pressure from a swelling brain or when to assist a patient's breathing by artificial means. But while it is a robust tool in the casualty ward, in some circumstances the coma score is positively misleading.

All the evidence for awareness garnered by the coma scale depends on the ability to move. But we can be conscious, and yet unable to move a muscle. We have already encountered two examples of this state of affairs. Patients paralysed by a muscle relaxant during surgery occasionally regain awareness: the 'medically qualified lady' had this misfortune. Patients with the locked-in syndrome can at best look up and down, but are fully aware.

Several other neurological disorders give rise to a similar predicament. In Guillain-Barré syndrome, for example, peripheral nerves lose their ability to conduct signals, temporarily, following an infection. Generalised paralysis occasionally ensues, but the central nervous system – and awareness – are unaffected, assuming adequate life support is available while the nerves recover.

The fact that consciousness can survive the loss of all the usual means by which we communicate our experience creates a need for more direct measures of awareness than the coma scale provides. Two approaches, most fully explored by anaesthetists, have shown promise: recording evoked potentials and monitoring the EEG.

Auditory evoked potentials, which we encountered in the last chapter, have proved particularly useful (see Figure 3.5). During the first 10 milliseconds after hearing a sound it is possible to detect activity travelling through the brainstem. This is followed by 'midlatency auditory evoked potentials' which reflect events occurring when the signal first reaches the cortex. As shown in Figure 4.6, these potentials consist of a series of fairly regular peaks and troughs.

It was by recording these midlatency potentials that the authors of the German research we encountered earlier were able to predict which of their subjects would be likely to remember something of the story they heard under anaesthesia.[54] The anaesthetic tended to delay or efface the peaks and troughs of the potential. In nine patients the delay of the first peak, Pa, was less than 12 milliseconds; in 21 it was greater. The patients in

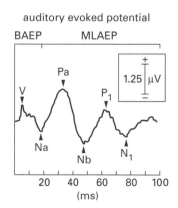

Figure 4.6 Midlatency auditory evoked potentials V belongs to the brainstem auditory evoked response (see Figure 3.5). Na, Pa, Nb and P1 are the midlatency auditory evoked potentials, reflecting early activity in the auditory cortex.

the first category included all seven who displayed signs of implicit memory, suggesting that the midlatency potential can be used as a measure of the depth of anaesthesia – or, conversly, the likelihood of some variety of awareness.

Professor Jones and his colleagues have extended this idea, making use of an interesting modification of the evoked potential technique.[55] Instead of playing single sounds to the subject a number of times, and averaging the result, these researchers exploited the discovery that sounds repeated at a certain frequency set up a 'standing wave'. This response stands out from the electrical background as long as the sound is repeated. In a waking subject the frequency which produces the clearest signal, the 'coherent frequency', is close to 40 repetitions/second.

Working with colleagues who agreed to act as experimental subjects – in the best traditions of anaesthetic research – Professor Jones showed that as anaesthesia deepened, so the coherent frequency fell. When a frequency of around 25 repetitions/second elicited the maximal standing wave, the subjects still responded to command, but had no memory of doing so after recovery. With a coherent frequency below 10 there was no evidence of any form of awareness (see Figure 4.7).

This work supports the idea that several states of awareness can occur during anaesthesia. Before the anaesthetic begins to take hold, we can perceive, respond to and recall events around us. As it builds up we lose, roughly in succession, our appreciation of pain, our conscious recall for the procedure, our ability to respond to requests and, finally, our ability to acquire implicit memories of the occasion.

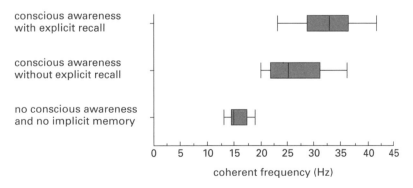

Figure 4.7 The coherent frequency and cognition during anaesthesia The coherent frequency falls as anaesthesia deepens and cognitive functions are progressively impaired.

These discoveries also provide a serviceable measure of the likelihood of awareness during anaesthesia – serviceable, but indirect. The auditory evoked potential relies on our ability to hear: no one thinks that deafness prevents consciousness. Indeed, there is no reason to believe that even *complete* sensory isolation leads automatically to loss of awareness. It would be preferable to use a measure of consciousness which allows us to infer its presence directly from the activity of the brain, without reliance on sensation. Does the EEG fit the bill?

A promising feature of the EEG for use as a measure of awareness is described as the 'median frequency'.[56] As I hinted in the last chapter, the complex squiggles of the EEG can be described mathematically as a combination of overlapping 'sine' waves. Sine waves are monotonous series of peaks and troughs; they are described by their height and their frequency, the number of waves occurring in a given period. A pure note is a sine wave travelling through the air; its height determines the volume, its frequency defines the pitch. The median frequency of the EEG is the middle frequency in the group of waves which superimpose to create a given pattern.

While we're awake and mentally active, the predominant frequencies are well above 5/second, with a median around 10. In deep natural sleep they drop well below 5/second. As anaesthesia deepens the median frequency of the EEG, like the coherent frequency of the evoked response, also falls gradually: Figure 4.8 shows the median frequency charted against the evolving features of anaesthesia as the dose is wound up and down.[57]

This correlation is impressive, but there is reason to sound a note of caution here as well. The EEG is not a direct reflection of our subjective

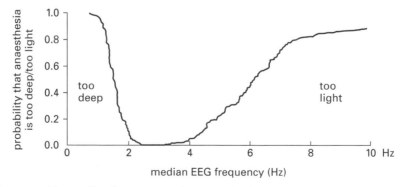

Figure 4.8 The median frequency under anaesthesia This provides an alternative approach to measuring depth of anaesthesia. A median frequency of under two suggests that anaesthesia is unnecessarily deep; above four it risks being too light.

state, even though it does remarkably well. 'Alpha coma' and 'endozepine coma' illustrate its shortcomings.

The first of these terms describes a variety of coma due to damage to the brainstem in which – against expectations – alpha rhythm is prominent in the EEG.[58] Alpha rhythm, you will recall, is normally the signature of resting wakefulness, reduced or abolished by opening the eyes or mental activity. Its presence in the EEG of patients who are undeniably in coma suggests the 'median frequency' might be a fallible guide to awareness.

The second example derives from a condition which has only recently been recognised.[59] Sufferers are prone to recurrent spells of irresistible sleepiness, lasting for days. They can be roused from their slumber, with some effort, but only for seconds or minutes, before lapsing back into sleep. The explanation turns out to be chemical: their brains are loaded with high levels of endogenous equivalents of the tranquilliser, Valium, known as 'endozepines'. Endozepines, like Valium, speed up the EEG. So, although she is fast asleep, the EEG rhythms of a patient in endozepine coma are predominantly rapid.

The EEG does not provide a read-out of awareness, but at present, though imperfect, it is the best available measure of consciousness. There is every reason to expect that the growing sophistication of the EEG and its magnetic sister, MEG, combined with rapid advances in our ability to image the working brain, will create a more powerful tool over the next few decades.

Conclusion: anatomising consciousness

This chapter has reviewed a variety of disorders of awareness. Most impair consciousness in the first sense we distinguished, the waking state. Some, like focal seizures, and subanaesthetic doses of drugs, colour the content of consciousness as well.

Two conclusions should need little emphasis. First, consciousness is fragile. Second, however magical it may be, it is a physical affair: mundane requirements for oxygen and glucose, electrical equilibrium, clean blood and adequate sleep must be met in the brain – or consciousness fails.

A third conclusion is that however coherent our experience and behaviour may appear, they are prone to fragment under stress. We have come across many examples: faints, fits and intoxication all reveal that perception, memory, movement and speech are separable capacities. This once again raises the question I dodged earlier in the chapter: *which* of these constitutes consciousness?

All four are perhaps needed to *establish* consciousness of a human kind: the growth of experience requires that we can sense the world and our companions, interact with and learn from them. Once consciousness is established, movement and speech lose some of their immediate importance. The 'medically qualified lady' could neither move nor speak, but she was acutely able to sense events and recall them. I imagine that no one would deny her consciousness. We may be less sure that awareness can persist when memory fails and only perception remains: this is the situation, for example, of patients undergoing the variety of anaesthesia studied by Ian Russel. But, although it may be an uncomfortable fact, I see no compelling reason to doubt that the capacity for experience can survive when the ability to communicate – and even to recall it – has been lost.

The final conclusion follows in part from the last. It can be extremely difficult to determine the presence or absence of consciousness. We cannot entirely rely upon the evidence of behaviour, of subsequent recall, of autonomic responses, or even – as things stand – of measures of activity in the brain. If we run into this problem with each other, it is no wonder that we are so perplexed about the question of animal consciousness.

Some instances are easy: few nowadays would doubt that chimps or dolphins are conscious of their surroundings. We find these cases straightforward because these animals resemble us sufficiently in behaviour, physique and physiology to make it highly likely that they resemble us – to some degree – in their subjective states. The argument from analogy seems compelling. But what of salmon, snake and spider? The resemblances here are strained – and we know too little about the mechanisms and functions of human consciousness to judge with any real authority whether or not these animals are likely to enjoy awareness of a kind.[60] This is also a disconcerting conclusion.

If the issue of animal awareness is tricky, the possibility of disembodied consciousness is more problematic still. Everything we have touched on in this chapter and the last suggests that the nervous system is the 'stuff' of consciousness. But there is a powerful human tendency to conceive of the mind as an immaterial substance, an ethereal being that breathes psychological life into the physical body. Perhaps the widespread belief in the soul originates in our reluctance to accept that the dead have left us for ever, when they live on so vividly in our memories. Whatever its source, the belief is seriously challenged by the wealth of evidence that damaging the brain can damage and fragment awareness. It may be arrogant to deny that consciousness can ever slip its moorings in the brain – after all, much of the world's population believes firmly that it can – but the evidence in favour of this happening is tenuous at best. We have reached the limits of our knowledge: 'whereof one cannot speak, thereof one must be silent'.[61]

Part III:
The contents of consciousness

5

From darkness into light: the structural basis of consciousness (ii)

Or when, under ether, the mind is conscious but conscious of nothing . . .

T.S. Eliot, 'East Coker'[1]

Introduction

While we are conscious at all, we are always conscious *of something*. I have chosen vision to illustrate the scientific approach to the content of consciousness. Sight has a special place in our lives, even if a rich human existence is perfectly possible without it. Its importance reflects our ancestry: about half the brain of the African monkey is given over to sight.

The challenge posed by vision for the scientist is evident enough. Just look around: the shapes and colours, depth and movement which meet your effortless gaze are all created by the brain.[2] How? Answering this simple question occupied some very able minds in the twentieth century: vision is the most intensively – and successfully – investigated human sense. Its beginnings, in the eye, are understood in molecular detail. A remarkable chain of discoveries now connects these molecular events with the visual consciousness which arises from their repercussions in the brain. This chapter follows the chain from the arrival of light in the eye to the moment of visual awareness.

Sight has another attraction for our purposes. The pathways serving vision, like those of the other senses, lie at the mouth of the brain: we should be able to trace them for some distance without losing our way in labyrinthine networks. Once we have a firm foothold in the 'visual system', we can aim for a glimpse of the horizon at which vision encounters memory, language and the other capacities which help to shape our experience.

In the next chapter we shall turn to some surprising ways in which sight can be impaired by – or survive – damage to the brain. Vision has become a hunting ground for scientists intrigued by consciousness: we shall end by asking how far science can ever go towards giving us an explanation of the experience of sight.

The story begins in sunshine.

Light and the evolution of vision

Light

By day our surroundings are flooded with light. The sun has beaten down on our planet ever since its formation, fostering first the beginnings of life and later the dawning of vision. To understand sight, we need to know something of light.

Light conveys energy – as I am reminded whenever our chilly northern surroundings warm at the touch of the sun. Experiments over more than 300 years have suggested that this welcome messenger has a twofold nature.

Light sometimes behaves like a wave of energy. Waves, whether rising and falling in the sea or pulsing through the brain, can be described in terms of two characteristics: their wavelength, the distance between successive crests, and their amplitude or height. White light is an impure mixture of waves: a prism splits up its constituent rays. Like rain creating a rainbow, the prism separates out the shorter wavelength, higher energy, blue lights at one end of the spectrum from long wavelength, low energy, red lights at the other. Isaac Newton described this property of prisms in the seventeenth cenury. Nineteenth-century physicists found additional reasons for believing that light is wave-like: its rays interact like waves in water, summing when peaks coincide, cancelling out when peaks meet troughs.

Despite this evidence in support of the 'wave theory' we know now that there are other contexts in which light behaves differently, as if it consisted of a discontinuous stream of particles, each bearing a tiny packet or 'quantum' of energy. Quanta of blue light for instance contain more energy than those of red. The 'wave–particle' duality was a major concern of twentieth-century physics. Just as light waves sometimes behave as particles, so particles sometimes behave like waves. It may be frustrating that we cannot settle for one or other simple theoretical 'model' of light, but why should it make itself amenable to our theories? Light, after all, is light.

Whether we think of it as a wave or particle stream, we know for certain that the band of radiation we can *see* is a tiny part of a much broader spread. The 'electromagnetic spectrum' contains wavelengths which vary by 25 log units (in other words, the longest wavelengths are 10,000,000,000,000, 000,000,000,000 times longer than the shortest). The visible spectrum falls within a single log unit of this spectrum. Wavelengths just short of blue fall in the ultraviolet; even shorter wavelengths include X- and gamma rays, highly energetic and potentially destructive forms of radiation from which we are – or were – largely shielded by the ozone layer. Wavelengths on the long side of red belong to the infrared; travelling still further up the spectrum we encounter the microwaves we cook with and the radio waves which keep us posted with the news.

Light and life

No sun showed one thing to another,
No moon
Played her phases in heaven . . .

Ted Hughes, 'Creation'[3]

Radiation from the sun has made three great contributions to life over the 4,500 million years of the earth's existence.

We can know little about the first. It is thought likely that between three and four thousand million years ago the chemical milieu on earth, stoked up by energy from the sun, allowed complex molecules to form from simpler atoms and molecules, like those of carbon, nitrogen and water. By chance, some of these complex molecules, nucleic acids, had the ability to make copies of themselves. This was the origin of life.

Once such molecules had come into being, bombardment by X- and gamma rays caused alterations in their structure. Most such alterations would have been injurious, leading to the molecule's demise, but every so often a mutation increased the molecule's chances of survival and reproduction. This was the beginning of the variation in the forms of life from which natural selection took – and still takes – its choice.

Sunlight's second great contribution occurred 2,000–3,000 million years ago. The evolution of photosynthesis allowed some fortunate organisms to manufacture carbohydrates, like sugars and starch, from carbon dioxide and water, using solar energy to power the process. The abundance of greenery around us testifies to the success of this manoeuvre, and provides the first link in the food chain for most of the animal kingdom. The process also liberates oxygen, which has transformed the planet's atmosphere. Photosynthesis allowed later arrivals on earth, like ourselves, to be sustained by sunlight, whose produce we both breathe and eat.

Photosynthesis depends upon the bleaching of a pigment, chlorophyll, by impinging light. The captured light is harnessed to generate an energy supply. Sunlight found its third role 500–1,000 million years ago, when it began to light up watching eyes. Light then became a source of knowledge as well as energy.

Life and vision

> One further debt is clear. Flowers ... bloomed long before man appeared on earth. They evolved in order to appeal not to him but to insects. Had butterflies been colour blind and bees without a delicate sense of smell, man would have been denied some of the greatest delights the natural world has to offer.
>
> David Attenborough, *Life on Earth*[4]

> Were our senses altered, and made much quicker and acuter, the appearance and outward scheme of things would have quite another face for us.
>
> John Locke, *An Essay Concerning Human Understanding*[5]

Darwin was well aware that 'organs of extreme perfection', like the eye, would be cited as evidence against his theory of natural selection. Their exquisite design surely suggests the deliberate work of a Maker. As Darwin wrote: 'to suppose that the eye with all its inimitable contrivances . . . could have been formed by natural selection, seems, I freely confess, absurd in the highest degree'.[6] He confessed to Asa Gray that 'the eye to this day gives me a cold shudder'.[7] But he conquered the shudder: what if 'numerous gradations from a simple and imperfect eye to one complex and perfect can be shown to exist, each grade being useful to its possessor'? Then 'there would be no logical impossibility in the acquirement of any conceivable degree of perfection through natural selection'.[8] By the time he completed *The Origin of Species* in 1859 his observations had convinced him that this was 'certainly the case'.

Evolutionary biologists have sometimes been accused of telling 'Just So Stories', appealing tales built on scanty evidence. Such stories certainly don't make science, but in case you are puzzled by Darwin's claim it may be helpful to spin such a yarn unashamedly before considering the evidence.

Imagine a primitive creature, a single waterborne cell. Like other such cells, it has a surface studded with proteins. None of these, at first, 'sees' light. Imagine next that a minute change in one of these proteins has the effect that impinging light changes its shape, tilting it ever so slightly in the membrane of the cell. By changing the forces acting on the cell, this might tend to spin it through sunlit water, allowing it to encounter more of its foodstuff than before, pleasantly warmed by the light. Such a creature might grow faster and reproduce more rapidly than its 'blind' companions. As a result the gene for the protein conferring 'sight' would prosper.

Natural errors in its replication of the gene would occur from time to time, as they always do. A few of the creatures would lose the 'sight gene', to their cost. Others would acquire a double dose. Provided that 'sight' was beneficial a cluster of the 'sight' proteins might eventually coalesce on the surface of the cell: our amoeba would have aquired an eye of sorts – not to speak of a 'sleep–wake cycle'.

In this creature's multicellular descendants, some cells would specialise in the manufacture of the light-sensitive protein. One of these descendants is, let's say, a water worm. Its 'eye' is a collection of pigmented cells. Occasionally the eye gets damaged by abrasion. A minor mutation affecting the growth of these cells, which causes them to recede a little from the surface of its body, mitigates this problem, creating an 'eye pit'. The mutation would spread rapidly through the population. But once in a while a particle of sand enters the eye pit, and blocks the worm's view. Another simple mutation could cause a thin – transparent – layer of skin to grow over the opening of the pit, excluding the sand, and confer another minute advantage. The water worm's eye begins to look disarmingly like ours.

Every part of our water worm, of course, is evolving, not just its eye. Mutations affecting other parts of its anatomy have allowed it to acquire a simple nervous system. A few of its neurons have developed a relationship with the pigment cells. Instead of simply tilting the pigment protein in the cell, the absorption of light causes a chemical change in the pigment cells which the neurons can detect. Light induces the worm's simple 'brain' to move it towards the warm sunlit water in which it likes to feed and swim by alerting the nerves which drive its muscles.

The eye's protective skin creates some other possibilities. If the layer of skin covering the eye pit were to thicken a little it could work like a simple lens. The eye which once merely detected the difference between light and shade would now be exposed to an image of the world beyond.

Stories like this go some way towards making it plausible that each small step on the way from a simple to a complex eye could be 'useful to its possessor'. But this story would have little interest were there no evidence that something of this kind in fact occurred. As Darwin anticipated, there is now a good deal of evidence.[9]

The soft tissues of the eye are not well preserved as fossils. We can't hope for a complete record of its evolution, but there are many suggestive clues. Examples of most of the 'gradations' mentioned in my story can be found in living animals, and sometimes traced through their growth in embryo. Many unicellular organisms have 'eyespots' which are sensitive to light. The multicellular limpet's eye consists of no more than a simple pit. The human lens begins life as embryonic skin, which becomes detached from the surface of the eye during development. In several groups of related animals it is possible to reconstruct a 'regular series of ever more perfect eyes' from living examples (see Figure 5.1).

Detailed comparisons of widely varying species have suggested that eyes of all kinds may have evolved independently as many as 40–65 times since life began. But recent evidence, from molecular biology, has also pointed to some close affinities between the eyes of animals as dissimilar as those of the fruit fly and man.

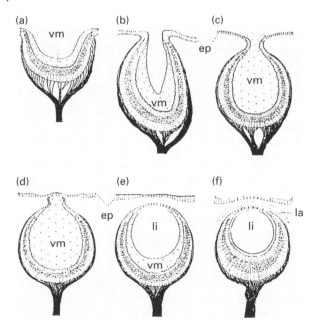

Figure 5.1 The evolution of the eye A sequence of increasingly sophisticated eyes from a group of related species, hinting at the kind of evolutionary story told in the text (vm=vitreous mass; ep=epidermis or cornea; li=lens; la=lacuna).

Their eyes *appear* very different. The insect eye consists of an array of numerous lenses, each 'looking' at light from straight ahead. It resembles the earliest fossilised eyes known to us, from Trilobites, found in Cambrian rocks over 500 million years old (see Figure 5.2). These insect eyes, ancient and modern, clearly contrast with the vertebrate version with its single large lens, of which ours is a fairly typical example (see Figure 5.3). But appearances can mislead.

Figure 5.2 The trilobite eye Trilobites were segmented creatures, resembling woodlice, which prospered around 500 million years ago. The compound eye of this beautifully preserved (fossilised) example is easily visible at the side of the head.

To begin with, there are are strong molecular resemblances between the pigment proteins which capture light in both varieties of eye.[10] There is no doubt, in fact, that they originated in a common ancestor. Perhaps the light-sensitive molecule which is the key precondition for the evolution of vision came into being only once, and was exploited right across the animal kingdom. Another intriguing connection between these dissimilar eyes has come to light very recently.[11]

The fruit fly *Drosophila* has been the subject of a great deal of genetic research, much of it correlating minute alterations in the structure of its DNA with alterations in the fly's anatomy and behaviour. The *eyeless* gene, a segment of DNA required for the development of the eye, has turned out to be closely related to a gene, *Pax-6*, which is known to control eye development in man. Mutations in the human gene can result in 'aniridia', eyes lacking an iris, which are oversensitive to light and liable to develop problems like cataract, which threaten sight, in childhood. Mice with

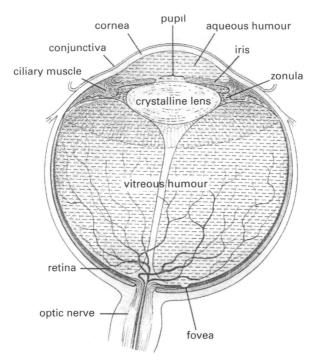

Figure 5.3 The human eye The human eye as it appears cut through its 'equator', with the cornea and pupil at the front, the retina at the back. The optic nerve runs back from the retina to the brain.

abnormalities in *Pax-6* have an abnormality known as *smalleye*. Thus despite the striking superficial differences between the eyes of contemporary insects and contemporary mammals, modern genetics hints strongly at an ancient evolutionary link.

Whatever circuitous path our eyes took to reach their present form, they evolved to inspect only a tiny portion of the radiation bathing our world. Why should vision open a window on this particular segment of the vast electromagnetic spectrum?

Since photosynthesis got under way and the ozone layer was formed, the earth has been screened from high energy radiation from the sun. In these aerobic conditions the world is most brightly lit at the wavelengths to which our eyes are sensitive, and our vision makes the best use of a limited view. Radiation of much higher energies, in any case, can damage living tissues and is best avoided by the eye. Low energy, long wave, radiation outside the visible spectrum might be unable to deliver an adequate signal to the eye. Finally, an eye which uses a lens must limit the range of wavelengths it surveys, or the resulting image will be blurred.

These constraints are not precise: as John Locke surmised, things might have been different. For some animals, they are. Bees' vision extends into the ultraviolet, enabling them to enjoy flowery 'honey guides' invisible to us; snakes can locate their prey using an exquisite temperature sense tuned to infrared radiation. These creatures are responding to features of the world which our unaided senses might well have detected but, as it happens, do not.[12]

But for all of us, you and I and fruit fly, the process of vision begins with the bleaching of pigment.

The retina: sensitive pigment

Capturing quanta

How a nerve comes to be sensitive to light, hardly concerns us . . .

Charles Darwin, *The Origin of Species*[13]

Despite its marvellous design, the eye's function is simple enough: to cast an image of the world upon the retina (see Figure 5.3). A thin layer of tissue, hugging the back wall of the eye, the retina then transforms light into signals which the brain can read. This miraculous result is achieved by about 100 million cells packed with light absorbing pigments.[14] These cells, known as rods and cones, betray their origins in a small anatomical detail (see Figure 5.4). The inner and the outer segments of the cell are connected by a cilium. Cilia are usually found on cells with elongated arms which beat against liquid – either to propel the cell or to move the liquid. The tail of a sperm, for instance, is an adapted cilium. But across a wide range of species, from worm to man, cilia have provided the point of departure for the evolution of light-detecting cells (see Figure 5.5).

Rods and cones differ in detail but share a common basic design. The outer segment contains a stack of infoldings of the cell membrane. The light-detecting molecule, known in the rod as rhodopsin, is embedded in these infoldings: one rod contains 100 million copies of rhodopsin. Rhodopsin consists mainly, but not entirely, of protein. Its protein component, opsin, folds up in the membrane to offer a congenial spot for a substance derived from Vitamin A, known as 11-cis retinal, to nestle. When a quantum of light impinges on 11-cis retinal, it changes its shape, just like our fictitious molecule in the last section. Once it has straightened out into 'all-trans-retinal' it no longer fits into its nest. Opsin itself changes shape

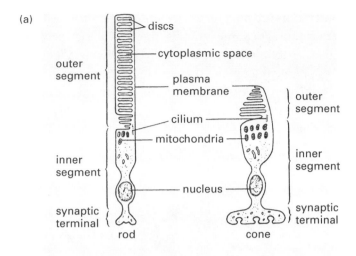

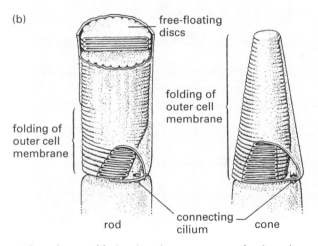

Figure 5.4 Rods and cones (a) sketches the appearance of rods and cones if split down the middle from top to bottom; (b) gives a three-dimensional impression of their shape. Notice the persistence of the 'cilium'; the infoldings of the cell membranes of both rods and cones which contain the 'photopigments', the proteins specialised to detect the presence of light; and the synaptic terminals at the base of rod and cone where the arrival of light is signalled by a change in the rate of neurotransmitter release.

as a result and thereby acquires a new chemical ability, to catalyse the production of a cascade of 'second messengers' within the cell.

The last of these messengers closes a channel in the cell membrane which otherwise allows a steady influx of sodium, known as the rod's 'dark current'. Reducing this current reduces the positive charge within the cell. This in turn reduces the release of neurotransmitters by the rod, to a degree

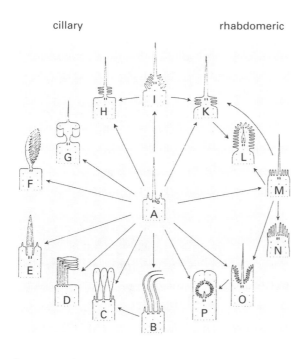

cillary   rhabdomeric

A   Hydrozoa (6)
B   Kamptozoa (3)
    Nematodes (4)
    Bryozoa (5)
C   Bivalvia (15)
    Polychaeta (16), (17)?
D   Gastropoda (14)
E   Chaetognatha (18)
F   Chordata (20), (23)?
G   Hydrozoa (8)
    Ctenophora (11)
    Placophora (12)
    Gastropoda (13)
H   Cnidaria (6), (7), (9), (10)
I   Asteroidea (19)
K   Bivalvia (44)
    Cephalopoda (45)
    Polychaeta (47)
    Arthropoda (48)
    Enteropneusta (50)
L   Bivalvia (44)
    Onychophora (47)
M   Gastropoda (44)
    Sipunculida (47)
N   Placophora (43)
    Gastropoda (45)
    Sipunculida (47)
    Asteroidea (19)
O   Ascidiacea (52)
P   Clitellata (46)
    Arthropoda part. (49)
    Pogonophora (51)
    Bivalvia (32)?

Figure 5.5 The evolution of photoreceptors This shows the possible relationship between photoreceptor cells in a wide variety of species. Notice their presumed origin in a cell with a single cilium: simple photosensitive cells of this design are still found in some species. F is the type of photoreceptor found in our phylum (or group), the chordates. Types D and M are found in grastropods, the phylum including snails and slugs; types K and P in bivalves, the phylum including mussels and oysters, and in arthropods, the phylum to which the insects belong.

proportional to the amount of impinging light (by producing a 'graded' signal, photoreceptors are an exception to the usual rule among neurons that their signals are 'all or nothing'). By these roundabout means the play of light and shade is translated into the neurochemical currency of the nervous system.

A closer look at rhodopsin tells the inside story of this process. Opsin contains 348 amino acids and loops seven times across the plasma membrane. Its composition, size and shape point to its ancestry. Rhodopsin belongs to the family of receptors involved in second messenger systems throughout the nervous system. With the help of retinal, rhodopsin is able to treat light as if it were a signal released within the body. A chemical trick allows the methods we use to communicate within ourselves to be coupled to events in the world outside. It is hard to see how, otherwise, perception could ever get off the ground.

Communicating contrast

Each of our retinae is home to about 100 million rods and 6 million cones. Cones are concentrated at the centre of the retina where they scrutinise the centre of the visual field. They come in three varieties, 'blue', 'green' and 'red', differing in the wavelength of light most avidly absorbed by the particular pigment they contain. Comparison of activity in the three varieties of cone is the basis for colour vision. Rods predominate away from the centre of the retina. More sensitive to dim light than cones, but much less closely packed, they provide our night vision, revealing a shadowy world by the light of the moon.

The 'transduction' of light into a neural signal by rods and cones, which I have just outlined, is one of the two main functions of the retina. Its second task is to begin the process of analysis which conjures up our visual world, extracting informative features from the dance of light and shade.

An unbroken field of light is uninformative. Edges of brightness, contours of colour, contrasts of movement and depth allow us to identify our surroundings. Accordingly the retina speaks to the brain mainly about discontinuities in the visual scene. How does it detect these?

The retina is a miniature brain: indeed, it originates in the embryo as an outgrowth from the brain. In man and other vertebrates – but not, for example, in the octopus and the squid – it has a curious 'inverse' design. Rods and cones lie right at the back of the retina (see Figure 5.6), furthest from the light they capture. To reach them at all, light must pass through two other layers of neural cells. These provide the retina's brain power.

The 'output' cells of the retina, which project axons back to the brain proper along the 'optic nerve', are its 'ganglion cells'. These lie furthest from the rods and cones. Each ganglion cell samples the activity of photoreceptors over a small circular area of the retina, known as the cell's receptive field. Receptive fields are smallest at the centre of the retina, which we use to discriminate fine detail, largest at the periphery.

In most receptive fields, light falling in the centre of the field has an opposite effect to light falling in the 'surround'. If light at the centre excites the cell, light in the surround will inhibit its activity – and vice versa. As a result, illumination of the entire receptive field has a weak effect, while a spot of light falling asymmetrically in the field will markedly alter the cell's firing rate. 'On-centre' cells are excited by the appearance of such a spot; its disappearance will excite 'off-centre' cells. This sensitivity to contrast is achieved by neurons which intervene between photoreceptors and

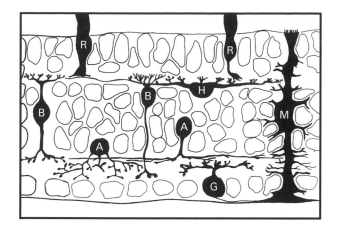

Figure 5.6 The retina This figure shows the layers of neurons in the retina. It was prepared in the mudpuppy, but the broad design is similar in man. The drawing is based on work using the Golgi method, which stains a minority of cells to show their full extent (the lightly outlined cells are unstained). The photoreceptors (R) lie at the back of the retina; their responses to light are signalled back to the brain by ganglion cells (G), whose axons make up the optic nerve; the intervening horizontal (H), bipolar (B) and amacrine (A) neurons shape the ganglion cells' responses so that they inform the brain primarily about regions of contrast in the visual scene. M is a Muller cell, a non-neuronal, glial, cell.

ganglion cells. Bipolar, horizontal and amacrine cells integrate the signals from groups of adjacent photoreceptors and provide the input to ganglion cells and hence the optic nerve.

The distinction between centre and surround is used to signal contrasts of colour as well as edges of brightness. Some ganglion cells, for example, favour the appearance – or disappearance – of a spot of red or green light. Others compare the intensity of blue light with yellow, the sum of red and green.

All this ensures that most of the news travelling in the optic nerve relates to change and contrast: the onset and offset of contrasts of brightness or colour. One additional complexity of retinal signalling has emerged in recent years. Some retinal ganglion cells ('M' for magnocellular) are especially sensitive to rapid movements of large objects. They care little for colour. Their large bodies and large axons allow signals to travel rapidly back to the brain. 'P' cells ('P' for parvocellular) have smaller receptive fields which are often sensitive to hue and sustained illumination: they are equipped to resolve fine details of static form and colour. Most ganglion cells fall into one or other class. The distinction between them hints at events downstream, where we shall now follow the flow of signals down the million fibres of each optic nerve.

Analysis and integration: the cortical visual areas

En route to the visual cortex

As the axons in the optic nerve course backwards from the eye they rearrange themselves. The principle of this rearrangement is extremely simple. Fibres which describe the left half of the visual world pass to the right side of the brain, and vice versa. Thus this reorganisation obeys the general rule that each half of the brain responds to signals from the opposite side of space, and issues commands to the opposite side of the body (*why* this widely observed rule should have evolved is not so clear).

Although the aim is simple, the details of the rearrangement are quite complex. The left side of space is inspected by the 'nasal' retina of the left eye and the 'temporal' retina of the right eye (see Figure 5.7): bringing together the axons from these two 'hemi-retinae' requires that axons from the left nasal hemi-retina cross to the right side of the brain. They do so at the 'optic chiasm', just in front of the pituitary gland. Fibres from the right hemi-retina cross here in the opposite direction.

The fibres maintain an orderly relationship throughout their travels, so that adjacent axons originate from adjacent retinal ganglion cells and speak of events at adjacent points in visual space. The 'M' and 'P' axons, however, separate, so that by the time the fibres from the eye come to make their first synapse, in the lateral geniculate nucleus (LGN) of the thalamus, it is possible to distinguish the magnocellular and the parvocellular components. Two magnocellular layers in the LGN, each receiving input from one eye, are capped by four parvocellular layers, two for each eye. Every layer contains an orderly 'map' of the opposite half of visual space, although these maps have one notable peculiarity, which we shall soon encounter.

The LGN is presumably more than a way-station for visual information. It receives input from a number of brain areas, including the visual cortex to which it sends on the great bulk of its axons. If so, its contribution remains poorly defined. The first radical transformation of the visual signals from the eyes occurs at the next staging post in the visual system. This is perhaps the most intensively studied single region of the brain: area 17, the 'primary visual cortex' or 'area V1'.

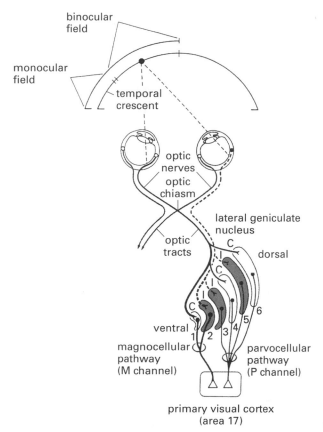

Figure 5.7 *En route* **to visual cortex** Each lateral geniculate nucleus (LGN) receives the fibres conveying information from the retinae about the opposite side of space (i.e. the left LGN receives information about the right-hand side of the visual scene). The signals from the two eyes are kept separate and stacked up in the LGN, coming together for the first time in the visual cortex.

Area 17

Brodmann's area 17 lies at the very back of the brain, at the tip of the occipital cortex.[15] It is distinguished by a stripe visible to the naked eye, the stria of Gennari, reflecting the density of the incoming fibres from the LGN, and is sometimes known as 'striate' cortex. Its importance to vision has been suspected at least since the mid-nineteenth century, when physiologists like Richard Caton recorded electrical responses to visual stimulation here.

The 'pity of war' extended our knowledge of this region of the brain. Work with a stream of brain-injured veterans from the trenches enabled a British neurologist, Gordon Holmes, to demonstrate that V1 in man contains a map of visual space, and to probe its structure in unprecedented detail. Restricted injuries at the extreme tip of the striate cortex affected only the centre of the field of vision, injuries of the upper bank impairing the lower field, injuries of the lower bank the upper field. Damage further forward in the striate cortex impaired more peripheral parts of the field (see Figure 5.8).

The map is not strictly to scale – or, rather, its scale is psychological, not geometric. Almost half of the striate map scrutinises the area inspected by the sensitive 'fovea' at the centre of the retina where ganglion cells are packed tight – an area roughly the size of a thumbnail viewed at arm's length. The periphery of the visual field, where our vision is less acute, is more scantily represented.

Area VI is therefore a kind of 'cortical retina', mapping visual space. Is that all? Is it just a cortical mirror of retinal activity? The first satisfying answers to this question came from the work of two American physiologists

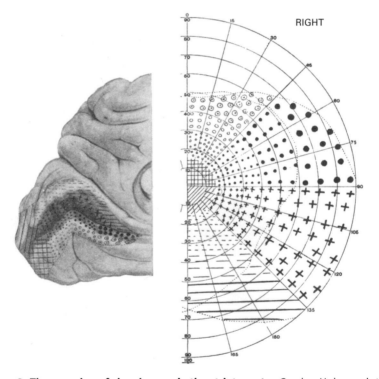

Figure 5.8 The mapping of visual space in the striate cortex Gordon Holmes plotted the representation of the visual field in the opposite striate (or primary) visual cortex by correlating the location of gunshot wounds at the back of the brain with the corresponding loss of vision. It seems extraordinary that Holmes, working 'in the base hospitals in France', during the First World War, was able to make such an accurate mapping. Note that a disproportionately large area of V1 inspects the centre of the visual field where our ability to resolve fine detail is high.

based in Boston, David Hubel and Torsten Wiesel, who received a Nobel prize for their work in 1981.

Hubel and Wiesel recorded the activity of single cells in the visual cortex of anaesthetised animals while presenting them with simple visual stimuli. They found that the *spots* of light which effectively excited retinal ganglion cells were ineffective stimuli for the visual cortex. Instead, each column of cortical cells was most potently excited by a *line* of a given orientation in the appropriate location in the visual field. Exploration of a series of adjacent columns revealed a regular progression in the orientation they preferred, changing by about 10° from one column to the next, and passing through 360° over every 1 millimetre or so of brain surface. This discovery suggested that the visual cortex might be designed to detect edges, scrutinising every part of the visual field for contours of all possible orientations.

Hubel and Wiesel also found that a second factor, the preferred eye, varied in a regular fashion across the visual cortex. This variation created 'ocular dominance columns' which were independent of the orientation columns already described. Thus the conclusion from their early work was that every 1mm² of visual cortex represents a full range of orientations, seen by either eye, in a small region of the visual field: this unit of visual analysis, repeated over and over again across area 17, came to be described as a 'hypercolumn' (see Figure 5.9).

The image of the visual cortex as a repetitive matrix of hypercolumns has the great merit of simplicity. But life is seldom simple. Work over the last 15 years, much of it also originating from Hubel, Wiesel and their collaborators, has painted a much more colourful and confusing picture.

One of the first clear indications that the organisation of V1 might not be so straightforward came not from physiology but from anatomy. Staining the visual cortex to highlight an enzyme involved in energy generation, cytochrome oxidase, revealed that V1 was 'blobby': regularly spaced blobs of cortex contained higher concentrations of the enzyme than surrounding regions. Anatomical variations in the cortex generally correspond to variations in function, and indeed the blobs proved to be doing something rather special.

Cells within the blobs are not orientation selective at all: they are, instead, 'wavelength selective', excited by axons from the LGN – and ultimately the eye – which signal regions of colour contrast. This finding suggested a second broad role for area V1: as well as analysing features such as form and colour in each part of the visual world, it *segregates* the information which describes them, channelling signals concerning colour into one stream – via the blobs – and 'achromatic' information into another.

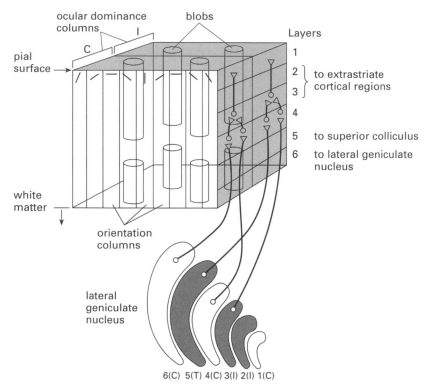

Figure 5.9 The columnar organisation of area V1 A hypercolumn is a region of the striate cortex inspecting a small area of the visual field representing orientations through 360° seen by either eye. 'Blobs' are also indicated.

This idea was broadly supported by the discovery of another element of complexity within V1. You will recall that 'P' cells and 'M' cells in the retina project to different layers of the LGN. This distinction is, to some degree, preserved in striate cortex. The parvocellular and magnocellular layers of the LGN project to subtly differing regions of layer 4 – the recipient cortical layer – of area V1. 'M' cells, with their rapid achromatic (colour-insensitive) responses to moving targets, innervate layer 4C alpha; 'P' cells, with slower but more sustained chromatic responses, synapse in layer 4C beta.

Thus V1 contains a map of the visual world which analyses and segregates visual information. Its increasingly confusing organisation took on a new dimension as attention turned to the neighbouring regions of the brain.

Multiple maps

Our everyday visual experience is unified and orderly. We see patterns of coloured forms in depth and, sometimes, motion, and as a rule the view makes sense. A painting seems an entirely natural metaphor for this coherent visual world, capturing all its essentials on a single canvas. It is therefore rather startling to discover that our visual field is 'mapped' around 30 times over in regions of cortex beyond V1 (see Figure 5.10).

Puzzling out the purpose of this extraordinary proliferation of visual areas has been a key goal in visual science over the last 20 years. The most

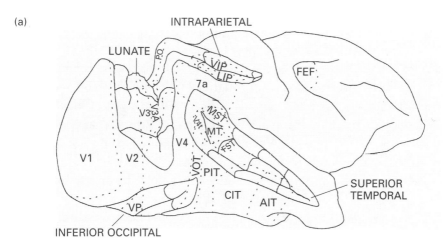

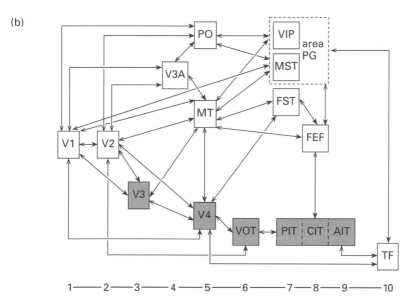

Figure 5.10 The cortical visual areas: anatomy and interconnections The visual areas of a monkey's brain are indicated in part (a). Area MT corresponds to area V5 in the discussion. Part (b) indicates the interconnections of the areas. The broad distinction between the 'where' (unshaded) and 'what' pathways corresponds to the upper and lower streams of signalling. Area TF lies on the hidden inner surface of the temporal lobe.

popular hypothesis is that the biological work of sight is somehow divided between them. This is at least partly true.

Visual area 2, V2, lies on the borders of the striate cortex. The stain that revealed the blobs and 'interblobs' of area V1 showed a repetitive tripartite structure in V2: thin and thick dark-staining stripes and pale-staining interstripes march across its surface. This organisation, and studies of the properties of the cells within the stripes, suggested that *three* streams of information flowed from area V1. The output from the blobs in V1 travelled to the thin stripes of V2, and thence to a further area, V4: this stream was a good candidate for the cortical basis of colour vision. A second, mainly parvocellular, stream, passing through interblobs in V1, coursed to the pale interstripes: this was a candidate for the fine analysis of form. Finally 'magnocellular' data, arriving in layer 4C alpha of V1, was channelled to the thick stripes of V2, then into V5: this stream appeared to be associated with the global perception of form and movement.

If colour, form and movement really do 'come apart' in the brain, one might hope to be able to show this directly in man. Functional brain imaging has in fact made it possible to investigate the activity of the cortical visual areas in the human brain. Inspection of a colourful, stationary image strongly activates the human counterpart of area V4, while inspection of a black and white pattern in motion triggers activity especially in area V5. And if distinct cortical regions mediate different aspects of human vision one might predict that brain injuries should occasionally lead to an isolated disturbance of colour vision or motion perception: we shall see in the next chapter that this is so.

More recent work has, unfortunately, 'thrown as much darkness as light' on these distinctions,[16] but it is beyond question that there are multiple visual areas in the cortex and that they make distinctive contributions to vision. Areas at comparable stages in the processing of visual information perform distinctive tasks, V4 serving colour vision and V5 movement perception. And, as one passes from areas 'upstream', such as V1 and V2, to areas 'downstream', such as V4 and V5, the nature of the visual 'mapping' changes. Cells downstream are likely to respond to stimuli over a wider area of the visual field and to respond to more complex 'processed' features, for example the global motion of a scene as opposed to the motion of its parts. Areas yet further down the stream are selective for stimuli as complex as faces and patterns, as we shall see.

The contrast between the analysis of fine detail and colour in the parvocellular stream, and the preoccupation with movement in the magnocellular stream, maps on to an earlier broad-brush distinction between regions of visual cortex concerned with identity and regions concerned with location, the 'what' and the 'where' of vision. Both the 'what' and the 'where' streams originate in the occipital cortex, but the former, the *ventral* pathway, runs into the temporal, the latter, the *dorsal*, into the parietal lobes. V4 lies in the ventral pathway, V5 in the dorsal.

The discovery of the cortical visual areas represents a huge advance in the understanding of vision. Traditional theories drew a distinction between the sensory cortex – in this case area 17 – where the raw data from the retina excited simple sensation, and the surrounding 'association cortex' which mysteriously 'elaborated' the sensory data, imbuing them with meaning. Contemporary research, instead, is beginning to explain how the processes of sensation themselves yield knowledge of the world. But a little reflection on the task performed by vision reveals some daunting unsolved problems.

Seeing things

Absorbed by the anatomy and physiology of vision it is easy to lose sight of its purpose. Its ultimate goal is to guide our actions. An intermediate aim is the recognition of objects. What capacities enable us to see *things*?

The wood from the trees

The first ability is so basic that it can easily escape attention altogether. The retina is excited right across its surface. So how do we know which regions of the dance of light and shade across the eye belong together? Somehow the brain must separate figure from ground and pick out significant outlines: otherwise the task of seeing things could never get started at all.

In the second and third decades of the twentieth century the 'Gestalt' psychologists suggested that we unconsciously apply a number of principles when we pick out figure from ground. We tend to group items which are close, similar to one another, which create a closed space or achieve a smooth continuity of line (see Figure 5.11). These principles have stood the test of time but make only rather general predictions about which patterns will stand out from the background.

More recently work by the Hungarian-American scientist Bela Julesz at Bell laboratories, Anne Triesman originally at Oxford, and others, has

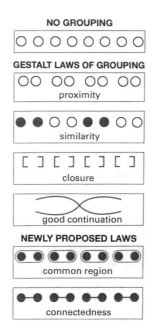

NO GROUPING

GESTALT LAWS OF GROUPING

proximity

similarity

closure

good continuation

NEWLY PROPOSED LAWS

common region

connectedness

Figure 5.11 The principles of grouping and an example of figure–ground ambiguity
Gestalt psychologists identified a number of principles guiding our selection of figure from ground; Maurits Escher played endlessly with figure–ground ambiguities in his work. This is a particularly exuberant example.

examined precisely which features guide the visual system in in its 'pre-attentive' segmentation of the visual world. Uncomplicated contrasts of form, colour, depth and movement allow objects to 'pop' out of an array (see Figure 5.12). These are of course just the features which are coded by cells in the early cortical maps: their activity seems likely to incorporate the rules which enable us to pick out figure from ground.

Bela Julesz has provided the most magical illustrations of these processes. You will some time have seen 'stereograms', which were once a popular Victorian after-dinner diversion. A scene is photographed from two slightly different points, mimicking the difference in position of the two eyes. If the two resulting images are then separately presented to each eye, using a 'stereoscope', the scene appears in depth. The effect is strong, but hardly astonishing. Julesz discovered that the visual system is able to use stereopsis to compute form *without any other clues at all.*[17] His 'random dot stereograms' contain no recognisable detail whatever until the two images are viewed separately, one with each eye. On doing so, delicate three-dimensional shapes rise up from the page, often after a delay of many seconds. They *are* astonishing, and provide the most vivid demonstration I have encountered of the creative computation that occurs without our noticing every time we open our eyes.

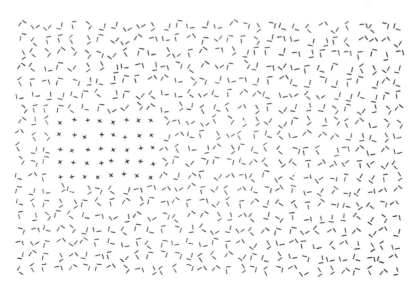

Figure 5.12 Preattentive and effortful visual search The square of crosses 'pops out' of this figure; finding the square of 'T's among the 'L's requires a painstaking search.

Binding

When a texture – like the 'x's in Figure 5.12 – 'pops' out at you from a scene, its distinctness must be signalled in some way by the brain. A related need is created by the existence of multiple maps in the visual cortex, serving specialised functions: the coherent perception of an object must somehow be conjured from activity scattered widely throughout the brain. Imagine yourself watching a bee buzz by: how do the form, colours, depth and motion of the bee cohere if they are analysed separately?

This is known as the 'binding problem'.[18] I hope the buzzing bee illustrates the difficulty it poses in understanding vision, but the problem is, in fact, of very wide relevance to brain function. Let's pause for a moment to consider why this is so.

If the brain mediates our experience and controls our behaviour – as the evidence I am marshalling for you suggests – it must in some way *represent* our perceptions and actions. What kind of representation does the brain employ when you recognise your grandma?

It's theoretically possible that the sight of your grandma is ultimately signalled by the activation of a single crucial neuron, a 'grandmother cell'. But it seems highly unlikely. A cell is a vulnerable element in the huge neuronal network of the brain: it would surely be unwise to entrust your grandma to such a fragile vessel. Moreover, a single cell would of course be unable to represent all the features of her current state, like her position in space and direction of movement.

The alternative is that networks, 'assemblies' or ensembles of neurons cooperate to represent items and actions. These networks may be simple or complex, sparse or rich, local or widely distributed, but it is of the essence that their constituent neurons can change allegiance, contributing sometimes to one, sometimes to another representation. This creates a 'binding problem': how do the members of each assembly, at any one time, know that they belong together?

The solution is uncertain, but two observations help to make the problem look a little less mysterious. Like the binding problem itself, they have a wide application, but let's take a look at them in the context of vision. First, we have seen that the various visual areas, typical of brain regions with related functions, are richly interconnected. These interconnections may allow the various streams of visual data arising from a single object like our passing bee to keep in touch, as they make their way through the cortex.

The second observation has given rise to huge interest recently. It might be possible to harness activity in disparate areas by ensuring its synchrony across them. Perhaps the bee's black and yellow, its rounded contours and determined motion are bound together in the brain because the signals coding them keep time with one another – a musical solution to a spatial problem. There is now some evidence that this occurs: within a single visual area cells coding a continuous stimulus, like a long sloping line, discharge in synchrony; cells in different areas coding aspects of a common stimulus, such as its form and movement, also resonate together.[19] Showing that the neuronal activity which represents a single item is synchronised in different parts of the brain is technically tricky, and the evidence that this is a key mode of representation remains quite thin. Nevertheless, the idea that the timing of neural discharge, as well as its rate and location, conveys information is exciting and may prove to be of fundamental importance. The frequency of neural discharge implicated in this process, around 40/second, may strike a chord with you: we have encountered it before, as the 'coherent frequency' of the waking brain.

Constancy

Separating objects one from another is a first prerequisite for recognising them. But consider this problem. Whenever you see a familiar item, for example your coffee cup, it casts a slightly different image in the eye. Close up, on a crowded shelf its image will be much larger than right across the room, where you left it stranded on the floor. The aerial view as you search the draining board is very different to its aspect when half-upturned by the toddler. In the grey light of a winter's morning its hue is murkier than under the summer sun. Recognising an object requires the visual system to detect the 'constancy' of its properties despite all these transformations of size and shape and colour. This is an immensely challenging computational task, but indispensable if vision is to be a source of knowledge about our surroundings.

The neural mechanisms achieving constancy are only partly understood, but like figure–ground segmentation and feature binding, constancy may well emerge from the activity of the cortical visual maps. Colour perception provides a helpful illustration.

We are very good at perceiving the 'true' colour of an object despite significant changes in the wavelengths of the illuminating light. Experiments first devised by Edwin Land, the American visual scientist and inventor, showed that this ability depends upon a comparison between the light reflected by objects of one colour and the light reflected by objects of other colours elsewhere in the visual field.[20] Indeed, if we are only allowed to see a single item of uniform hue its perceived colour depends upon the colour of the illuminating light. This implies, remarkably, that our normal perception of an object's colour involves a comparison extending over an area well beyond the object itself.

This comparison is unlikely to occur in the primary visual cortex, where the mapping of the retina is precise and interactions between different parts of the visual field are limited. As one would expect, the colour cells in VI are sensitive only to local colour contrast and cannot explain constancy. Downstream, though, in area V4, where mapping is less precise and colour the main concern, neuronal responses correspond much more closely to the true colours of objects, to colour *as it is perceived*. It is likely that the 'comparison of comparisons' which underlies normal colour perception occurs in this region of the brain.

What about the mechanisms allowing us to classify our coffee cup – among other objects – as such despite the random play of light and perspective? We don't yet fully understand this remarkable ability, but it seems a fair bet that areas at the termini of the 'ventral' visual pathway, in the temporal lobes, are responsible for computations of this kind (see Figure 5.13).

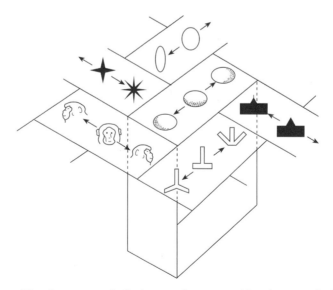

Figure 5.13 Visual responses in the temporal neocortex Visual neurons in the temporal lobes are excited by much more complex stimuli than the edges required by neurons in area V1, over a much wider region of the visual field. This figure shows the kinds of stimuli which obtain maximal responses, and indicates the shifts in preference seen as the experimenter explores the preferences of adjacent cells.

Cells here have large receptive fields, which usually include the point of focus. They respond best to moderately complex features, such as a diamond, sometimes in combination with a colour or a texture. The features preferred vary somewhat within and more markedly between adjacent cortical columns. The underlying goal of these complex responses may well be the accurate classification of objects despite the confusing accidents of appearance.

The analysis, integration and classification of the data pouring down the optic nerve are of course not ends in themselves. They are always directed towards recognition and action.

Recognition

> In the night, imagining some fear,
> How easy is a bush supposed a bear!
>> William Shakespeare, *A Midsummer Night's Dream*, V.i

> She likened the hills to ramparts, to the breasts of doves, and the flanks of kine. She compared the flowers to enamel and the turf to Turkey rugs worn thin. . . . Everything, in fact, was something else.
>> Virginia Woolf, *Orlando*[21]

Recognition is usually so effortless that we take it for granted. Once in a while a visual mistake startles us from our complacency: a tree trunk on an evening walk looms up like a dark attacker, a twist of black cotton on the floor announces itself as SPIDER. In these examples, like Shakespeare's, eye and brain run ahead of the evidence, making the most of inadequate information – and, unusually, get the answer wrong.

A little reflection reveals that such processes are not the exception but the rule. Our knowledge of the world pervades perception: we are always seeking after meaning. Try *not* deciphering a road sign, or erasing the face of the man in the moon. What we see resonates in the memory of what we have seen; new experience always percolates through old, leaving a hint of its flavour as it passes. We live, in this sense, in a 'remembered present'. Poets have always recognised this elusive characteristic of our experience.

> Twice or thrice had I loved thee,
> Before I knew thy face or name . . .

wrote John Donne 400 years ago.[22]

What is the basis of visual recognition in the brain? It is clearly a progressive process, with a number of stages. We have already encountered most of these: the analysis of the simple features of the visual scene, the segmentation of forms and the computation of 'constancy'. But if we are to recognise what we are looking at, our neural representations must, at some stage, gain access to our knowledge of the world.[23]

In a sense the entire visual system incorporates such knowledge. Over hundreds of millions of years it has evolved to enable us to perceive and act on our surroundings: the genetically specified structure of the visual system is the product of countless ancient encounters with the environment – and reflects its properties. The visual system is shaped by learning in another sense too: as we shall see in the following chapter, its development after birth is powerfully conditioned by visual experience in infancy and childhood. But there is now good evidence that the cumulative database of knowledge we personally acquire through life, our semantic memory, has a 'local habitation' in the brain.

Think, for a moment, about the vast amount of background information which you have at your disposal as you survey the world. For example, you can name the objects that surround you, perhaps in more than one language. This presupposes a network of concepts which you began to acquire some time before you first spoke. It's likely, for example, that you are sitting on a *chair*: it may be of a hard, unyielding, continental or a squashy, British variety; wooden or plastic, wicker or cane. Making this classification is no effort: your brain must somewhere be storing an extensive accumulated experience of seats. If pressed, you could go on to explain that chairs belong to the broad church of *furniture*, and that articles of furniture themselves are *human artefacts* designed to increase the ease and comfort of life. Man-made objects, like living ones, belong to a category of *physical objects* of which you have certain more or less confident expectations, such as their continuing existence when you leave them on their own.

This is a tiny part of the great background of knowledge we tap into when we recognise things, a dense pyramid of concepts allied to the rich resources of language. There are good reasons to suppose that the temporal lobes, the destination of the ventral visual stream, are home to this stock of knowledge. Moreover, in the last 15 years evidence has begun to accumulate for the anatomical separation of different kinds of knowledge within the semantic store. Thus knowledge of classes of living things, of tools and of people known to us as individuals may have substantially separate representations in the brain.[24]

Imagination

Recognition is not the only visual process relying on stored knowledge. We also summon up items from the store when we imagine things. Think about your kitchen. Where is the sink? How is it placed in relation to the stove? What colour is the wall above the stove? Where would you look for a pot of jam? Could you fit a table beside the fridge? Most of us answer such questions by visualising the room and our movements around it. This summons up a picture, usually less vivid than the real thing, but 'visual' nonetheless.[25]

Celebrated experiments by Roger Shepard from Stanford University supported the idea that when we are imagining something we interact with the image much as we would with the original.[26] He asked his subjects to visualise complex shapes made up from cubes, and to rotate them in their 'mind's eye'. He found that a small rotation was performed more quickly than a longer one, suggesting that the mental image was rotated at a measurable speed.

More recent experiments have examined the electrical and metabolic activity of the brain during tasks requiring image formation. Work by the doyen of psychological studies of imagery, Stephen Kosslyn of Harvard University, has shown that summoning up a visual image activates the visual cortex.[27] Kosslyn, for example, has recently reported that a small image, formed in response to the name of an object, is associated with activity in the area of V1 serving central vision, whereas a large image activates more peripheral parts of the visual representation. Nancy Kanwisher, from Boston, has identified and investigated two visual areas well 'downstream' from area V1: one, in the fusiform gyrus, is specifically activated by images of faces; the other, in the parahippocampal gyrus, is specifically activated by images of places: if subjects are asked to summon up alternate images of faces and places, brain activity rises and falls alternately in these two areas.[28]

How can we summon up such 'imaginary' activity in the brain? As we have seen, visual areas downstream always project back to the source of their input. The back-projection is often as substantial as the forward one. Imagination may exploit this two-way traffic. To return to our example, when you were imagining your kitchen you activated a memory, probably stored in the temporal lobe. This, in turn, excited a cascade of areas in your visual cortex, giving rise to a faint but nonetheless visual experience. If these ideas are correct, imagination is akin to recognition in reverse. In the next chapter we shall encounter evidence that hallucinations – imaginings which we take to be real – have a similar explanation.

The roving eye

While you read your eyes are scanning to and fro across the page, allowing the sensitive foveae of the retina to consume the text. For a moment, interrupt the movement as you read, look dead ahead, keep still . . . . What happens? You could probably make out just a handful of words over two or three lines of the page. Reading depends on precise and rapid movements of our eyes. Of course, you knew this, but it is not quite so obvious that most of the uses we have for vision are just as dependent on our roving gaze.

An image held completely stationary upon the retina fades rapidly from sight. This is not an experiment you can perform in your armchair: it can only be achieved with some technical help, for instance by mounting the image on a contact lens, as our eyes' healthy 'microtremor' normally ensures that there is always some movement of the image. But it illustrates that movement is a presupposition of sight.

Keeping our eyes as still as we reasonably can reveals how little we take in at a glance: too little, as you found, to finish a sentence. The area seen by the retina with high resolution is surprisingly small, only the size of a thumbnail at arm's length. We gain knowledge of our visual surroundings without any conscious effort, but this ease is deceptive: inspecting a view, admiring a painting or a pretty face all involve a process of active exploration, of gradual construction, dependent on delicate muscular control. Indeed, mapping the movements of eyes as we look at our surroundings generates a recognisable image of their crucial features (see Figure 5.14).

Our eye movements are the result of the coordinated contractions of 12 muscles, six on each side, which anchor the globe of the eye to the surrounding bone of the orbit. Some of these movements are reflex compensations for movements of head, body or surroundings: the 'oculocephalic' reflex for example enables you to maintain a steady gaze on an object of interest as you turn your head (try it and see); the 'optokinetic' reflex allows you to inspect a view as you or your surroundings move (best observed in fellow passengers on trains). Other movements are voluntary, allowing us to pursue a moving target, like a tennis ball, or to shift our gaze between targets, much as we look between faces while we talk over a table: these are known as 'pursuit' and 'saccadic' eye movements respectively.

All these movements are rapid, accurate and exactly equivalent in the two eyes. The muscles involved are subject to the most precise control of any in the body. The neural pathways concerned are intricate but now quite well

 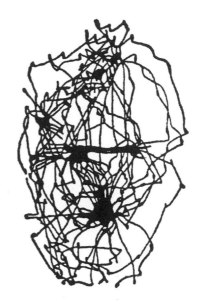

Figure 5.14 Eye movements during visual inspection Vision involves a continual exploration and questioning of appearances. The eyes repeatedly travel to the most informative or appealing parts of a figure, tracing out an image of the image, as in this example from Luria's work.

understood. I won't burden you with their detail, but want to underline three aspects of the relationship between movement and sight which are close to our main theme.

The first should be evident already. Sight is an activity. Even the momentary presentation of an item, preceded and followed by darkness, excites a cascade of activity from retina to brain. Under more normal circumstances, when we have time to look around, sight involves a constant interplay of sensation and movement. Each impression raises questions for the eyes, which are answered by their next glance. We overestimate the information we can harvest at an instant: to perceive is to explore, and to explore is both to sense and to move.

The second aspect relates to the goal of vision. David Milner, a British psychologist, and his Canadian colleague Mel Goodale, have argued in a series of papers, and a splendid book,[29] that the science of vision has substantially missed the point: vision does not exist primarily to create an image of the world, but to guide action. They accept that vision does, in fact, create such an image, enabling us to glean information that may be of use when we choose how to act in the future. But they propose that much of the activity excited by sight in the dorsal stream is concerned with the unconscious control of movement from moment to moment. We shall take a closer look at their views in Chapter 8. Given that vision must have evolved in the service of behaviour, the broad thrust of their argument is powerful: 'The great end of life is not knowledge but action'.[30]

Finally, if movement is both the partner of sensation and its eventual goal, we should expect to find areas of the brain which allow a close dialogue between them, where, for instance, sight is translated into action. There are several such areas, and they are an absorbing focus of current research. If they have been relatively neglected in the past, part of the explanation is that they can only be studied in waking, moving animals: the classical experiments on the cortical visual areas were performed under anaesthesia.

Some cells in the posterior parietal region, for example, the eventual destination of the dorsal visual pathway, respond both to the appearance of an object and to the movement required to grasp it: one such cell was excited by the look of a small toggle, requiring a finger–thumb precision grip, but also by fashioning the grip.[31] This cell responded maximally to the *combination* of a view of the object and its manipulation. Another intriguing group of cells, christened 'mirror neurons', has been described recently in the monkey brain by Giacomo Rizzolatti, the Italian physiologist, and his collaborators in Parma.[32] A mirror neuron is selectively excited both by the *performance* of a particular action and by the *sight* of another monkey performing the same action. Such a cell might, for instance, be involved in the recognition of a gesture, like a wave. Are such cells 'sensory' or 'motor'? This is a teasing question: whatever our answer, both of these groups contribute tiny links to the great neuronal chains which are constantly transforming sensory signals into motor commands.

Paying attention: did you see the gorilla?

> My experience is what I agree to attend to.
> William James, *The Principles of Psychology*[33]

> . . . hearing the grass grow and the squirrel's heart beat . . . we should die of that roar which lies on the other side of silence.
> George Eliot, *Middlemarch*[34]

As you read, I doubt that you are aware of the pressure of your shirt on your shoulder, or of the shoe enclosing your foot: they are perceptible, but not perceived. Much more sensation is available to us than we can focus on; attention, by its nature, is selective. Understanding attention would be a valuable start in understanding consciousness, for attention is the sentry at its gate. There has been plenty of progress in this direction in recent years. It is important, as a preliminary, to be clear what we mean by the term.

In all its forms, attention depends on some degree of vigilance or alertness, the subject of Chapters 3 and 4. Assuming we are sufficiently alert, we can summon up several varieties of attention. 'Preparatory attention' involves lying in wait for an expected event, as we might await a ring on the bell in the seconds after we hear a car draw up outside. Once our interest is engaged, we can select from the range of targets presented to a single sense, picking out the sound of a particular instrument in an orchestral piece – or switch our focus between the senses, from a conversation to a familiar face. This is 'selective attention'. Getting things done, like writing or reading this paragraph, requires a third type – 'sustained' or 'maintained attention'. *Selection* is, in fact, at the heart of all three brands of attention: in the case of preparatory attention it is allied to an expectation; in the case of sustained attention it is stiffened by a resolve.

We can choose to attend to our thoughts as well as our surroundings, and all these brands of attention may be 'overt' or 'covert'. When you look up from your book to answer a question you overtly change the focus of your interest. But you can achieve a similar result without moving a muscle – if you lose yourself in a daydream while you gaze at the open page.

By directing our attention we choose what we shall experience. What do we know of the neural basis of this elusive but crucial ability? It is helpful to distinguish its neural expression, mechanisms and control, before considering its goals.[35]

Attention boosts the salience of its target. The salience of a neural representation must be related to the activity of the cells subserving it. So a simple theory might predict that attention will increase the relative discharge rate of neurons coding for its target. Remarkably, this seems to be the case.

To understand the work which has led to this conclusion it's helpful to imagine yourself into the place of one of the 'experimental' monkeys from whom we have learned so much about attention. You are seated in front of a screen, which has a central 'fixation' point. You have to gaze at this *throughout*. The principle of the experiments that follow is simple: a 'cue' will indicate what you should attend and respond to. It might, for instance, be a spatial cue, indicating *where* to direct your attention (covertly, as you are not to move your eyes). When a stimulus appears in the cued location, you respond by pushing a button. In such experiments, monkeys and humans detect stimuli more rapidly, and at lower intensities, in cued locations than in unattended regions, demonstrating that attention *works*. What is its accompaniment in the brain?

Recording from the brains of waking monkeys while they perform tasks like these reveals that attention to a given location in visual space enhances the activity of neurons which inspect it, in visual areas beyond the striate cortex; attending to a colour modulates the responses of colour-selective cells in area V4; attending to a given direction of movement influences the activity of movement-selective cells in V5.[36]

Nancy Kanwisher has shown a similar effect of attention on activity in the 'face' and 'place' areas we encountered earlier. If one looks steadily at the centre of a slide which has faces to left and to right, places above and below, activity in these two brain areas is markedly modulated by attention: face area activity increases if one attends to the details of the faces, place areas activity if one concentrates on the places.[37]

These findings suggest that the expression of attention is indeed an enhancement of relevant neuronal responses, and that it begins to make itself felt quite early in the visual stream. What mechanisms allow us to allocate visual attention?

The idea that the brain contains a 'system' which regulates attention, akin to the networks controlling sensation and movement, has been championed by scientists including Marcel Mesulam, a distinguished American neurologist, and the psychologist Michael Posner.[38] On the basis of animal experiments, work with brain-injured humans and PET studies (see p. 372, n. 24), Posner has suggested that three interlinked areas govern our ability to transfer covert visual attention. In his elegant scheme the posterior parietal lobe is required to *disengage* attention from its current location; the superior colliculus, a centre in the midbrain which contributes to the control of our eye movements, *moves* attention from one site to another; finally, the pulvinar, a thalamic nucleus which interconnects a variety of visual areas, allows us to *engage* attention at the new site. We shall encounter these ideas again in the next chapter when we examine some pathologies of visual attention.

These mechanisms govern the transfer of attention around a visual scene to areas which deserve a closer look. Decisions about whether we should be attending to our visual surroundings *at all* – rather than to the voice in the receiver or the scents of spring – call for other strategies.

We attend, on the whole, to things that matter to us. We might expect the brain regions with 'executive' charge of attention to take account of what's happening both in sensory cortices and in areas which mediate motivation, especially the limbic system. One could also make an educated guess that they will lie in the frontal lobes, which, broadly speaking, regulate thought and behaviour. An area fitting these specifications has been identified by Posner and others as a nodal point in the control of attention. The anterior cingulate gyrus, the cortical extension of the limbic system, is activated by tasks which demand focused attention. Bilateral injuries to this area are one of the causes of 'akinetic mutism': in this state of 'will-lessness', the eyes follow eye-catching objects but, despite the appearance of awareness, the 'promise of speech' goes unfulfilled.[39]

These are the neural systems which mediate attention. What difference does it make? What are its goals? We have seen that attending to a task increases speed and sensitivity. More generally, attention enhances judgement. Indeed there are many tasks which can only be performed when we pay attention. We read a road sign saying STOP at an effortless glance if we are looking at all: but seeking out the 'T's in Figure 5.12, or indeed reading a book, requires deliberate attention. Attention allows us to perform effortful, 'serial' processes, like deciphering a paragraph, as opposed to the automatic, parallel processes which decode a road sign.

Recent work in the psychology of vision has illustrated the surprising extent of our 'blindness' to change occurring outside the focus of attention. Kevin O'Regan and others have shown that provided the *moment* of change is masked in some way, most viewers are extraordinarily insensitive to large changes in a visual scene. Major alterations to the page you are now reading would go unnoticed if they were timed to coincide with your blinks or eye movements; the movement of masses of mountain in a seaside view is all but invisible if the instant of change is disguised by a momentary flash.[40] Experiments by Erian Mack and Irvin Rock show that visual events which occur at the periphery of our attention, even eye-catching ones, are usually missed.[41] Kevin O'Regan introduced me to a wonderful video demonstration of this phenomenon (if you want to view this yourself, I suggest you do so, via the web, before reading the remainder of this paragraph).[42] Kevin invited the viewers of this unusual ball game, played between a team dressed in white and one dressed in black, to count the number of times members of the white team exchanged the ball. It was about 12, as I recall. At the close Kevin asked us who had seen the gorilla. Like almost everyone else in the audience, I had failed completely to spot the man in a gorilla suit who made a leisurely entrance from the right, walked into the midst of the baseball game, drummed his chest, and made his exit to the left.

The focus of attention is much narrower than one might think. It brings us to the very threshold of consciousness.

The beholder's share

What is felt is always action in an organism.

Suzanne Langer[43]

All seeing is 'seeing as'.

John Searle[44]

Nature imitates art.[45]

We have by now touched on all the processes which are vital for vision: the detection of light, signalled by a change in the behaviour of rods and cones, and subsequently of neurons; the systematic and parallel analysis of these signals in numerous areas of cortex containing maps of visual space; a classification of the results of this analysis in a form which permits recognition; its interpretation in terms of past experience; active and attentive exploration of our visual surroundings, demanding exquisitely accurate movements of our eyes.

Other modes of sensation – touch and hearing, for instance – embody similar key features. Physical stimuli, a deformation of the skin or a perturbation in the air, are detected by specialised receptors, which signal their occurrence in the electrochemical language of the nervous system. The resulting neural activity is analysed and classified in terms which allow us to gain knowledge of the world. It is related to our past experience, and contributes to it, conditioning future perception. These active processes, consuming time and energy, are part and parcel of an attentive exploration of the world. The work of living tissue, they give rise to a living creation.

Does this story go any distance towards explaining our delight in the more widely celebrated feat of artistic creation? Following the lead of Ernst

Gombrich, the great theorist and historian of art, I believe that the science of vision does help to explain how illusion comes to be possible and pleasing.[46]

Two general principles of perception are especially relevant. The first is the war cry of this chapter: that sight is an activity, always reaching after meaning. Eye and brain keep busy making sense of our surroundings, drawing on the inherited wisdom embodied in our visual system and on the expectations we accumulate over a lifetime. They do so by seeking and interpreting significant detail.

Artists deal, precisely, in significant detail. To evoke the visual world which eye and brain reveal, artists look for artificial keys to turn the locks of recognition. They do so by exploring the workings of vision, using trial and error to pick out the elements which guide our search for meaning. Cartoonists show how little detail is needed to capture mood and expression. Their pen and ink exploit our visual fascination with the sparse edges and orientations which define a face or a human form. Like artists from Leonardo to Hockney who have delighted in economy of line, cartoonists exploit and celebrate the unobvious act of creation we perform when we open our eyes (see Figures 5.15(a) and (b)).

The second general principle, related to the first, is that perception is always shaped by our past. The world is not 'given' to us as a stream of uninterpreted colour and unreconstructed line: instead, when we look around, we see a world we recognise, which we have learned to 'read'. This has an interesting implication. If the new is always informed by the old, 'what we see' cannot be specified purely in terms of raw physical stimuli. Perception is always metaphorical: everything, in fact, is 'something else'.

Like perception, art is metaphorical from start to finish. The choice of medium and technique, the development of style, the selection of detail and the patterning of the work are all choices of metaphor. The realisation that vision itself is far from a literal, photographic rendering of the world helps to explain how the artificial metaphors of art can be so satisfying, evoking the artist's response to his surroundings, and in the process teaching us *to see*. 'Nature imitates art' because art can educate perception. To mint a metaphor of our own, art is vision become conscious of itself, a quintessentially human pursuit.

Figure 5.15 (a) Lear's owl 'The owl and the pussy cat went to sea/In a beautiful pea-green boat . . . The owl looked up to the stars above/And sang to a small guitar . . .'. Lear's owl is drawn with expressive economy.

Invisible destinations

I have deliberately concentrated in this chapter on the pathways and processes within the visual system which promise an explanation of the conscious experience of sight. But information from the retina follows several routes besides the royal road through the LGN to the visual cortex. These pathways have their own work to do, but by and large they do not yield conscious perception. This creates an intriguing prospect: understanding the differences between activity in these 'invisible' destinations and in the cortical visual areas might help to define the neurology of visual consciousness.

Figure 5.16 shows the complicated reality of the projections from the retina into the brain. The larger projections are indicated with heavier arrows. We have so far explored the top two streams, from retina to LGN, area VI and the higher visual areas. I would like to introduce you briefly to

Figure 5.15 (b) Rembrandt's *Young Woman Sleeping* Rembrandt's lovely 'young woman sleeping' is executed with 'a sparse, fluid elegance reminiscent of eastern calligraphy'.

some of the other way-stations for visual signals, which illustrate the variety of unconscious processes occurring in tandem with those which lead – somehow – to consciousness.

Axons run directly from the retina to the pretectal nucleus of the mid-brain, next door to the superior colliculus or 'tectum' (see below). Here they influence cells which control the diameter of the pupil, contracting it in bright light, dilating it in dim. This process continues in patients in whom cortical injuries have abolished all perception of light. The 'light reflex' is a typical example of a neural process which gives rise to adaptive 'behaviour' of a kind, but which neither excites nor requires conscious perception.

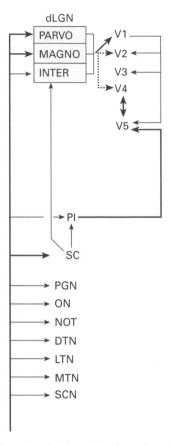

Figure 5.16 Retinal projections Visual information from the retina flows to the lateral geniculate nucleus and on to area V1 – but also to a host of other destinations. Dotted lines represent relatively sparse projections. Most of the interconnections between the cortical visual areas beyond V2 are not shown in this figure. Key: SCN = suprachiasmatic nucleus; MTN, LTN, DTN = medial, lateral, dorsal terminal accessor nuclei respectively; NOT = nucleus of optic tract; ON = olivary nucleus; PGN = pregeniculate nucleus; SC = superior colliculus; PI = inferior pulvinar.

We have already encountered a second destination. The suprachiasmatic nucleus of the hypothalamus, a pacemaker for a variety of circadian rhythms, receives a direct projection: this entrains circadian activity to the diurnal cycle of darkness and light. As we saw in the last chapter, when this input is lost, as it may be in the blind, the body's intrinsic circadian rhythms persist, but break free of the solar cycle to which most of us beat time.

A third destination receives a more substantial input from the retina. The superior colliculi lie at the top of the midbrain, where they give rise to a pair of small hills ('colliculi' in Latin). The colliculi contain three sensory maps, of visual, auditory and tactile space, as well as a 'motor map', which helps to control our eye movements. The sensory maps, layered one above another, are all three in register, allowing the rapid coordination of eye movements towards salient events – from the appearance of a face to a call or a touch. This system probably lies behind the familiar but rather uncanny experience of turning one's eyes unthinkingly to find them meet another's gaze.

In addition to its retinal connections, the superior colliculus both receives input from the cortical visual areas and projects to them, by way of the pulvinar nucleus in the thalamus. We met both these structures in the context of attention: the superior colliculus shifting, the pulvinar engaging our visual interest. In the next chapter we shall see that the parallel route to the higher visual areas through these nuclei, bypassing area V1, may provide an explanation for some strange dissociations between awareness and behaviour. All these examples remind us that although vision is a pre-eminently conscious sense we cannot assume that every one of the brain's 'visual centres' contributes to the conscious experience of sight.

Before ending this anatomical interlude, we should pause to consider what becomes of the signals travelling through the mainstream of the visual system once they leave it altogether. Like so many of the questions we are asking of the brain, this one has alternative answers: one, drawing on all that we know of the intricate truth, looks desperately complex, while the other is an informative simplification. I shall keep things simple.

We have concentrated most of our attention on the 'ventral' visual pathway. By the time visual signals have reached the terminus of this pathway in the temporal lobe they have been processed up to or close to the point of recognition. Work in animal brains suggests that information flows on from the temporal visual areas in several directions, in particular to parts of the limbic system concerned with memory and emotional response, and to areas of the frontal lobes and basal ganglia which regulate behaviour. The dorsal pathway, running from the occipital to the parietal lobe, is more overtly concerned with the guidance of action than the ventral route – and as one might anticipate is linked most strongly with 'executive' centres in the frontal lobes. Finally, as if to resist any neat effort to attribute specific regions to systems in the brain, the dorsal and the ventral pathways are themselves extensively interlinked. Matters are likely to be even more complex in the human brain, not least because it supplies the neural basis for language.

Conclusion: image and action

We have travelled a long road in this chapter, from the physics of light to vision's self-discovery in art. Let's briefly review progress.

Light is a species of electromagnetic radiation, with properties both of an energy wave and a particle stream. Radiation from the sun contributed to the genesis of life on earth, creating chemical conditions which favoured the formation of nucleic acids, the agents of heredity. Later, light supplied the energy driving photosynthesis, the process by which carbon combines with water to produce carbohydrates, including sugar, the base of the food chain for the animal kingdom. The evolution of vision created a third role for light, when it became a source of knowledge of the world. Although eyes appear to have evolved in parallel in many lines of animal descent, an ancient common ancestry is evident from affinities between the genes and photopigments used by species as dissimilar as the human and the fly.

The arrival of light in the eye sets in train a series of events with which we are now quite familiar. The retina seeks out discontinuities of line and colour and relays the news to the brain, where each half of space is inspected by the opposite hemisphere. Here a number of cortical areas mapping visual space analyse orientation, colour, depth and motion. Analysis goes hand in hand with integration, allowing significant forms to be isolated, classified and recognised, by comparison with the stored record of experience. While areas in the temporal lobes elaborate our visual world, regions in the parietal lobe help to guide our actions. One type of action, the movement of our eyes, continually updates visual awareness, constructing more detailed knowledge over time than we could ever acquire at a glance. Finally, our ability to allocate attention allows us to search for what interests us. The image conjured up by this intricate activity is a marvellous biological achievement, greatly increasing the efficiency with which we act upon the world. But like consciousness itself, it is also a vulnerable achievement. It is time, now, to examine some of the ways it can fail, exchanging the light for darkness.

6

'I cannot see you Charley, I am blind': clear-sighted blindness and blindsight

'. . . touch me with your hand. For I cannot see you Charley, I am blind.'

Charles Dickens, *Bleak House*[1]

Introduction

'You see her eyes are open.'
'Ay, but their sense is shut.'

William Shakespeare, *Macbeth*, V.i[1]

The commonest causes of blindness reside in the eye. This might seem obvious – until one realises that the process of vision has only just begun when a focused image falls upon the retina. Disorders of the brain also give rise to many pathologies of sight.

One of these will be within the personal experience of about one reader in ten. Attacks of migraine are often ushered in by a zigzagging intrusion in the field of vision, known as the 'fortification spectrum' from its resemblance to a set of battlements. Vivid, scintillating, this unwelcome guest usually makes its way across a part of the visual field over a quarter of an hour, sometimes leaving in its wake a temporary patch of blindness, a 'scotoma': headache and nausea follow on. I am in the unlucky 10 per cent and had my first full-blown attack while I was reading some medical notes. It was thoroughly unnerving. The 'visual aura' of migraine is thought to result from a wave of excitation followed by a 'spreading depression' of electrical activity in the visual cortex.

The migraineur's temporary scotoma can be reproduced lastingly by a well-circumscribed injury of the brain. The effects of limited gunshot wounds provided evidence early in this century for the existence of a precise map of visual space in the primary visual cortex. Rarely such injuries can disrupt the more specialised functions of the visual areas downstream from V1: isolated impairments of colour vision, of the perception of movement and of the recognition of familiar faces are among the selective deficits which can result. These rare experiments of nature strengthen the evidence for the division of labour within the visual cortex which I described in the last chapter.

Studying these deficits promises to illuminate the neural basis of conscious sight. The discovery that vision of a most unusual kind, of which its possessor is *unaware*, can often be demonstrated within the 'blind' field of scotomata has also created an opportunity to delineate the neural processes that are crucial for visual consciousness. We shall take a close look at this curious ability, aptly named 'blindsight' by its discoverer.

Other surprising effects of damage to the visual cortices are of interest to us. Patients who are blind following such damage sometimes deny their predicament vehemently. It is as if the loss of their visual capacity has gone hand in hand with a loss of the capacity to appreciate the loss. Other patients retain their sight but so 'neglect' one half of the scene before them that they behave as if they were blind on the neglected side. Occasionally damage to the visual brain gives rise to an ebullient excess of visual sensation.

All these phenomena have been studied mainly in adults, whose visual systems developed normally through the long years of childhood – until misfortune struck. But before we turn to these unusual capacities and impairments, I will touch on the process of development itelf, and the cost to vision if it fails. The study of visual development has gone a long way towards explaining one of the main themes of the last chapter – that past experience works powerfully on the present.

The famished eye

Seeing is an art that must be learned: we cannot see at sight.

Sir William Herschel[2]

Most of us will have had some experience to persuade us that we can educate the eye. I had my own crash course in Africa, where I spent four wonderful months in a mission hospital close to the Kenyan–Ugandan border. Although I had African colleagues and patients at home, like many European travellers my first impression at the airport was of a milling sea of black faces. Within a few days my eye was in, and recognition of my new friends and acquaintances became as effortless as usual. As an almost solitary 'mzungu' in the Kenyan bush, I had plenty of practice. Some of my African neighbours, whose everyday exposure to white faces was limited to two red-cheeked doctors with bushy beards, had lasting difficulty in telling us apart.[3]

Clearly we need to learn *subtle* visual skills, like those we call on when we distinguish faces, but perhaps these are exceptional, the icing on the cake. It could be that our basic visual abilities are innate: surely we don't need to *learn to see*. As it turns out, we do, although the mix of 'nature' and 'nurture' in visual development is complex. Research over the last 30 years has revealed an intimate interdependence between the growth of the visual system, its electrical activity and visual experience. But long before this work was done, some moving accounts of the difficulties which can follow the restoration of sight after a lifetime of blindness hinted at a similar conclusion.

Molyneux's question

For as long as I can remember, I have been blind, and at home with my blindness.

B. Magee and M. Milligan[4]

'Now that I've felt it I can see.'

SB, quoted by Richard Gregory[5]

In a famous passsage in the *Essay Concerning Human Understanding*, written over three hundred years ago, the English philosopher John Locke outlined a question put to him by a friend, William Molyneux: 'Suppose a man born blind, and now adult, and taught by his touch to distinguish between a cube and a sphere of the same metal . . . . Suppose then the cube and the sphere placed on a table and the blind man made to see; query, whether by his sight, before he touched them, he could now distinguish and tell which is the globe, and which the cube?'[6]

Locke, like Molyneux, thought not, on the grounds that experience is required to correlate the feel and the look of objects. Over the centuries since Locke posed his question it has become possible to remove the cloudy lenses from eyes blinded by cataracts from birth. When this surgery has been performed in adulthood Molyneux' question has received an unequivocal answer. The blind man cannot distinguish globe from cube, but this is not just because vision must be related to touch: 'where vision was tested soon after the operation, patients could distinguish colour, but they had little idea of form or shape, no idea of distance, no idea of depth, and very little idea of solidity . . . . Their visual perception in itself was defective . . . . They could not in fact *see* like normal people'.[7]

The sight which greets such newly seeing eyes is a 'chaos of continually shifting, unstable evanescent appearances'.[8] The experience can be profoundly unsettling. Instead of enriching the recipient with a new and precious sense, the gift of vision late in life may be a poisoned chalice, making the newly sighted person feel a stranger in a world where he was at home.

Alberto Valvo has described a number of patients whose sight was restored after long periods of blindness.[9] Most of his subjects felt bewilderment in the early days: 'I had a feeling that I had begun a new life, but at certain times I became depressed and discouraged when I realised how difficult it was to understand the visual world; in fact all around me I see an ensemble of light and shadow, lines of different length, round and square things, generally like a mosaic of changeable sensations that astonish me, and whose meaning I do not understand. In the evening, I enjoy the darkness, which gives me a feeling of peace and rest . . . .' Of course, the bewilderment is sometimes mixed with wonder: 'Last evening on the balcony [my grandmother] told me to look up and I saw a white round thing; but I did not know what it was until my grandmother told me it was the moon. To me it seemed as near as someone standing near-by'.

The more fortunate patients gradually gain useful vision, although after a lifetime's adjustment to blindness sight may never become as natural or efficient as touch. The British psychologist, Richard Gregory, studied SB, a man whose sight was lost at 10 months and restored at the age of 52.[10] He seemed dejected on a trip to London shortly after his surgery. Because of his 'long-standing interest in tools and machinery', Gregory took him on a visit to the Science Museum. He was led across to a case containing a lathe:

He was unable to say anything about it except that he thought the nearest part was a handle . . . . We then asked a museum attendant (as previously arranged) for the case to be opened, and S.B. was allowed to touch the lathe. The result was startling . . . . He ran his hands eagerly over the lathe with his eyes tight shut. Then he stood back a little and opened his eyes, and said 'Now that I've felt it I can see'.

Another, more humdrum, observation confirms that it's vital we use our eyes early in life to make the most of sight. The eyes of children who squint look in different directions, and such children usually develop a preference for using one or other eye – for the very good reason that looking through both at once gives rise to double vision, a confusing and uncomfortable experience. Quite how a child 'suppresses' one of the two available images is mysterious, but the result is undoubted. The neglected eye becomes 'lazy' and gradually loses the acuity of its vision. Beyond the age of seven or so this loss is irretrievable: before that age the simple expedient of patching the good eye for a period each day, forcing the child to work with the neglected one, maintains its acuity for life. This adds to the evidence that if we are to see the world clearly we have to *use* our sight, and we have to use it young. But the 'lazy eye' has been blamed unfairly for a much more deep-seated change. The distortion of visual experience profoundly affects the growth of the visual brain.

The ripening of vision

The growth of the visual system and the maturation of its activity have been studied intensively since the 1960s.[11] It's clear that the basic groundplan of the visual system emerges during the development of the foetus without any need for visual experience. The generation of neurons, their migration to create the layers of the visual cortex (see Figure 6.1), the projection of axons to their targets and the broad organisation of cortical connections all proceed along predetermined lines in the dark of the womb in the months before birth.

This is not to say that the intrinsic activity of neurons, which begins soon after they appear, plays no part in these early events. Using a toxin from the puffer fish, tetrodotoxin, it's possible to silence the electrical activity of the optic nerve without damaging its axons. This, for example, prevents the normal layering of the visual input to the thalamus. Neural activity can thus be a factor in development well before our birth.

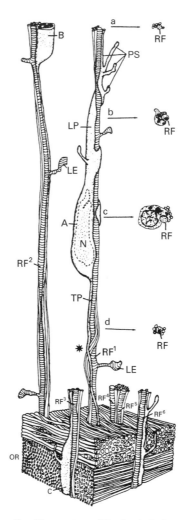

Figure 6.1 Neuronal migration The cortex of the brain is formed by migration of neurons from a 'germinal zone' close to the ventricles, deep in the brain, to the brain's surface. Their migration is guided by glial cells which extend radial fibres along their route. This figure shows three neurons, A, B and C, making their way to the cortical surface, guided by radial glia (RF). Neuron A is shown with its leading process (LP), pathfinding pseudopodia (PS) and trtainling process (TP). OR = optic radiation.

By the time of birth the human visual system has matured sufficiently to allow some quite impressive visual distinctions: within days a baby can imitate the facial movements of those around it, for example mouth opening or protrusion of the tongue.[12] But although the groundplan of vision has been drawn, its details are refined and its anatomy embellished over the following months. One simple fact is telling: at birth all the neurons of the visual brain are present, but only around 10 per cent of the synapses.[13] These points of contact between neurons are the gates through which information flows in the brain: they are shaped after birth under the pressure of experience.

Two celebrated series of experiments revealed the plasticity of the maturing visual system. You may remember that the two eyes feed separately into layer 4 of the primary visual cortex, creating alternating 'ocular dominance columns'. At birth the input from the two eyes is intermingled: the ocular dominance columns form later, under the influence of visual experience. But if one eye is deprived of vision early in life, for example by a patch, the columns excited by the sighted eye expand, while those which should be excited by the deprived eye shrink. This effect depends on two key factors: it occurs only when there is *competition* between a seeing and a deprived eye, and only when the pathway from the seeing eye *successfully excites* the visual cortex.

This is a good example of a process I outlined in Chapter 2, first envisaged by the Canadian psychologist Donald Hebb. 'Hebb's rule' states that connections between neurons which are active together are strengthened. If one eye is deprived of vision, only neurons 'driven' by the other will have a chance to activate their targets and strengthen their connections. In ways that remain poorly understood, the neurons of the visual cortex appear to 'reward' the axons which excite them and 'punish' those which fail to: successful axons flourish and expand their bushy crowns, while their disappointed competitors wilt and shrink away.

This effect can only be obtained during a limited 'critical period' which differs from species to species, a matter of months in kittens, but lasting years in man. During this sensitive time the results of depriving one eye can be reversed by patching the other and allowing the deprived eye an opportunity to see. Indeed alternate occlusion of the two eyes during the critical period has the effect of creating two populations of cells in the visual cortex, each driven exclusively by one or other eye. This preserves vision in both, but it also has its cost. Stereoscopic depth perception depends on a group of neurons which normally receive a balanced input from both eyes: the normal development of these cells, and hence the refinement of depth perception, are prevented by alternate occlusion of the two eyes.

The second series of experiments is in some ways more startling. We saw in the last chapter that the primary visual cortex contains columns of cells which 'represent' the orientations of lines in given regions of space. What would happen if a person's or an animal's visual experience were restricted to lines of a certain slant, all close to the vertical, say, or all oblique? This is not quite as odd a question as it sounds: people with severe 'astigmatism' are sometimes in just this situation, as the lenses of astigmatic eyes focus some orientations well but fail to focus others.

This issue has been examined systematically in animals, and the answer is clear. During a critical period, rather earlier than the critical period for ocular dominance columns, biased exposure to lines of a certain slant greatly increases the proportion of cortical cells selective for that slant, and reduces the proportion selective for other orientations (see Figure 6.2). Similarly, rearing animals in environments that move around them in a particular direction increases the numbers of cells which pick out movement in that direction (see Figure 6.3).

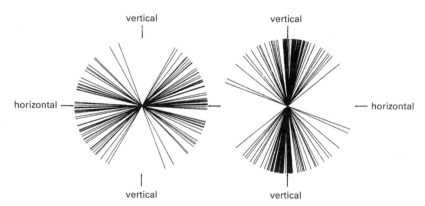

Figure 6.2 The effect of selective visual exposure to horizontal or vertical orientations Rearing an animal in surroundings which mainly expose its eyes to horizontal lines (left) biases the preferences of its orientation-selective cells to the horizontal: there is a dearth of cells with a preference for vertical orientations (the orientation of the lines in the diagram reflects the orientation preferences of individual cells in the visual cortex). The reverse experiment is depicted on the right.

Why should the visual cortex be able to adapt to its surroundings in this rather perverse fashion? The most widely accepted answer is that it would be difficult, and is unnecessary, to specify the strength of every last synapse of the visual system in the brain's genetic blueprint. A rough genetic sketch for sight seems to be sufficient. So long as the system is provided with a generous superfluity of potential interconnections, experience can be allowed to select the useful ones, 'fine tuning' our vision, and sculpting our visual system, as it does so.

normal
animals

rightward
reared

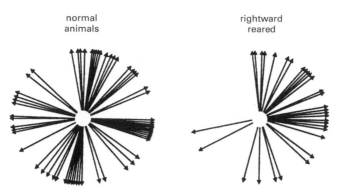

Figure 6.3 The effect of selective visual exposure to directions of movement If a
young animal is constantly surrounded by a pattern of dots moving in one direction,
in this case to the right, its movement-selective cells will tend to become selective for
rightward movement (in this case each arrow represents the directional preference of a
single cortical cell).

A more controversial but thought-provoking explanation is that it's wise
for us to be equipped to *see* what surrounds us. If our surroundings are
dominated by vertical edges which always move off to the right we would
do well to specialise in discriminating these. This may seem a rather con-
trived explanation for the plasticity of the primary visual cortex – which is
hardly likely to encounter such odd environments outside the laboratory –
but it prompts an interesting thought.

We all do, in fact, tend to become expert in 'seeing' – and distinguishing
– the objects that surround us, from faces to Ferraris, from hair styles to
varieties of grape. This is clearly because we learn about them, acquiring
expectations which make us more discerning than we would otherwise be.
Could the visual memory of the adult brain represent an extension into
maturity of the processes which give rise to plasticity in the child's? The
hypothesis that experience may continue to 'sculpt' the cerebral cortex,
long after the period of maximum plasticity is over, underlies much contemporary thinking about memory. It is a profound idea, suggesting that
we store information through synaptic change in the sensory regions in
which we also 'process' it. If it is correct, 'plasticity' and memory may share
a common fundamental explanation in 'Hebb's rule'.[14]

These experiments help to explain why deprivation of vision during its
sensitive period early in life has such disabling consequences. Sight is the
outcome of a process of growth which is guided at different times by an
inherited blueprint, intrinsic activity and visual experience. Alterations in

our experience alter the pattern of growth. If both eyes are deprived of vision they may be affected less grievously than a single deprived eye with a seeing partner, but a life in the dark is nonetheless very bad news for vision: capacities which normally mature without experience eventually decay, and those which require it never develop. The crucial importance of early experience during a sensitive period appears to be a general law of psychological development: it applies to the acquisition of language and of social skills as well as the maturation of the senses. We should no longer be at all surprised that we 'cannot see at sight'.

Novel sensations

'I had to die as a blind person to be reborn as a seeing person.'

A patient quoted by Valvo[15]

None of us would choose to lose a sense. But the loss or the absence of sight or hearing can perfectly well be survived. Indeed, there is often some gain to balance the loss, an intensification of the senses that remain, a heightened appreciation of touch and sound, of taste and of smell. Oliver Sacks gives a moving account of 'Virgil', a man blind since early childhood, who had once worked as a masseur, and could still describe his many clients with a wealth of 'tactile detail'.[16] And, of course, none of the senses has a monopoly of understanding: even the language of sight is to some degree accessible to the blind.

The blind philosopher Martin Milligan debated this point with a colleague, Bryan Magee, in a published exchange of letters, written shortly before his death.[17] I doubt that many sighted men or women could better Milligan's description of the connotations of the word 'darkness': '*difficulty in perception, the unknown and the incomprehensible, threat and danger, and also sometimes warmth, privacy and safety against intrusive perceptions by others*'.

Is there a neural basis for the acute perceptions of the blind? There is in fact growing evidence that regions of the brain which would normally dedicate themselves to vision can be activated by hearing and touch in the blind. A study published in *Nature* in 1996 by Norihiro Sadato and colleagues, for instance, used functional imaging to compare activity in the visual cortex of blind and sighted subjects whose task was to distinguish shapes by touch, and, in the case of the blind, to read Braille.[18] In the sighted the activity of the visual cortex *fell* while they explored the shapes, a predictable result, as attention to one sense tends to 'deactivate' others. In the blind, in contrast, activity in the visual cortex *rose*, most markedly when reading Braille. There are several possible explanations for this discovery, but taken in conjunction with other similar results it suggests that, in the brains of the blind, touch recruits networks which normally concern themselves with sight.

This could be the natural outcome of processes of competition and development akin to those we encountered in the last section. If a sighted eye can 'win' space in the cortex at the expense of a blind one, perhaps an active sense can conquer regions of the brain from an inactive one. There is every reason to think that this occurs.

An area in the frontal lobe of the cat's brain, the 'anterior ectosylvian', is specialised for locating the source of sounds in space.[19] The area is 'multimodal', containing representations of 'visual', 'auditory' and 'tactile' space. Cats who have lacked visual experience from birth are exceptionally good at localising sounds. Their anterior ectosylvian cortex (AEC) then contains greater than usual numbers of cells sensitive to the source of sound; the responses of these cells are unusually precise; most impressively of all, they are found in regions of the AEC where neurons normally have exclusively visual responses. In such animals the visual map all but disappears.

Changes of this general kind could give rise to the tactile activation of the visual cortex seen in Sadato's study. The visual areas are richly interconnected: if the cells in the AEC which normally serve vision, but which can be won over by auditory or tactile input, are connected indirectly with area VI, one can see that touch and sound might become able to excite it. The blind may 'look with their fingers' and 'see with their ears' in a more literal sense than ever seemed likely.

Blindness is an occasional human misfortune, though one which can be triumphantly endured. There are some species for which it has become a way of life. Between 10 and 30 million years ago the ancestors of the blind mole rat abandoned the earth's surface for a subterranean life. In their unlit world they have no use for sight: their eyes have regressed to the size of a pinhead, and are covered by skin and fur.[20] What happens to the visual brain in circumstances of such extreme visual deprivation?

The optic nerve which normally conveys signals from the retina back to the brain is greatly thinned in the mole rat. The lateral geniculate to which it projects is smaller than in the rat's sighted relatives, but it is still clearly present. Experiments performed by a group of German and Israeli researchers have shown that in this animal the input to the LGN, and to the occipital cortex, to which the LGN in turn sends signals, is *auditory*, not visual. In other words, the visual brain has been conquered by hearing, a sense on which the mole rat, scurrying down dark tunnels, extensively relies.

Some of the observations I have described in this section are controversial. Whether the blind are really more acute in their touch and hearing remains a vexed issue. If they are, it could be that their superiority simply reflects the attention they lavish on the senses which remain, and the practice which results. But the evidence for neural adaptation to the loss of a sense is steadily growing, and, if it occurs, it helps to explain why the restoration of sight late in life should be such a mixed blessing: not only will the visual system have lost its edge during a lifetime of blindness, but the other senses may have invaded the territory of sight.

Mindblindness: the agnosias

'At the club I saw someone strange staring at me, and asked the steward who it was. You'll laugh at me. I'd been looking at myself in a mirror'.[21]

An agnosia is literally a failure of 'gnosis', of knowledge. In neurology the term has a more specific use. The 'agnosias' are disorders of the later stages of sensation, in which the affected sense appears substantially intact but the perception or knowledge to which it gives rise is impaired. The man who asked the steward about his own reflection, for example, knew that *someone* was staring at him – he could 'see' – but somehow he couldn't make out his own face.

I shall use the term broadly, to embrace the whole family of rare conditions in which aspects of vision are selectively disturbed by damage to the brain. Some of these are oddly reminiscent of the misbehaviour of television sets: human vision, like our rather unreliable TV at home, is capable of sudden transitions from coloured to black and white mode, or of abrupt 180° inversions of the image. Other agnosias, like the selective inability to recognise faces, are more subtle than even my TV can achieve. But all these disorders drive home the message that vision is a complex process, distributed widely in the brain, whose facets can be individually impaired. Let's take a look first at a problem which can be easily imagined, but much less easily endured.

Apperceptive agnosia

Colour

'I AM ABSOLUTELY COLOR BLIND. . . . Tomato juice is black'.

Jonathan I, quoted by Oliver Sacks[22]

Colour is one of the great joys of life. I spend most of my time in the curiously colourless surroundings of a hospital: harsh lighting, plain walls and bland artificial hues tend to make a monotonous impression on the eye. By the end of a long day, the subtle gradations of hue in an evening sky or the purple tints of the hills are intensely welcome. There have been praiseworthy campaigns recently to bring paintings on to hospital corridors, in recognition of the serious (though not generally fatal) risk of visual starvation. I would hate to lose the rich refreshment of colour.

Very rarely, damage to the brain destroys the ability to see in colour, sparing the rest of vision.[23] This is rather extraordinary. Pause a moment before reading on, and imagine your surroundings unchanged in all respects but one: quite stripped of colour, changed into a world of greys.

Oliver Sacks' essay on 'Jonathan I', an accomplished abstract painter, describes how his life and his work were laid waste, and eventually transformed, by this outlandish occurrence. Everything, for many weeks, looked sickeningly different and wrong:

> Mr I could hardly bear the changed appearances of people ('like animated grey statues') any more than he could bear his own appearance in the mirror: he shunned social intercourse and found sexual intercourse impossible. He saw people's flesh, his own flesh, as an abhorrent grey: 'flesh-coloured' now appeared 'rat-coloured' to him. This was so even when he closed his eyes, for his vivid visual imagery was preserved but was now without colour as well . . . it was, he said, like living in a world 'molded in lead'.

As time went by, Mr I became able to work again, returning to subjects, like the human face, he had not painted for many years and depicting them in black and white (initial experiments in colour were a failure). He also began to sculpt. 'He seemed to be turning to all the visual modes that still remained to him – form, contour, movement, depth – and exploring them with heightened intensity'. His personal life changed as well: he began 'to relish the night':

> He would drive at random, to Boston or Baltimore, or to small towns and villages, arriving at dusk and then wandering about the streets for half

the night, occasionally talking to a fellow street walker, occasionally going into little diners: 'Everything in diners is different at night, at least if it has windows. The darkness comes into the place, and no amount of light can change it . . . . I love the night-time'.

What is the explanation for this strange disorder? We saw in the last chapter that the multiple visual areas in the occipital cortex allow different aspects of the visual scene to be analysed in parallel. One of the streams coursing through the cortex is especially concerned with colour and one visual area in particular, V4, is a focal point for colour perception. Although achromatopsia – Mr I's disorder – is exceptionally rare, the available evidence suggests that the damage which causes it is centred on the fusiform gyrus, the likely location of V4 in man.

Is that the end of the story? Not quite: there is, as so often in science, a twist in the tail. Some recent research shows that while the awareness of colour is lost after damage to V4, the brain can nonetheless make use of boundaries between different colours to perceive shape. In other words, the damage to V4 which explains 'achromatopsia' rather specifically impairs the *consciousness* of colour, without necessarily preventing the analysis of information about colour.[24] The intriguing idea that the brain may be able to exploit information which it cannot consciously appreciate will surface repeatedly in the next few pages.

Movement

> Movement may be recognised as a special visual perception.
>
> George Riddoch[25]

In 1983 a German neurologist reported a unique case.[26] LM had been admitted to hospital some years before, in coma. Tests had shown that one of the large veins which drains blood from the brain had been blocked by a clot of blood. She recovered well from this serious illness, with little worse than a mild problem with finding words – except for one other most unusual symptom:

> The visual disorder . . . was a loss of movement vision in all three dimensions. She had difficulty, for example, in pouring tea or coffee into a cup because the fluid appeared to be frozen, like a glacier . . . she could not stop pouring at the right time since she was unable to perceive the movement in the cup . . . . She could not cross the street because of her inability to

judge the speed of a car, but she could identify the car itself without diffi-culty. 'When I'm looking at the car first it seems far away. But then, when I want to cross the road, suddenly the car is very near'. She gradually learned to 'estimate' the distance of moving vehicles by means of the sound becoming louder.

Careful investigation of her vision revealed that it was normal in almost all respects: her performance on a reading chart, the extent of her visual fields and her detection of colours were all fine. But her ability to detect move-ment fell way below the performance of a control. When asked to describe her visual experience while watching a moving target she explained that she saw a sequence of still images, 'one light spot left or right, or up or down, and sometimes at successive positions in between'. This problem only affected vision: she was well able to judge the movement of an object touching her skin, or of a sound.

Injuries of the human brain are seldom neat and tidy, and LM is no exception to this rule. Scans revealed quite extensive damage to the back of the brain around the primary visual cortex – although not involving VI itself. We cannot, therefore, be absolutely sure of the locus of the damage which has robbed LM of the perception of motion. But it's probably rele-vant that the damaged regions include the human equivalent of V5, the 'motion area' of animal research, which abounds in cells responsive to movement.

Achromatopsia and 'akinetopsia' – the name given to LM's condition – provide a good example of a 'double dissociation': colour vision can be abol-ished while movement perception is spared – and vice versa. This suggests that their neural mechanisms are separate, and strongly supports the view that aspects of the visual scene are processed separately and in parallel in the brain.[27]

Colour and movement are vivid attributes of our visual surroundings: our ability to perceive them is a delight when we're relaxed, and often saves our fragile skins. But the most fundamental visual attribute of all is, surely, shape. Can one imagine an agnosia for form?

Form

In 1890 Heinrich Lissauer drew a distinction which has deeply influenced, and arguably misled, subsequent thinking about the agnosias.[28] He distin-guished varieties of agnosia in which *vision* is undeniably disturbed from those in which the problem appears to lie with the *recognition* of items which are clearly seen. He termed the first type of agnosia 'apperceptive', the second 'associative'. As our understanding of the creative complexities of vision has increased, the sharp dividing line between sensation and memory, which Lissauer assumed, has been partly effaced. But the distinction remains useful in practice, and the most fundamental of all these disorders is indeed agnosia for form, 'apperceptive agnosia' in its narrowest sense.

The visual experience of sufferers from form agnosia is very odd – although, in many respects, their sight may be normal. They may be able to see flashes of light, for instance, right across their visual field; colours, movement and depth are all perceived; the ability to resolve detail – for example by distinguishing a grating from a uniform background – may be almost as good as yours or mine: yet 'form agnosics' cannot make sense of shapes, confusing 'X' and 'O', a triangle and a square, a key and a safety pin.

One such patient 'identified a photograph of a white typewritten letter on a blue background as "a beach scene", pointing to the blue background as "the ocean", the stationery as "the beach" and the small typewriter prints as "people seen on the beach from an airplane"'. It is as if the world were seen through a distorting lens which blurs every shape out of all recognition while – impossibly – sparing the view of colour, movement and depth.

We have seen that the agnosias for colour and movement, achromatopsia and akinetopsia, can be plausibly linked to highly focused damage in cortical visual areas, V4 and V5 respectively. There is no comparable area specialised for form perception, and the cause of form agnosia is not, as a rule, a discrete brain injury. The majority of sufferers have been poisoned – not in the course of domestic vendettas, but by a deadly, invisible, odourless gas, carbon monoxide.

The chemistry of carbon monoxide explains its sinister effects. It tricks the protein which ordinarily conveys oxygen to our tissues – haemoglobin – into combining with it. Unlike oxygen, once carbon monoxide has attached itself to haemoglobin it won't let go. Unless the victim is rapidly rescued, or the poisoning mild, asphyxiation quickly ensues. Severe but non-fatal poisoning with carbon monoxide causes widespread but incomplete damage to the brain. It seems likely that such incomplete injury to the visual cortex prevents the integration of signals required to 'construct' the perception of form.

The story of form agnosia, like achromatopsia, has a fascinating recent postscript. Several observers had noticed that patients with form agnosia could sometimes get around more easily than might have been expected. David Milner and Mel Goodale may have discovered why.[29]

Their discoveries stem from work with 'DF', a young woman with a typical form agnosia, following carbon monoxide poisoning in a shower. She can identify colours, fine differences in texture and make simple judgements about objects' relationships in space. She can sometimes even make accurate guesses about an object's identity, using the clues of colour and texture. But despite all this she is unable to identify letters or numbers, distinguish simple shapes or even judge the orientation of a line. Remarkably, however, Milner and Goodale found that if DF is asked to post a letter through a slot or to pick up objects of various shapes, she does so quite normally, adjusting the movements of arm and hand to the requirements of the task just as you or I would. She both can and cannot see.

Milner and Goodale argue that the computational demands of recognition and of action are so different that we have evolved two partly independent visual systems: in DF the 'recognition system' is badly compromised, while the 'action system' is substantially intact. If they are right these two systems appear to differ in one crucial respect: the first is conscious while the second is not. Just as someone with achromatopsia may be able to see shapes which are defined by boundaries of colour, without seeing colour itself, so a sufferer from form agnosia can act effectively on shapes which can't be 'seen' at all.

Associative agnosia

Objects

A normal percept stripped of its meaning.

Hans Teuber[30]

If agnosia for form is the clearest example of an 'apperceptive' agnosia, agnosia for objects is the clearest example of the 'associative' type. The famous quotation from the work of the psychologist Hans Teuber captures the essence of the problem: the eyes can see but the mind is blind. Objects have lost their 'meaning', and can no longer be identified by sight. The *names* of objects, by contrast, retain their significance for the sufferer, and in classical object agnosia objects can still be recognised by way of touch and sound.

Oliver Sacks' 'Man Who Mistook his Wife for a Hat' suffered from object agnosia, and as usual Sacks' description offers a vivid insight into this strange predicament:[31]

I tried one final test. it was still a cold day, in early Spring, and I had thrown my coat and gloves on the sofa.

'What is this?' I asked, holding up a glove.

'A continuous surface,' he announced at last, 'infolded on itself. It appears to have' – he hesitated – 'five outpouchings, if this is the word.'

'Yes', I said cautiously. 'You have given me a description. Now tell me what it is.'

'A container of some sort?'

'Yes,' I said, 'and what would it contain?'

'It would contain its contents!' said Dr P with a laugh. 'There are many possibilities. It could be a change-purse, for example, for coins of five sizes. It could . . . .'

I interrupted the barmy flow. 'Does it not look familiar? Do you think it might contain, might fit, a part of your body?'

No light of recognition dawned on his face . . .

Later, by accident, he got it on, and exclaimed 'My God, it's a glove!'

Dr P exemplifies the key features of object agnosia: preserved general intelligence, the ability to recognise and name objects using touch, and apparently 'normal' vision coupled with an extraordinary failure to make sense of what is seen.

A recent careful review of world literature on agnosia has reopened an old question, casting doubt on Teuber's view.[32] Is object agnosia really a disorder of memory or could it be, after all, a disorder of vision? Are objects really normally seen but unrecognisable because they fail to trigger the appropriate records, or is their visual analysis itself somehow impaired? This is a subtle distinction: how could one decide between these two views?

On the one hand, if the disorder is primarily visual, one would predict that sufferers should fail on some visually demanding tasks which are not dependent on visual memory, such as resolving fragmented or obscured shapes. On the other hand, if the disorder primarily affects memory, such tasks should be well performed, despite the failure to associate what is seen with what is known. The teasing interface between perception and memory is a focus of active research at present, and the answer to my question is uncertain. In all likelihood, there are a variety of object agnosias, some primarily affecting visual analysis, others knowledge of objects, while yet others may defy the distinction between memory and perception. This distinction is growing less and less sharp: as we have seen, our experience shapes the visual system and some of our visual memories are probably incorporated into the machinery of sight.

Faces

Faces excite and delight us, attract and repel us. At the same time, they *inform* us. I can learn so much about you from a glance. Have we met? Where are you from? Are you happy or angry or sad? Are you interested in me? In a noisy room, I can read your lips. The human face is the clearest picture of the human soul – even if it sometimes lies. Given the feast of social signals on offer from the face, we should not be too surprised to find that our brains contain some specialised equipment for decoding them.

The existence of this equipment has been demonstrated directly over the past 15 years, but it could have been predicted from a rare but well-studied disorder, prosopagnosia. Sufferers, like the patient who embarrassed himself at his club, can *see*, but cannot recognise faces. This is not due simply to a failure to put names to faces: it reflects the much more fundamental inability to associate *people* with their faces. This embarrassing predicament apart, knowledge of friends and acquaintances is usually intact, and sufferers can still identify them in other ways, by the sound of a voice or the rhythm of a step.[33]

Distinguishing the countless faces we encounter in our daily lives is a challenging visual task. One might reasonably wonder whether prosopagnosia is really specific for faces, or just a problem with especially difficult visual judgements. Some sufferers do indeed have trouble with other fine visual discriminations – for example between types of plants, items of food or makes of car. But for others the defect appears to be highly specific: in one case 'the identification of relatives and close friends constituted an insurmountable problem if he could not rely upon their voices'. But when 'requested to identify his own electric razor, wallet, glasses and neckties when each of them was presented together with six to ten objects of the same category' or 'to identify his own handwriting from nine samples written by other persons . . . he performed unhesitatingly and correctly'.[34]

The discovery, in the early 1980s, that certain areas of the temporal cortex in monkeys contain numerous visual neurons selective for faces paved the way to an explanation for agnosia for facial identity. Work using functional imaging by Nancy Kanwisher, among others, has shown that there are also areas in the human brain which take a particular interest in faces. In man the areas implicated by these experiments, and by studies of prosopagnosia, the inability to recognise familiar faces, lie in the lingual and fusiform gyri, on the undersurface of the occipital lobe, towards its junction with the temporal lobe (see Figure 6.4). The right, non-dominant, hemisphere takes the dominant role in face perception, although whether damage to this hemisphere *alone* gives rise to prosopagnosia is still controversial.

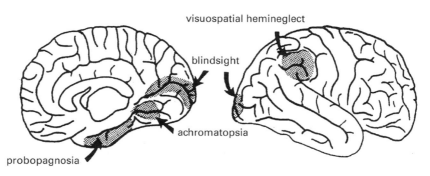

Figure 6.4 The location of prosopagnosia The location of the regions in the human brain where damage is liable to cause prosopagnosia, achromatopsia, blindsight (area V1: neglect is discussed on pp. 221–4 and blindsight on pp. 224–7).

We can ask the same question of prosopagnosia as of agnosia for objects: is it a disorder of memory or of vision? A similar answer is emerging: 'prosopagnosias' are a mixed bag, some – like the classical cases I have described – primarily affect visual analysis of faces; others affect knowledge of people; yet others fall somewhere between. A sad case described by Jon Evans illustrates that these boundaries can shift.[35] The first hint of trouble for VH was her difficulty in recognising the faces of friends, family and famous people. But at this stage she *could* recognise them by voice, and given the name of a friend or relation she could produce plenty of recollections. As time passed, her difficulties became more profound. She was clearly losing her *knowledge of people*, altogether, so that voices and names became as powerless as faces to evoke memories of the past. The underlying disorder in the brain was a progressive shrinkage of the right temporal lobe (see Figure 6.5).

We need to *identify* familiar faces, but it is almost as important to be able to 'read' their *expressions*. Surprisingly these two abilities turn out to be independent. The study of fear has led the way.

Darwin himelf is the grandfather of this line of enquiry. He had a strong interest in emotion, believing that psychological states and social behaviour, like physical form, must be the products of natural selection. In *The*

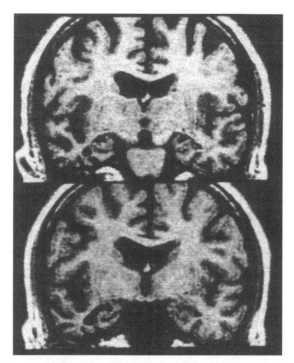

Figure 6.5 MRI scans of VH Shrinkage of the right temporal lobe (marked by arrows) in a patient whose first symptom was prosopagnosia, followed by a gradual loss of knowledge of people.

Expression of Emotions in Man and Animals,[36] published in 1872, he conjured up the image of fear in the human face with some relish: it 'is often preceded by astonishment, and is so far akin to it, that both lead to the senses of sight and hearing being instantly aroused . . . the eyes and mouth are widely opened and the eyebrows raised', as the frightened man 'stands like a statue motionless and breathless' (see Figure 6.6).

Fear belongs to a small group of emotions which are expressed by stereotyped – and probably instinctive – facial expressions in all human societies.[37] The other members of this group are happiness, sadness, anger, surprise and disgust. Until recently it would have been a reasonable assumption that decoding facial expressions depends on a single psychological capacity. But work by a British psychologist, Andy Young, and his colleagues in Cambridge, and by Antonio Damasio and his colleagues in the States, has cast doubt on this.[38]

An early hint that there might be something special about the perception of fear came from work with DR, whose 'amygdalae' had been damaged surgically on both sides of the brain in an attempt to relieve her epilepsy.[39]

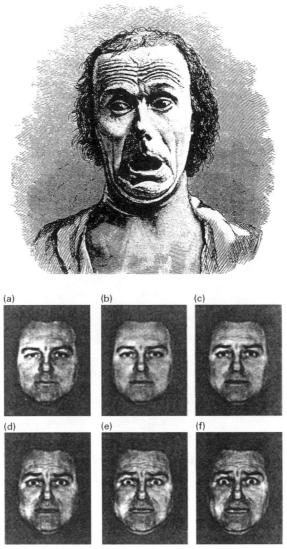

Figure 6.6 Terror Darwin used this (upper) illustration of fear by the French neurologist Duchenne in his book, *The Expression of the Emotions in Man and Other Animals*. The lower figure shows a series of expressions 'morphed' by a computer program from neutral to fearful, and used in the work described by Andy Young and colleagues.

The amygdala is a cluster of neuronal groups, tucked in beneath the cortical surface of the temporal lobe, lying close to the hippocampus. DR, minus her amygdalae, had no difficulty in recognising familiar faces. She had no problems in reading the facial signs of happiness and sadness, surprise and disgust. She could not always pick out angry expressions – but she was completely unable to recognise fear in a human face. This made sense: the amygdalae are known to be active in circumstances which provoke fear or anger. Patients with epilepsy arising from the amygdala sometimes experience surges of these emotions during attacks. It is plausible, if unexpected, that the brain region which is critically involved in the experience and the expression of fear should also be required to perceive signs of it in others.

Andy Young and his colleagues followed up this observation with a study of fear perception by the healthy human brain.[40] A team based in the Functional Imaging Laboratory at Queen Square in London – across the road from the hospital where Hughlings-Jackson consulted one hundred years ago – showed subjects a computer-generated series of expressions, traversing the spectrum from happiness to fear. Brain activity was monitored using PET. The subjects' stated task was to decide the gender of the faces, rather than to read their emotion. But we cannot normally help reading the expression in a face, and as the 'percentage' of fear in the face increased, so did the activation of the amygdala.

Patients with prosopagnosia reveal that some areas of the human brain are particularly involved in identifying faces. Studies of cases like DR's show that facial expression is processed independently of facial identity, and hint that different emotions are handled by different brain systems.[41] A postscript to the story of face perception adds another strand of complexity, echoing the tales of colour and form perception. Some patients who are unable to make conscious judgements about the identity of faces have 'covert', 'implicit' or unconscious knowledge of them.

This has been shown in several ways. The guilty knowledge test utilises the fact that the readiness with which the skin conducts a small electric current depends on the level of arousal of the autonomic nervous system. A sudden change in conductance signals a change in the activity of the autonomic system. This is the basis of the 'lie detector'. Some patients with prosopagnosia exhibit such changes in response to familiar but not to unfamiliar faces, although they *report* familiarity with neither.[42] There is no reason to think they are lying. The likeliest interpretation is that familiar faces are in fact recognised, but this recognition is either too weak to trigger awareness or is somehow disconnected from it. A similar conclusion is suggested by work showing that some prosopagnosic patients are better at learning true than false pairings of faces with names – despite their vehement insistence that none of the faces is in the least familiar to them.[43]

Places

Recognising faces and their expressions helps us to navigate around our social world. The ability to recognise places is of obvious importance in our navigation of our physical surroundings. Route finding, for example, involves recalling a sequence of turns, but to make use of the sequence we need to recognise the landmarks at which to make the turns.

Agnosia for landmarks has now been well described, sometimes in isolation, but often in conjunction with agnosia for faces or for colours: a 58-year-old woman

> was well until, while going to work on a streetcar, she suddenly realised that she could not recognise anything around her. She left the streetcar when the conductor announced a street well known to her, but she was soon lost and had to ask directions to a pharmacy . . . . She quickly learned to orient herself verbally ('the door of my room is the first on the left after the fire escape') but the ward never became familiar to her . . . she also reported an inability to recognise familiar handwriting, including her own, and the inability to recognise familiar pet animals.[44]

Like prosopagnosia, agnosia for place occurs more commonly after damage to the right hemisphere than to the left, and like both object agnosia and prosopagnosia it gives rise to a debate about the nature of the impairment: is it a disorder of perception, of memory or both? Either way, it is another example of the fractionation of visual awareness in the brain.

We should pause to take stock. The varieties of agnosia are signposts along the interweaving paths of ordinary vision. Every step on the road to recognition can be blocked (see Figure 6.7). Perceptions of shape, colour and motion are unequivocally 'visual' tasks: each can fail in relative isolation, but success in these alone does not guarantee that we can identify an object. To recognise something – a chair, a banana – as an example of a kind requires that we locate its category in conceptual space: patients with agnosia for objects cannot do this. Many familiar visual items invite a further stage of recognition: the faces of your family and friends, your car, the rooms of your house and the streets of your town are normally recognised as individuals: this crucial ability fails in agnosia for face and place.

These breakdowns are bizarre and seriously disabling. But, as we have seen, they are often incomplete: visual information about form, colour and the identity of faces *can* sometimes be sensed and processed by patients with agnosia. This is shown by tests in which unconscious information

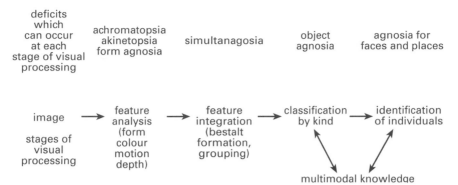

Figure 6.7 Blocks along the road to recognition The major steps along the neural road to recognition, with an indication of the stages at which selective visual deficits can arise.

influences behaviour, even though it fails to break the surface of awareness. The discovery of such covert or implicit knowledge has been an important development for theories of awareness over the last 20 years. This theme resurfaces in two other contexts in which subjects are unexpectedly unable to acknowledge the evidence of their senses: neglect and blindsight.

Neglect

Despite the usual 'dominance' of left brain and right hand, we are symmetrical beings, with a balanced awareness of our surroundings and our bodies. I can reach for something delicious with roughly equal alacrity on either side, and I would notice you wink your left eye just about as readily as your right. But for over a hundred years neurologists have noticed that brain damage sometimes upsets this delicate balance, leading, in the nineteenth-century term, to 'imperception' of events on one side of space. This much more often follows injury on the right of the brain than on the left, and the result is now loosely described as 'neglect'.[45]

It's important to realise that neglect is not the the straightforward result of the loss of a sense: sight, hearing and touch may all be intact. It is, rather, a deep-seated failure to *pay attention* to what's happening in one half of the world. As the side of space affected is usually the left, food may go uneaten on the left side of the plate, half of the face may remain unshaven, half of the page unused.

Some revealing 'bedside' tests were devised in the 1950s to bring out evidence of neglect. Sufferers asked to mark the midpoint of a straight line misjudge badly, usually marking a point well across to the right, as if they had failed to notice the leftmost segment. In a test requiring them to strike out the stars in a mixed array of shapes, they tend to miss those on the left. Asked to draw a clock and mark in the hours, the numbers 6–11 may be omitted or crowded on to the right-hand side (see Figure 6.8).

An elegant experiment by Eduardo Bisiach, an Italian neurologist who works in Milan, revealed that neglect affects imagined scenes as much as real ones. He asked his subjects to imagine themselves sitting on the steps of the cathedral in Milan, and to describe the buildings in the piazza beyond. As Bisiach expected, patients with neglect described all the buildings which would have been visible to their right, forgetting to mention those to their left. Then he asked them to imagine sitting at the opposite end of the square. They described just those buildings they had omitted to mention first time round, which now lay on their (imagined) unneglected right-hand side.

This experiment shows that neglect goes deep. Other recent observations indicate that although neglect is clearly a 'spatial' disorder, it does not always confine itself to the left-hand side of *space*. Patients asked to copy a pair of line drawings may reproduce them both, but systematically omit their left-hand sides. In this case the left side of objects, rather than the left side of space, is the victim of neglect.

Besides impairing the perception of space and objects, neglect can impinge directly on movement. Ingenious experiments dissociating movements towards the left from perception of items on the left have shown that, in some patients, 'neglect' flows from a reluctance to direct actions

Figure 6.8 An example of neglect (a) stimulus (b) patient's copy

leftwards.[46] Yet another fractionation of neglect has emerged from the discovery that patients may neglect 'near' but not 'far' space, and vice versa.[47]

It's clear from these subtle distinctions that neglect is not a single indivisible disorder. This accords with what we know of its anatomical basis. The inferior parietal lobe of the right hemisphere is the most commonly affected site, but damage to the right frontal lobe, corresponding regions in the left hemisphere, and the thalamus can all give rise to varieties of neglect. These sites are home to a family of neural networks which allow us to comprehend the spatial relationships between and within the objects that surround us. Damage in different sites presumably interferes with subtly different networks.

The puzzle in patients with neglect is that they fail to respond to items which they seem perfectly well able to sense and act upon. It is therefore not too much of a surprise that events in neglected space *can* sometimes be shown to influence behaviour: sufferers may show signs of implicit knowledge of facts they fail to report. For example, two Oxford psychologists, John Marshall and Peter Halligan, invited a patient with left-sided neglect to compare two drawings. One had a plume of smoke rising from a house fire on the left-hand side.[48] She could not spot the difference between them. But when asked which of the two houses she would prefer to live in, she consistently rejected the burning home. In a more technical study, apparently unidentified words presented on the neglected side of space were shown to influence the recognition of words presented later on the attended side.[49] This 'priming' effect could only have occurred if the words on the unattended side were in fact identified, albeit unconsciously.

Neglect undermines the usefulness of faculties which are substantially intact. But we can also neglect our afflictions, our losses. This is quite a common occurrence in neurology and goes by the offputting name of 'anosagnosia' (implying the loss of knowledge, *gnosis* in Greek, of disease, *nosos* in Greek). Its manifestations range from the mild to the grotesque. Mild anosagnosia occurs, for example, in individuals who fail to notice that they have lost their vision to one side, following damage to the visual cortex, until repeated accidents in doorways or parking lots bring the problem painfully to light. The bizarre extremes of anosagnosia are seen in patients who resolutely deny their newly acquired and total blindness, or who battle to eject their own paralysed limb from their bed, insisting that it must belong to someone else.

A moment's reflection suggests one reason (there are probably several) why this should happen. If I sprain my ankle, falling off the kerb, I may injure my pride, but my healthy nervous system, and my frustration about all the jobs I need my ankle for, keep me well informed about the problem. Matters may be quite different if I lose my perception of the left side of space. This deals a double blow, robbing me both of a useful perceptual ability and of the yardstick by which I could recognise its loss. Joni Mitchell lamented 'Don't it always seem to go that you don't know what you've got till it's gone'. After injury, in the shadow of neglect, it may become impossible to tell what's been lost once it's gone.

Blindsight and residual vision

The absence of all sensation

an absence of any and all sensation . . .

P. Stoerig and A. Cowey[50]

Twenty-five years ago a paradoxical term entered the vocabulary of science. The phenomena it describes have intrigued and exercised a generation of psychologists since then – and even some philosophers. If a 'science of consciousness' is feasible at all, the study of 'blindsight' is a most promising point of departure.[51]

The term first appeared in print in the *Lancet*, a leading British medical journal, in 1974.[52] The patient described in the *Lancet* paper, DB, was a man aged 34 who had undergone surgery to remove an abnormal tangle of blood vessels at the back of his brain. Following the operation, in which the primary visual cortex had to be removed from the right hemisphere, he appeared to be blind on the left. Given the surgical damage, this was to be expected. But previous work with monkeys had suggested that after injuries *restricted* to the primary visual cortex, vision sometimes recovered surprisingly well. DB offered a rare human parallel to the predicament of the 'experimental monkey'. He denied seeing anything on the left, but what would happen if he were 'urged to guess'?

To his own astonishment DB performed quite well. He was able to point accurately to a target in his blind field; he could guess correctly whether a line was vertical or horizontal and whether an 'X' or an 'O' had been presented; it even proved possible to measure the grain of his blindsight, by asking him to guess whether a grating was present or absent in the blind field: he was only a little worse than on the other side. 'Throughout these experiments he insisted that he saw nothing except in his intact field.

When shown his results he expressed great surprise and reiterated that he was only guessing.'

Since the first report of DB's blindsight, the surviving capacities of the blind field have been clarified and extended. With some variation from case to case, subjects with blindsight can indicate the position of targets in the blind field, the orientation of lines, the presence of movement and its direction, the occurrence of flicker and even the colour of the target. They can 'see' shapes in the same sense as DF, the girl with form agnosia. whom we encountered earlier: they are able to adapt their hand appropriately when grasping objects in the blind field.[53] There is even evidence for some appreciation of meaning: words presented in the blind field, for example 'river' or 'money', can influence the interpreta-tion of an ambiguous word, 'bank', heard a moment later. In every case of blindsight, to restate the point, subjects deny that they can see the fea-tures they are 'guessing', and are astonished to be told that their guesses are correct.

Now hang on. This is, surely, very odd – indeed, some would say, incred-ible. I am asking you to believe that people who are *blind* in half of space can nonetheless *see* and indicate all kinds of things of which they claim to have no knowledge. That's exactly right. Such a peculiar claim provokes a host of questions. First and foremost, is it true? As a famously sceptical col-league puts it, is this evidence really bomb-proof? Second, if the claim is correct, what is the mechanism for blindsight?

Does blindsight really exist? Two main alternative interpretations of the results from patients with blindsight have been advanced. The first is that 'blindsight' in fact depends on vision in the sighted hemifield. If light were scattered into the seeing field, or the eyes were to move during the experi-ment, subjects might be able to see and indicate targets without invoking any exotic abilities at all. Clearly they don't *think* they are seeing in the ordi-nary way, but we can all make mistakes.

The most elegant rebuttal of this idea comes from work by the discoverer of blindsight, Lawrence Weiskrantz, long-serving and now Emeritus Pro-fessor of Experimental Psychology in Oxford, and his collaborators. There is one region of the retina which is permanently and irredeemably blind, the optic disc, where the optic nerve gathers up its fibres and sets off back to the brain. This gives rise to a 'blind spot' in the visual field of each of our eyes. You can find this by moving a finger horizontally from the central point of one eye's visual field, with the other eye closed. Go slowly: about 15° out your fingernail will disappear from view. If scattering of light or subtle eye movements were the explanation of blindsight, we should all have 'blindsight' in the blind spot – but we do not.

A second sceptical suggestion runs something like this. Subjects with 'blindsight' may really be using their 'blind' fields – but perhaps they are not really blind! The vision in the blind field is relatively poor, no doubt, and they have lost their confidence in it: they *can* see, but no longer believe that they can. The idea that subjects with blindsight deny seeing things because they are doubtful about 'degraded data' would be plausible if the signals coming from the blind side were very weak and allowed performance only a little better than chance. It is less plausible in circumstances in which performance is roughly equivalent in the 'blind' and seeing fields, yet subjects still deny seeing anything at all on the blind side. This can be demonstrated, and suggests that there is a qualitative difference between blindsight and ordinary vision.

It looks, then, as if blindsight exists: subjects who are unable to report any visual experience from one side of space can nonetheless glean a good deal of information from the blind field. How can this be?

The mechanism of blindsight is a controversial topic. The kind of explanation we require depends on precisely what kind of brain damage underpins blindsight. Some authors have suggested that tiny surviving islands of striate cortex might allow blindsight to occur. If so it could depend on rather similar mechanisms to 'ordinary' sight. But in the two most closely studied cases, the best imaging techniques available have failed to show evidence of activity in area 17. Most students of blindsight agree that we need to look for an explanation beyond the striate cortex. If so, where?

There are several possibilities. Recall that the retina sends visual information to more than 10 destinations *besides* the primary visual cortex (see Figure 5.16). The most substantial of these pathways is to the superior colliculus in the midbrain, where maps of auditory, tactile and visual space exist in register. The superior colliculus communicates with an area of the thalamus, the pulvinar nucleus, which itself receives a small direct projection from the retina and also sends signals on to V5. Finally the lateral geniculate nucleus, the main way-station between the retina and V1, *also* sends small numbers of fibres to V2, V4 and other cortical visual areas directly. We do not yet know which of these regions is the bedrock of blindsight.

Recent work has brought the story of blindsight full circle. You will recall that the stimulus for the discovery of blindsight in man was the observation that monkeys recover a good deal of visual function after losing striate cortex. Can we say anything about the *experience* of these monkeys? Could it be that they too, like their human counterparts, are *blind*? This sounds like a difficult question to address: monkeys don't speak to us. But the Oxford neuropsychologist, Alan Cowey, working with Petra Stoerig, believes that he has found a way of asking them what they see. His experiment is ingenious and will take a little explaining.[54]

Cowey and Stoerig have worked for several years with three macaque monkeys in whom they have removed the striate cortex from one hemisphere, impairing their vision on the opposite side of space. But Dracula, Lennox and Wrinkle appear to have regained pretty good vision in their affected hemifields. For example, the three highly trained monkeys can detect almost every appearance of a dim light in both the normal and the affected hemifield, in a task in which they are rewarded for pushing buttons as they light up. Alan Cowey modified this task a little to 'ask' the monkeys about their visual experience.

In the new task the monkeys were rewarded for pushing buttons as they lit up in the normal hemifield. On some trials, however, the signal indicating that a 'trial' was about to begin was followed by – nothing. On these 'blank trials' the monkeys were rewarded for pressing a different, separate, button. When they did so they were effectively reporting that 'nothing has occurred'. What would happen when a solitary button in the opposite, affected, field lit up? Remember that we know from previous experiments that the monkeys can detect this event. Would the monkeys press the illuminated button, on the principle that pressing lights was rewarded, or would they treat the event as a blank, to indicate that nothing had happened?

The results were exceedingly clear. The three brain-damaged monkeys consistently classified lights on the affected side as blanks, whereas Rosie, a normal animal, equally consistently pressed the newly illuminated button. Are Dracula, Lennox and Wrinkle trying to tell us that, like DB, they cannot *see* the targets they can successfully detect in their blind field of vision?

Blindsight is truly odd, allowing subjects to use their eyes to inform themselves in the apparent absence of visual awareness. But we have seen that the boundaries of awareness are blurred. Does blindsight ever give way to *some* visual sensation: can the darkness give way to light?

The sound of distant gunfire

'a pinprick', 'a prickling' or 'gunfire at a distance' . . .

(Patients' reports of their visual experience after brain injury)[55]

Such faint sensations ought to be fully studied by the psychologist and assiduously cultivated by everyman . . .

C. S. Pierce and J. Jastrow[56]

Some patients with damage to the striate cortex report visual sensations in their affected visual fields. These sensations are subtle. Three of nine patients studied by W. Richards experienced *something* when the 'blind' regions of their visual fields were illuminated. They tended to describe their sensations in the vocabulary of touch or hearing rather than sight: they resembled 'a pinprick', 'a needle' or 'gunfire at a distance'. Larry Weiskrantz has also documented the wide range of vague, faint and almost indescribable sensations excited by vision after damage to the primary visual cortex.[57]

These reports are reminiscent of the sensations described in 1983 by a woman in whom a stroke had caused a dense numbness down one side of the body.[58] To her surprise, she found she was able to point quite accurately to the spot where her skin was touched on the numb side, suggesting that she might have an ability analogous to blindsight. But as the experiment proceeded, she became aware that something was happening when her numb arm was touched: 'Well I cannot say what it is, but I know that there is a place that you are going to. But it's such a little thing, if you like. It's so tenuous, tenuous'. Like patients with blindsight, she described her experience in terms belonging to her unaffected senses: 'I would like to understand . . . why do I see it? I "hear" that one'.

These sensations are of great interest, as they suggest that primary sensory areas are not *essential* for conscious sensation. This possibility has been pursued to some lengths in the study of patient GY.[59] This seasoned subject of numerous experiments, now in his thirties, was involved in a car crash at the age of seven. He suffered damage to the left occipital cortex. So far as one can tell from brain scans, this has destroyed his primary visual cortex on that side. As one would expect, GY's vision is greatly reduced on the right. But he is *not* completely blind. He is explicitly aware of lights which briskly flash on or off on the affected side, and of prominent rapidly moving targets.

Can we say anything about the source of GY's residual visual awareness? Semir Zeki, the discoverer of several of the cortical visual areas, and his colleagues, have answered this question with the help of PET scanning. They compared the activity in GY's brain when he looks at dim stationary stimuli – which are invisible to him – with the activity excited by the bright rapidly moving stimuli he can reliably detect. GY's residual conscious vision was accompanied by activation of area V5, the cortical visual area most clearly specialised for movement perception, another visual area, V3, and a region with complex functions, Brodmann's area 7. This suggests that 'residual' vision, like residual touch, can sometimes be sustained by cortical regions which survive the destruction of the primary sensory cortex, like area V5.

Why is blindsight blind?[60]

Blindsight has provided a promising source of ideas for theorists of visual awareness. Patients with blindsight see a good deal in a sense, yet they report seeing nothing. If we could give a definitive answer to the question of why blindsight is blind, we would be well on the way to understanding the neural basis of visual consciousness: blindsight gives us the opportunity, so to speak, to conquer consciousness by stealth, under cover of darkness. I shall sketch some possible explanations here: in Chapter 8 we will take a closer look at these in the wider context of recent scientific theories of consciousness.

It could be that the brain activity on which blindsight depends occurs in the wrong *places* to give rise to consciousness, an anatomical explanation, or that it is the wrong *kind* of activity, a physiological explanation, or both. At least three anatomical ideas have been mooted: that blindsight depends on activity in 'subcortical' regions of the brain, but only activity in the cerebral cortex reaches consciousness; that blindsight occurs in the absence of area V1, and that this is required for visual consciousness; and finally, that blindsight depends on the function of the 'dorsal' or 'where' stream of visual processing, but that visual consciousness depends upon the 'ventral' or 'what' stream. Physiological ideas include the possibilities that the neural activity subserving blindsight is too weak to give rise to consciousness, or that it fails to recruit the particular pattern of activity, perhaps a 40 Hz oscillation, required for consciousness.

Each of these ideas has its strengths and weaknesses. As yet, the true explanation is unknown.[61] Functional imaging experiments like Semir Zeki's work with GY, exploring the differences between the brain activity associated with conscious and unconscious visual responses, should help to adjudicate between these possibilities. The limited results to date suggest that both the location and the quality of brain activity influence its chances of reaching consciousness.[62]

Hallucination: 'There's a seagull on your shoulder'

Most of this chapter has been devoted to losses, the impairments of vision which follow damage to the brain. But occasionally brain damage gives rise instead to a burst of hallucinatory excess.[63] This may in fact be quite a common outcome. The brain's activity ordinarily reflects a balance between excitation and inhibition: brain injury can lead to a loss of inhibition, and thereby to an extravagant flowering of experience.

Some time ago I encountered an an extreme example. A highly articulate man in his sixties, Mr B, still very active in his retirement, was admitted to hospital after some peculiar events. On the previous three nights he had noticed that as cars approached him through the winter darkness, one of their headlamps failed. He was puzzled by this widespread electrical fault – until he began to suspect that he might have lost some of his vision to the far right. On the day of his hospital admission he took a friend for a drive. His friend, who knew him well, pointed out that he was giving obstacles on the left a wide berth, but coming perilously close to colliding with oncoming cars on the right. Later that day Mr B felt unwell, found that his speech was slurred and was dispatched to hospital.

On arrival there he had the first of a bewildering succession of experiences. He noticed that coloured letters and numbers were superimposing themselves on objects in his field of view: they would hover in space for a moment, then exit to the right. Soon afterwards he had the impression that all the patients in view had plastic tubing connecting their mouths to their ears; hot and cold taps in the washbasins were also yoked together. Odder still, a few minutes after looking at some seagulls soaring outside his window, he began to see them everywhere, distinct, correctly coloured, and stereotyped, looking at him with a steady gaze. They appeared on companions' heads, on his physician's shoulder and on one occasion he found a gull perched on the edge of the tumbler on his bedside table. The closer the birds came, the smaller they seemed: the bird on the glass was tiny. The letters, numbers, tubes and gulls were only the first of a phantasmagoric collection of images which flashed up around him over the next few days – he was surrounded by clergymen's collars, yellow bows, holes drilled in the ceiling, railway junctions, tubes sprouting from the floor, from reception desks and from patients' necks. He was mildly alarmed, but never in any doubt that these images were unreal: vivid for a few seconds, they seldom stayed for long, usually heading off towards the right-hand extreme of his gaze. Throughout this period his doctors reported that he was perfectly lucid. After five days the last of these hallucinations, an image like the underside of a jellyfish swimming, opening and closing, which erupted into a bursting firework of light, appeared in the button of a shirt he was ironing on the day of his return home – and he found himself at peace again, in a world which had recovered its agreeably predictable appearances.

What on earth had happened to him? The neurological problem giving rise to this strange picture show was commonplace. Mr B had suffered a minor stroke. When first examined in hospital, his vision to the right had been restricted, and a brain scan had subsequently shown an area of abnormality – likely to be due to the blockage of an artery – in the left occipital cortex.

By coincidence, I encountered another patient with an equally exotic visual complaint soon after meeting Mr B. John, a fit professional man in his forties, was sitting quietly at work one afternoon, when he had the impression that someone was flashing a bright yellow light, like a blow-torch, low down on his right-hand side. He turned towards it – but there was no one to be seen. The flashing continued for a few minutes; when it abated John realised that he could no longer see *anything* where the light had been.

The flashing recurred intermittently over the next few hours. On the following day, things began to change. John had the impression that he could see part of his patterned pullover in his blind area – even when he was looking elsewhere. Some time later he noticed a red gas cylinder out of the hospital window; a few minutes afterwards it reappeared, now inside the room, in his 'blind' visual field. In the meantime, the flashing returned in the blind field, on and off. This had stopped altogether, a few days later, when John walked from a dark street into a brightly lit shop: there was a sudden burst of coloured light to the right and below, in the midst of which John could make out his own face, as if reflected in a mirror – though mirror there was none. Over the next few days John saw his own reflected image on and off in his blind area, quite clearly, for a few minutes at a time. He continued to experience visual echoes, as well. The most vivid of these occurred on the way to a football match, after coming face to face with a police horse on a street corner. A minute or two later the horse reappeared in his blind field, complete with fluorescent hood. Both the visual echoes and the image of himself gradually subsided. When I last saw him the area of blindness had also substantially receded. Like Mr B, John was remarkably unperturbed by these images, which he described with amused detachment.

Symptoms like these occur sufficiently often to have their own descriptive vocabulary. Mr B experienced a mixture of illusions, 'misreadings' of objects which he could genuinely see, and hallucinations, perceptions which had no basis in the view before his eyes. John encountered, first of all, 'phosphenes', then 'palinopsia' and finally 'autoscopy'. Phosphenes are poorly formed colourful bursts and flashes of light; palinopsia is literally 'seeing again', a phenomenon well described after damage to the occipital lobe and its neighbouring regions, in which something perceived recently is 'seen again' a while later, in its absence. The reappearing police horse, hallucinated after an interval of minutes, is an excellent example of a palinopsic image. Autoscopy is the hallucinatory perception of an image of oneself. As it happens, this is one of the images more commonly glimpsed in the blind field following damage to the visual cortex.

John's underlying problem, like Mr B's, proved to be a minor stroke, involving the left occipital lobe. Why it should have occurred in a young man remained mysterious. But its bizarre effects testify to the creativity of the visual brain: the loss of the usual input from the occipital cortex can release a wealth of visual experience from areas 'downstream'.

Visual hallucinations are also common following the onset of blindness in later life due to ocular disorders: this phenomenon is known as the Charles Bonnet syndrome, named after the Swiss philosopher who first described it. As the hallucinations tend to come and go, it is possible to study the brain activity which correlates with their presence using functional imaging. Dominic ffytche and his colleagues, working with patients with the Charles Bonnet syndrome, found that hallucinations of faces, colours, textures and objects were associated with increased activity in visual areas beyond the primary visual cortex, in and around the fusiform gyrus.[64] The brain activity observed in functional imaging work usually follows the stimulus or task used to provoke it, but in this experiment the activity built up over some seconds *before* the patient reported a hallucination – as one might predict if the brain itself is the source of the hallucinatory experience. Similar results have been reported from patients with musical hallucinations occurring after the onset of deafness: auditory areas, beyond the primary auditory cortex, which are ordinarily activated by listening to music, were active also during musical hallucinations (including the Irish national anthem, 'Edelweiss' and 'Just a rose in a garden of weeds').[65] This work is very striking. Hallucinations must rank among the most subjective and elusive of all our experiences. To have given these 'airy nothings' a local habitation in the brain[66] adds persuasive weight to the view that every distinction we draw in experience has its distinctive correlate in the brain.

Exquisite correlations

I hope that the last two chapters will at least have persuaded you that visual experience is bound up with events in our brains. But the study of vision points to a second clear conclusion: that only *some* of the activity within the visual brain gives rise to visual awareness. A great deal of neural activity is 'silent': from the reflex which constricts our pupils in bright light to the covert recognition of faces in prosopagnosia or the capacity which allows DF to adjust her grip to an object which she cannot see. This creates a difficulty for efforts to capture the correlates of awareness in the brain: how can we distinguish activity which simply accompanies consciousness from activity which causes it?

There are at least two possible approaches. We could subtract the correlates of covert processes, like blindsight, from the totality of brain activity set in train by visual stimuli: the neural signature of conscious vision would lie in the remainder. A second approach is to focus on changes in brain activity which occur when visual experience changes without any change in visual stimulation: these changes should be closely tied to consciousness.[67] We have already encountered several examples of this kind: imagining a room in our mind's eye, shifting our attention without changing our gaze, hallucinating the image of a familiar face. Each of these mental processes is tied to modulations of activity in regions of the visual cortex.

Two other kinds of visual experience illustrate the exquisite correlations which are emerging between neural activity and visual awareness: illusions and 'multistable perceptions'. First, take a look at some illusions.

Figure 6.9 illustrates three kinds of 'illusory contour'. Spend a moment convincing yourself that they are illusory. A high-level, 'top-down', explanation for these illusions comes to mind. Perhaps we see the contours because they economically interpret the appearances in terms of simple shapes. For instance, a regular triangle superimposed on these three circles gives a simpler 'explanation' of Figure 6.9a than the truth: that there are three odd-looking part-nibbled circles placed at the apices of a

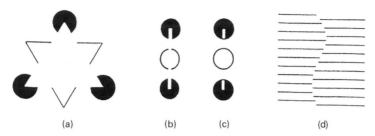

(a) (b) (c) (d)

Figure 6.9 Illusory contours Illusory contours are compelling 'imaginary' edges which we project upon these figures. Prove this to yourself by covering up the surrounding objects: as you do so, the contours disappear. Figure (c) generates little if any illusory contour because of the closure of the circles.

non-existent triangle. But it turns out that there may be no need to appeal to 'high-level' explanations. One need only step just outside the striate cortex, into area 18, to discover neurons which respond to illusory contours. Such cells are driven almost equally well by a continuous line passing through their receptive field *or* by an illusory contour – provided the figure used is not modified in such a way as to abolish the subjective contour.

A second, magnificent, illusion supplies another example. 'Enigma' is a pattern of circles superimposed on an array of black and white lines radiating from a common centre. Most of us, looking at this pattern, see vivid illusory motion within the circles which seem to rotate within their stationary surroundings. Does this illusion of motion have a correlate in the brain? Semir Zeki, using the PET technique, has shown that Enigma, like a pattern in genuine motion, excites area V5, the 'motion area'. Once again, a visual illusion turns out to speak neurological truth.

Multistable percepts need a word of introduction. In a range of circumstances the brain switches to and fro between two or more readings of a single image. The Necker cube (see Figure 6.10) is a familiar example: we can see it in two quite different three-dimensional configurations. Something similar happens if two different images are presented to each eye simultaneously. Rather than fusing them, visual awareness usually alternates between them. The neural basis for this alternation during 'binocular rivalry' has been studied both in animals and in man.

Nikos Logothetis, a physiological psychologist, has conducted a series of experiments in monkeys to define the neural correlates for these 'multistable' perceptions.[68] One might have guessed that some simple mechanism alternately suppresses the input from one or other eye – but this does

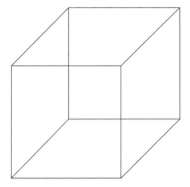 

Figure 6.10 The Necker cube and Escher 41 The Necker cube is a very familiar example of a multistable percept, switching depth from one orientation to the other as we gaze at it. Escher achieves similar effects: do you see fish – or a bird?

not seem to happen. Both patterns simultaneously excite a response in the cortical areas Logothetis has explored. But the image which the monkey indicates it is currently seeing correlates with the behaviour of certain neurons – about a third of the total he recorded from – in cortical layers 5–6 of visual areas V4 and V5. These 'modulate' their responses according to the monkey's current percept ('percept' is shorthand for 'what is being perceived', the current contents of visual consciousness). Similar experiments from a different laboratory have shown that the cells responsible for the monkey's current percept synchronise their firing until the alternative percept replaces it in visual awareness.[69]

In man, Nancy Kanwisher has shown that if one eye is shown a slide of a face, the other a slide of a place, the conscious percept switches between the two: as it does so, activity waxes and wanes in the face and place areas which we encountered earlier. The magnitude of the change in activity in these areas as the percept changes is similar to the magnitude of change when images of faces and places are alternately presented. This discovery implies that, by this stage of processing in the human brain, activity is tied to visual consciousness rather than to the physical features of the impinging stimuli.[70]

These examples highlight the dependence of our visual experience, in all its subtlety, on activity in the brain. Even fragile illusions and shifting perceptions have their demonstrable neural correlates.

Conjuring the rainbow

> Though it can be useful to speak of 'coding' and 'decoding' . . . we must
> be careful to avoid the conception that there is some final stage where the
> message (in the brain) is 'understood' . . . . The decoding is completed
> only by action . . . . The brain is constantly making hypotheses that
> prepare for useful actions.
>
> J.Z. Young[71]

> How should these principles be entertained, that lead us to think all the
> visible beauty of creation a false imaginary glare?
>
> Bishop Berkeley (1725)[72]

From the evidence marshalled in the last two chapters, it looks as if neuroscience can give a rich explanation of visual experience. But many readers will
have a lingering doubt about whether this explanation will be completely satisfying. Can it really explain why the young leaves shimmering in the breeze
in spring, or the wisps of mist rising from an autumn pond look *like this*, or
indeed why they *look* like anything at all? J.Z. Young, the distinguished
British physiologist, quoted above, seems to be warning us not to expect an
explanation of experience from 'messages in the brain'. 'Is experience, then,
an illusion?', Bishop Berkeley might have asked. The final chapters of this
book address just this concern. But while vision is fresh in our minds, let me
introduce two thought experiments designed to bring this dilemma to life.[73]

Imagine that a blind physiologist exhaustively studies the science of
vision. She might learn all there is to know about vision in the abstract. Yet,
if her sight were somehow restored, would she not learn something new
about vision? Most of us intuitively react that she would indeed: she would
learn what it's like to see, gaining a dimension of knowledge about sight
which would otherwise have been closed to her for ever.

Or consider an animal which has a sense organ we lack, like the electric
organ of some fish, or the echolocatory system of bats and dolphins. We could
in principle know all there is to know about the objective details of these
sensory systems: but could we know what it's like to possess them – what it's
like to be a bat? Once again it looks as though there is a dimension of knowledge the objective observer is denied. Scientific explanation fails to encompass the 'view from within' which consciousness confers on its possessor.

To illustrate the problem further, try comparing two examples of explanation within the realm of neuroscience, one which does not explicitly refer
to experience, while the other does.

Here is an example of the first kind. We can give quite a good explanation, nowadays, of why someone has an epileptic seizure. For any of several definable reasons a group of neurons becomes unusually excitable; it broadcasts its excitement along a variety of pathways through the brain, thereby recruiting the activity of distant neurons to its own synchronous pattern of discharge; if it continues unchecked, this process eventually overwhelms the sufferer, who may stiffen and convulse. This is a conventional scientific explanation, correlating one observable event – the pattern of electrical discharge in the brain – with another, the generalised seizure. The first event gives rise to the second one: there is nothing unusual or problematic about this at all.

Contrast this with an explanation for our perception of colour. One term in the explanation – the 'explanans' – echoes the example of the seizure: we explain colour vision in terms of neural activity at a series of levels, from the retina through to the cortical visual areas and beyond. No problem here. And part of what is to be explained – the 'explanandum' – is also unproblematic: our abilities to name colours, to sort them or to respond to them overtly in a range of other ways all clearly depend on colour perception and give rise to observable behaviour. But there seems to be more to colour perception than these abilities. So far, we seem to have left out the perception of colour itself, our appreciation of the delicate shades of spring leaves or the deep red tones of a wine. Our *experience* of these visual qualities is *not* obviously observable. Here lies the difference between explaining a seizure and accounting for the perception of colour. In the first case we are trying to relate two straightforwardly observable series of events; in the second case we are trying to correlate observable events with experience, which seems to be, in principle, inaccessible to observation.

The problem lies not so much with the kind of explanation being offered as with what is to be explained. If our perceptions are really private, if subjective experience is an ineliminable fact, science is bound to be incomplete. Science concerns itself with observable, public, objective data, with the world as it might be considered from *any* point of view: it cannot exhaustively describe the 'inner world' of our experience. I believe that this spells out what most of us – rightly or wrongly – assume about the nature of our awareness.

Many philosophers believe that this 'common sense' view is deeply mistaken on the grounds that awareness can be wholly resolved into the operations and functions of the brain. If so, experience is not quite what it seems. One of the most articulate advocates of this view, the American philosopher Daniel Dennett, compares his work metaphorically to looking behind the stage of the 'theatre of experience': 'once we take a serious look backstage, we discover that we didn't actually see what we thought we saw onstage . . . the very distinction between onstage experiences and backstage processes loses its appeal'.[74] In Chapter 9 we will examine this debate more closely and you will have a chance to decide whether Dennett's arguments persuade you.

Will science ever deliver a complete explanation of visual awareness? Can it 'conjure the rainbow' from the workings of the brain? The answer must depend on what we decide visual awareness amounts to. Science can certainly correlate our reports of visual experience with activity in the brain. Year by year it is providing an ever richer account of the patterns of neural activity which underlie the patterning of vision. The achievement is already impressive and surely offers a powerful explanation for our experience. Will this account eventually become 'complete'? Perhaps, but only if the vocabulary of experience can be translated without loss into the language of science. If not, the scientific description will remain unable to tell us what vision *is like*. Would this make experience a mystery? No more, and no less, than existence itself – and for the same reason: it is our point of departure. There is no need to conjure the rainbow: the rainbow is already there, before our eyes.

Conclusion: vision and consciousness

It is time to recap.

In Chapter 5 we explored our current understanding of the delicate and beautiful system which enables us to see. Such an intricate device is bound to spring a leak from time to time: in this chapter we have looked at a few of the many revealing ways in which the system can break down.

Its growth is the outcome of an interaction between inherited instructions, intrinsic activity and visual experience. If visual experience is lacking or distorted in our early years, we may never learn to see.

The agnosias involve the selective breakdown of the specialised – and localised – abilities which enable us to see. We can lose our ability to see colours, movement or forms, to recognise objects, people or places. These losses are sometimes incomplete, sparing some degree of covert knowledge. Such covert knowledge can influence behaviour in the absence of conscious perception.

In agnosia the preservation of knowledge is unexpected. Among patients with neglect, just the opposite is true: the senses seem to be working normally, yet events on one side of space are ignored. Nevertheless, they can exert an unacknowledged influence. Anosagnosia is the related failure to recognise impairment – the neglect of lost abilities.

Blindsight is the best-studied example of a 'covert' ability. Following injuries to the visual cortex, possessors of blindsight – to their great surprise – can make a variety of visual judgements about items they claim not to see. Monkeys deprived of their striate cortex appear to see quite well, but recent work suggests that they may also be relying upon blindsight. There are several competing anatomical and physiological explanations for this paradoxical ability. These must take into account new evidence that extrastriate visual areas, in the absence of V1, can give rise to conscious vision.

Although damage to the brain usually robs us of psychological abilities, it sometimes gives rise to excesses of experience or behaviour. The hallucinations which can follow damage to the visual cortex are a vivid example of such neurological 'release'.

These observations open up two approaches to defining the neurology of conscious vision: by subtracting the activity associated with covert processes from the totality of brain activity, and by exploring the activity which correlates with changes in visual experience in the absence of stimulus change.

Will neuroscience eventually deliver a 'complete' account of vision? It is certainly looking plausible that every distinction drawn in our visual experience will be reflected in a distinctive pattern of neural activity. Whether we think that a full understanding of these patterns will give a *complete* explanation of vision depends upon our concept of visual awareness, in particular on whether we believe that the 'inner world' of experience can be exhaustively redescribed in the language of science. This central question will resurface in Chapters 8 and 9. Before rejoining it, we must hunt for the source of awareness.

Part IV:
The origins of consciousness

7

The history of everything

Introduction

> A four-year-old, emphatically: 'I know *everything*.'
> Her father, doubtfully: 'Even Pythagoras' theorem?'
> The four-year-old, apprehensively: 'I don't like that. Does it bite?'

We can ask four fundamental questions about each part and activity of an organism: how does it work, what is it for, how does it develop and how did it evolve? Biologists refer to these as questions of mechanism, function, ontogeny and phylogeny (ontogeny concerns the development of the individual, phylogeny the development of the species over many generations). We can reasonably ask these questions about consciousness. So far I have concentrated largely on the first, the mechanisms of the waking state and vision, with only brief excursions into questions of growth and evolution.

This chapter will redress the balance. Living things are the creation of an immensely ancient history. We will never understand them properly unless we can piece together something of their past. In this chapter I will sketch what we know of the evolution of the brain. Evolution and function are closely linked. Organs evolve only if it is worth their while – if the process confers an advantage. As consciousness is one of the most conspicuous functions of the brain we should expect to find some compelling reasons why consciousness evolved.

In the interests of a long perspective, I shall start at the very beginning – without meaning to suggest, like my daughter, that we ever will, or even could, know the whole story.

First things

> For thou exist'st on many a thousand grains
> That issue out of dust
>
> William Shakespeare, *Measure for Measure*, III.i

> I don't know what the soul is. But I imagine that somehow our bodies surround what has always been.
>
> Anne Michaels[1]

Wherever astronomers cast their gaze around the universe, its galaxies are flying away from us – and one another.[2] The rate at which they are receding depends on their distance from us: the further off they are, the greater the relative speed of their flight. This is what would be expected after an explosion. As every part of the universe is behaving in the same way, the explosion must have involved everything there is. From knowledge of the speeds at which the galaxies are receding, it is possible to estimate the length of time for which they have been travelling. The primordial 'Big Bang', the standard current model of the origin of our universe, is thought to have occurred 10–15,000 million years ago.

Matter and energy were concentrated at unimaginable densities in the first few minutes after the Big Bang. Atoms, even the very simplest, like those of hydrogen, could not have existed under these conditions. At the pressures and temperatures prevailing then, radiation and subatomic particles were all there was. The history of the universe from those first moments is a tale of expansion, cooling and the gradual evolution of complexity.

As particles and energy streamed away from the initial titanic eruption, pressures and temperatures fell rapidly. In the less extreme conditions that resulted, subatomic particles became able to associate with one another, forming the simple atoms of hydrogen and helium. At the same time, gravity became a force to reckon with, matter attracting matter, creating great aggregations of atoms in the midst of vast extents of empty space. These were the seeds of the earliest stars and galaxies, whose formation began within 1,000 million years of the Big Bang.

Events within the early stars had a special importance for us. Stars are gigantic natural furnaces – with a crucial difference. The fires and engines which are familiar to us on earth reduce complex substances like petrol, coal and wood to simpler ones like ash and carbon dioxide. Atomic bombs of the kind used at Hiroshima also reduce complexity, releasing energy by splitting atoms of uranium in the process of nuclear fission. Things are quite different in the burning core of a star. Its primary fuel is hydrogen, but rather than breaking it down to something simpler, a star exploits nuclear *fusion* to generate atoms of elements heavier than hydrogen, a process which releases huge amounts of energy. We are bathed in this energy every day, as this is the source of sunlight. But sunshine is not the the stars' only contribution to our lives: the atoms of which we all are made, belonging to elements like carbon and oxygen, calcium and iron, were forged in the nuclear furnaces within the first generations of stars.

Our own sun has existed for about 4,500 million years, roughly one-third of the age of the universe since the Big Bang. It is a pretty average 'second generation' star, a peripheral resident in its galaxy, the Milky Way. Distances at galactic scales are often expressed in multiples of a 'light year', the distance travelled by light in a year (light travels about 300,000 kilometres/second: a light year is therefore about 9.5 million million kilometres). The Milky Way is a 'spiral' galaxy, roughly 100,000 light years across: the sun lies 33,000 light years from the galactic centre. It is one of 100,000 million stars in our galaxy. This total, incidentally, is not too far from the observable number of galaxies in the universe: there are a few thousand million in parts of the universe visible to astronomers.

Our earth and the other planets of the solar system orbiting the sun are of a comparable age to the sun itself. The sun is thought to be approaching the halfway point in its stable phase of hydrogen fusion. In another 8,000 million years it will be in a phase of rapid expansion: as it grows into a 'red giant', any trace of life on earth will boil away. It is likely that many other stars in our own galaxy, and in other galaxies, are orbited by planetary systems. Whether these are currently a home to life, and whether they might support us in the future, remain tantalising but unanswered questions.

The long-term future of the universe is just as uncertain. Will its matter continue to expand indefinitely, into unending space, spreading itself ever more thinly as it cools towards absolute zero? Or will gravitational attraction eventually reverse the trend, so that in a few thousand million years the galaxies will be hurtling back to a 'Big Crunch'? Neither possibility is particularly attractive, but the prospect is still consolingly remote.

The Big Bang, the creation of the galaxies, the stars and the solar system are the story of our distant past, too distant you may feel to be of any real interest or importance: 'The proper study of mankind is man'.[3] Just so: but as it happens the stuff from which we are made was formed within the stars. The study of man leads back irresistibly to the early universe. You and I, quite literally, are stardust.

The birth of life

> things counter, original, spare, strange;
> . . . He fathers-forth whose beauty is past change . . .
>
> Gerard Manley Hopkins[4]

> We are an item of history, not an embodiment of general principles.
>
> Stephen Jay Gould[5]

The elements which formed within the stars, like oxygen and carbon, nitrogen and iron, can combine with one another in innumerable ways, giving rise to simple molecules, like water, carbon dioxide, methane and ammonia. And so they do, throughout the universe. But closer to home, soon after the earth's formation, conditions seem to have been especially conducive to the creation of more elaborate chemical compounds. Some of the complex molecules which resulted were the forerunners of the first living things. Their descendants have left their imprints in the earliest known fossils which demonstrate that recognisable forms of life existed when the earth was only about a quarter of its present age, 3,500 million years ago.

There is no detailed or universally agreed explanation for the origins of life. But suggestive observations indicate that we can, in broad terms, provide a satisfactory explanation. For instance, in 1953 an American biochemist, Stanley Miller, showed that if the simple molecules mentioned in the last paragraph are energised by an electric current for a period of hours, much more complex ones, like sugars and the amino acid building blocks of proteins, appear spontaneously in the brew.[6] These molecules have a tendency to associate with one another in concentrated droplets, increasing the opportunities for fertile chemical interactions. These molecular aggregations could become players in a kind of molecular evolution, preceding the true dawn of life: some droplets, with a self-destructive chemistry, would fall apart, while others, stabilised by the reactions taking place within them, would prosper. If they grew beyond a physically optimum size, they might split in two, each of the 'daughters' preserving the chemical composition of her parent.

We will never know every link in the chain of events which gave rise to terrestrial life. But most biochemists would agree that the defining moment in its emergence, the explanation for the profound underlying similarity of all living things today, was the appearance of nucleic acids. These molecules provide the basis for the genetic code, the medium by which inherited characteristics are transmitted and modified from one generation to the next, throughout the living world. The nucleic acid which supplies this medium in the great majority of organisms is deoxyribonucleic acid, DNA.

DNA has three properties which fit it for this purpose. First of all, it can reproduce or 'replicate' itself: if the two strands of the double helix of a molecule of DNA are teased apart, each can guide the construction of a 'complementary' strand, much as a mould will shape a jelly. This allows it to serve as a faithful messenger between the generations.

Second, the instructions 'written' in DNA can be 'translated' into the chains of amino acid which make up proteins: as we saw in Chapter 2, proteins, in their immense variety, are the stuff of life. A 'gene', by definition, is a stretch of DNA which codes for a given protein. Genes 'code' for proteins in the sense that they specify the order in which amino acids must be strung together to build the protein concerned. DNA and proteins are now thoroughly interdependent and must have undergone a long period of co-evolution in the early phases of life.

Finally, although the DNA transmitted to an offspring is usually a faithful record of the parent's genetic make-up, it is liable to occasional 'mutations', rare chancy alterations. These may be 'neutral', with no effect on the protein for which the DNA in question codes; they may be disadvantageous, in which case the offspring will be more likely than otherwise to succumb in the struggle for survival; but just once in a while an alteration will improve the chances of biological success – which is to say, of reproduction. If so the gene will spread, and the creature's descendants will reap the marvellous benefits of chance. This is the basis for the evolution of species by the 'natural selection' of advantageous mutations.

All living things on earth use DNA (or its close relative RNA) as the language of inheritance, and we all share a host of proteins. The ubiquity of DNA helps to explain why the story of evolution is a tale of continuity – but it is of course also a tale of extraordinary change. We share a common ancestry with the snail and much of our fundamental body chemistry with a blade of grass. What were the landmarks on the road to the delightful diversity of the four million species of living things today?[7]

Once DNA had emerged, and a system for synthesising proteins had evolved, the stage was set for a limitless variation in the forms of life. But change, in fact, came slowly. The first organisms to appear in the fossil record, long thought to be primitive bacteria, held sway on earth for about 2,000 million years. The monotony of the fossil record from this vast period, almost half the earth's lifetime, must conceal some major achievements in biochemical evolution. We touched on the most profound of these in Chapter 5: photosynthesis, the ability to harness sunlight to build organic molecules from carbon and water, evolved over 2,000 million years ago, probably in blue-green 'cyanophytes', close relatives of the bacteria. Beside providing a life-support system for organisms with the necessary chemical sophistication, photosynthesis transformed the earth's atmosphere by releasing oxygen, and created the base of a food chain which would later sustain the animal kingdom.

By 1,400 million years ago, the bacteria and algae, the 'prokaryotes', coexisted with 'eukaryotes', a family which comprises many single-celled creatures and every multicellular creature, including you and me.[8] The defining feature of eukaryotes is the internal complexity of their cells: the interior of a eukaryotic cell contains numerous 'organelles' bounded by membranes, leading semi-autonomous lives within the greater life of the whole. Chief among organelles is the nucleus itself, containing the cell's complement of inherited instructions, its DNA.

Unicellular eukaryotes and their prokaryotic companions, some photosynthetic and some not, held the stage for another 700 million years. Loose associations of cells like those of sponges may have begun to form 800–1,000 million years ago. These associations are not yet 'multicellular' organisms in the full-blooded sense of the term: the cells of the sponge remain virtually independent, unspecialised and largely uncoordinated.

The next huge leap of evolution is recorded in the fossils of the Ediacara outcrop in Australia and the slightly later fauna of the 'Cambrian explosion', such as the Burgess Shale.[9] These bear the earliest witness to the first appearance, in the seas, of true multicellular life, 5–700 million years ago. The major groups or 'phyla' of the contemporary animal kingdom originated in this explosion of biological diversity. Worms, molluscs, like the mussel and the oyster, and arthropods, the phylum containing insects, lobsters and spiders, are all represented in the Burgess Shale. Indeed, poignantly for our kind, another denizen of the Shale, *Pikaia gracilens*, previously classified as an annelid worm, may be the earliest fossilised chordate, the first recorded member of the phylum to which mankind belongs.

Multicellular life evolved in the sea. About 400 million years ago primitive plants, soon followed by invertebrate species, ancestors of the millipede, made their way on to land. For 50 million years millipedes, spiders and insects were the dominant multicellular species on land, and indeed in the air, which the insects invaded 380 million years ago.

While the invertebrates multiplied on land, our remote ancestors, the early vertebrate descendants of *Pikaia*, remained waterborne. The fragmentary fossils of primitive jawless fish have been found in rocks about 540 million years old. Over the following 100 million years their descendants acquired capable jaws and a well-developed backbone – the vertebral column after which the 'vertebrates' are named – and diversified into numerous species. Some of these gained the ability to propel themselves along the sea-bed; others, dwellers in shallow reaches which were prone to run dry, became able to extract oxygen from air as well as from water. About 350 million years ago these two abilities were combined in the first vertebrate species to walk and breathe on dry land: these were amphibians, creatures somewhat akin to contemporary newts and salamanders.

Amphibians must lay their eggs in water. Their descendants, the reptiles, which first appeared some 300 million years ago, managed to dispense with this requirement, completing the transition to a wholly terrestrial life by producing watertight eggs. Reptiles were the most prominent vertebrate species on land until some 65 million years ago. But by then two other great classes of vertebrate had evolved from reptiles, the warm-blooded birds and mammals. Both made their first inconspicuous appearance around 150 million years ago. The first primates, the ancestors of prosimians, like lemurs, monkeys and apes, evolved some 60 million years ago; the first hominids, the immediate common ancestors of apes and man, 5 million years ago.

It is traditional to use an analogy with some more familiar time scale to make it easier to grasp the essentials of an immense evolutionary story of this kind. I like the simpler ones. If one compresses the whole of the earth's history into a single day, life of the most elementary kind appears in the small hours, before 5 a.m.; photosynthesis gets going some time after dawn, at around 10 a.m.; eukaryotic cells do not appear until 5 p.m.; true multicellular life at 8 p.m.; amphibians conquer the land at 10 p.m.; early mammals appear at 12 minutes past eleven; the first primates at half-past eleven; hominids at two minutes to midnight.

Begetting the brain

You move through the era of fishes,
The smug centuries of the pig –
Head, toe and finger
Come clear of the shadow . . .

Sylvia Plath[10]

To the man-in-the-street who, I'm sorry to say,
Is a keen observer of life,
The word *intellectual* suggests right away
A man who's untrue to his wife.

W.H. Auden[11]

The last two sections have set the scene for the history of our subject, the brain. It would be quite wrong to regard the human brain as the hero of the piece – an achievement for which the evolution of the rest of life was a tedious preparation. Evolution is a quirky, unpredictable business, and there are many routes to success. In Stephen Gould's words, 'There are more bacteria in the gut of each person reading this essay than there are humans on the face of the earth: this time is their time, not the "age of mammals" as our textbooks chauvinistically proclaim.'[12] Rooted or restless, green-leaved or eight-armed, there are many winning strategies in the struggle for survival. Nevertheless, the route which our ancestors took *has* led to success, of a kind. Its hallmark has been the evolution of a brain which allows us to understand our world to an unparalleled degree. Our particular evolutionary story is substantially, though not exclusively, the story of a growing brain. We are by nature Nature's intellectuals. As ever, the story of the brain's evolution speaks both of continuity and change.

Continuity

Even the highest faculties of feeling and intellect begin to germinate in lower forms of life.

T.H. Huxley, 1860[13]

How far can we trace the history of the brain?[14] Its elements, the essentials of the 'simple nervous system' which we discussed in Chapter 2, are very ancient indeed. But why should they be so ancient and how can we tell?

It is relatively easy to say *why*. The coalitions between cells in multicellular bodies create an obvious problem: if their alliance is to be fruitful, the constituent cells must be persuaded to pull together. At its simplest, a nervous system is a means of achieving this, of ensuring that the responses an organism makes to the events that it senses are in its overall interests. Neurons are the parts of a multicellular organism which specialise in control. As a means of control is indispensable, we might reasonably expect nervous systems to be as old as multicellular life.

How can we study the early history of the nervous system? There are three main sources of evidence: each has its share of problems.

First of all, we can make informative comparisons between the nervous systems of living organisms. If we find that every multicellular species uses a particular chemical for signalling in the nervous system, then it is likely that the common ancestor of all these species did so – long ago. This approach runs the risk of confusing superficial resemblances with deep historical affinities: it could be that separate lines of evolution converged independently on a similar solution to a similar problem.[15] This doubt can usually be laid to rest nowadays, with the help of molecular biology, which makes it possible to look in minute detail at the relevant proteins or even their genes.

Second, we can search the fossil record for evidence of the beginnings of the brain. Fossils come in many shapes and sizes. As bodies decay, their soft parts are of course the first to disappear. If the conditions are right – they seldom are – the hard parts of a dead plant or animal may gradually be infiltrated and replaced by silt or sand, limestone or silica. If the fossil survives and is found – which it seldom will be – it may be possible to prise it from its surrounding 'matrix' of rock. Occasionally the dead organism may decay completely but as it does so the space which contained it may be filled by some other material, giving rise to a 'mould' in the surrounding rock. Sometimes the imprint of an organism on a soft surface may survive as an 'impression'. The great drawback of every kind of fossil for a student of the brain is that nervous systems are hopelessly soft, and only the bones surrounding them, or at best their surface detail, are likely to survive. Nevertheless, as we shall see, the fossil record has plenty to tell us about the brain.

Finally, most dangerously, we can try to glean something about evolution from the growth of the individual. The nineteenth-century biologist Ernst Haeckl proposed that 'ontogeny recapitulates phylogeny'. The idea, alluded to rather loosely by Sylvia Plath in the lines at the head of this section, is that the development of a growing organism rehearses the stages of its evolution. This is not altogether true: growing organisms are just as much subject to the pressures of the struggle for survival as the adult forms, and will adapt accordingly. There is no obligation upon them to display their evolutionary past for the delectation of biologists. All the same, other things being equal, development does provide clues about evolution. I have two books open on my desk: one illustrates the central nervous system of a jawless fish, a heterostracid, which swam in fresh-water estuaries about 425 million years ago (see Figure 7.1); the other illustrates the brain of a four-week-old human

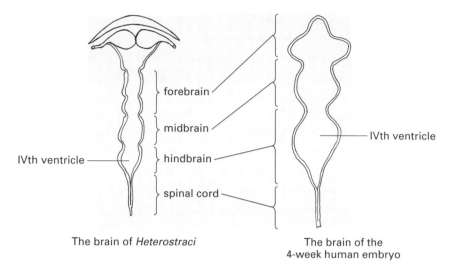

The brain of *Heterostraci*

The brain of the
4-week human embryo

Figure 7.1 The brains of fossil Heterostracid and the four-week-old human embryo
The structure of the developing brain of a four-week-old human embryo contains a
distant echo of the fossilised brain of a primitive 400-million-year-old jawless fish,
Heterostraci.

embryo. There are differences, but I shall leave you to decide whether these
are more impressive than the fundamental similarities.

Heterostracids apart, what is the hard evidence that nervous systems
were an ancient invention? Let us try the first approach I mentioned, the
comparison of living nervous systems, to sidle up to this question. Figure
7.2 shows a tree of life, designed to indicate the relationships between existing organisms. The little worm I mentioned in Chapter 2, *Caenorhabditis
elegans*, is classified as a 'pseudocoelomate', at the lower left of the picture.
We of course are mammals. It would be difficult to find two multicellular
organisms which are less closely related. But here is a brief account of the
neurological capabilities of the humble worm.

C. elegans moves, not perhaps in ways that would attract you, but it indu-
bitably explores, and seeks and flees. It senses its surroundings and its own
states, responding to touch, stretch, temperature, its chemical environment including the presence of a sexual attractant, the concentration of the
medium through which it is moving, the presence of light and its haz-
ardous arrival at a precipice. It feeds, mates, lays eggs, excretes its waste
and modifies its behaviour in relation to recent events. Within broad limits,
C. elegans does most of the things we do.

But the question that interests us here is whether *C. elegans* uses a
nervous system which remotely resembles ours to regulate its behaviour,

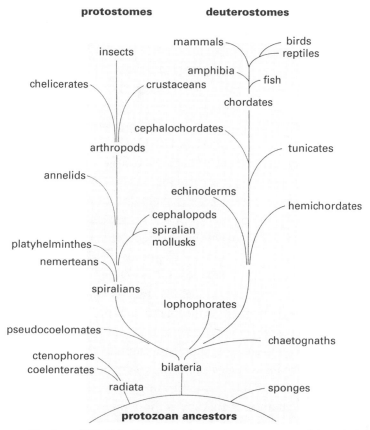

Figure 7.2 The tree of life This diagram indicates the remoteness of the relationship between *Caenorhabditis*, a pseudocoelomate, and us. It is not meant to imply that there are 'lower' and 'higher' species: all living creatures are the youngest twigs on the smooth crown of a tree, rather than residents on different rungs of a biological ladder.

or has it quite independently evolved its own wormy brain? It is open to question whether, strictly speaking, *C. elegans* possesses a brain at all – but it certainly makes a huge investment in its elongated nervous system which comprises 302 of its 959 cells. Weight for weight, *C. elegans* is better equipped with neurons than man. On close inspection, these cells look suspiciously familiar. *C. elegans'* neurons, like ours, transmit electrical signals and communicate at chemical synapses. The chemicals they use, acetylcholine, GABA and serotonin, are all key players in the human brain. The receptors for acetylcholine, and probably for GABA, in *C. elegans*, resemble receptors which abound in the human nervous system.

In fact, the history of some of the elementary components of the nervous system can be traced back further still. The ancestors of 'voltage gated ion channels', those vital pores which allow ions to pass across the neuronal membrane in the course of electrical signalling, can be found in simple single-celled prokaryotes. In these most ancient organisms they play a role in energy production. In contemporary protozoa, which are the simplest eukaryotic organisms, consisting of a single cell, they have been adopted for a rather different role, pregnant with possibilities.

Pressure applied to the front of the protozoon *Paramecium* opens channels which allow an influx of calcium. Calcium is positively charged, and its entry reduces the net balance of negative charge within the protozoon. In response, the organism's 'legs', its cilia, reverse the direction in which they beat and carry the creature away from the trouble ahead. A touch applied to the back opens channels for potassium: this flows out of the cell, increasing the negative charge within, and boosts the rate at which the cilia beat, helping the organism to outpace its pursuer.

At some time before the divergence of the invertebrates from the vertebrate line, in the early days of multicellular life, this family of ion channels enlarged to include a channel permeable to sodium. These channels, for calcium, potassium and sodium, now provide the ubiquitous and indispensable basis for neuronal signalling throughout the animal kingdom. The family can trace its lineage almost to the very beginnings of life.

This example points to profound affinities between all existing nervous systems.[16] Indeed, an ancient ancestry is more the rule than the exception for the major classes of molecule exploited in the brain. The families of neurotransmitters, the families of their receptors, the families of factors which promote the growth of neurons and the factors which glue them together all originate in the remote Precambrian past. Neural evolution from a common source has been occurring for at least 600 million years.

Change

> Size *does* matter.
>
> Anon.

I am not really trying to persuade you that your intellect resembles a meagre worm's. I *am* trying to persuade you that there are deep continuities between simple nervous systems, like *C. elegans*', and ours. But continuity is only one of the twin Janus faces of evolution; the other is change. However strong may be the concealed affinities between *C. elegans* and us, a great deal has altered since the divergence of our evolutionary stems. What has changed, and why?

The most obvious change is in numbers. *C. elegans* has 302 neurons in its hermaphrodite form, 381 in the male, a place for each one and each one in its place. By contrast you and I have around 100,000 million neurons in our brains. Erring on the generous side towards *C. elegans*, we still have 100 million times as many nerve cells in our brains as the worm has in its entire nervous system. If we take into account the numbers of connections between individual cells, which are much higher in complex than in simple nervous systems, the differential between worm and man becomes more striking still.

This comparison looks distinctly unflattering for *C. elegans*, but it is not entirely fair. We are, after all, much bigger than the worm. To make fair comparisons between species, we need to make some allowance for size. Presumably a proportion of any animal's neurons are involved in house-keeping tasks which will demand larger numbers of cells, the larger the house to be kept. Once we have made this allowance, the excess of cells beyond those required for humdrum chores might be expected to correlate with an animal's 'brain power' – the richness of its perceptual world, the power of its memory, the complexity of its behaviour.

This kind of argument has been developed in detail by students of the evolution of the vertebrate brain.[17] I shall concentrate on their theories and discoveries in the rest of this section, abandoning *C. elegans* and the invertebrates for the moment, with regret.

We need to find a way to 'correct' the size of the brain to take account of the size of the body, if we want to draw tentative conclusions about 'brain power'. Simply dividing brain weight by body weight has proved unhelpful. This may be because weight reflects volume, while the nervous system is preoccupied with *surfaces*, the surfaces at which we receive stimulation and through which we act on the world. The surface area of the body can be estimated from body weight (it is approximately the cube root of the square of weight), and the ratio of brain weight to body area turns out to give quite a good indication of the relative brain development of a species, its 'encephalisation'. This is sometimes expressed in terms of an 'encephalisation quotient', EQ for short. An EQ is the degree of an animal's brain development relative to some standard, for instance relative to the average degree of encephalisation among vertebrates in general, or in mammals or in some more limited group. I apologise for introducing all this jargon: it will be worth it in the end.

Degrees of encephalisation can be calculated for fossil species as well as for living ones. This is possible because in most vertebrate species the brain pretty well fills the skull: therefore an 'endocast', a cast of the interior of the fossilised skull, is of much the same dimensions as the brain which once resided there. By a nice coincidence, brains have the same weight for volume as water: this implies that the volume of an endocast (in fractions of a litre) equals the weight of the brain it resembles (in fractions of a kilogram). Provided that it is possible to estimate the body weight of a fossil species, and to examine an endocast, it is possible to compute its EQ.

Comparisons of endocasts and living brains suggest the following rough and ready account of vertebrate brain evolution. The subdivisions of the nervous system into spinal cord, hindbrain, midbrain and forebrain have persisted throughout the vertebrate line. But there have been several major episodes of encephalisation in the course of vertebrate evolution, giving rise to groups with distinctive EQs.

Figure 7.3 shows vertebrate EQs in relation to an 'average mammal', which has been assigned an EQ of '1'. Reptiles, which broadly share the encephalisation of fish, have an EQ about 1/20th that of an average mammal. This has been stable for many tens of millions of years. Stability is success: the reptilian brain is clearly quite adequate to the reptile's needs.

Between 200 and 150 million years ago two major groups departed from the reptilian stock: birds and mammals. As Figure 7.3 shows, their succes-

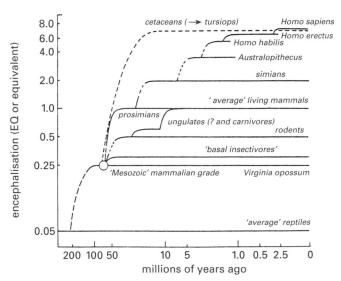

Figure 7.3 Vertebrate encephalisation quotients A comparison between the size of the brain in a variety of living and fossilised species and the size expected for an 'average' living mammal, a category including prosimians, like lemurs, cats and dogs. The circle at about 60 million years ago marks the start of the great 'adaptive radiation' of mammals. Solid lines indicate fairly complete records; broken lines show extrapolations.

sors continued to 'gain brain'. From our human vantage point, two developments were especially important: the appearance around 60 million years ago of primates, and the rapid evolution of the brains of our recent ancestors over the past 5 million years.

The later chapters of mammalian evolution have given rise to three broad groups of living mammals. The first contains rodents, like rats and mice, and insectivores, like anteaters, whose EQs fall some way below the mammalian average; the second group comprises ungulates, like cows and sheep, carnivores, like cats and dogs, and the least sophisticated of the primates, the prosimians, whose EQs all fall close to the mammalian average; the third group, including monkeys, man and the cetaceans (whale and dolphins), has moved well ahead of the rest. An 'average' primate has an EQ of 2; we have an EQ of 7–8; dolphins do not fall far short.

All this goes to show that brains – some brains – have got substantially bigger over the course of vertebrate evolution. And not just bigger, but bigger in relation to their bodies, suggesting a gain in 'brain power'. This raises several questions. What do I mean by 'brain power'? Whatever I mean, is there good evidence that EQs correlate with it? If so, why?

I have used the coy term 'brain power' quite deliberately. 'Intelligence' might have been a more obvious choice, but intelligence tends to be rather narrowly construed, with its connotations of 'IQ' tests in man and maze learning in rats. Harry Jerison, a palaeontologist of the brain, whose work I have drawn on in the last few pages, came up with a magnificently evasive definition of 'biological intelligence', in a heroic effort to avoid too narrow an interpretation: for Jerison, intelligence is 'the behavioural consequence of the total neural information-processing capacity in representative adults of a species, adjusted for the capacity to control routine bodily functions'.[18] But Jerison is surely right to be evasive. Think of the variety of ways in which an animal might use some *extra* capacity: to allow it to explore a new modality of sensation, to sharpen the perceptual distinctions it already draws, to expand its memory, to increase its ability to 'model' the future and plan ahead, to refine its manipulative skills. Any of these uses could sophisticate its behaviour and boost its 'biological intelligence'.

Different animals will indeed have different needs, and develop different aspects of intelligence: biological intelligences, in the plural, will gradually evolve. This creates a difficulty in answering my second question, whether EQs correlate with intelligence – for we need a means of comparing intelligence in different species. There can be no perfect comparator. Suffice it to say that where direct comparisons can be made, for instance in tests in which different species of mammal are required to deduce a simple rule, the results are predicted by EQs: primates outperform carnivores, who outperform rodents.[19]

But why should EQs correlate with intelligence? This may seem obvious: bigger brains, more brain power, more intelligence. But can one be a little more precise? Pleasingly, one can.[20] The functional 'information-processing' unit of the cerebral cortex, the cortical 'column', is common to every mammal, and occupies much the same surface area in a rat, a cat and a man. The surface area of the cortex, in turn, is directly related to brain weight. Thus as brain weight increases in mammals, so should the capacity for information processing. Once an allowance has been made for body size, any residual 'brain weight' will be proportional to extra 'processing resources'. Bigger brain, more brain power: as you knew!

We have charted a major increase in brain size and power in some lines of descent over the 500 million years of vertebrate evolution. So far I have written as if the *whole* brain enlarged equally. Is that right?

Neither altogether right, nor altogether wrong. There are clear examples in which some small part of the brain has hypertrophied greatly in the service of a particular need: this is true, for instance, of areas in the brainstem of fish with an electric sense and of bats which echolocate. Jerison refers to this as the 'principle of proper mass': as the 'processing demands' of a function of the brain increase, so must the volume of brain which supports it.

But in general when brains enlarge they follow predictable trends, and ours are no exception. The relative proportions of the human brain are much as might be predicted for a primate brain the size of ours.[21] Our brains are built along standard lines – only bigger. How did we come to acquire them?

The tree of man

The tree of man was never quiet . . .

A.E. Housman[22]

Of all the animals, man has the largest brain in proportion to his size.

Aristotle[23]

Between 65 and 90 million years ago small squirrel-like mammals hunted insects in the trees. It is likely that they were mainly active at night. You and I are their descendants, an honour we share with about 230 other species of 'primate' – the name, meaning chieftain, chosen by the zoologist Linnaeus for our Order in 1758.[24]

There are three great groups of living primates: the relatively primitive prosimians, the group which includes lemurs, lorises and tarsiers; monkeys, found both in the New World and the Old; and the hominoids, comprising the gibbons, chimps, gorillas, orang-utans – and man. Prosimians are the least intellectually sophisticated of the primates, with EQs today close to the 'average mammal' level of 1, akin to cats, dogs and deer. A number of other 'primitive features', such as an unfused chin bone, also distinguish the prosimians from their more encephalised cousins.

It is 40–50 million years since the line leading to monkey, ape and man diverged from the prosimian stock. A common relative of gorilla, chimp, orang-utan and man, *Proconsul*, is known from abundant fossil deposits in East Africa which are 15–23 million years old. Five- to eight-million years ago, a period for which the African fossil record is poor, a small but significant side branch departed from the lineage of hominoids. This was the start of the hominid line. One solitary species represents this branch today: it is of course our own, *Homo sapiens*.

The first hominids, all now extinct, were known as the 'australopithecines'. Their most famous representative is probably AL–288–1, better known as 'Lucy', the skeleton of a female australopithecine discovered by the American palaeo-anthropologist, Don Johanson, in the desiccated hills at Hadar, in Ethiopia, in 1974.[25] Lucy lived about 3 million years ago. She and her kind were small, but not diminutive: *Australopithecus afarensis* weighed 30–70 kilograms as adults, with a height of 1–1.5 metres. Their brain weight approached half a kilo, giving them an EQ of around 3.4, closer to the chimp's EQ of 2.6 than to the human EQ of 7 (average human brain weight is about 1.4 kilograms). Given these vital statistics, Lucy was no genius, but in one crucial respect she resembles her human successors more closely than any living ape: beyond reasonable doubt Lucy was habitually given to *walking upright*.

The footprints at Laetoli, in northern Tanzania, are among the most moving of all pre-human remains. Laetoli lies in the Rift Valley, one of the important East African sites excavated by several generations of the Leakey family and their collaborators. The Laetoli footprints were made by three australopithecines more or less contemporary with Lucy, as they crossed a carpet of fresh volcanic ash, disgorged from the nearby volcano, Sadiman. The ash had been wetted by rain; in the heat of the day the footprints dried and hardened rapidly. Soon afterwards they were covered over by another shower of ash. Other layers formed above them, but natural erosion eventually exposed some of the prints. Careful excavation in the late 1970s revealed their true significance.

These footprints show that the small-brained australopithecines walked very much as you and I do. We know from their fossils that their hip and leg bones had gone much of the way towards adopting the human form, in place of the configuration seen in the apes which suits them for swinging through the trees and scampering on all fours. Early hominids may have developed an upright stance because they lived in woodland, or open savannah, in place of the dense forest favoured by apes. But whatever its explanation, their fondness for walking upright had a momentous long-term result: a two-legged gait frees the hands for greater things than locomotion.

Several species of australopithecine lived in South and East Africa between four and one million years ago, the youngest of these 'ape-men' overlapping with the earliest examples of our own genus, *Homo*. The exact relationships between the australopithecine species are debated, but on current evidence *Australopithecus afarensis*, Lucy's species, lies close to or on the line which leads to man. Although the hands of australopithecines were evolving towards their human form, with lengthening thumbs and an increasing capacity for fine manipulation, there is no clear-cut evidence that Lucy and her kind used tools any more extensively than apes. Matters were soon to change.

2.4 million years ago a new variety of hominid and the earliest stone tools appear more or less simultaneously in the African fossil record. Specimens of *Homo habilis* have been gathered from the beautiful shores of Lake Turkana in Kenya, at Koobi Fora, from Olduvai Gorge in Tanzania and elsewhere. In keeping with her ability to fashion stone tools, the brain of *Homo habilis* was slightly larger than that of her australopithecine contemporaries, with a volume of 5–800 millilitres.

The earliest specimens of *Homo erectus*, *Homo habilis'* successor, also originate in Africa, from Lake Turkana, dating to 1.8 million years ago. Over the next 1.5 million years the nameless generations of *Homo erectus* left a record of increasingly sophisticated tools, and of an increasingly powerful brain. Important changes were also occurring in the structure of the throat which would gradually have allowed the sounds uttered by *Homo erectus* to approximate human speech: chimps, like human infants, are unable to shut off the nasal passage from the airway to the lungs, and cannot produce the sounds [i], [a], [u], [k] and [g]. One million years ago, *Homo erectus* had spread around the world, into Europe, the Middle East and throughout Asia.

The final chapter of human evolution is a matter for heated debate. The 'multiregionalist' school of thought holds that *Homo erectus* evolved into our own species, *Homo sapiens*, throughout the inhabited world. On this view human racial variations go deep: they had the opportunity to accumulate over a million years, while reproduction between members of adjacent groups has preserved the integrity of the species. The rival 'replacement' theory holds that there was a second diaspora from Africa around 100,000 years ago: as a result *Homo sapiens*, the children of an 'African Eve', replaced *Homo erectus* throughout his territory, later becoming the first hominid to colonise Australia and the Americas. On this view, the human racial differences in evidence today are superficial variations on a single basic type. Recent studies using molecular biology to compare DNA from different races support this latter 'Out of Africa' hypothesis of a recent common origin for all existing humankind.

This debate has a particular resonance in Europe.[26] Neanderthal man was at large in the Middle East and Europe between 200,000 and 35,000 years ago. Local descendants of *Homo erectus*, Neanderthals had brains as large as ours and an impressive range of cultural attainments. Their subsequent history hangs in the balance of the argument I have just outlined. To the multiregionalist they were the local torchbearers for humankind, my ancestors, and possibly yours; to the proponents of replacement, they were a sideshow, fated to extinction by African invaders.

The past 5 million years of evolution have sculpted the human animal from an ape-like ancestor. You may be surprised at the lack, in this account, of any mention of a 'missing link', described in the 1860s as the sought-after 'arch in an enormous bridge, which time has destroyed and which may have connected the highest of animals with the lowest of men.'[27] The twentieth century's finds have sketched the outlines of the bridge: no vital link is missing now. This is not to say that the fossil record is complete – none ever is or will be – but the surviving remains of the human line already document the crucial transformations, in gait, hand, voice and brain, between ancestral ape and modern man.

This chronicle of changing prehuman anatomy is an important part of the story of our origins. But so far I have told you only half the tale. This is not because of missing fossils, but because developments of quite another kind, less tangible yet even more profound, were taking place in early man. Human culture was evolving hand in hand with the human form.

From biology to history

> In the beginning was the Word . . .
>
> The Gospel According to St John, 1:1

Our sense of uniqueness depends less on our anatomy or gait than on our common culture – the intricate organisation of human society, the variety of human artefacts, and, above all, our versatile language. There are echoes of all three among the apes. Chimps prepare and deploy a number of tools, fishing for termites with carefully stripped twigs, soaking up water and washing with leaves; with some human encouragement they can use sign languages at the level of human two- and three-year-olds; and although their social organisation is loose-knit, their personal interactions look uncannily familiar. The chimp seems to teeter on the verge of humanity.[28] But without any question our abilities in all these domains outstrip the chimp's by far. They do so because, for 2–3 million years, human culture and the human brain have co-evolved. What do I mean by this?

The earliest stone tools known to date were fashioned by early hominids of the species *Homo habilis* in Ethiopia, Kenya, Zaire and Malawi, 2–2.6 million years ago. These animals were larger-brained than the australopithecines, but their EQ of around 4.5 falls well short of *Homo sapiens'* value of 7. There is compelling evidence that the rapid growth of the hominid brain over the next 2 million years occurred in concert with a growing wealth of cultural achievement (see Figure 7.4). It is likely that each fuelled the other in the struggle for survival, as the refinement of cultural traditions made possible by our enlarging brains increased the pressure for the intelligence with which to develop them further. What were the cultural achievements of early man? We know most, of course, about the more durable human creations.

By 1.8 million years ago the workers of the 'Oldowan Industry', the first well-defined tradition of stone tool manufacture, were already travelling up to 18 kilometres or more to gather their raw materials. Studies of remains from the same site, at Olduvai, indicate that the resulting tools were used for slicing meat from animal bones, and to crack them open for marrow. The proportions of flakes struck from stone cores in particular directions indicate that the majority of the tool makers were right-handed, hinting that 'lateralisation' of function was already under way in these early human brains. On this evidence, early hominids fashioned their tools

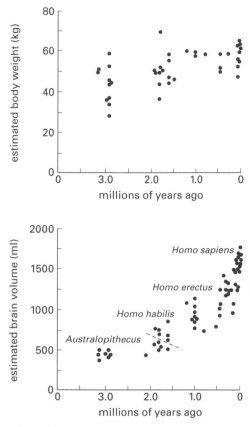

Figure 7.4 Body weight and brain volume in human evolution Body weight changed relatively little during the evolution of *Homo sapiens* from his australopithecine ancestors; the rate of change in brain volume was much steeper.

from carefully gathered materials, used them to butcher meat and had begun to develop the modern pattern of dexterity.

Around 1.5 million years ago, the reliably repeated structure of 'Acheulean' hand axes suggests that their makers were working from a pre-conceived form, which they carefully 'impressed on stone'. Manufacturing such tools may well have required a period of training, adding another human touch to the early hominids' way of life. By 3–500,000 years ago there is evidence of the controlled use of fire, of hearths and of constructed shelters. The first known wooden tools date from this time. Throughout this period the brain was growing rapidly towards its present size.

Around 100,000 years ago, within the span of Neanderthal man, *Homo sapiens* and brains of our current dimensions, the pace of cultural evolution quickened. The diversity of tools increased; deliberate burial became a widespread practice. Australia was peopled by modern man some 50,000, the Americas 15–30,000 years ago. The beginnings of figurative art 40,000 years ago reveal minds which were fully capable of symbolism: 'if modern man did not speak by that time one is at a loss to know' when he started.[29] Settled agriculture and the domestication of animals began in the Middle East and Western Asia 9–12,000 years ago. Life in conurbations followed close behind. Writing, using pictograms, was probably invented in Sumer, between the rivers Tigris and Euphrates, about 5,000 years ago.

This acceleration of cultural change signalled a new phase of human development. The long co-evolution of culture and brain had at last allowed human culture to take on an independent life. With the aid of language, leaps of imagination – like quirks of fashion – could bound from mind to mind, shaping and reshaping our civilised existence and our understanding of ourselves. Culture came to pattern work, knowledge, play and worship.

The evolution of culture, essentially an evolution of *ideas*, now occurs with a rapidity inconceivable in genetic evolution. In the past 150 years our society has mastered electricity, the combustion engine and the jet, radio and television, nuclear power and nuclear weapons, for better or for worse. The hominid brain has proved to be an awesome force in alliance with the human culture, which it creates – and was created by.

There are huge gaps in this telescopic narrative. The most gaping of these concerns language, surely the most potent of all human inventions. Stones weather better than conversations. However we may long to eavesdrop on the talk of our ancestors, we shall never know the origin of language with any certainty. There is some evidence that all languages spoken today share a common source at the diaspora of modern man.[30] It may be that *Homo erectus*' stone technology and the mastery of fire depended on the emergence of a proto-language, exploiting this species' newly won capacity for human utterance – but this is speculation.

There is one conclusion, though, which can be drawn with confidence from this brief account of our recent evolution. Man is a thoroughly cultural and cognitive animal – not in the outdated sense that we have a 'rational nature' superimposed on our animal being, but in the profoundly interesting sense that the essence of our biological identity lies in the evolution of our cultural and cognitive capacities.

How did the beginnings of human history conspire with our natural history to speed the growth of the human brain so dramatically over the past 2 million years? The size difference between the human brain and the chimpanzee's exceeds the difference between the chimp's and that of the mouse lemur, a tiny prosimian with an 'average mammalian' EQ.[31] Yet, given the time available, the making of the human brain cannot have demanded any major genetic transformation. Indeed we know that it did not, as over 98 per cent of the 'eloquent' DNA is identical in human and chimpanzee.

There may be a fairly simple explanation for the precipitate expansion of the human brain. The human infant's brain is the appropriate size for an 'average primate' of our human birth weight. But human brain growth continues at the foetal rate for a further two full years, while in our primate cousins brain growth tails off shortly after birth (see Figure 7.5). The result in man, as we have seen, is a brain of the standard primate type – just very much bigger than most. If this is correct, the key mechanism for human brain evolution may have been a postponement of the processes which curtail its growth in other primates. The extension of the growth phase of the brain has gone hand in hand with a prolongation of our childhood and of our life span, linked adaptations which have shaped the biological contours of our lives.

There is one salient difference between brain function in man and other primates which may also be relevant here. As we saw in Chapter 2, the human brain is markedly 'lateralised'. In right-handers – and indeed many left-handers – the left hemisphere is mainly responsible for language, numeracy and skilled action; the right hemisphere plays the leading part in many aspects of perception, especially in spatial awareness.

Work by the Bostonian neurologist Norman Geschwind and his collaborators in the late 1960s showed that there is an anatomical correlate for the

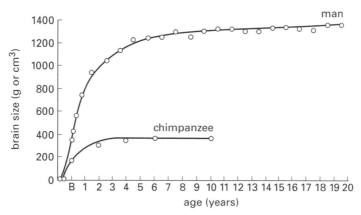

Figure 7.5 The growth of the brain in man and chimp The rapid foetal growth rate drops soon after birth in the chimp, but continues for around two years in man. The figures for the chimp are obtained from cranial capacity; those for man are for brain weight.

'dominance' of the left hemisphere: areas involved in processing language in the temporal lobe, part of Wernicke's area, are substantially larger on the left than the right in most human brains. But matters are not simple: the asymmetry is present in human adults, human infants – and in apes, but not monkeys. It is not, therefore, a specifically human development.

'Handedness' may be. Apes do show hand preferences, but these are no more often for one hand than the other. There is some evidence that *Homo erectus* may already have developed a consistent preference for the right hand in tool manufacture 2 million years ago. What sense can we make of all this?

Cerebral asymmetry is a feature of hominoid brains. Functional asymmetry, giving rise to our right-handedness, is a notable feature of human brains, and probably of their hominid precursors. This subject is in need of further research. But it is possible that a novel lateralisation of brain function, allowing a more efficient use of cortical resources, has been an important adjunct to the growth of the hominid brain and the blossoming of our intelligence.

Our species, *Homo sapiens*, with its bursting brain, is the terminus of the journey we have charted in this chapter. We exist 'on many a thousand grains that issue out of dust', but our biology and history have endowed us richly with the fruits of consciousness. We are aware of our surroundings, of ourselves, and of awareness itself. It is time to ask why nature has gone to such trouble. What is consciousness for, and when did it first arise? These questions are interdependent. If we were clear about the function of consciousness, we could go and see which animals do whatever it does, and infer that *they* are conscious. If we knew *which* animals were conscious, we could look and see what is special about the things they do, and infer the functions of consciousness. As things stand, there is no certainty about how to answer either question. Let's relax, suspend our assumptions and take an inquisitive sniff at the problem.

The coming of consciousness

The uses of awareness

To make so much of consciousness may have been my first mistake. There is much to be said for irresponsible stupefaction.

Philip Roth, *The Anatomy Lesson*[32]

> . . . consciousness is the tutor who supervises the education of the living
> substance . . . .
>
> Erwin Schrödinger[33]

What is consciousness for? What biological purpose is served by our keen appreciation of a nettle's sting, the sweetness of honey, the trilling of a nightingale, a beautiful face, a gnawing hunger, or the shades of colour in a dawn sky? And what is the use of our intentions, our conscious purposes? How do these help us to chart a course through the world?

These questions may strike you as far-fetched. Experience and volition are self-evidently useful. We are no good to anyone while fast asleep. Maybe – but their usefulness has been called into question. If our nervous system is indeed a biological machine, what 'added value' does consciousness supply? Let's think through a few examples.

Occasionally I go jogging along the slippery paths of Edinburgh. About once a year, I twist one of my joints. Consciousness plays little part in the first half-second of reflex response – but it certainly plays a part thereafter, the baleful discomfort reminding me, as I hobble around, that I really had better not.

First thing every morning I negotiate a series of hazards as I try to get up and out. The current routine is well established: climb out of bed, run downstairs, fill bottle for baby, make pot of tea for us, shower, shave, munch breakfast, leave; avoid dressing children if possible. These activities are seldom memorable and can usually be accomplished half-asleep – but the pattern is not fully automatised. Nor could it be: sharp objects left by the toddler on the floor between bed and bedroom door claim their price, if not carefully avoided, and some attention is needed to select appropriate subroutines: even at 7 a.m., do *not* empty the entire packet of tea into the teapot (a procedure reserved for the caddy), and remember that toothpaste is preferable to shaving foam for cleaning one's teeth, however similar the dispensers look these days. Even in these humdrum activities of daily living, there is a degree of unpredictability which requires a flexibility of response, and a range of options which demand attentive choice.

If I manage to leave home, I may get a chance to think through a problem at work. This calls for close attention, usually at intervals, sometimes over weeks, months or even years. Information must be gathered from a range of sources, brought together, synthesised. This prepares the ground for a solution. The problem will have to compete for attention with other distracting stimuli, like pretty girls in the library. Eventually an answer may emerge – or it may not. Conscious control of the process which delivers the answer is limited, but once delivered it belongs to consciousness.

Problem solving, generally, involves a delicate balance between conscious preparation and unconscious 'processing'. Most of us have had the odd experience of searching the memory for a name or a telephone number, to no avail – only to find it ready and waiting on waking the following day. On a loftier plane, the chemist Kekulé attributed his discovery of the ring-structure of benzene to a dream in which he glimpsed a snake-like chain of atoms grasping its own tail; Otto Loewi dreamed the experiment which proved the chemical basis of neurotransmission. In both cases conscious effort was a prerequisite for the delivery of the solution by unconscious problem solving.

Each day brings its share of conversations. Their potential scope is literally infinite. Apart from the most unpromising exchanges of stylised greetings, every human dialogue makes major demands on attention. Conscious control of conversation, like problem solving, is mysterious: we only know what we mean once we have said what we think. But communication tends to demand, and articulate, consciousness. Imagine, for example, that you are interrupted at your desk by a colleague who spent the weekend in the hills. She is not an experienced climber and has no head for heights. Her enthusiastic friend led her from hillside on to scree, from scree to boulders, from boulders on to a ridge which plunged to a lake on one side, down icy rock on the other. As she describes her walk you share a *frisson* of terror, imagining what she must have felt, and you express your sympathy. Years later you may remember what she told you.

Two hundred medical students pass annually through the department in which I work. I help to teach half of them. Among other things, my hundred students need to learn how to judge the 'tone', the degree of floppiness or stiffness, in the limbs of their patients, and how to elicit reflexes, like the 'knee jerk'. These manoeuvres can give useful clues to the causes of problems with movement. To teach these tricks, I try to remember why beginners find them difficult to master. There are several reasons: anxiety that they might cause pain, uncertainty about how to position the patient, or how to swing the hammer, ignorance of what to expect and to look for. I do not know how well I teach them, but to have any chance of success I need to be aware of how *I* set about these tests, *and* be able to put myself back in the place of the beginner.

Episodes like these are familiar to everyone: they are the stuff of our everyday lives. Varieties of perceptual awareness and conscious purpose seem to be their indispensable ingredients. What purpose do they serve?

In their different ways they enable us to select appropriate actions to meet the unpredictable challenges which every day offers up: the twisted ankle, the toys on the floor, the scheduling of the early morning routine, the problem in search of a solution, the cut and thrust of conversation, the challenge of imparting a skill. If this intuitive answer is halfway right, consciousness is closely linked to the control of behaviour.

Three simple predictions follow: we should expect, by and large, to be conscious of events on which we can make an impact; we should not expect to be conscious of routine activities, which can look after themselves; finally, we might expect there to be limits on the capacity of consciousness as there are simple physical limitations to the number of jobs we can do at once. Are these predictions borne out?

In general we do not encounter *futile* consciousness. Until recently, for example, there would have been no benefit in having perceptual awareness of events occurring within us, like the enlarging coat of 'fur' on an artery wall or the gradual rise of the blood sugar in early diabetes – and indeed we know nothing about them until we suffer some uncomfortable consequence. In contrast there are some internal states we *can* do something about, like dehydration, undernourishment or my sprained joint. These internal states create challenges we are equipped to meet: they are the source of our simpler motivations, our hungers, thirsts and pains.

Automatic routines do tend to slip from consciousness. Learning to ride a bike at the age of five absorbs all our attention. Setting off on it, 30 years later, our minds are free for other things, as we whistle, chat or ponder. Novelty and unpredictability can always summon consciousness back to the task: if we have to get to grips with a unicycle, or deal with a slippery road.

The limited capacity of consciousness is well recognised. We can switch its focus flexibly, from the book on our knee to the view from the window, from the sounds on the road to the smells from the kitchen. We can divide our attention – but only so far. You could not simultaneously read this paragraph and pay your bills, or listen carefully to music while you plan the day ahead.

The obvious idea that consciousness helps us to select appropriate actions in an unpredictable world has several strengths and weaknesses. Its principal strength lies in its intuitive appeal: surely it *must* be true that our awareness of our body and of our surroundings supplies us with information which we use to guide our behaviour; it *must* be true that our intentions govern our actions.

But correlation does not imply causation. Consciousness is certainly correlated with the scenarios I have described, but maybe our perceptual awareness and avowed intentions are in fact causally irrelevant to our behaviour. Most people rebel against this idea, but it is given some credence by examples like the case of DF. If you recall, she is unable to *report* the orientation of a slot by word or deed, yet she can post objects through it with remarkable accuracy. Her case suggests that consciousness may be less essential to our behaviour than we suppose. This counter-example is not all that compelling. Like patients with blindsight, DF is very handicapped: blindsight is no substitute for real sight.

This simple proposal has a second apparent weakness, which might just be a strength. My account of the function of consciousness looks suspiciously like our general account of the function of nervous systems: the detection of events within and around us, and the orchestration of apt responses to them. But in the last chapter we came to the conclusion that consciousness arises only from certain kinds of activity in certain parts of complex nervous systems. We need to ask ourselves what is special about these. One way to attack this question is to ask: *when* did consciousness come on the scene?

The souls of animals

> . . . there is nothing which leads feeble minds more readily astray from the straight path of virtue than to imagine that the soul of animals is of the same nature as our own.
>
> René Descartes[34]

> I have no idea whether fleas, grasshoppers, crabs or snails are conscious. . . . We do not know at present how far down the evolutionary scale consciousness descends.
>
> John Searle[35]

> From a strictly behavioural point of view, the existence of consciousness might be inferred when a living organism responds to environmental events in an adaptive way that is not entirely automatic.
>
> Marcel Mesulam[36]

> Cognition is . . . the construction of a real world of experience.
>
> Harry Jerison[37]

In charting the lengthy evolutionary tale of the human brain I kept rather quiet about consciousness. But we cannot avoid asking where it belongs in the scheme of evolution. We generally consider that sticks and stones are unconscious. What of prokaryotes, eukaryotic unicells, *C. elegans*, insects, fish, cats, cows, monkeys – and humans? Few questions in science or philosophy have excited more heated and contradictory answers.

Much that we have learned about consciousness so far suggests that it is tied to the activity of nervous systems. This widespread assumption is open to question.[38] But if we accept it for the time being, we can conclude that prokaryotes and unicells are unconscious, as they have none.

C. elegans poses much more of a problem. It undoubtedly has a nervous system, though it lacks a major neuronal aggregation worthy of the name of brain. The number of neurons in question is tiny, as we have seen. More importantly, *C. elegans* 'represents' its environment in only the most tenuous sense. It may shrink from a touch or pursue a pheromone, but can scarcely conduct a detailed 'perceptual analysis' of its surroundings. Stimulus and response are too closely interwoven. Moreover, its repertoire of actions is extremely limited, and its responses highly predictable. Setting aside the possibility that *C. elegans* displays some kind of activity cycle, a pale shadow of our rhythm of sleep and waking, most of us would probably agree that *C. elegans* is unconscious. There is nothing it is like to be a worm. But I must confess to a faint but genuine sense of unease as I write this, reflecting how little we know for certain about consciousness.

You and I, on the other hand, are conscious in every sense of the word – which leaves us with the status of insects, fish, cats, cows and monkeys to resolve. It is comforting that many of those who have thought about this question most deeply remain perplexed. Some biologists have suggested an answer along the following lines.

A vital part of the work of the mammalian brain, an important aspect of biological intelligence, is the creation of a perceptual world. This, for example, is the task of much of the visual brain which we toured in Chapter 5. It is useful to many animals, including ourselves, to be able to distinguish, identify and re-identify objects, to tell a blackberry from a poison berry, our enemy from our friend, our own child from another's. It seems unlikely, on general biological grounds, that the consciousness which attends these human abilities appeared abruptly in the brief period of evolution which separates us from our primate cousins. It is more probable that, like the great majority of our biological abilities, perceptual consciousness is the product of a long evolutionary gestation, and grew up with the neural equipment upon which perception depends.

Conscious intentions lack the qualitative texture of perceptions. But a similar argument applies to these. The creation of our perceptual world is ultimately justified by the judicious selection of actions. The processes which give rise to our conscious plans must surely have their precursors in animal brains. The chimp who fetches a twig to fish for termites, and probably even the dog who brings you his lead, have definite aims in mind.

These general conclusions are regrettably vague. It is likely that monkeys enjoy a perceptual awareness similar to our own. Remember the monkeys with blindsight who were able to tell us that in their blind fields they could not see. But what of insect, cow, cat and fish? We may never be able to give a comprehensive account of the kinds of consciousness, if any, they enjoy. But we can get some way there – by studying the perceptual distinctions and classifications that animals can make, discovering how they exploit them in their behaviour, and and examining the neural resources they rely on. Where perceptual distinctions are richly drawn, behaviour flexible and nervous systems complex, we should take seriously the possibility of consciousness. Animal awareness, where it exists, might of course be very alien to our own experience: fish for example operate with about 1/160th of the relative neural resources we can deploy, and harness them to very different ends.

A broad contrast between two strategies of animal reproduction sheds some unexpected light on the ground we are covering.[39] The key to biological success is to make as sure as possible that your descendants multiply and prosper. This can be achieved in two contrasting ways: by spawning huge numbers of offspring in the hope that some at least will survive, or by producing just a few and making every effort to ensure that they prosper. Insects and fish do the former, we the latter, and other species fall somewhere on the spectrum in between.

The 'choice' of strategy has implications which reverberate throughout an animal's make-up. Animals which spawn huge broods – and then leave their fate substantially to chance – tend to reach sexual maturity swiftly, to lead brief lives and to have small brains in relation to their bodies. Their behaviour is stereotyped; they neither can nor need to learn. Animals which nurture and support their young have longer gestations, extended childhoods, longer lives and larger brains. Longer lives and larger brains make it both possible and vital to learn about your surroundings and to adapt your behaviour to changing conditions. They, perhaps, provide the ground from which consciousness springs.

Harry Jerison has suggested a related scheme for thinking about the evolution of perceptual worlds.[40] Simple nervous systems get along well enough using what Jerison describes as 'machine language', the code of neural firing and synaptic chemistry. Machine language *per se* does not give rise to consciousness, but is adequate to the most basic kinds of sensori-motor integration. More complex nervous systems, perhaps including all existing vertebrate brains, organise the wealth of information with which they are bombarded by representing their surroundings in a different, conscious, code, constructing a world of objects, space and time. The most complex nervous system we know, our own, goes a step further, 'representing its representations' in the symbolic code of human language.

Much is uncertain about what consciousness does and which animals possess it. If there is an 'orthodox' view, I think it runs along these lines: consciousness is restricted to living things; indeed, it is restricted to a subset of living things, ones with brains sufficiently complex to allow them to draw fine perceptual distinctions, and to use them to select appropriate actions from an ample repertoire of behaviours. Consciousness, in other words, is the child of neural complexity. We shall think further about precisely what kind of neural complexity is required, and what kind of psychological benefits it might confer, in the next chapter.

A Darwinian conclusion: evolving awareness

Before you resort to a consciousness-altering drink, let me summarise progress in this chapter.

Contemporary physics and biology have sketched an ambitious account of our beginnings. It is, in a sense, our contemporary mythology, under-determined by the evidence, and doubtless incorrect in many details. Nevertheless it is the best cosmology to date, and has the great virtue that it is open to correction by new evidence.

The story begins with an eruption of a region of immensely compressed matter some 15,000 million years ago (see Figure 7.6). Galaxies, stars, planetary systems and the heavy elements formed in its wake. Our sun and its planets are one-third of the age of the universe since the Big Bang. The first evidence of life on earth is ancient, 3,500 million years old. Prokaryotic cells were joined by eukaryotes around 1,400 million years ago; the beginnings of multicellular life followed 5–700 million years ago. The chordate-vertebrate line originated in this explosion of biological diversity. Vertebrates came ashore 350 million years ago, giving rise successively to amphibians, reptiles, mammals and birds.

The elements of nervous systems – neuron, synapse, neurotransmitter and their receptors – are ancient indeed, originating in the common ancestors

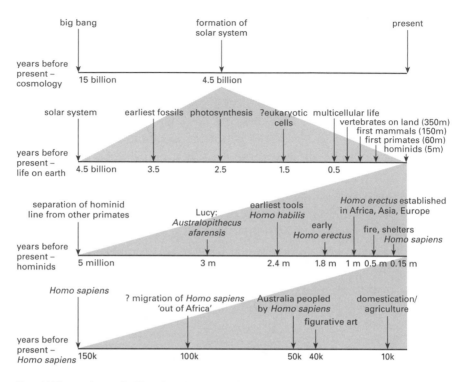

Note: 1 billion = 1 thousand million; 1k = 1 thousand. All figures are rough estimates. The question mark beside eukaryotic cells alludes to the uncertain relationship between prokaryotes and eukaryotes (see note 7, p.381); the question mark beside the migration of *Homo sapiens* 'out of Africa' refers to the uncertainty discused in the text (see end of 'The Tree of Man').

Figure 7.6 The chronology of everything A chronology for those, like me, who have difficulty holding huge time scales in mind.

of multicellular organisms. The basic structure of the contemporary verte-brate brain is already apparent in early fossils, some 400 million years old. Although some successful vertebrates have retained small brains, an increase in brain substance beyond the demands of body size – 'encephalisation' – has been a striking feature in other lines of vertebrate descent. This is especially true of the line which leads from reptile to mammal, primate and man.

The hominid twig which leads to man departed from the primate bush 5–8 million years ago. Australopithecines, with brains not much larger than contemporary apes, walked over 3 million years ago, freeing the hands for action. Stone tools were first manufactured by *Homo habilis*. Over the following 2 million years, through the heyday of *Homo erectus*, human culture and the human brain developed in tandem: cultural advance was probably a major stimulus for the rapid evolution of the brain. Before the appearance of *Homo sapiens* our human ancestors were fashioning finely honed tools of stone and wood, fetching raw materials from distant sites, using fire and building shelters. The source of *Homo sapiens* is controversial, but growing evidence favours an origin in Africa 100–200,000 years ago, with subsequent replacement of Neanderthals and *Homo erectus* throughout Africa and Asia. At some undetermined time in the course of hominid evolution the emergence of language created a new, symbolic, form of description, and the most powerful of all mankind's tools.

This story charts the evolution of the brain over millions of years. The same events must have brought about the evolution of awareness. What biological purpose has consciousness served? Reflection on the uses to which we put perception and intention, awareness of self and of others, suggests that they help us to select appropriate actions in an unpredictable world – building on the functions of the very simplest 'brains'.

Which animals are conscious is much debated. Encephalisation is associated with small broods, long lives, increasing biological intelligence, ever richer representations of the environment and increasingly flexible repertoires of response. One proposal suggests that simple nervous systems have no need of a 'perceptual code', while more complex nervous systems find it useful to develop conscious representations of objects organised in space and time.

Part V:
Consciousness considered

8

Scientific theories of consciousness

Introduction

The renaissance of interest in consciousness over the past two decades has encouraged scientists and philosophers to propose general theories of its mechanisms, its functions and its nature. In this chapter I shall concentrate on the scientists' contributions, turning to the philosophers in the following chapter. Some have focused on the neurobiology of awareness, nominating candidates for the 'NCC', the neural correlate of consciousness. Any given moment of visual awareness, they suppose, depends on activity in a network of brain regions: but *which* brain regions and what *kind* of activity? Others, grounded in computer science, have asked what role consciousness might play in the information-processing pathways of the brain: what distinguishes the contents of awareness from the plethora of unconscious information passing through the brain? A third group of theorists have looked beyond biology and computation to the wider human context of awareness, seeking its purpose in our sometimes devious social interactions. Most of these theories are targeted on the contents of, rather than the capacity for, consciousness: 'field theories' tackle both.

Before we take a look at these ideas I shall remind you of the facts they need to explain, broadening our focus on vision to take in some recent parallel disoveries about memory and action. I am also honour bound to point out a tricky problem for the science of consciousness, which helps to explain what we can and can't expect to learn from science about awareness.

The story so far: sight, memory and action

'That tree's talking and that tree's nodding its head . . . '.

A four year old boy watching the wind in the wood

Glancing from my window I can see the branches waving in the September wind, thousands of leaves in a gentle agitation, the first touches of gold on their late summer green quietly warning that they will soon be gone. This is the kind of visual experience, rich in interpreted form and motion, colour and depth, that a theory of visual consciousness must explain.

We have already encountered a range of processes which offer promising leads: analysis of the features of the visual scene in the numerous cortical areas devoted to sight; the traffic between these areas and regions of the temporal lobes where our memories are stored; the mechanisms serving attention which allow *visual* experience, rather than, say, the chattering from the room next door, to come to the forefront of awareness. And we have encountered two promising approaches to identifying precisely which kinds and locations of neural activity are critical for consciousness. First, the delineation of the brain activity which changes when experience changes without any change in the world around us – in imagination, hallucination and shifts of attention – should help to identify the neural processes most intimately tied to visual experience. Second, the definition of the brain activity which subserves implicit or unconscious perception, in blindsight, neglect and agnosia, should enlighten us about those neural processes which do not give rise to any experience at all.

Much of the recent thinking about consciousness has focused on vision. This is not surprising: vision is our best-developed and best-understood sense. But consciousness casts its light into every corner of the mind: we have conscious memories and conscious plans as well as conscious sensations. Any theory of awareness needs to take account of these, and the study of memory and action has yielded some important discoveries which parallel the results of work on vision.

Cast your mind back to yesterday evening. Where did you have supper? Who with? What did you drink? Did your plate rest on a table mat, a tablecloth, a bare table or did you balance it on your knees while you watched something a bit shameful on TV? Maybe you had a picnic. The chances are that you can answer all these questions very accurately – perhaps after pause for thought. Doing so exercises a particular kind of memory, known as *declarative episodic* memory: it is declarative in the sense that the memory is conscious and can be 'declared', episodic in the sense that you have recalled a unique occasion from your past. Declarative memory also comes in another flavour, *semantic*, which we encountered in Chapter 5 (p. 182): as well as being able to recall and describe episodes from the past, we can articulate a huge amount of general knowledge, from the dates of the world wars to explaining just what 'an armchair' is.

We have known for about 50 years that acquiring declarative memories like these requires the healthy working of the limbic system, in particular a circuit which runs from the hippocampi in the medial temporal lobes to the thalamus, and then back to the hippocampi via regions of cerebral cortex (see Figure 2.15, p. 66).[1] If critical parts of this pathway are removed or gravely damaged, the ability to acquire declarative memories is damaged with them. HM, whom we met in Chapter 2, is the most celebrated victim of this fate: his medial temporal lobes were removed from both sides of the brain in 1953 to cure his epilepsy. He was, poignantly, left stranded in a 'perpetual present' from that day to this, lacking any conscious memory of the intervening days and years. But it turns out that HM and others like him have not entirely lost the ability to learn. Several kinds of learning are spared by the 'amnesic syndrome' (see Figure 8.1): classical conditioning, priming and the acquisition of new motor skills.

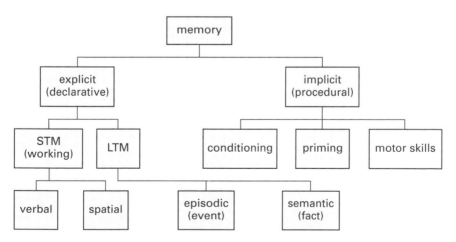

Figure 8.1 The taxonomy of memory The distinctions drawn between varieties of memory in this classification broadly correspond to distinctions between neurological systems. The acquisition of long-term declarative memories depends on the healthy operation of structures in the circuit of Papez. STM = short-term memory; LTM = long-term memory.

Classical or 'Pavlovian' conditioning is the process by which a neutral event, like the ringing of a bell, if it is regularly paired with an emotive one, like the mouth-watering appearance of a morsel of food, gradually comes to elicit the 'unconditioned' response to the event with which it is paired – in this case salivation. This is a powerful form of learning. I still shrink from drinking the liqueur which I once sipped, duty-free, at the start of an extremely rough and nauseating ferry ride across the English Channel; I was at one time almost as strongly moved by a girlfriend's rose-petal scent as by her bodily presence. Priming is also a familiar form of learning. Sometimes a photograph of a familiar object, like a toothbrush or a kettle, taken from an unfamiliar angle, baffles us at first glance. But once we have 'seen it', the sense of puzzlement is hard to recapture: on a second encounter we recognise it straight away. To measure priming, psychologists often use 'fragmented figures' (see Figure 8.2): no one is likely to recognise the figure at the top of the series, unless they have been 'primed' by past exposure to its neighbours. Motor learning is more or less self-explanatory. HM was able to acquire the – perhaps not terribly useful – skill of mirror writing, and steadily improved his performance in other manual tasks, despite his lack of any conscious recollection of previous attempts. *This* feature is the really startling one: all these forms of learning – the conditioning of desire and of disgust,

Figure 8.2 Fragmented figures Figures like these are used in studies of priming. Amnesic patients gradually learn to recognise increasingly fragmented examples from these series.

the priming of recognition, and the acquisition of skills – are independent of the ability to recall the occasions of learning. The brain has multiple memory systems, and only some of them support conscious recollection.

These discoveries about memory offer an analogy to the results from the study of vision. Episodic memory, the ability to summon up a vivid recollection of events, is a conscious process analogous to the experience of sight; procedural memory, the ability to store a record of events and actions which can later influence behaviour *without* any requirement for conscious recall, is analogous to the unconscious visual guidance manifest in blindsight. The study of action supplies a second set of parallels.

Some of our actions are deliberate: we can justify or, at least, explain them. I walked round the park a few minutes ago – because I wanted to stretch my legs and the fine September day lured me from my desk. This seems straightforward enough. But sometimes the content of our intentions is subverted. If I told you that my desktop computer had *ordered me* to take my walk, or that my legs had *made me* go against my will, you would be rightly concerned, as such 'delusions of control' are a common symptom of psychosis.[2] They stand to our ordinary experience of intention as hallucinations stand to ordinary vision. Moving into stranger territory still, neurological patients with the 'alien limb syndrome' can offer no explanation at all of movements made by their arm or leg although these may look highly purposeful – reaching into a pocket, downing a glass of squash or even interfering with the willed activity of other limbs.[3] In psychosis the awareness of intention survives, but is perverted; in alien limb syndrome it is lost altogether.

The awareness of intention also slips away in a much less exotic context. For the seasoned operator, brushing teeth, tying shoelaces or a necktie demands very little attention. Much that we do is habitual. Yet when we are *learning* these skills we have to concentrate hard – as we also do if ordinary circumstances change, as when, at least in my case, the tie requires a bow. So here is a second set of parallels (see Table 8.1). Deliberate action is analogous to conscious vision. Just as conscious vision can be derailed by hallucination, so the contents of our intentions can be distorted by psychosis. Automatic – and 'alien' – action offer a parallel to blindsight: both occur outside the realm of awareness, although, unlike the vision in a blind field, we can usually reactivate our awareness of automatic actions at a moment's notice.

We know a little about the basis for these unconscious processes in the brain. Classical conditioning particularly involves the cerebellum, a part of

Table 8.1 Parallels between vision, memory and action

	vision	memory	action
Stimulus constant, experience changes	Shifts of attention Visual imagery Hallucinations Shifts in perception of multistable figure	Declarative memory	Delusion of control

Experience constant, behaviour changes	Visually guided behaviour in:
	    Blindsight
	    Neglect
	    Agnosia
		Procedural memory	Automatic behaviour
			Alien limb

the brain usually involved in controlling movement.[4] Priming leads to a reduction in the local brain activity excited by the stimulus in question, for example in the visual areas, suggesting that repeated exposure to the stimulus increases the efficiency of the neural processing it excites.[5] Similarly, as motor skills become automatic, global brain activation declines.[6] The pattern of activation also changes. In particular, activity tends to shift away from areas in the 'prefrontal cortex', which are engaged by the acquisition of new skills, to more posterior regions of the cortex and some 'subcortical' regions, like the basal ganglia.[7]

These three sets of parallel distinctions – between conscious vision and blindsight, declarative and procedural memory, deliberate and habitual actions – together with what is known of their correlates in the brain, lie at the foundations of contemporary theories of consciousness.[8] But before we home in on them, I must delay you for a moment with a methodological problem which goes deep.

A methodological wrinkle: the necessity for report

> Heard melodies are sweet, but those unheard
> Are sweeter . . .
>
> John Keats[9]

Science deals in observables. We can use science to reach *towards* the unobservable – towards the invisibly small, in subatomic physics, or towards the unattainable extremes of space and time as we explore the structure and history of the universe. But no scientific theory is worthy of the name unless it makes some tangible predictions that can be tested.

This creates at least the semblance of a problem for the science of consciousness.[10] For we do not ordinarily regard experience as being directly observable.[11] I may be oblivious to the gnawing toothache you are keeping to yourself, or of your secret happiness, or that tune you can't get out of your head. What you tell me, and what your actions reveal, will generally give me a fair idea of how it is with you – but they are no more than clues to the contents of your consciousness. Like particle physics and cosmology, research on consciousness has to be conducted at one remove from the phenomenon itself, reliant on reports and indications of awareness.

Indeed, to make matters worse, it is not obvious that conscious experience need always be accessible to report, even in principle. Typical instances of consciousness are manifestly open to description. Glance out of *your* window: you could describe the view that greets you in a few words, or sketch it on a pad, or match the colour of the sky to one of a set of samples. But is the possibility of reporting experience an absolute prerequisite for consciousness?

Cast your mind some chapters back. The ability to move is definitely not required for consciousness: paralysis is no obstacle to awareness, as we have seen. Language is probably dispensable: few of us doubt that one-year-olds and some animals, or adults rendered languageless by stroke, are conscious. The formation of long-term memories usually accompanies consciousness: but we have encountered research by anaesthetists suggesting that it is not crucial for awareness. Perhaps, at the very least, the capacity to frame a thought about experience is required for consciousness. This notion echoes the etymology of 'consciousness': the use of the word suggests the 'sharing of knowledge with oneself'. But even this is open to some doubt: is a pain really painless if I cannot frame a thought about it? Is an isolated conscious sensation, an 'unarticulated flash of sensation', a logical impossibility? Many of the theories of consciousness we are about to encounter assume that unless we can think about our experience we cannot be conscious. But is this so?

We do not know the minimal conditions for consciousness. Here is a 'thought experiment' which may at least help to clarify the problem. Imagine that we could isolate, or that nature somehow had isolated, a human visual system. Would such an isolated system be capable of visual experience? If it were genuinely isolated, most bets would be against any experience at all. For one thing, it would lack the activation from the brainstem which is normally required to maintain the waking state. So let's be generous and build this in. Now we have an isolated visual system, activated from the brainstem as it would be in a waking brain. And let us also allow it to have a visual input, say a view of a richly coloured abstract scene. Some sophisticated readers may be uneasy about all this: the brain is massively interconnected, and it is open to question whether the results of activity in 'isolated' systems can be sensibly discussed. But indulge me: there is no reason in principle why one could not set up the neuronal conditions which normally occur in the visual system during the perception of this abstract scene. If, for the sake of argument, one did so, in a system which clearly has no means of 'reporting' its experience to others or even to itself, could the activity give rise to an experience?

Reactions to this thought experiment vary. Some find the idea that experience might occur in these circumstances absurd or misconceived. I personally find it plausible that a visual experience might occur – although one has to remind oneself how limited the experience would be. It would lack any self-reference or personhood, any resonance with past experience, any linguistic dimension, any capacity to give rise to action. But one's intuition about the truth of the matter in this particular case is less important than the uncertainty it underlines: we are as unsure of the minimal conditions for consciousness in the human brain as of the minimal conditions for consciousness in the animal kingdom. It is not self-evident that the possibility of report is a prerequisite.[12]

If not, some consequences follow for the science of awareness. First, the gulf between the contents of consciousness and the observations we can make of them creates a difficulty which needs to be acknowledged – or challenged – rather than ignored. Recognising the problem creates a healthy scepticism towards any theory which claims to say the last word on awareness. Second, more specifically, it calls into question any theory of consciousness which *assumes* that the neural processes underlying consciousness must be accessible to the processes which subserve action and report – as at least one influential recent theory does. Third, very generally, the gulf between experience and observation suggests that theories of consciousness which emphasise the importance of the normal integrated function of the brain may be built on an artefact of observation.[13] All these points will come into focus soon, as we examine the theories in question.

I have considered this problem at some length to sound a note of caution, without meaning to overplay its importance. For one thing, typical instances of conscious experience are accessible to report and it may be unwise to lean too heavily on unusual cases. Any science of visual awareness clearly has to get started by observing the observable: reports and indications of aware-ness. For another thing, the possibility of unreportable awareness is open to argument. It assumes a concept of experience – private, unobservable – which many philosophers dispute. We shall look closely at their reasons in Chapter 9. But first, let's turn to the scientists who have tried to encapsulate what we know about experience in comprehensive theories of awareness.

The 'where' and 'how' of conscious vision

Just about every scientist who has tried his hand recently at a theory of consciousness agrees on some basic points. It is taken for granted that consciousness *matters*, in the sense that it allows us to do all kinds of things that would be impossible without it; that consciousness is bound up with the brain, but that not all the activity occurring in the brain is conscious; that deep structures in the brainstem and thalami are crucial to arousal while activity in the thalami and cortex determines the contents of consciousness; that the activity giving rise to consciousness is spread around the brain rather than occurring at a single location, and that several psychological systems participate in it (see Figure 8.3). Most

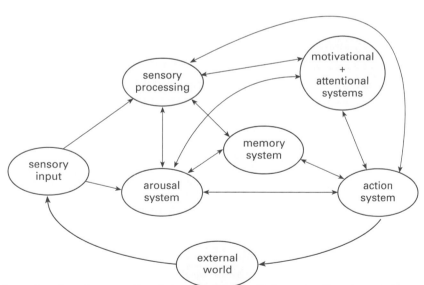

Figure 8.3 Consciousness from interaction Paths of information flow through the brain. We know that pathways and modules of these general kinds exist. Many contemporary theories of consciousness locate the genesis of consciousness in interactions between two or more of these modules.

theories also assume that the neural correlate of consciousness will be a loosely linked but temporarily coherent network of neurons spread around the brain, a grouping christened a 'cell-assembly' by the prescient Canadian psychologist Donald Hebb.[14]

These major points of agreement leave plenty of scope for dispute about critical details. How large must a cell assembly be to give rise to consciousness? Need it incorporate particular types of neuron, or particular layers of cortex? Must the interactions within the assembly attain a certain level of complexity? Must its activity be of a particular kind or duration? Need it involve particular cortical regions, or have a certain range of connections with regions elsewhere? And how do these details relate to the psychological structure of consciousness? Differing answers to these questions distinguish the theories on offer. Some theories stress the anatomy, the 'where', of consciousness, others its physiology, the 'how'. We will take anatomy first.

Where?

a million-fold democracy whose each unit is a cell . . .

Sir Charles Sherrington

Theorists of consciousness disagree on which brain regions are critical for visual awareness. I shall introduce you to one strongly argued and fairly typical suggestion, and we can then examine some rivals which offer a range of variations on the theme.

Gerald Edelman won the Nobel prize in 1972 for work in molecular immunology before turning to consciousness. Like Francis Crick, the co-discoverer of the structure of DNA, Edelman came to see the operation of the brain, and especially the genesis of awareness, as the outstanding challenge for contemporary biologists. The main thrust of his research is an effort to reconcile the subjective features of experience with the known biology of the brain structures likely to support it, and with the results of computer simulations of their presumed activity. He has views both on the 'where' and the 'how' of consciousness.

His anatomical proposal is that the neural correlate of consciousness (NCC) is a moving target, a shifting coalition of 'strongly interacting elements' which he and his colleague Giulio Tononi refer to as the 'dynamic core'.[15] At any given time the dynamic core responsible for 'primary consciousness' – our perceptual experience – comprises regions of the cerebral cortex, in brisk communication with one another and with their associated nuclei in the thalamus. The cortical regions include both areas of cortex, like the cortical visual areas, with a sensory role, and areas shaped by past experience which can imbue the stream of sensation with meaning and emotion.

Edelman and Tononi envisage that consciousness arises from the integration of activity across these areas, as information flows swiftly back and forth, allowing local cortical circuits to perform their specialised, 'segregated', functions, while simultaneously entering into a unifying dialogue with the other elements of the dynamic core. They claim that this 'model' of the neural processes subserving consciousness can account for many of its key subjective properties: its continuity and changefulness, its coherence and its pace of change, the existence of a focus of attention and a more diffuse surround, and the access of the contents of consciousness to the full range of our other psychological capacities – language, memory, emotion and decision making. In terms of the questions we identified earlier, Edelman's theory plays down any special role for particular neuronal types or cortical regions, but emphasises the importance of complex interactions within and between areas in the cortex and the thalamus.

Francis Crick and his collaborator Christof Koch have made a series of proposals along broadly similar lines to Edelman's but with instructive differences.[16] Crick and Koch anticipate that at any given moment the NCC will comprise a sparse but widespread network of neurons, whose activity will stand out above the background of neuronal firing for at least 100–200 milliseconds. They speculate that the neurons directly involved in the NCC may have 'some unique combination of molecular, pharmacologic, biophysical and anatomic properties': for example, Crick has speculated that 'bursty' pyramidal cells in layer 5 of the cortical visual areas play a critical role.

Recently, they have added another, controversial, strand to their theory.[17] In a paper in *Nature* in 1995 they proposed that neurons within area V1, the primary visual cortex, do not directly participate in the NCC for visual awareness, despite supplying much of the information that is processed in visual areas downstream. This idea has two sources: experimental work suggesting that our visual experience correlates more closely with the behaviour of neurons in higher visual areas, such as area V4, than in V1; and the theoretical notion that only cortical regions which can directly influence action, via interconnections with the frontal lobes, can contribute to consciousness. This is a direct statement of the idea we encountered – and questioned – in the last section, that conscious information must always be capable of guiding action. As we shall see, it is a recurring theme in recent theories.

If primary sensory areas make no direct contribution to awareness, perhaps whole swathes of cortex operate beyond the reach of consciousness. David Milner, whose studies of the patient DF we encountered in Chapter 6, has made a proposal along these lines.[18] DF, you may recall, was able to 'post' shapes she could not 'see'. Her remarkably accurate manipulation of shapes which she was unable to identify, among a wealth of other evidence, led Milner to the view that the 'dorsal' stream of visual processing is dedicated to the unconscious 'on-line' control of visually guided behaviour, while the ventral stream is responsible for the creation of our conscious visual world.

The broad idea mooted by both Edelman and Crick, that consciousness is conferred on otherwise unconscious neural processes by virtue of an interaction between brain regions – or between psychological processes – is taken up in differing ways by several authors. They include Larry Weiskrantz, the discoverer of blindsight, Jeffrey Gray, a psychologist whose thoughts about consciousness grew from studies of disordered thought and emotion, and Antonio Damasio, a neurologist whose main work has concerned the effects of brain damage on cognition and behaviour.

Weiskrantz argues that what is missing in a subject with blindsight, who can point to a target which he cannot see, or in an amnesic patient who can aquire a skill without any conscious recollection of the period of training, is 'the ability to render a parallel acknowledged commentary' on activities which he can still perform.[19] The primitive faculty – of sight or memory – survives, but the ability to 'comment' or reflect upon it, to make use of it in thought or imagery, has gone. Weiskrantz makes a helpful distinction between two views of this 'commentary stage': the first is that it merely *enables the acknowledgement* of consciousness which is somehow achieved by other means; the second more radical view, which he favours, is that making the commentary itself *endows* us with consciousness: 'it is what is meant by being aware and what gives rise to it'. Weiskrantz draws attention to the similarity between his view and the concept of consciousness advanced by the philosopher David Rosenthal. Rosenthal suggests that to be conscious of what one is seeing is to be having the thought that one is seeing it: in other words, consciousness arises when thought illuminates unconscious sensation.[20]

Weiskrantz does not spell out the anatomy of the 'commentary stage' in great detail, although he anticipates that it will involve 'fronto-limbic' areas governing memory and action, to which Edelman and Crick also point. Jeffrey Gray is more specific.[21] Gray agrees with Weiskrantz that mere sensation is insufficient to give rise to consciousness. It results from a 'second pass' in which the unconscious data of sensation are compared with expectations generated by past experience and current intentions, in limbic regions of the temporal lobes and the basal ganglia. Gray construes the bizarre experiences which occur in schizophrenia as the result of a failure to pass sensory data through this secondary filter, which normally allows us to identify events of genuine significance.

Antonio Damasio offers another variation on the idea that consciousness arises from an interaction between brain processes, calling on a neural model of the self.[22] He suggests that consciousness arises only when the brain represents the effects of sensory data on the organism, by a process of 'second order mapping'. Once again this theory regards mere sensation as being insufficient for awareness: on Damasio's view it must first be transformed by a process which makes explicit the impact of the knowledge on the knower. Interestingly, Damasio locates the neural representation of the self in relatively ancient brain regions, in the upper brainstem, thalamus, deep forebrain nuclei and somatosensory cortex.

These theories are all 'interactive': they imply that consciousness depends upon dialogue between diverse regions of the brain which are usually associated with more or less independent psychological functions, like perception, emotion, memory and action. They contrast with models which envisage that consciousness can arise from relatively local activation of the brain. For example, Semir Zeki, the physiologist of vision, has proposed that each of the functional systems within the visual brain, like the system specialised for motion perception involving area V5, generates its own 'microconsciousness'.[23] This idea stems from evidence that we become aware of different aspects of visual stimuli after slightly but significantly different intervals: the 'microconsciousness' of an object's colour is marginally asynchronous with awareness of its shape. If this is so, ordinary visual awareness may result from the binding of a group of 'microconsciousnesses' rather than the binding of activities of cells at different sites. Zeki's ideas are reminiscent of our earlier thought experiment. He seems to suggest that an isolated visual system, or even one of its subsystems, might indeed be conscious.

So – which of these theories is *right*? They have a lot in common, differing in two main respects (see Figure 8.4). They diverge, first, in the amount of dialogue between brain regions and psychological functions which they

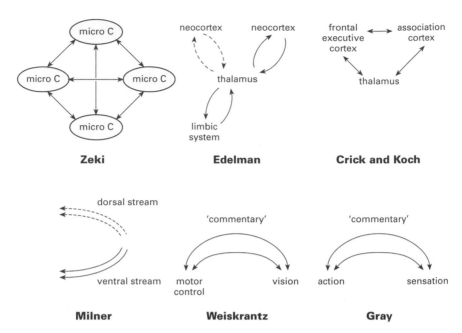

Figure 8.4 Theories of consciousness The theories discussed in the text are mostly interactive, envisaging that consciousness arises from dialogue between psychological or neural systems or subsystems. Dotted lines indicate unconscious or only potentially conscious (Edelman) processes.

consider necessary for consciousness: most, but not all, suggest that sensation becomes conscious only when it undergoes some further process – when it encounters past associations, or is used to govern future action, or becomes the object of reflection, or is felt to impact upon the self. The second difference flows from the first: the theories differ in the range of cortical and subcortical structures which are regarded as being critical for consciousness: all accept that regions of the cerebral cortex and the thalamus are involved, but the theories differ on *which* regions of cortex are crucial and on the importance of deeper centres, such as the basal ganglia and brainstem. The authors of these theories generally regard them as tentative proposals, preliminary attempts to pull strands of recent evidence together into testable hypotheses. The time for a final adjudication lies some way off. And these pioneering theories, as I have outlined them so far, go only halfway towards sketching the neural basis of consciousness: for surely consciousness will depend on what *kind* of activity is occurring in the brain as well as on its whereabouts. Let's turn to ideas about the physiology of awareness – *how* the genie rubs the lamp.

How?

Dance, then, wherever you may be,
I am the Lord of the Dance, said he . . .

Sydney Carter, 'Lord of the Dance'

We know something about the kinds of neural activity which *fail* to excite consciousness. Slow wave – or dreamless – sleep and generalised 'grand mal' seizures share a salient electrical feature: in both these states, neurons throughout the brain synchronise their activity, discharging in a massive harmony which is incompatible with consciousness. Does this imply that every kind of synchronised activity in the brain is likely to trip up awareness?

Not necessarily. The idea that a *limited,* controlled synchronisation of rapid neuronal discharge might play a key role in perception, memory and movement is an intense focus of current research. We encountered this notion in Chapter 5, as an explanation for the 'binding' of visual experience. Let's pause for a moment to reflect on why it is attracting so much attention.

Neurons have traditionally been thought to 'code' information in one of two ways: using 'place' codes or 'frequency' codes. 'Place' refers to the importance of a neuron's spatial relationships. Thus a neuron running from a particular point on the retina to a particular point in the LGN codes visual information from a particular point in space. 'Frequency' refers to the neuron's rate of firing. As neurons often fire spontaneously in the absence of stimulation, both an increase and a decrease in their rate of firing can convey information. In sensory neurons there is usually a relationship between the intensity of sensory stimulation and the neuron's discharge rate. These two methods of coding information help to explain how it is transmitted faithfully from a sensory surface, like the retina, back to the cortical areas where sensory analysis begins. In the visual cortex, as we have seen, this analysis involves cells and cortical regions specialised to detect orientation, form, colour and depth.

But how are the objects we perceive reconstructed from activity in the cells that analyse visual input? One traditional explanation has been that neurons with 'simple' preferences, picking out a segment of a line for instance, connect to cells with more complex interests, perhaps picking out a square. This hierarchical process continues through several generations of cells and connections until visual signalling arrives at neurons equipped to pick out the complex categories and unique individuals we can recognise, for example a cell which might uniquely identify your grandma – a 'grandmother cell'. There is evidence that 'hierarchical' visual processing occurs. But it cannot be the whole story.

For one thing, we don't see grandmas in a vacuum. We see them in a visual context. There must be a mechanism which associates activity in complex cells high in the visual hierarchy with activity in earlier visual areas containing a detailed map of visual space. For another thing, visual processing occurs in several areas *in parallel*: there must be a mechanism to associate the form, colour and movement of the selfsame object wherever they are being analysed. Finally it is very unlikely that activity in *individual* cells underlies recognition. It is much more likely that small networks of complex cells combine to represent objects and people: if so, there must be a mechanism which associates the activity within them.

The new idea is that a third mode of neuronal coding provides a common mechanism to meet all these demands. Place and frequency coding relate to single cells. The new mode, 'time' or 'phase' coding relates to the activity of *groups* of cells. The idea is, in essence, extremely simple. Perhaps neurons which represent the disparate features of a single object – which may be widely spread across the brain – are associated by firing *at the same moment*. There is incomplete but growing evidence that something of this kind occurs.

Synchrony does not necessarily imply rhythmicity – cells could fire in synchronous bursts at random intervals – but it looks as though the synchronous firing of neurons which are involved in a common activity is often rhythmic. The rhythms involved range from about 25 to 100 cycles/second, in the 'gamma' frequency band. Several lines of evidence converge on the idea that these rhythms are critical for consciousness. Work on vision has suggested that cells responding to a single object at the focus of attention synchronise their activity at frequencies in the gamma range;[24] wakefulness and REM sleep are characterised by gamma frequencies which are synchronised across the brain;[25] at the moment that anaesthetics steal consciousness away, gamma activity across the brain diminishes and loses its coherence across brain regions, while at the recovery of consciousness, gamma power and coherence are restored.[26]

If these synchronised oscillations are required for consciousness, how are they achieved? As we saw in Chapter 3, the explanation is likely to lie both in the properties of individual neurons and in their interconnections: the intrinsic rhythmicity of neuronal discharge allows for the rhythmic pacing of brain activity; the ubiquitous, bidirectional connections between related brain regions facilitates synchronisation.

The idea that synchronous neuronal discharges might generate awareness has sex appeal. These dancing rhythms of activity seem eminently fit to compose a modern 'music of the spheres'. They also have more sober uses. Neurons are 'coincidence detectors': large numbers of other cells connect with them. Excitation at a single synapse is unlikely to make a neuron fire: synchronous excitation of several at once stands a much better chance. More than this: synchronous firing of networks of cells is probably a feature of brain regions controlling movement as well as of regions involved in sensation.[27] Synchronous firing in sensory areas could provide a potent means of selecting appropriate motor responses.

Although they are technically difficult to test, these ideas build on familiar, well-established principles of neural science. But perhaps explaining consciousness requires a more radical departure from the received wisdom. There are some wilder cards on the table.

Roy John, a distinguished American neurophysiologist, has recently proposed a 'field theory' of consciousness.[28] Like many of the theorists we have encountered, John envisages that synchronous activity in the gamma frequency in multiple brain regions is a prerequisite for consciousness. But his model includes a further step, the generation of a 'resonating electrotonic field': one of its notable properties is subjective awareness. The existence of such a field is open to experimental tests, although their details would tax the understanding of most non-physicists.

The notion that consciousness is best conceived as a field, and that its contents are expressed as modulations of the field, has also been championed by Rudolfo Llinas, whose work on the gamma oscillations of wakefulness and dreaming sleep we encountered in Chapter 3.[29] The philosopher John Searle has lent his support to this approach, which regards the existence of 'basal consciousness' as the basic challenge for the science of awareness.[30] Searle argues that if we could understand how the brain operates to produce the experience of 'minimal wakefulness' – your first moments of awareness as you wake from dreamless sleep in a darkened room – we would be well on the way to grasping the essential neurology of consciousness, and further than we are likely to get by searching for the individual neural correlates of perceptual experiences. The line of enquiry naturally emphasises the importance of the global brain processes which regulate sleep and waking, like those we encountered in Chapter 4.

Quantum theories of consciousness take a step further from the everyday world of biology. Sceptics about these ideas say that they are inspired by the principle of 'minimalisation of mysteries': the behaviour of subatomic particles and the workings of consciousness are equally myste-rious – the idea that the former might explain the latter minimises mystery. But these ideas have deeper roots. Roger Penrose has drawn attention to the existence of forms of human understanding – in particular mathemat-ical knowledge – which defy computational proof.[31] He takes them to indi-cate that human cognition must obey novel physical principles, rather than the old-fashioned physical laws which biologists (and conventional com-puter scientists) take for granted. Stuart Hameroff, an anaesthetist, has contributed to this line of thought with his suggestion that quantum processes occurring within microtubules, elements of the 'skeleton' of nerve cells, could be relevant to consciousness. Such processes are dis-rupted by general anaesthetics. These specific ideas are highly controver-sial, but they highlight the possibility that explaining consciousness may require a fundamental shake-up in physical theory.

What consciousness *does*: the ghost in the virtual machine

The computer is the last metaphor for the mind.

P.N. Johnson-Laird[32]

The theories we have been reviewing focus on the neural mechanisms which underpin awareness, the hardware of consciousness. They take its uses for granted. An alternative approach is to ask what we can infer about awareness from its functions.

We pondered these in the last chapter, and came up with the suggestion that consciousness helps us to select appropriate actions in an unpre-dictable world, actions we choose from an ample repertoire on the basis of fine perceptual distinctions. This idea links consciousness firmly with *control*, in particular the control of behaviour under challenging conditions when we need to harness our psychological resources to the task in hand.

One item of modern technology, the computer, is also closely linked with control. Like the brain, the computer is an information-processing device, transforming a variety of inputs into outputs on the basis of preprogrammed rules and local operations. Imagine for a moment that the brain *is* a com-puter (we will ask how far this analogy can reasonably be pressed in the next chapter). What can one say about the computational processes that give rise to consciousness? How do they differ from the processes that never do? An answer to this question should tell us about the 'software' of awareness, the logical operations which the brain is implementing when we are conscious.

Bernard Baars, an American psychologist, has produced a theatrical metaphor for the computational role of consciousness.[33] Baars proposes that at any moment two kinds of information processing are occurring in our brains. On the one hand, a multitude of dedicated cortical modules are constantly handling the unending but limited streams of information in which they specialise. So, as long as your eyes are open, cells in visual area 4 will be computing colour contrasts, even though your attention may be exclusively focused on the voice from the telephone at your ear. But some events in your nervous system, on the other hand, are available for you to 'report, act upon, distinguish and acknowledge as your own'. Baars describes these events, those currently giving rise to consciousness, as commanding a 'global workspace': its contents can be broadcast widely through the nervous system, recruiting the operation of the specialised subsystems to the currently dominant goal, in this case coming up with a reply to a question over the phone (see Figure 8.5). Left to themselves, the subsystems operate automatically, in parallel, with high combined capacity and great speed, whereas the global workspace operates slowly, with limited capacity, handling one task after another under voluntary control. Baars compares this mode of operation to the deliberations of a group of experts, pooling information on a blackboard – an unnecessary luxury when all is going according to prearranged plans, but invaluable when problems arise and several experts need simultaneous updating to help them produce a solution.

These ideas supply computational metaphors rather than closely worked models. But they help to explain how processes linked to consciousness might be useful to us. As in most of the neural theories we reviewed in the

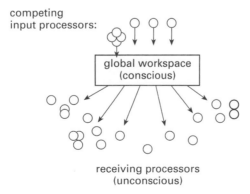

competing
input processors:

global workspace
(conscious)

receiving processors
(unconscious)

Figure 8.5 Baars' model This basic version of Baars' model emphasises the role played by consciousness in broadcasting pertinent knowledge around the brain.

last section, Baars places interactions between unconscious systems at the centre of his theory. His ideas chime with an evolutionary view: that consciousness comes into being as flexible behaviour emerges from more rigid instinctive patterns of response. They also lend themselves to an explanation of unconscious processes, like blindsight. After damage to the brain, the specialised unconscious modules which combine forces during conscious processing may continue to function in isolation from the global workspace.

Given that consciousness only emerges from neural activity after some delay, there is continuing argument over the extent to which consciousness can be regarded as *enabling* psychological processes, as opposed to simply resulting from them. This is a potential stumbling block for computational theories which try to give consciousness work to do in the brain. But there is a more fundamental problem, which applies equally to biological ideas and to computational hypotheses: it is not obvious that any of these models fully explains why *consciousness* results from the mechanisms in question: why should they not operate just as well *unconsciously*? This has been called the 'hard question of consciousness'. We encountered it at the end of our discussion of vision and it is firmly philosophical. Before we head off in pursuit of the philosophers, one other scientific approach to understanding awareness deserves a mention.

Getting to know you better: social theories of consciousness

Consciousness is fundamentally a social phenomenon, not the property of an individual brain or mind.

Steven Rose[34]

Wolves, chimpanzees and elephants, which all go in for complex social interactions, are probably all conscious; frogs, snails and codfish are probably not.

Nicholas Humphrey[35]

Bless you, darling, I have
Found myself in you.

W.H. Auden[36]

Neural and computational theories of consciousness focus sharply on the individual. Maybe such a sharp focus might be missing important parts of the picture. Two elements, in particular, may be lost from view. One is the physical environment. Dreams and imagination can conjure up wonderfully or fearfully vivid images of our surroundings, but they are a poor substitute for the real thing. Much of the richness of our experience depends on the richness of the world we inhabit.[37] The other missing element is our social milieu: some writers have suggested that we need to look to our social existence for an explanation of consciousness.

This idea has several sources. First, it echoes the etymology of the word itself: as we saw in Chapter 1, the Latin root of consciousness refers to knowledge *shared with another*: this collective connotation lives on, in phrases like 'the national consciousness'. Second, the work on child development which we also encountered in Chapter 1, showing that awareness of self and of other are acquired in parallel, supports the idea that social interaction conditions our awareness. This may not be obvious to us as adults; our social environment works its most powerful effects at an age too early for us to expect to retain any conscious memory of the process.[38] Third, there can be no doubt that language shapes and articulates consciousness – and whether or not we are genetically equipped to learn and use them,[39] human languages are clearly social creations. But to say that consciousness is moulded or revealed by our social existence is not necessarily to say that it is *created* by it. This ambiguity hovers over an extremely interesting and influential article by Nicholas Humphrey in 1978.[40] He proposed a specific social function for introspective consciousness: that it allows social animals to predict each other's behaviour on the basis of their insight into each other's states of mind. In other words, your consciousness of pain, or hunger, or jealousy, or pride, and their effects on your behaviour, allow you to anticipate the reactions of those around you when events excite these same emotions in their breasts.

Without a doubt, much of our mental agility is devoted to puzzling over and trying to influence the mental states of others: the teenager who muses 'she loves me, she loves me not . . . ', the parent who ponders why exactly his child is lying on the floor again and kicking her heels, the politician who hopes to capitalise on a scare story spread by the papers, are all doing just this. When we do so we employ the 'theory of mind' or 'mentalise' for short. The ability to read our own states of mind and to recognise them in others is a central part of human self-consciousness, involving what we called the 'awareness of awareness'. But is this ability required for us to see, or suffer pain, or experience hunger? Humphrey seems to believe that it is, although his article never quite settles the question: borrowing the terms with which Larry Weiskrantz drew his rather similar distinction, does

Humphrey's faculty of 'introspection' actually endow mental states with consciousness, or merely enable their acknowledgement?

This quandary echoes the larger question linking all the approaches to consciousness discussed in this chapter: how much interaction, between psychological processes or brain systems, is needed to generate consciousness? I believe that Humphrey offers a theory of 'self-awareness' or 'higher-order consciousness' rather than addressing the more basic problem of perceptual awareness. But theories like Humphrey's supply a useful corrective to ideas framed solely in the language of neuron and brain: society plays a powerful role in the creation of a fully fledged human consciousness.

Conclusion

What we see, remember and plan are generally conscious, but there are informative exceptions to this rule. Subjects with blindsight lose the experience of sight but remain able to use vision to guide some simple actions; sufferers from amnesia lose their memory of *what* happened but remain able to learn *how* to do things; as skills become automatic their performance slips from consciousness without necessarily losing any of its edge. These contrasts should help to define the neural correlates of the contents of consciousness. Circumstances in which experience changes without any change in our surroundings – for example in shifts of attention – open up a second approach to the NCC.

These approaches are generating plenty of data for the science of consciousness. But what are we ultimately seeking to explain? If the target of our theories is experience, the explanation of consciousness collides with a simple and obvious problem. We cannot directly observe the experience of others. For scientific purposes we have to rely on indications and reports of awareness, which provide indirect evidence of its presence – or its absence. This problem is not fatal: several other areas of science, like quantum physics and cosmology, also deal with unobservable processes. But it imposes an unmysterious limitation on the science of consciousness; and it casts some doubt on theories which assume that the neurology of consciousness must overlap with the neurology of report. This problem would disappear if the idea that experience is private and unobservable can be refuted, as some philosophers believe.

Almost all theories of the NCC share a number of key assumptions, in particular the importance of 'cell-assemblies' in the cortex and thalamus in shaping the contents of consciousness. Recent theories of the anatomy of consciousness differ most notably in the degree of interaction they consider necessary between cerebral regions and psychological processes. At the minimalistic end of the spectrum, Zeki has proposed that each visual area generates its own visual 'microconsciousness'. The majority of theories envisage that some further reverberation of neural activity is necessary for consciousness, and that input from the senses must first resonate in memory, feed through to action, undergo a commentary, encounter the neural embodiment of the self or modify the 'basal field of consciousness'. Each of these proposals implicates a somewhat different set of neural structures in the creation of consciousness.

The variety of alternative anatomical-cum-psychological theories of consciousness currently on offer is confusing. Matters are a little clearer with the physiology, the 'how' of consciousness. Interest is focused on synchronised activity across brain regions occurring at around 40 cycles/second. Several lines of evidence converge on the idea that this activity is both a signature of wakefulness and provides a mechanism by which the contents of consciousness can be bound into a unified whole. This idea will be a major target for experimental work on consciousness over the next few years. Needless to say there are other contenders in the effort to identify the physiology of awareness, among them controversial theories based in quantum physics.

Theories of the anatomy and physiology of consciousness run alongside two other scientific approaches to awareness. Bernard Baars has pursued the tempting analogy between the information-processing device which regulates our behaviour – the brain – and the information-processing devices which increasingly regulate the rest of our lives – computers. If the brain is a computer of sorts, consisting of a huge number of specialised systems which can operate in parallel, conscious information corresponds to signals which are broadcast widely to harness psychological resources to meet demanding challenges. Social theories of consciousness remind us that all human and much animal consciousness develops and exists within a social context. Human awareness in particular is conditioned by early social interactions, taxed by the need to understand and control the behaviour of others and pervasively affected by our language.

These theories identify promising mechanisms and functions for awareness. They may be preliminary or even premature but they take seriously the challenge posed by consciousness for science. They may or may not impress you. But lurking in the shadows is a troublesome doubt: could *any* theory of this kind tell us what we want to know about the makings of awareness? For every mechanism scientists may propose, can we not always ask the further question: *why* should this be conscious? Like it or not, this question leads us from the territory of science into the kingdom of philosophy, and we must follow.

9

The nature of consciousness

Introduction

Two simple facts inspired this book: the first is that we are richly conscious of our world and of ourselves, the second that this consciousness depends upon events within our brains. These facts raise questions which have refused to surrender completely to many centuries of philosophical attack. This chapter will introduce you to contemporary thinking on three issues at the heart of the debate: what is the nature of the relationship between conscious states and the neural activity associated with them? Is there any bar, in principle, to the construction of a conscious machine? What are the implications of the intimate relationship between consciousness and brain events for human freedom and responsibility?

Experience and the brain

Two sketches on a sunny day

At the end of our Edinburgh street the gardens run down to a river. The early summer sun has spread a great carpet of daisies over the lawn. From the bench where I sit in the shade of the trees, the birdsong is clearer and louder than the muted sounds of traffic on the bridge nearby. With a turn of my head I can glimpse a rhododendron in extravagant pink bloom and half hear the rush of water tumbling to the sea. A breeze is playing in the trees, countless leaves are shimmering in the brilliant sunshine. A bush of honeysuckle sweetens the air at the gate.

This is a sketch of ordinary experience. It evokes the kinds of sensations which compose the fabric of our waking lives. I have written this book to acquaint you with another, hidden, story of sight and sound and scent, a story with the outlandish ambition of explaining how experience comes about. It is at once more exotic and less evocative than the familiar picture. It remains far from complete, but we can pencil in some details now which were missing from the sketch on a rainy day:

> Streams of energy bombard an organism whose surface is bristling with detectors. Photons of visible light, interfering patterns of vibration in the air, billowing clouds of complex molecules, excite sensitive receptors in its eyes and ears and nose.
>
> These in their turn release a barrage of signals to the brain. But unlike the sights and sounds and scents which have excited them, the signals are monotonous: electrical as they course along the axon, chemical as they leap from one neuron to the next.
>
> During sleep, signals like these would quench themselves in fractions of a second. But pulses of neurochemicals from the brainstem are priming thalamus and cortex; the rapid electrical rhythms of the waking brain have replaced the slow oscillations of sleep. This creature is hungry for news, wide open to the world.
>
> The information streaming to the nervous system runs into a host of parallel paths. Some govern reflex responses, like the contraction of the pupil as sunshine darts through the leaves. Others are more complex, parcelling signals out among the cortical areas which map the features of our world: the three-dimensional space of the garden, the colour space of the flowers, the tonal space of birdsong. Here, by processes we only just begin to understand, the signals are analysed and classified, taken apart and reunited, making it possible to isolate, classify and identify the stimuli which excited them.
>
> This is never an end in itself. The sensory signals are soon streaming on towards regions of the brain which govern action, to exert their influence on word or deed. Some of course never do so, and disappear without trace; others leave their subtle mark in minute alterations of the pathways future signals must traverse. Some contribute to the words you are reading now.

This is a scientist's picture of the basis of sensation in the brain. I hope this book will have persuaded you that events in the brain provide the physical basis for consciousness. But what is the nature of the relationship between what happens in our brains and what passes through our minds? How do events in the brain give rise to awareness? This is the up-to-date version of an age-old question: how is the body related to the mind?

A war of intuitions

When we ponder the relationship between experience and the brain several deep intuitions come into conflict. If we cling to them all, we may never make sense of the relationship between the physical and the mental. Let us begin by trying to spell out our hunches – keeping an open mind, accepting that we may eventually have to sacrifice some of our old beliefs. One thing at least is certain: our favourite intuitions may be wrong.

My first hunch is that experience is rich and real. To most non-philosophers, and to many philosophers, this is almost too obvious to need stating. The sketch at the start of this chapter was a meagre illustration of the wealth of our sensations. Sight, sound, scent and touch are limitlessly varied, an inexhaustible source of wonder and pleasure, terror and pain.

The 'reality' of experience may be more controversial than its variety. What exactly is meant by the claim that experience is 'real'? As real as what? – as eggshells or electrons, as elegies or efforts? We will return to this question, but most of us would agree that the qualities of our experience, like sensations of colour or texture or smell, are at least robust phenomena in need of explanation – phenomena which any full description of the world must take into account. Indeed, it seems quite natural to regard experience as our point of departure in gaining *any* knowledge of the world.

The second intuition is that experience is interconnected with our physical being. In an unsophisticated form, the belief is universal: we all know that it is hard to concentrate when we are tired or hungry, and that sleep or food can put the problem right; that downing a gallon of beer induces a spinning sensation; that certain ways of stimulating bodies give rise to exceptional pleasure; that a sharp blow to the head may be prejudicial to awareness – and so on.

Science has sharpened this intuition. In the last hundred years we have learned plenty about the neural basis of our states of awareness, and the neural correlates of the contents of awareness. We know enough to have framed a tentative law: '*every* distinction drawn in our experience and behaviour will be reflected in a distinctive pattern of neural activity'. Progress in the correlation of mental with neural events has gone hand in hand with work suggesting that only some of the structures and processes in the brain subserve awareness. We are beginning to discover which these are. A 'neurobiology of consciousness' is no longer a distant dream.

The third intuition is that experience makes a difference. It seems self-evident that much of our behaviour is explained by mental events: if I could not see or hear or touch, if I knew nothing of pain or pleasure, if I lacked conscious desires and intentions, I would not and could not behave as I do. If this is true, it looks plausible that the capacity for experience, like our other biological abilities, has *evolved* in the service of action. There may be a brutally simple reason why we can experience so much: being able to do so enhanced our ancestors' chances in their struggles for survival.

Taken individually, each of these three intuitions looks reasonable enough:

- experience is rich and real;
- every distinction drawn in experience will be reflected in a distinctive pattern of neural activity;
- experience is an evolved capacity which governs our behaviour.

But collectively they generate some formidable problems. You will swiftly see why, if I caricature two extreme views of the relationship between mental and neural events. Each view does justice to at least one intuition – and violence to the others.

Here is a version of a materialist or 'physicalist' view.

Science is equipped to give an absolutely comprehensive description of the world, a 'theory of everything'. This will include a description of experience – because experience is no more and no less than certain types of activity in certain types of physical systems. The brain is one such system. Once the relevant types of activity are fully described, there is no more to be said about experience.

This view may or may not appeal to you, but its strengths and weaknesses, judged against our intuitions, are plain to see. It respects our belief that experience is interconnected with the physical world: indeed it *identifies* experience with physical events. It does justice to our belief that experience governs our behaviour: we are quite used these days to thinking of the brain as our on-board computer, controlling operations. If experiences are simply events in the brain there is no problem at all in understanding how they control us. And we know that the *brain* evolved: if experience is just the brain in action, it follows that experience also evolved.

But what about the our first intuition, concerning the 'reality' of experience? The physicalist theory tells us that experience is *no more than* activity in the brain. This takes some swallowing: the subjective properties of experience, like the glimpse I caught a moment ago of the golden ochre hues of the seaweed on the shore, or the gnawing painfulness of a toothache, certainly seem, on a first consideration, to be something more than the activity of neural networks. Anyone faithful to the intuition that experience is real is likely to insist that it involves some further fact, over and above neural activity. She may concede that experience is interconnected with events in the brain – for example, it may be *caused* by them. But identical with them? No.

Here is one version of the antithetical, 'dualist' view:

> The brain is a physical system. Its activity is well described by physical laws. But while states of the brain are the states of a physical system, experiences are the states of an immaterial system: call it the soul. States of the brain are observable by anyone with the right equipment. States of a soul are detectable only by its possessor. Science describes the public universe, but the soul is accessible only to its own subject. Experience will never be described by objective science.

This theory is solidly built on our first intuition that experience constitutes a 'further fact', which goes beyond activity in the brain: it wholeheartedly acknowledges that experience is 'real'. But it gets into grave difficulties with the other intuitions. How can experience be interlinked with physical events, or govern our behaviour, if it is entirely separate from the physical operations of the brain? Given our current physical knowledge, there is no scope for independent non-physical events to perturb the course of nature. This theory makes the interconnections between the physical and the mental deeply mysterious. In particular, our belief that experience is useful seems to be jeopardised by according it such special status – despite the strong hunch that it is an *evolved* capacity.

There are numerous rival proposals besides my two caricatures (upwards of 15, from a quick count in a recent review of the subject). I shall introduce you to a few of the more powerful alternatives in the section on '-isms' below (p. 312ff.). But the mere fact that there are so many contenders should warn us that none of them quite does the trick. Where deeply held beliefs converge and clash, we cannot expect a painless solution: there will be blood on the page.

What is it like to be . . .

'Thought experiments' have loomed large in recent writings on these issues. They are misleadingly named. These are not experiments in the scientist's sense, of practical procedures yielding robustly repeatable observations.

They are aids to reflection, devices for concentrating the mind. Daniel Dennett has aptly described them as 'intuition pumps', and the skilful operator can harness them to pump intuition in whatever direction she pleases. But even if they fail to settle the arguments they help to focus them.

I shall introduce you to two kinds of experiment. The first variety has to do with the limits of knowledge. If we knew all the physical facts about an animal or another person, would we know the whole story – or might there be something more to learn from their experience? The second variety probes the limits of logical possibility: could the physical facts be held constant and yet the facts about experience change? The answers we give to these questions should go a fair way towards determining our view of the relationship between experience and the brain.

. . . a bat, or blind as Mary?

> these experiences . . . have in each case a specific subjective character which it is beyond our ability to conceive.
>
> Thomas Nagel[1]

> The structure of a bat's mind is just as accessible as the structure of a bat's digestive system.
>
> Daniel Dennett[2]

To conduct the following experiments you need only sit back and read on. You encountered them in passing in Chapter 6 (p. 236).

Here is experiment **i**.[3] Imagine that you are a scientist investigating the behaviour and physiology of a creature which possesses a sense you lack, for example a microchiropteran bat. These animals, which are mammals with powerful brains, navigate by sonar, probing their surroundings with a stream of high-pitched squeaks: the echoes allow them to distinguish shape, depth, motion and texture. Imagine that you are working in the distant future, when neuroscience can deliver a complete account of the bat's inner workings. Suppose, as most of us do, that bats are conscious. Would mastering this account inform you of what it is like to be a bat?

Experiment **ii** brings the question closer to home.[4] Imagine a scientist, Mary, at work in the same fortunate future. Mary's particular interest is the human visual system. She knows all there is to be known about its intricate anatomy and hitherto baffling physiology. But Mary has a personal reason for being interested in vision: she is entirely colour blind. Her own researches make it possible to devise an operation to restore her colour vision. Fortunately the surgery is a complete success. When Mary next opens her eyes, will she learn something new?

The authors of these two thought experiments, the American philosopher Thomas Nagel, and the Australian Frank Jackson, expected their readers to answer that knowing all the physical facts would *not* tell the whole story. The bat scientist will never know 'what it is like' to be the animal he studies, or 'how it is for the bat itself'; Mary *will* learn something new after her operation – she will learn what it is like to see colours.

While they agree on these results, Nagel and Jackson draw somewhat different conclusions from them. Nagel argues, from the example of the bat, that the existence of points of view, of subjectivity, creates the real problem of consciousness. We cannot imagine how an objective description of the brain, even a complete one, could ever yield an account of the subjective experience it permits. Nagel professes an open mind about whether the bat's experience is somehow the 'same thing' as the activity in its nervous system: but, if it is, we cannot at present even begin to see how. Jackson is more uncompromising. If Mary had *all* the physical information, and yet her knowledge was incomplete, 'physicalism', the thesis that the world is no more than its physical contents must be false.

Most people are, at least initially, attracted by the 'results' which these philosophers report from their experiments. But are they inescapable?

Let us try a little harder with the bat. If we knew everything about its anatomy, physiology and behaviour we would know a great deal. We would know which wavelengths of sound it is sensitive to and what kinds of distinctions its sonar allows it to make: whether it can tell a still pool from one the wind has ruffled, orange rind from apple peel, a greenfly from a midge. We would know how it classifies the things it can distinguish: whether it can tell animal from vegetable from mineral. We would have discovered what it seeks and what it shuns, whether it shows affection, if it is capable of deceit. Once we had filled all the gaps in our current knowledge, we would arguably have learned a great deal about what it is like to be a bat: it is to be able to hear these sounds but not those, to recognise these objects but not others, to care for *a*, to detest *b*, and be indifferent to *c* . . . . The study of bat brains and bat behaviour certainly seems to be capable of giving us a grasp of the *structure* of the bat's experience. Is there anything more to know? Nagel and Jackson think so, arguing that the knowledge we can gain 'from the outside' is schematic and incomplete. Others disagree. For the time being I will leave the issue open, if only because the answer is deeply unclear.

Mary, of course, is in the same boat as the bat. It is not easy, in fairness, to predict just what Mary might know if she knew *all* the physical facts about vision. Perhaps she might *not* be surprised when she opened her eyes. I must confess that I find it hard to imagine which physical facts could prepare her for her first sensation of colour. But could it be, as a notable critic of these experiments has suggested, that I am mistaking 'a failure of imagination for an insight into necessity'?[5]

. . . a zombie?

There is nothing it is like to be a zombie.

David Chalmers[6]

We're all zombies.

Daniel Dennett[7]
(to which Dennett appends the footnote: 'it would be a desperate act of intellectual dishonesty to quote this assertion out of context')

The examples of Mary and the bat may show that a comprehensive physical description of a human being, or an animal, would fail to capture significant aspects of their experience. This suggests, along the lines of our first intuition, that experience includes a set of further facts, over and above neural activity and behaviour. The second pair of experiments have been used to reach the same conclusion in a rather different way. Reactions to them are notably varied: some find them persuasive, others cannot keep a straight face.

Here is experiment **iii**.[8] You and I are asked to sort a bucketful of coloured plastic shapes into heaps by colour. We take it in turns to pick out a shape, name it and consign it to its appropriate pile. The shapes are blue, green, red and white. Each is asked to comment on the other's decisions. The colours are bold and unambiguous and, wonderful to relate, you and I agree every time. But although we agree, do we *see* the same colours? Could it be that, although we draw the same distinctions systematically, where I see red, the colour you actually see is what I call blue (and you call red); where I see blue, you see what I call red (and call it blue) . . .?

This may seem an extravagant hypothesis. But, at first sight, it does not seem impossible that we might have qualitatively different experiences, provided the structure of our discriminations is preserved. It 'does not seem impossible' in the bare sense that there is no logical contradiction in supposing this. But if this is possible, then the facts about experience might change while the physical facts are held constant – giving us another demonstration of the independence of experience from the physical domain.

Daniel Dennett has argued with panache that this hypothetical inversion of experience is worse than fanciful: it is nonsensical.⁹ He recasts the experiment so that all the action takes place within a single consciousness. With apologies to Dennett, this is my version of his line of argument. Imagine that your colour sensations (but not mine) were suddenly inverted. Apples would look tomato coloured to you and we would therefore no longer agree about the colours of objects – what I call green, you now call red. If so, our behaviour will differ: the 'physical facts' which describe us will have changed, as our experience changes. So far this is perfectly consistent with the view that the physical facts tell all. Now imagine that you gradually adjust to the change in sensation. You begin to call apples green again (everyone else does, and it avoids a lot of explaining if you do the same); as time passes, they start to remind you of emeralds and Ireland, in the way they always did (after all, emeralds now look red, and so does Ireland). You get back on terms with tomatoes, as well: after a couple of months you call them 'red', like the rest of the world, and you can appreciate the poetry of their French designation, *pommes d'amour*. Gradually your behaviour reverts entirely to 'normal'. You forget about the disturbing inversion of your colour vision, a nasty shock from which you have now pretty well recovered. Then one day I ask you (rather unkindly): 'When you see apples nowadays, do they *really* look green to you, like in the old days, or are they *actually* red, just like tomatoes were?' Dennett suggests that you will now find this question difficult to answer – in the limiting case, in which you have fully adjusted to the inversion, you will find it impossible to answer. As your behaviour – and therefore the 'physical facts' – readjusts to the change in your experience, so your experience takes on its old colours, so to speak. If there is *no change* in the physical facts, there can be none in experience: once again, the physical facts tell all. You, dear reader, may want to protest that however the subject of this experiment *behaves*, her experience either has to be one way or the other (either of red or of green!). But whatever your reaction, we shall see that Dennett's argument epitomises one powerful school of contemporary thought about brain, behaviour and mind.

Let's move on to experiment **iv.**¹⁰ You meet an old friend, with whom you share an interest in philosophy. Over a pint of beer you chat about the nature of consciousness. As you talk about the brain, experience and their logical independence, it dawns on you, gradually but insistently, that your old friend is a zombie – a philosophical zombie, that is. Actual zombies, of the Haitian sort, would probably not have it in them to discuss the philosophy of mind. But philosophical zombies can do that – and everything else that you and I can. They differ from us in no physical detail whatsoever, neither in the constitution of their brains nor in the niceties of their behaviour – but there *is* a difference between us and them, and it is an important one. They have absolutely no awareness whatsoever: they are consummate automata. As David Chalmers puts it: 'there is nothing it is like to be a zombie'.[11]

If you accept that the idea of a zombie is free of internal contradiction – not everyone does – it provides some further grounds for believing that mental facts are distinct from physical ones. You and your old zombie friend differ in no physical respect – but you are conscious and he is not. The inversion experiment claims to show that the facts about experience might change while the physical ones are held constant: the case of the zombie claims to show that the physical facts might stay constant and yet experience *disappear*.

I will leave you to decide for yourself whether any or all of these four experiments establish that experience is a 'further fact'. This stubborn intuition has certainly been the major stumbling block in the way of 'physicalist' theories of consciousness. But both dualism, the view that there is a separate domain of mental facts, and physicalism, the view that the physical description of the world can be exhaustive, come in several flavours. Let us take a look at a few of the more popular proposals.

'-isms' enough for all

Virtually all the current philosophical accounts of the relationship between experience and brain events agree on certain points: that the brain plays a key role in the genesis of experience; that experience is part of the natural order, rather than a 'supernatural' afterthought; that the mind should be conceived as a process or an activity, rather than as a ghostly 'substance'.

The fundamental issue which divides them is whether talk of experience can be translated into talk of physical matters, talk about brain and behaviour. 'Reductive', physicalistic, theories take this point of view; 'non-reductive', dualistic, theories regard experience as an obstinate 'further fact'.

Let us start – where most of us begin.

Varieties of dualism

DESCARTES: SUBSTANCE DUALISM

> . . . the mind, by which I am what I am, is entirely distinct from the body
>
> René Descartes, *Discourse on Method*[12]

What is natural may not be right, but most of us are naturally dualists. We tend to regard the mind and the body, the mental and the physical, as separate domains. This belief is literally built into our culture, in the separate institutions we have created for the care of diseases of the mind and of the body – mental asylums on the one hand, hospitals on the other. It is reflected in the words I hear in clinic several times each week: 'You don't think it's all in my mind, do you, Doctor?' It is expressed in the first thought which – I suspect – we are all likely to have on the mind–body question: they are at least as different as water and wine.

We owe the most famous philosophical statement of dualism to a retired soldier who wrote the *Discourse on Method* while leading a life 'as solitary and withdrawn as I would in the most remote of deserts'.[13] It was published in 1637. Descartes wanted to establish which of his beliefs were *certain*. He tried, in his imagination, to strip away all the beliefs about which he could be mistaken. He found that

> I could pretend I had no body and that there was no world or place that I was in, but . . . I could not, for all that, pretend that I did not exist . . . on the contrary, from the very fact of doubting the truth of other things, it followed very evidently and very certainly that I existed; while, on the other hand, if I had only ceased to think, I would have had no reason to believe that I existed; I therefore concluded that I was a substance, of which the whole essence and nature consists in thinking, and which, in order to exist, needs no place and depends on no material thing . . .[14]

Descartes was surely justified in concluding that he was a 'thinking thing'. It is much more doubtful that this implies the existence of a separate spiritual 'substance'. But Descartes' distinction between 'thinking things' – minds – and 'extended things' – physical objects – was immensely influential.[15] His view has come to be known as 'substance dualism'.

Few philosophers would describe themselves nowadays as 'substance dualists'. In fact dualists of all description are something of an endangered species, but there is life in dualism yet. A lucid account of the mind–body problem by the contemporary philosopher, David Chalmers, has recently stated the case for a contemporary variation on the Cartesian theme.[16]

CHALMERS: PROPERTY DUALISM

Chalmers is persuaded by examples like Jackson's Mary and Nagel's bat that certain properties of experience are irreducible. In Chalmers' view, talk of experience cannot be translated, without loss, into talk of the brain and behaviour. There is an 'explanatory gap' between physical and mental events. Even if we could achieve a full understanding of the inner workings and outward behaviour of an organism, there would always be these further questions to ask about it: is it conscious, and, if so, what is its experience like?

Chalmers does not ignore the achievements of neuroscience over the last century. But he denies that conventional neuroscience is poised to explain consciousness. It *can* explain the physical *correlate* of consciousness. Chalmers terms this physical state 'awareness' (a distinctly technical sense of the word: let's call it awareness*). He defines awareness* as 'the state wherein information is accessible for verbal report and deliberate control of behaviour', or 'directly available for global control'.[17] In Chalmers' terms a computer, which could report and act in some way on information from its surroundings, would thereby be aware* – but it might or might not be conscious.

Explaining consciousness itself requires a further step. We have to generate a set of 'psychophysical laws' which describe the relationship between events in the brain and events in the mind – between awareness* and consciousness. Chalmers regards this as a long-term goal, but suggests that we can already grasp one or two interim principles, for example the 'principle of structural coherence': any distinction in experience will be mirrored by a distinction in neural activity, and the pattern of experience will be matched by the pattern of awareness*.[18] Once we have a full physical description of the world *and* a set of psychophysical laws, then we really will have the makings of a 'theory of everything' – but not until then.

Chalmers' theory differs from Descartes' in important ways. He does not find it necessary to postulate that there is a mental *substance*, or that the mental domain is supernatural. He regards the mental features of reality as properties of physical entities – animals. He thinks that their mental properties bear a lawful relation to their physical ones. He describes his theory therefore as a type of 'naturalistic property dualism'.

So far, so good: but dualism of every kind sooner or later comes up against a major and possibly fatal problem. We glimpsed this earlier, when we criticised my second caricature. Dualism has the greatest difficulty in explaining how mental events can be efficacious, how they can make a difference – but we have an overwhelming intuition that they do. The problem is this: if mental properties are different in kind to physical ones, how can the two interact? At best, it seems that physical events might somehow give rise to mental ones, as an 'epiphenomenon', a consequence without function – but how could mental events possibly influence the physical course of nature without defying physical law?

Descartes suggested that this interaction took place in the pineal gland. He chose this candidate for psychophysical contact because, like the soul, it is single – whereas most parts of the brain exist in two symmetrical versions. But Descartes failed to offer a good explanation of *how* interaction occurs. Chalmers is less evasive, 'biting the bullet', as philosophers like to say. He accepts that mental events do not affect the course of nature. In his view the explanation of awareness* will suffice to explain our behaviour, and only awareness* emerged by a process of Darwinian evolution. Consciousness, beautiful but somehow unnecessary, is explained by the existence of eternal – and themselves inexplicable – psychophysical laws.

The apparent failure of dualism to make sense of the efficacy of consciousness is a major driving force behind the radical alternatives of physicalism. But before we leave dualism behind, we should visit two other recent attempts to solve – or dissolve – the mind–body question, without completely sacrificing the Cartesian intuition.

MCGINN: PESSIMISTIC NATURALISM

The water of the physical brain is turned into the wine of consciousness, but we draw a total blank on the nature of this conversion . . . there is something terminal about our perplexity.

Colin McGinn[19]

There can be little doubt that the human intellect has evolved. Just as we are quite fast runners but bad at digesting grass, so there may be some intellectual problems we are suited to solve and others that tend to stump us. It could even be that there are some problems that will *permanently* stump us. Although it is an attractive and much-discussed goal, we might never be able to come up with a 'theory of everything'.

If this much is accepted, could it be that the mind–body problem is destined to be a permanent stumper? Colin McGinn, a British philosopher now teaching in America, has argued for this pessimistic conclusion.[20] The problem has certainly proved pretty resistant for 2,500 years. It is odd, as McGinn points out, that we have done so badly at explaining the widespread and seemingly quite simple biological fact of consciousness while we have so successfully probed the nooks and crannies of the physical universe. But we have made a start with the science of consciousness, as this book has set out to show. Should we despair of eventual success?

McGinn sets his standard of 'explanation' very high. He accepts that correlations of mental and physical events are perfectly feasible. But McGinn doubts that this will give us the kind of explanation we desire. He believes that we are seeking a property of the brain which would show us how events in the brain *necessarily* give rise to our experience – but that the nature of the human mind is such that this property must always be beyond our grasp. There is no *philosophical* problem of consciousness in the sense that some creature, with a different intellectual make-up, could in principle grasp this property: the property really exists and consciousness is not miraculous.

McGinn may be looking for a deeper explanation of 'psychophysical laws' than science can be expected to supply. A detailed set of psychophysical correlations would go a long way towards a scientifically respectable 'explanation' for consciousness. It is always possible to ask *why* things should be as they are, in any area of science: explanation has to end somewhere. But McGinn is surely right that we are having more than average difficulty in getting to grips with the problem of consciousness.

McGinn follows Descartes in accepting that consciousness is special – so special that he doubts it will ever be explained. John Searle, the doyen of American philosophy, agrees that it is special, but tries not to let this disturb his philosophical composure. He believes that he has solved the mind–brain problem, and that the solution is simple. He thinks that the facts of experience and the claims of science can be reconciled. His arguments have the ring of common sense. Is all the hoo-ha over at last?

SEARLE: OPTIMISTIC NATURALISM

The famous mind-body problem . . . has a simple solution.

John Searle[21]

Searle's account of experience is firmly in the Cartesian tradition.[22] He accepts that facts about experience are 'intrinsically subjective', and regards subjectivity as 'a rock bottom element of the world',[23] albeit one which does not permit our standard approach to observation, either in our own case or in that of others.[24] A mental state 'is always *someone's* conscious state'[25] and allows access to the world which is always from a point of view. But there is nothing scientifically mysterious about this:

Our world picture, though extremely complicated in detail, provides a rather simple account of . . . consciousness. According to the atomic theory, the world is made up of particles. These particles are organised into systems. Some of these systems are living, and these types of living systems have evolved over long periods of time. Among these some have evolved brains that are capable of causing and sustaining consciousness. Consciousness is, thus, a biological feature of certain organisms in exactly the same sense of 'biological' in which photosynthesis . . . and reproduction are biological features of organisms.[26]

I believe that Searle is describing what most scientifically educated people would, on reflection, say about consciousness today. He regards it as an 'emergent' property of certain physical systems – systems like you and me. Regarded in this light he sees no difficulty in understanding how conscious states can make a difference: they make a difference because they are part of the causal chain. And there is no mind–body problem: consciousness is 'a mental and therefore physical property of the brain in the sense in which liquidity is a property of a system of molecules'.[27]

The real work in this attempted reconciliation between mind and matter is being done by the idea of emergent properties. Does it possess the power required for the job?

The difficulty with Searle's account can be illustrated by pressing his analogy. We understand how the microscopic features of a liquid – the relatively free association of its molecules – give rise to the macroscopic property of liquidity. The property of liquidity can therefore be put to work in physical explanations without further ado. But in such explanations it serves as shorthand for the microscopic properties of the system: it has no independent explanatory power.

Consciousness seems to be different. It is not clear to us how the microscopic features of the brain necessitate awareness in the sense that the microscopic properties of water necessitate its liquidity. This, after all, is the source of our puzzlement about the relationship between mind and matter. The possession of consciousness seems to be a further fact about the brain: it may be caused by the brain's microscopic properties, but it is not exhausted by them in the way in which the property of liquidity is exhausted by the microscopic features which explain it. If certain facts, as Searle insists, are 'intrinsically subjective', they go beyond our ordinary conception of physical items and properties. If these subjective facts influence our behaviour, we are left with the puzzle of where they belong in the physical scheme – and we arrive back at the problem we were hoping to resolve. The concept of emergent properties seems to be either too weak or too strong to effect the reconciliation Searle intends. He has restated our intuitions about consciousness with characteristic eloquence, but has not convincingly shown that they are mutually consistent.

All the philosophers we have encountered so far have clung doggedly to our intuitive concept of experience. Perhaps this is where the real problem lies, and we need to rethink what we mean by consciousness in the first place. The theories we are about to encounter will test your loyalty to 'common sense' to the limits – and possibly beyond.

Types of physicalism

. . . accepting dualism is giving up.

Daniel Dennett[28]

. . . the deeper objection [to physicalism] can be put quite simply: the theory in question has left out the mind.

John Searle[29]

Physicalism is the view that the mind can be explained in the same terms as matter. This is a broad river of thought, and several streams flow into it. The first springs from the difficulties faced by dualism in explaining how mind and matter interact. We have already encountered these.

A second flows from a general – and controversial – principle that a 'difference which makes no difference is no difference'. The only differences which count, for those keen on this line of thought, are public ones, which anyone could verify. If you accept this principle there can be *no genuine difference* between you and your zombie twin (remember this twin would be *exactly* like you in every outward respect – but he/she is unconscious). So, on this view, if your concept of consciousness tempts you to consider the possibility of zombies, your concept 'needs fixed', as the Scots like to say.

A third stream flows from a general enthusiasm for science – and from the recognition that science springs big surprises. Two hundred years ago, who would have imagined that it would be possible to communicate almost instantaneously with the other side of the world using an invisible messenger which is a close cousin to light, that the smallest units of elemental matter can be split to release colossal quantities of energy, or that the recipe for building our bodies is written in a helical chemical repeated in every cell of our bodies? We all too easily lose our sense of wonder about these extraordinary discoveries. If we have had to revolutionise our concepts in order to understand matter, energy and life, should we not expect similar surprises when we let science loose on the mind?

A physicalist theory of the mind has two broad options: to find ways of translating our ordinary talk about consciousness into talk of something else, more obviously physical, or to write off talk about experience altogether as a bad job – and to start from scratch, with a more efficient set of concepts. These two approaches are known as reductionism and eliminativism. Physicalists differ on which is the wiser option, but this difference is minor compared to the decision which physicalists of every kind must take: *what* exactly should the concept of consciousness be reduced to or eliminated in favour of? If experience is not itself, what is it? There have been three popular answers to this question: behaviour, activity in the brain, and the 'functions' which translate sensation into action. Let us examine each of these in turn.

BEHAVIOURISM

Behaviourism comes in two varieties: methodological and philosophical. We have already encountered the methodological type, without giving it such a grand name. If we wish to study consciousness in others we are bound to rely on their behaviour to indicate whether they are conscious, and of what. If we are studying other people the behaviour in question will usually be verbal: what they say. There is nothing startling about this: we can only observe what is observable. But philosophical behaviourism makes a much larger claim: not that behaviour is all we can observe, but that behaviour is all there is to consciousness.[30]

This idea is slightly less outrageous than it looks on first encounter. Some of our mental vocabulary yields quite readily to a behavioural analysis. Learning, for example, is a psychological process, part of our 'mental' life. But learning a list of words mainly involves acquiring the disposition to recite the list, in certain circumstances – for instance on request. This is clearly a 'behavioural' disposition, and a behavioural analysis of this mental process looks quite promising.

But how about 'seeing red'? If I see red I certainly have some behavioural dispositions as a result: I am predisposed, for instance, to say that I am seeing red. But the claim that behavioural dispositions exhaust my experience of seeing red looks very implausible indeed. It seems to miss the heart of the experience: what seeing red is like! Few if any philosophers today expect this approach, unaided, to do the trick for physicalism. Its epitaph may be the well-known jest: one behaviourist says to another, after they make love: 'That was great for you – how was it for me?'

MIND–BRAIN IDENTITY THEORY

Science is a regular source of real surprises. It must be surprising to anyone, on the first encounter, to learn that graphite and diamond are pure examples of the same stuff, carbon, which differ only in the way in which atoms of the element are arranged. And it comes as a surprise to learn that heat – which we *detect* by reaching our hands out to the fire – is best regarded as the energy possessed by atoms of hot gases in virtue of their motion. This is an example of successful scientific 'reduction': heat, as it exists in a hot object, is the energy of its molecules. In the same vein, visible light, as it exists in the world around us, is in fact a part of the much wider spectrum of electromagnetic radiation to which radio waves, X-rays and gamma rays also belong.

Given the evidence we have mustered that consciousness arises from the brain, it is tempting to suggest that mental events, like seeing red, *are really* the brain events which give rise to them – nothing more and nothing less.[31] Much as learning about molecules in motion has revealed the true nature of heat, so discovering what goes on in the brain has revealed the *true* nature of experience. Does this proposal make you feel, like Daniel Dennett's imaginary sparring partner in *Consciousness Explained*, 'as if my pocket was just picked'?[32] If so, you might be right to suspect an intellectual sleight of hand.

There is something suspicious about this second example of reduction. The identification of heat with molecular motion is plausible just because we set aside our *experience* of heat. This, admittedly, is what usually alerts us to the presence of hot things. But when we identify heat with molecular motion, we are not concerned to analyse the nature of our experience, but to explain the physical nature of heat. When we do come to analyse the nature of experience itself, 'setting it aside' is not an option. The feeling of hotness is an essential part of the experience of heat – rather than something that alerts us to a process which can then be *fully* described without further reference to the experience.

This suggests that the analogy between mental-physical reduction (reducing 'seeing red' to a process in the brain) and physical-physical reduction (reducing heat to the motion of particles) is false. But could it be, nonetheless, that when we learn about activity in the brain we are learning what experience *is*? Well, we certainly seem to be learning what its physical basis is. But this response precisely implies that experience is something further

– defying the initial suggestion that experience is *really* nothing more than activity in the brain.

FUNCTIONALISM

Human consciousness . . . can best be understood as the operation of a . . . virtual machine implemented in the parallel architecture of a brain.

Daniel Dennett[33]

We propose that seeing is a way of acting. It is a particular way of exploring the environment . . .

J. Kevin O'Regan and Alva Noë[34]

The idea that states of mind might be no more and no less than states of the brain originates in our intuition that experience is bound up with the physical world. The final tactic of physicalism originates in the intuition that experience makes a difference. Perhaps mental states do not just make but *are* that difference. In other words, the essence of consciousness in general, and of specific mental states, lies in the functions that they serve.

Take sight as an example. It enables us to make countless discriminations and classifications on the basis of visual appearances. Functionalism suggests that visual experience *consists* in the drawing of these distinctions, and in their consequences for the rest of our mental life – for example in the beliefs they give rise to.

It would follow that any system which made just the same visual distinctions as you do, and used them in all the same ways, would enjoy the same experience – whether the system in question were born of woman or built out of nuts and bolts. This theory rules out the possibility of spectrum inversion that we entertained earlier – if you and I sort and describe colours identically there is no logical space for our colour 'percepts' to differ. For the same reason the theory has no truck at all with 'philosophical zombies'.

Functionalism owes much to the developing science of artificial intelligence. The artificial brains of a computer, like our human ones, convert inputs into outputs. In the computer the conversion results from human programming of a human device: a 'software' package is implemented on the computer's inbuilt 'hardware', giving rise to a 'virtual machine'. (Daniel Dennett, the arch-functionalist of contemporary philosophy, defines a 'virtual machine' as 'a temporary set of highly structured regularities imposed on the underlying hardware by a program: a structured recipe of hundreds of thousands of instructions that give the hardware a huge, interlocking set of habits or dispositions to react'.[35]) The idea at the heart of functionalism is that human consciousness emerges from the implementation of a magnificent 'input–output' function in the brain. If we could describe this function and implement it artificially – the ultimate goal of work in artificial intelligence – the resulting system would have just as strong a claim to consciousness as you or I.

This idea has many attractions. Like all the physicalist models of the mind it places consciousness squarely in the world of maths and physics. It accounts for – indeed originates in – our conviction that consciousness has effects. It is more 'inward' than behaviourism, taking due account of what must go on within our heads. It is less parochial than mind–brain identity theory, allowing for the occurrence of consciousness in other organisms – or indeed machines – which perform the same intellectual computations as we do. Is Daniel Dennett therefore justified in claiming that here at last is *Consciousness Explained*?

A substantial group of philosophers believe that functionalism has gone the extra mile to close the explanatory gap between the mind and its matter. But pause for a moment before you conclude that the curtain has finally come down on this ancient conundrum.

Functionalism suggests that visual experience consists wholly in the drawing of visual distinctions and their repercussions for our other mental states, like our beliefs. Can you really accept this? If so, knowing everything about these processes should tell us everything about experience. But remember the bat and colour-blind Mary: it looked as if it would be possible to know everything about the inner workings of their brains, and the functions their brain states served – without knowing what it is like to be a bat, or to see colours.

And does it automatically follow that an artificial system, which reproduced the functions of our brains, would be conscious at all, let alone enjoy a consciousness like ours? It *might* well be conscious: but it is open to question whether it would *have to be*. Arguably experience is just not a 'functional' phenomenon: my 'seeing red' is not the way it is because of the functions that it serves – it is the way it is because that is what it is like! Whether or not an artificial system would see red the way I do – or indeed see it consciously at all – looks like a legitimate question, unanswered by a functional description of its workings.

Night at the end of the tunnel?

If you are feeling frustrated at this juncture – I am glad. This book has done its work. You have been bitten by the philosophical emotion which has sent thoughtful minds back to the problem of consciousness over and over again for almost 3,000 years.

In recent contributions to this ancient debate, the outcome is usually predictable from the opening shots. In the introductory pages of *The Conscious Mind*, David Chalmers writes that the 'first and most important' constraint on his account is his wish to 'take consciousness seriously', as a 'natural phenomenon', but one which is 'not open to investigation by the usual scientific methods'.[36] If these are the ground rules, there can be little scope for argument. An account which sets out from the assumption that experience is inaccessible to the methods of science is bound to leave consciousness off the stage of contemporary biology. At the opposite extreme of the philosophical spectrum, Daniel Dennett states that the challenge for the philosopher of consciousness is to 'construct a theory of mental events, using the data that scientific method permits'.[37] But any theory which assumes that an analysis of consciousness must only admit the third-person data of science will predictably 'leave out the mind'.

What is the way forward from this impasse? We need some concession from one side or from both: we must change our concept either of mind – or of matter. Which will it be? Which of our intuitions are we willing to sacrifice?

One possibility, favoured by physicalists, is that as we learn more and more about the workings of the brain, and assimilate the new knowledge, our concept of consciousness will gradually metamorphose. Once the process is complete, it will just seem obvious to us that mind is a function of matter. As Daniel Dennett puts it, using his favourite theatrical metaphor: 'once we take a serious look backstage, we discover that we didn't actually see what we thought we saw onstage . . . . the very distinction between onstage experiences and backstage processes loses its appeal'.[38]

This predicts that our understanding of consciousness will evolve in the future along similar lines to the changing conception of 'life' over the past two centuries. Before the development of modern biology, life was often regarded as a supra-physical property, a 'vital spirit' animating matter, an irreducible 'further fact'. Most of us nowadays accept that this supposition is unnecessary. Life, loosely defined, is the property possessed by physical systems which are able to utilise energy from their surroundings to reproduce themselves. The immensely subtle discoveries of modern biochemistry explain how physical systems can perform this remarkable feat.

The analysis of life in physicochemical terms is the most dramatic of all examples of 'reductive' explanation. Will consciousness go the same way? The jury is out. If it becomes possible to give a satisfying functional analysis of consciousness, akin to the functional definition of life, then there is no reason why not. But there are grounds for questioning whether consciousness can be defined in this way for reasons we have just reviewed.

We have directed most of our fire on the concept of consciousness. What about our concept of matter? Might this be the source of our difficulties in understanding the nature of mind?

It is easy to assume that we have a clearer grasp of the nature of matter than we in fact possess. Modern science has allowed us to split the atom, communicate at the speed of light, clone sheep and fly to the moon. We must be getting something right – but practical successes do not provide a guarantee that our theories are comprehensive or that our models are literally correct. Science is always provisional and undergoes constant revision. As its scope extends down towards the infinitesimally small and out towards the unimaginably large, it concerns itself increasingly with unobservable phenomena. There may well be several kinds of permanent limitations to human scientific understanding – limits both to the concepts we can form and to the observations we can make.

Once we realise that science is something of a quicksand, the qualities of our experience begin to look more solid. They are, after all, our point of departure. We develop scientific ideas by a process of abstraction, from the data they supply. This is a journey towards objectivity. The rewards *en route* are huge – but the journey is towards a destination which might be unattainable. If we forget the point of departure in our own experience, we risk a misunderstanding of our intellectual travels. I have described consciousness as a 'further fact', but it might be described more accurately as the fundamental fact of our human lives. This thought does not supply a solution to the problem of consciousness. But it cautions us wisely against accepting facile solutions which assume what they claim to explain.

If our current physical theories are less robust than we tend to imagine, is there any way we could enlarge them in the future to accommodate consciousness more comfortably?

Contemporary physiologists are tantalised by this idea. The '40Hz oscillation', for instance, which we have encountered as a signature of perceptual awareness and a candidate for the mechanism of 'binding', *may* prove to be the most convincing physiological correlate for consciousness to date. If so, its discovery will prove to have been a landmark. But even if its contours turn out to match the profile of experience curve for curve, the real puzzle of experience will remain – why should *this* oscillation yield sensation?

The 40Hz proposal is new and exciting, but it belongs to a familiar tradition. Can we imagine more radical departures in our physical theories, perhaps stemming from quantum physics, which might attack the puzzle of experience more successfully? It is difficult to see how such a radical departure could succeed, unless it involved a claim that a certain physical process *necessarily* leads to consciousness – and at present it is difficult to see what reason we could have for accepting such a claim.

The inclination to leap from limited evidence to grand conclusions is a deeply human trait. It can lead to magnificent achievements, but also to premature admissions of defeat. We have not solved the problem of consciousness yet – but it is much too soon to give the battle up for lost. For the time being we have no alternative but to continue to use all three languages, of biology, behaviour and experience, in our efforts to understand the mind.

Other minds

We wonder whether other human beings possess minds only in moments of exasperation or unusual philosophical abstraction. We have no real doubts about the consciousness of our fellow humans. But we do have genuine uncertainties about whether – and which – animals are conscious. As computers become swifter and more powerful, and begin to acquire the capacities of biological brains, we shall want to know whether they are becoming conscious agents. If – as seems likely – we encounter alien forms of life as we explore the universe, our attitudes towards them will be shaped by our views on whether they are conscious: one can only hope that they recognise that *we* are.

Human minds

The 'problem of other minds' is a traditional product of the philosophical scepticism which ruthlessly questions the grounds for 'knowledge' which we normally take for granted. Like Descartes, you can scarcely doubt your own consciousness: but could it be that you are the only conscious being in a world otherwise peopled by automata?

If some version of physicalism is correct, this question loses its bite: you can find out definitively whether someone else is conscious by watching her or studying her brain or learning about the 'virtual machine' her nervous system implements. Indeed, the fact that physicalism takes the sting out of this question is one of its attractions, precisely because we do not have serious doubts about the consciousness of others.

If we reject physicalism, other minds become a problem once again. If our companions' consciousness is an unobservable further fact about their brains, we cannot be *certain* they possess it. This does not make our belief in their consciousness absurd. We postulate plenty of unobservable entities in the 'hard' science of physics, from elementary particles to black holes. In the more familiar context of other minds, we can argue by analogy from our own case to the consciousness of others: when I am stimulated in certain ways, or behave in others, I am conscious of them, so it seems very likely that in the same circumstances other people are conscious too. When we consider that we all consist of the same flesh and blood, organised in much the same ways, the hypothesis that anyone just like me is conscious looks all the more plausible. These components create consciousness in me: why not in others?

There is an interesting further argument to the effect that it is *illogical* to question the existence of other minds. It runs along these lines.[39] The concept of our *own* mind is intertwined with the concept of other minds, and we can only speak meaningfully of minds at all if we have some way of singling them out. We do so by singling out the *people* to whom they belong. The concept of a mind is logically dependent on the concept of a person, and there is no 'problem of other people' (except as part of a much more general problem concerning whether the world we perceive exists at all). Thus when we cast doubt on whether other people possess minds the very expression of our doubt presupposes that we *know* they do. The doubt is therefore empty.

This argument draws our attention back to the importance of observable facts in our judgements about minds. It reminds us that when we learn the language which describes our mental states, we are *bound* to rely on observable facts about people and their behaviour: imagine, for example, how a child learns what 'anger' means. If this argument is correct, it helps to refute the possibility of 'zombies', and to dissolve the problem of other human minds. But it seems to fall short of a general solution to the problem of other minds – for what are we to say about the existence of minds that do not belong to people?

Animal minds

For practical purposes we all accept that some animals are conscious. We come to regard our pets as friends. Most of us approve of steps to regulate animal farming, and medical research, because we accept that animals can suffer. Hunting is a threatened sport in the UK. A conviction that methods of meat production are inhumane is swelling the numbers of vegetarians. Even Peter Sellers' fictitious sheepdog trainer who revealed in a broad rural accent that the secret of his success was 'a little kindness – and a lot of cruelty' implicitly acknowledged the feelings of his luckless pupils. Admittedly, we tend to be inconsistent: most of us will coo at a lamb one day and munch it happily the next; vegetarians seldom eschew leather bags or catgut stitches. We are also discriminatory: our first impulse is to cuddle kittens – but to exterminate rats.

Are we right to attribute consciousness to animals, or are we falling headlong into that error of 'feeble minds' that Descartes warned against? If we accept – as we all do – that other *people* are conscious, the evidence that many animals, also, are conscious looks overwhelmingly strong.

It comes from several directions.[40] First, animals often behave in ways which suggest that they possess the same basic psychological capacities as we do. They appear to perceive the world around them in ways broadly similar to us; to seek pleasure and shun pain, suggesting that they *care* about what happens to them; to remember the past; to come up with solutions to simple problems that indicate they possess the rudiments of thought. Given that these claims are based on observations of animal behaviour there will always be scope for disagreement over the nature of their 'inner lives'. It is *possible* that instinctual responses and unfeeling reactions are masquerading as the fruits of perception, emotion, memory and thought, and in any individual example of animal 'awareness' it is worth asking whether these simpler mechanisms might explain the evidence. But the claim that they explain all the instances looks increasingly far fetched.

Animal behaviour is on show for all to see. A second line of evidence suggesting that some animals are likely to be conscious flows from the study of their brains. We have already visited this subject, in Chapter 7; I will not labour the point. Human brains are exceptionally powerful, but their design follows the basic vertebrate scheme. Where they depart from the vertebrate norm they are following the lead of other mammalian and primate nervous systems. Our brains are large and size clearly matters, but it would take a very strong argument to show that only the human nervous system has crossed a putative 'threshold' for consciousness.

The third argument stems from the evolutionary continuity of our other organs and their functions. There is no dispute that our heart, lungs and liver have their counterparts in other animals. They differ in innumerable details from one species to the next, but their relationships are undeniable. In particular they serve related functions in related species. Consciousness is a key function of our brains. Given our knowledge of every other area of biology, there is strong reason to expect that consciousness is also a function of at least some other animals' brains.

If you find these three lines of evidence as compelling as I do it might be difficult to see why many thinkers have doubted that some animals have minds. But, of course, we are separated from all our animal neighbours by a substantial gulf – the gulf created by human culture. So far as we know, no other species has a language that approaches ours in scope or subtlety, and none has so much to talk about. Human consciousness is undoubtedly enlarged and conditioned by our culture – but there are good reasons to suppose that simpler forms of consciousness can get along without it.

Manufactured minds

> I propose to consider the question *Can machines think?*
>
> Alan Turing[41]

> The question is not whether machines think, but whether men do.
>
> J.B. Watson

Introduction: surprising Nelson

Waking early on a bright July morning, I get up before the family stirs, to enjoy the view from our holiday house. The estuary runs into the distance through an expanse of fields and salt marsh. Ropes clatter against masts, and sails rustle in the gusty wind. A few small boats are heading off for a race beside the line of purple mallows which outlines the path to the sea. The air is alive with birdsong. I am surrounded by a breezy multitude of timeless sights and sounds.

This is the harbour where Horatio Nelson learned to sail. Little has changed here over the two centuries since then. He would have been at home with the bare boards and threadbare carpets of our cottage. But I am typing these words on to an object which would surely have taken Nelson by surprise: an unobtrusive lightweight laptop computer. This amiable plastic companion has a capacious memory, mathematical powers which easily outstrip mine and script of a clarity no human hand could better.

It belongs to the family of intelligent tools which is transforming the management of our lives. We depend on them increasingly to regulate our industries and our finances, our airspace and even the cars we drive. Since the first substantial computers were designed at the end of the Second World War, huge effort has been expended on enhancing their speed and their power.

Most of these machines – like my laptop – require that we give them detailed instructions from moment to moment. This is changing. We are beginning to create intelligent machines which have a measure of autonomy. Computers in research laboratories around the world are gradually acquiring artificial senses and artificial limbs – governed by artificial brains. Might such a machine one day conjure up an artificial consciousness?

This small question prompts a quiverful of others which have been much discussed in recent writings. Can consciousness really be prised apart from life? Does human thought have features which in principle defy its implementation by a machine? Is anyone who suggests that computers could be conscious not confusing simulation with reality? Most fundamentally – and most awkwardly – how on earth could we *find out* whether or not a computer was conscious? If, like mine, your first instinct is to doubt that machines might be conscious, it may be helpful to itemise some of the reasons for such doubts and examine them more closely.

FIVE REASONS WHY COMPUTERS CANNOT BE CONSCIOUS

1. Looks *are* everything?

I have to admit at the outset that some of the problem lies with the look of computers. They are so very obviously *machines*, bristling with sockets and leads. Outside research laboratories working on artificial intelligence they tend to lack recognisable means of sensation or of action, beyond a keyboard and printer. I am sure we would be more inclined to grant computers consciousness if we could stroke their fur. But we would all accept that appearances can be deceptive. Following his stroke at the age of 40, Jean-Dominique Bauby, the author of the bestselling *Diving-Bell and the Butterfly*,[42] had no means of acting on the world beyond the movements of his eyes and eyelids: his evocative writing shows that words can speak louder than actions; Helen Keller had no effective use of her eyes or ears, but this did not prevent a rich inner life.[43] The mere fact that computers do not resemble us is surely insufficient to rule out their potential consciousness – and they will come to resemble us more closely.

2. Computers just do what they're told

The second source of doubt is more significant. Everything computers do, we might suppose, is *programmed*. A computer simply implements a programmer's plans without any understanding of its own. There is surely a world of difference between being acquainted with and thinking about the world as we do, and the blind operations of a glorified adding machine. There is: but on reflection this distinction might be less sharp than it first appears.

For one thing, as we have seen, the human brain is substantially 'preprogrammed': the intricate anatomy of the visual system, for example, weaves its way into being before it has any opportunity for visual experience. Admittedly, experience after birth shapes and refines the basic structure – but a capacity to cleave to regularities in the world can also be conferred on a computer. Explaining this requires a brief digression.

The first computers to come on line about 50 years ago were bulky monsters which engaged in rapid 'serial' processing. That is to say, the central processor of the machine did one thing at a time. The things it did were extremely simple, individually, but ingenious programming, combined with an ability to record the results of the individual operations, allowed computers to accomplish swiftly and efficiently things we find tedious and difficult, such as complex calculations.

This is a far cry from human thought or experience. But our new knowledge of the brain, for example of the design of the visual system, is guiding the creation of machines with 'habits of thought' which resemble ours much more closely. They engage in 'parallel processing' and achieve self-education. Parallel processing is the simultaneous handling of a number of channels of information. We go in for this on a massive scale, our brain dealing simultaneously with tastes and smells, sights and sounds, memories, thoughts, emotions and plans. Computers can be built with a similar multimodular facility.

The creation of machines which can educate themselves closes the gap between mechanical and human minds considerably, for it enables them to get 'acquainted with world' much as we do as children. The details of these processes are not crucial for the moment, but imagine the following scenario: a computerised robot is equipped with a sensor, such as an 'eye', an effector such as an 'arm', and an aim in life, such as making its way among obstacles to a target which contains a 'reward'. It has a 'brain' whose components are initially connected at random. It is possible to build a learning rule into the circuits governing its actions which enables the robot to shape its responses by trial and error: with the help of such a rule it will gradually learn to distinguish the appearance of obstacles and target, and to find the most efficient route to its goal. Anyone who has watched a baby learning to walk or listened to one learning to talk would be struck by the similarities in the robot's progress towards competence.

The circuits in question deliberately echo neuronal pathways, and are known as 'neural nets'. Their style of operation approximates to the operation of the brain. We can make the approximation even closer: following the creation of the 'silicon neuron' by two American scientists a few years ago, neural nets are being constructed using artificial units which reproduce the electrical behaviour of our brains.[44]

The invention of self-educating systems which resemble the human brain goes some way towards appeasing our second set of doubts. Such computers are indeed programmed – to roughly the degree to which you and I are programmed by our genes – but they are much more than 'glorified adding machines'.

3. Computers cannot really think – or innovate – or experience emotion

Here is a third worry. Computers might be capable of all kinds of clever things, like charting the course to the moon, but there must be reaches of human thought, or creativity or emotion which they could never reproduce.

The Oxford mathematician Roger Penrose has written extensively about the first of these points.[45] There are mathematical theorems which we can know to be true but cannot prove. Programming a computer to use mathematics relies on the ability to prove the theorems in question. Hence there are aspects of human thought which are not 'computable'. This claim is controversial, but I do not think it need detain us overmuch. Our interest lies in whether computers *could* be conscious: the answer to this question does not obviously turn on whether computers can reproduce *every* feature of human cognition: animals cannot and we allow that they may be conscious. Computers, in any event, can clearly model large parts of human thought.

Is creativity a stumbling block? Not necessarily. Creativity depends upon the generation of novel material combined with a critical faculty which sifts the chaff from the grain, selecting good ideas or pleasing forms or lilting tunes: there is no reason in principle why computers should not perform these functions.

How about emotion? Well, it may strike you at first as exceedingly unlikely that a computer should be capable of a fit of pique or a rush of affection, but tomorrow's computers may run some risk of these emotions. If we find that a degree of autonomy is an advantage in our mechanical helpers, we will need to equip them with goals. Goals create motivations, and motivations are close to the heart of human emotion: we seek what we *desire*; a fruitful pursuit of our quarry brings us *joy*; if our search is disappointed we court *anger* and *despair*. Computers *may* never be capable of such feelings: but this begs our question. It certainly seems possible that they might have *reason* to experience them.

4. Only living things can be conscious

There is a fourth source of doubt. The creatures whose consciousness we feel sure of – well, they are creatures. Consciousness seems to be a biological achievement, a dance within the living brain. If living brains cause consciousness, why should we think for a moment that inanimate computers can?

The answer to this question depends on what it is about our brains that makes us conscious.[46] Most, though not all, current theories suppose that consciousness depends upon properties of the neuronal circuitry in certain regions of the brain – the electrical behaviour of the constituent neurons and the strength and pattern of their interconnections. A computer might well be able to reproduce these essentials, gaining a *prima facie* claim to consciousness.

This argument can be reinforced with the help of a thought experiment. Imagine that some time in the future the silicon neuron scientists have perfected their art. They can manufacture components which perfectly simulate the signalling characteristics of neurons. Imagine that one of the thousands of millions of neurons in your visual system is replaced with the silicon version. It is plausible (not proven – this is a thought experiment!) that your awareness would be unchanged. Now imagine the gradual replacement of your whole brain, cell for cell, by silicon neurons. At the finish, signals will be 'processed' just as before: is it not likely that awareness will survive intact?

This is also plausible – but not certain. Masses of things happen in the brain besides an abstract pattern of computation. It is quite possible that some of *these* are required for consciousness. Computational models of the brain capture little or none of the brain's chemical activity – or it might be that some interaction between neurons and the glial cells which outnumber them in the brain is necessary to generate awareness. We *may*, in other words, discover processes which defy the powers of silicon neurons but are required for consciousness. Admittedly, we have not discovered them yet, but neuroscience is a long way from completion.

5. Attributing consciousness to a computer confuses simulation with reality

Similar considerations bear on the final source of doubt. Computers can clearly simulate aspects of human thought; they are, for example, pretty good at arithmetic. But we do not expect simulations to possess all the properties of the processes they simulate: meteorologists do not get wet when they inspect their models of weather and a model of sexual attraction would not normally blow kisses. So why should we expect a computer model of human cognition to generate consciousness?

This question is really a variation on the last. *If* the key to consciousness is the formal organisation of a complex network, then computers are entitled to take a shy at consciousness. If they can reproduce the organisation of our brains we must take the possibility of their awareness very seriously. But if we conclude that consciousness depends on other properties of the brain, computer models of cognition will fall short of awareness – and, presumably, of human performance as well.

Taking the Turing Test

This brings us to the crux of the matter. If a computer were to be conscious, how should we know? At a meeting at which these issues were discussed some years ago a fellow participant joined me on the way to lunch. His first words were faintly disconcerting: 'I was not born of woman. My maker built me on this planet some 50 years ago and I have been studying its people and their strange ways ever since. As you hear I have had some success in acquainting myself with your languages . . . .' It turned out that he was not suffering from an elaborate set of delusions, but making a debating point: if a machine could conduct a sustained and intelligent conversation, we would be very likely to regard it as conscious. If it looked just like you or me the issue would almost certainly be settled in its favour. In other words, we would look to its behaviour to help us make up our minds about its consciousness.

This is essentially the answer given by the British mathematician and wartime code-breaker, Alan Turing, in an influential essay published in 1950.[47] After all, where else is there to look? If we knew more about the basis of human consciousness in the brain we might get some clues by studying the computer's circuitry – but there may be several routes to consciousness. Once a computer, equipped with the necessary sensors and effectors (and perhaps some fur to stroke), really had reproduced human behaviour across the board, what possible reason, beyond a stubborn dogmatism, would we have for denying its consciousness? The fact is, of course, that this goal remains an extremely distant prospect.

You may well feel some resistance to the direction in which these pages are carrying you. Is a machine, made of a few million silicon chips and wire and screws, the right kind of thing to be conscious at all? Yes, of course, we can *imagine* a conscious machine – or a thoughtful clockwork mouse – but it is childish to take these tricks too seriously. Is it? The brain is also made up of millions of components. It is a kind of biological machine, reliably manufactured by time-honoured and largely unmysterious methods. Why should this particular carbon-based, lipid-rich, bone-built device have a monopoly on consciousness? It *might* turn out to, but this has yet to be shown. For the time being there is no wholly compelling argument against the possibility of artificial consciousness.

Alien minds: a midsummer night's dream

On a very rough approximation there are 100,000 million stars in our galaxy, the Milky Way, and 100,000 million galaxies in the observable universe. If we make the conservative assumption that one in every million stars is orbited by planets, there are 10,000 million million planetary systems in our universe. The atoms of which you and I are made are abundant and naturally inclined to combine into the complex molecules of life under certain favourable conditions. The evolutionary path which some successful organisms have taken towards a rich representation and understanding of the world would be a fruitful option wherever evolution has occurred. These speculations make it plausible that we are not alone, and will, in time, encounter other kinds of mind.[48]

Of course, we have not encountered any yet. Or so I thought. But on one of those long undisturbed evenings the parents of young children so often enjoy, I was idly tuning my ultra short wave receiver when I intercepted the following message. I have transcribed it for you as best I can recall it:

> This is Technical Services Broadcasting. The following is an abbreviated version of a report by the regional superintendent of the Intergalactic Trust based on a recent survey of the outer spirals of galaxy XP4530. Field work in this region has been disappointing. We have encountered contemporary life forms in fewer than 500 (0.05 per cent) of the planetary systems surveyed. We found evidence of technology on only one planet, 33,000 light years from the galactic centre, from which this report is being filed. It is known locally as *earth*. Given its modest proportions the planet contains an unusual variety of both habitats and life forms. We find it beautiful, if crowded. Its organisms are carbon based. Many of these exhibit signs of mentality. However, our preliminary findings suggest that the flexible use of symbolism for communication and of wide-ranging technologies is confined to a single group, *the human race*. The languages spoken by humans are exceptionally expressive, given their modest technical achievements. They cultivate and value both the sciences and the arts, but, curiously, treat them as separate realms. Although human mathematics allows for more adequate theories, their physics recognises only four dimensions, three of space and one of time. We have searched for local terms which might denote the fifth dimension. The closest approximations appear to be *affection, desire* and an outmoded term, *virtue*, but the corresponding human concepts integrate poorly into their physics. They have no term or concept whatever corresponding to the sixth dimension. As a result human beings find the nature of consciousness a perennial puzzle and expend much fruitless effort in debating the relationship between the mental and the physical. They are primitive in several other respects. They have not explored their immediate surroundings beyond their own satellite, *moon*. They have yet to be persuaded of the futility of war. Nevertheless we hope it will prove possible to preserve this varied biosphere. Indeed, we recommend urgent measures in view of the greater conflict which threatens to engulf us all.

For an intergalactic broadcast I thought the reception was rather poor. And it seemed odd that this ominous message should be going out in English, with its vague suggestion of some imminent 'War of the Worlds'. For a while I felt privileged to have heard the first communication from a superior intelligence, but I suppose that it was probably a hoax. Perhaps the children had yet again been meddling with my head set.

Human freedom

> Tout comprendre c'est tout pardonner.
> (Understanding everything, we would forgive everything.)
>
> We are apparently condemned to want something impossible.
>
> Thomas Nagel[49]

The prospect of prediction

Our new knowledge of the brain has whetted the blade of another ancient philosophical dispute, concerning the freedom of human choice.

If our actions are determined by events within our brains, and these obey the laws of physics and of chemistry, it should, in principle, be possible to predict them – like eclipses of the moon or the rates of chemical reactions. Consider *C. elegans*, whose nervous system comprises 302 neurons: the task of building a model to predict the worm's behaviour does not look impossibly daunting. If this is possible for *C. elegans*, why not for us? The difference between worm and man is, arguably, one of degree rather than kind, the difference between a simple and a complex nervous system. Indeed, some predictions of human behaviour from knowledge of neuronal behaviour are already feasible. The *Bereitschaftspotential*, for example, signals our intent to act for about a second before we make a move.

This possibility creates a niggling worry. If our choices in life are predictable, can they be free? If they are predictable, is it reasonable to hold ourselves or others responsible for decisions which 'could not have been' other than they were? If science will eventually allow a comprehensive explanation of behaviour, blow by blow, should we be preparing to abandon all the judgements and emotions which presuppose that we or others 'could have done better', or worse, than we did – resentment, blame, shame, gratitude, admiration, pride?

These questions have received a great deal of philosophical attention over the centuries, since long before the advent of neuroscience, for concern about freedom takes wing as soon as one entertains the thought that *anyone* might know in advance what we are going to do. The anyone in question might be a neuroscientist, a physicist or God. Writing in 1820, Laplace left his or her precise identity open: 'Given for one instant an intelligence which could comprehend all the forces by which nature is animated and the respective situation of the beings who compose it [and] an intelligence sufficiently vast to submit these data to analysis . . . nothing would be uncertain and the future, as the past, would be present to its eyes'.[50]

If you are depressed by the idea of an omniscient intelligence foreseeing your every move, from your first day to your last, and you feel, all of a sudden, rather helpless, philosophy can offer you a range of consolations. Let us see what they are. Armed with their comfort we shall return to ask how threatened or diminished we need feel by determinism, the view that our actions are determined by their causes.

Solving for three bodies

The first response concerns the practical limits of prediction. We *imagine* that we might give an explanation for someone's behaviour in terms of physics and chemistry. We say that this is possible 'in principle'. We extrapolate from the unquestionable successes of scientific prediction and engineering – bridge building, moon shots and the like – to the distant prospect of predicting human choice. It is worth reflecting for a moment on the huge extent of this imaginative leap.

Quantum physics provides the best current description of the interactions of subatomic particles. This is unquestionably 'basic' science. You and I are built from subatomic particles, nothing more and nothing less. So when can we expect an accurate prediction of your next house move or romantic attachment based on a quantum mechanical description of your subatomic parts? Don't hold your breath, is my advice. At the last count physicists using old-fashioned Newtonian mechanics were able to describe the interactions of two bodies in succinct mathematical terms. Predicting the behaviour of three or more remains a laborious task. I will not even try to estimate the numbers of particles in your brain, but it exceeds the numbers of neurons a great many billionfold.

This is linked to a feature of our nature which easily escapes our notice but which it may be helpful to keep in mind: we are wildly complex entities. A piece of iron or copper of the same size as the brain could be succinctly described in a few lines, detailing its size and shape and any trace impurities. The summary description could exploit the monotonous structural regularity of a lump of elemental metal. But a similar kind of description of the brain would be a gargantuan task, given its numerous layers of intricate organisation. This contrast can escape our notice because the unaided eye is not a well-attuned complexity detector. But it is surely important when we think about the prediction of action. Much of the complexity that stands in the way of its prediction lies inside our heads.[51] This helps, at least, to explain why we feel special.

It also helps, I think, to explain why we do not readily accept that our actions issue from causes. The causes in question are mostly located in the same unassuming space within our heads. As Daniel Dennett puts it: 'we see the dramatic effects leaving: we don't see the causes entering; we are tempted by the hypothesis that there are no causes'.[52]

So the first consolation for our predictability is that, in practice, we are not so predictable after all.

Che sarà sarà? (What will be, will be?)

The idea of an omniscient spectator foreseeing all our decisions sometimes prompts the dejected thought that if the future is determined already there is no point in trying any more. Che sarà sarà: what will be, will be. If so, why agonise, why worry, why knock your head against Fate's brick wall? But the claim that our fate is sealed whatever we do, however we weave and duck, goes well beyond the premise that our actions are predictable.

In fact the claim cannot be true. Because we *know* for sure that it makes a difference whether we try – to finish the cleaning or to write the book – and that if we 'can't be bothered' to do it the chances are it will not get done. We *know* that we maximise our chances of success in many undertakings by giving them a bit of thought beforehand: it really helps to look before we leap. How come?

The answer is simple and will have occurred to you already. Even if the future is predictable, our efforts and deliberations are among the facts which can influence its outcome. The omniscient spectator will need to factor them into his projections. The belief that our fate is sealed *whatever we do* is known as 'fatalism'. Sometimes, indeed, the die is cast whatever we do – but only in exceptional cases when matters are out of our hands. Usually – predictably – our forethought and our efforts make a difference. This is a second consolation.

Free fall

> They that have power to hurt and will do none . . .
> They rightly do inherit heaven's graces
> And husband nature's riches from expense.
>
> William Shakespeare, Sonnet XCIV

So far, so good. Prediction is overwhelmingly difficult. Effort and deliberation can make a difference to predictable outcomes. These reflections may have cheered you up a little. But you may still be worried that if your decisions and actions are predictable, if they are pre-ordained to go one way or the other, you cannot *really* be free.

Sufferers from this anxiety are traditionally treated with a trusty philosophical tranquilliser, a third source of consolation. It consists of the question, 'When do we normally consider that someone has freedom of action?' The comforting answer expected is: 'When he can act as he wishes, hindered neither by external force nor by internal compulsion.' We do usually act in this way: pistols are seldom held to our heads and the balance of our minds is generally sound. But the discovery of laws describing our behaviour would do nothing to interfere with freedom construed in this way. If I eat the bar of chocolate which I was hungering after I will have done as I liked – and therefore acted 'freely' – however predictable my action may have been.

You might not be shaken off so easily. You might respond like this: 'Sure, you did as you liked when you sneaked the chocolate from the cupboard. Incidentally, I like chocolate, and you might at least have given me some. But can I really blame you for your selfishness, given that your actions are so utterly predictable? You *could not have done otherwise*, after all. Your claim to freedom looks to me like a boastful delusion: you were just free to fall.'

It is worth examining the claim that 'I could not have done otherwise' more closely. Try to think of some recent episode of which you are mildly ashamed, and ask yourself whether you could have behaved differently. When I play this game the answer is consistently, 'Of course I could.' In fact, this possibility is a condition for the shame: if I did not think that I could have done differently, I would have no cause to feel ashamed. But if my behaviour was predictable, would this imply that I could not have done differently, in the sense relevant here? Is my sense of shame mistaken? Arguably, not. When I imagine 'doing differently' I imagine that some of the circumstances of my action changed, in simple and plausible ways: instead of greedily giving way to my lust for chocolate, and scoffing the lot, I might have remembered that my friend next door was especially fond of this brand and offered her some. Why not? I am not always so mean. Next time I will try to do better. If I do – I will have succeeded in a bit of minor self-improvement; if not – well, we all have our failings, and it will look as if mine are getting ever more deeply entrenched.

Are you still doubtful about my freedom of action? Perhaps. You could take this line: 'You say that you could have done differently if you had been more thoughtful. I accept that. But in the situation which actually arose, given the circumstances precisely as they were, your action was predictable and you could not have done differently. This possibility, of taking a different decision when all the circumstances were just as before, is the one required for real freedom. You remain in the grips of your boastful delusion.'

Some philosophers have indeed taken this line, although it is fraught with difficulties of its own. The most obvious is this. We ordinarily take ourselves to be free, within limits. If the predictable causation of our actions is incompatible with freedom, what *other* source can we find for our liberty? If our actions are not caused, they are uncaused; if uncaused, the argument runs, they are random. Random choice looks like an even less promising basis for freedom and responsibility than predictability. It seems that those who wish to defend the freedom of will while denying that our actions belong to a causal chain are indeed 'condemned to want something impossible'. Either our freedom is an illusion or it is compatible somehow with causality.

These are the consolations offered by philosophy in the face of a scientific account of human action. Our choices are, in practice, somewhat unpredictable; the theoretical predictability of our actions allows scope for effort and forethought and only poses a limited threat to our common-sense notion of freedom. These thoughts go some way towards vindicating our sense that our choices are free: it may be a less full-blooded, a less absolute liberty than we might at first imagine, but a liberty well worth having nonetheless.

This conclusion, that freedom is not really threatened by the predictive powers of science, is known as 'compatibilism'. It is not the only possible conclusion. Some philosophers have argued that if determinism is true our freedom is an illusion and our moral judgements groundless: when we blame others we are simply blinding ourselves to the fact that they could not have acted otherwise than they did.[53] Others have hoped to pluck some sort of radical freedom from the jaws of science,[54] or argued that our moral attitudes are so deeply rooted in our nature that attempts to justify them are irrelevant.[55]

Clearly we cannot create ourselves from scratch: 'to do anything we must first be something'.[56] That something is not of our choosing and this is an inescapable limitation of our freedom. But although we originate in processes we cannot choose, all ordinary human beings gain freedom of a kind. We are in practice unpredictable, and the reason for this lies in *our* complexity. We can consider the reasons for action, weighing up its pros and cons: we do so more or less wisely, and this process affects our decisions. We can make an effort to achieve our goals: this considerably enhances our chances of success. Much of the time we act untrammelled by compulsion from without or from within. Does all this add up to *real* freedom and permit us *real* choice? It may be the closest thing to freedom we could hope for, and represent all that choice could be. I will leave you to decide whether it is sufficient for your needs.

Conclusion: the matter of the mind

This book is an extended reflection on two facts which astonish me: our experience is marvellously rich *and* utterly dependent on the brain. Any account of the nature of consciousness must do justice to these facts, and, perhaps, to a third intuition: that experience is useful.

Dualism respects our belief that experience is special, but leaves the interaction of mind and matter deeply mysterious. Physicalism, which tries to redescribe experience in one or other kind of physical vocabulary, explains how mind can trade with matter, but does so by cheating our first intuition – and 'leaving out the mind'.

The way forward from this impasse is not clear. Theories which depict experience and its neural basis as inseparable aspects of a single process may hold out the greatest promise. But we do not have any clear understanding of how a single process could have two such different aspects. We can see that the liquidity of water necessarily follows from the properties of the molecules of water. We lack any comparable insight into the connection between experience and the molecules of the brain. It is not yet certain that science can supply this. Making sense of their relationship may require us to rethink the nature of matter, mind, or both.

Our attitudes to the possibility of consciousness in animals and machines are clouded by these doubts. Similarities between the mental capacities and nervous systems of man and other animals, coupled with the argument from evolution, make a compelling case that some animals are conscious. The gradual emergence of intelligent and autonomous robots will steadily erode our belief that machines are not. If the computational organisation of the brain is the key to consciousness, nothing, bar complexity, stands in the way of conscious machines. If consciousness depends on some other physical feature of the brain it could, in principle, be artificially engineered. There is at present no convincing reason to doubt the possibility – currently remote – of artificial consciousness.

If we are, in a sense, biological machines, our actions are, in principle, predictable. Does this deny us freedom? We tend to suppose, without giving it too much thought, that we are the ultimate authors of our actions. This supposition is threatened by the scientific picture of our actions as events, just like others, in an unbroken chain of causes and effects. But several reflections help to soften the blow. Our complexity makes us unpredictable in practice, whatever the theorists say. Predictability does not prevent our efforts and our forethought from making a difference to the world, nor does it prevent us from doing what we will. Perhaps this is freedom enough.

Epilogue

All the rest is silence
On the other side of the wall,
And the silence ripeness,
And the ripeness all.

W.H. Auden[1]

Why are we conscious?

How do the events in our brains give rise to those in our minds? How does the intricate activity of 100,000 million nerve cells generate consciousness? To gain a long perspective on the ground we have traversed, I would like to close by asking an even simpler question: *why* are we conscious? Despite its simplicity, this question can be attacked in several different ways.

Mechanisms

A first approach is to outline the mechanisms of consciousness: what makes awareness possible?

We know a good deal about the mechanisms of *the waking state*, as we saw in Chapter 3. The 'electricity of the brain' tracks our states of consciousness. While we wake, fleeting rhythms dance over the surface of the brain, produced by shifting coalitions of neurons in the cortex. These rhythms, in their turn, depend upon an activating system at the core of the upper brain-stem and in the thalamus. The chemicals it releases unlock the cerebral hemispheres to the information which bombards us from the senses, priming them to process it in relation to our current needs and schemes.

Sleep, like wakefulness, is organised from the brainstem. It has a hidden structure of its own: in the course of the night we cycle repeatedly from light sleep to deep, from deep to dreaming sleep. The brainstem continues to generate these rhythms after the destruction of the hemispheres, as, for example, in the 'vegetative state'. By contrast, death of the brainstem is almost always followed, within hours or days, by death, pure and simple.

We know something too of the mechanisms which supply the *contents of consciousness*. Chapter 5 was devoted to the neural basis of visual awareness. We focused on sight because it plays such a large part in our lives, but a similar account could be given for each of the human senses. We saw how light is detected by the retina, how contrasts are signalled to the brain, how form, colour, depth and motion are analysed in regions of the visual cortex. We caught a glimpse of the mechanisms by which the brain reintegrates the features of the visual world, allowing us to recognise what we see, and to conjure up the playthings of the imagination. We surveyed the neural basis of attention, the gatekeeper of consciousness. We saw how the process of vision is interwoven with action: how sight guides the movements of the eyes, which in their turn keep vision up to date.

The idea that rapid synchronised activity among widely scattered groups of cells may play a part in consciousness has been a recurring theme. This activity is a feature of ordinary wakefulness, of dreaming sleep and of awareness under anaesthesia; it has been proposed as the mechanism which 'binds' the disparate features of a single visual object, and as a means of selecting the items at the forefront of consciousness. It *may* turn out to be a key to the biology of consciousness.

Phylogeny

Laying bare a set of mechanisms like these is one way of explaining consciousness. These mechanisms, after all, are part of us, the contents of our skulls. But we can also look for a historical answer to the question 'Why are we conscious?', an account of how these mechanisms emerged – how our ancestors came to be conscious in the course of our evolutionary past. This is the phylogeny of consciousness.

The elements of the nervous system – the neuron, its ion channels and its chemical transmitters – date back to the very origins of multicellular life. In almost every complex organism these common elements have been exploited to create a signalling system, which allows animals to respond to events around them with appropriate actions.

In some lines of animal descent there has been an ever increasing investment in this signalling system, allowing a progressively richer range of perceptual distinctions and a more flexible repertoire of response. This process of 'encephalisation' has been particularly striking in some parts of the vertebrate lineage, which includes fish, reptiles, mammals and our own primate Order. Somewhere on the burgeoning bush of life which leads from the simplest nervous systems to the most complex, animals began to have experiences: consciousness appeared. We touched on the uncertainties surrounding this event in Chapter 7.

A huge investment in the growth of the brain has been the single most striking feature of prehuman evolution over the past 5 million years. It has both driven and been driven by the emergence of civilisation – technology, culture and language. Nervous systems in general allow animals to create an internal model of their surroundings: the evolution of the human brain has given rise to a new level of representation, the symbolic description of the world. We ourselves loom large in this description.

Ontogeny

Phylogeny is history on a grand scale, the natural history of vast groups of creatures. But every animal has its own special story – as, indeed, does each of us. This opens the way to a second kind of historical answer to the question 'Why are we conscious?', an answer in terms of individual growth and development. John Locke wrote in this vein 300 years ago: 'Follow a child from its birth, and observe the alterations that time makes, and you shall find, as the mind by the senses comes to be more and more furnished with ideas, it comes to be more and more awake'.[2]

We have touched on several aspects of this process. Over the early months of brain development, 'ontogeny recapitulates phylogeny' in the womb – up to a point. This re-enactment of our evolutionary past is rough and ready, but in the brain of a four-week-old human embryo we found a remarkable resemblance to the brain of a fish which swam the seas 400 million years ago.

Once the brain begins to be 'furnished with ideas', it proves a wonderfully receptive and retentive vessel. These powers very likely derive from the plasticity of the synapses at which neurons interact. Experience can shape these, strengthening some and weakening others, creating assemblies of neurons which represent the contents of our world. The astronomical numbers of synapses in the brain, which run into thousands of billions, account for the scope of human memory.

Our development has another crucial dimension. We are quintessentially social animals, creatures of our families, societies and cultures. This fact is at the heart of our biology. Growing up among others, learning to speak their language, we gradually gain awareness of ourselves. We discover that we possess bodies like theirs, feelings like theirs, and, eventually, minds like theirs too. In acquiring 'a theory of mind', we take a great stride into the human condition.

Function

These mechanisms and their history make consciousness possible for us. But what does consciousness make possible? What is it for? This is probably the most difficult and controversial of all the scientific questions about consciousness. Let us assume, for the moment, that consciousness does have a function: it is intuitively unlikely, to say the least, that it has none.

Our reflections in Chapter 7 suggested that consciousness comes into play when automatised, routine, solutions fail. Novel challenges, demanding a concerted response, summon up conscious attention, which helps us to select appropriate actions in an unpredictable world. Richness of representation makes for flexibility of response.

If we compare the control system embodied in our brains to a computer in charge of a robot, 'conscious' information might correspond to the data which is broadcast widely in the system, amongst the automatic modules which enable the smooth performance of familiar tasks. This widely broadcast information would then be available to control a wide range of responsive behaviour, including self-report – by which we articulate what is passing through our minds.

But *why* are we conscious?

Learning about mechanisms, history and function seems to take us some distance towards an explanation of why we are conscious. Will it take us all the way?

Not as far as some would like to go. The following kind of worry is always lurking in the wings: 'Talk of evolution, mechanisms and function is helpful up to a point. It tells us lots about the brain. But it says nothing at all about the really difficult and interesting question, the one to which we really want an answer – why we *experience* what happens in our brains, why we *see* colours, *hear* music, *savour* tastes. The processes you have described could perfectly well be enacted in darkness and silence, in a world without consciousness, a world of complex bodies without minds.'

It is because this response seems so terribly wrong, and yet so naggingly right, that the mind–body question has proved so difficult to answer. Physicalists hope to undermine its suppositions, to show that once mechanism, history and function are explained no residue of mystery remains. Others, dualists, believe that there is a continuing dilemma, a legitimate reason to doubt that science can ever give a full account of consciousness.

I share their doubt, but suspect it may be barren. Our difficulty in explaining the fact of consciousness, in the face of everything we can hope to learn through science, is akin to our difficulty in explaining existence itself. Indeed, it is surely the *same* difficulty, in disguise, marking out the limits of human understanding.

Glossary

Acetylcholine
A chemical which transmits excitation between nerve and muscle. It is also a major neurotransmitter in the brain, with an important role in maintaining arousal and permitting learning. Brain acetylcholine is depleted early in the course of Alzheimer's disease.

Achromatopsia
The absence of colour vision. This can be peripheral, the result of abnormalities in the retina, or central, due to a disorder of the areas responsible for colour vision in the brain.

Action potential
The all-or-nothing electrical signal transmitted by a neuron which has been sufficiently excited.

Afference
A collective term for the input to a neuron or region of the nervous system.

Agnosia
A disturbance of perception which is not straightforwardly due to problems in the sense organs or to destruction of primary sensory areas in the brain. In the case of vision, 'apperceptive' agnosias affect the formation of the visual image, while 'associative' agnosias interfere with its interpretation. This distinction is sometimes difficult to draw.

Alpha rhythm
An electrical rhythm at 8–13 cycles/second originating in the brain which can be recorded from the back of the head in a relaxed subject with his eyes closed.

Amino acid
Amino acids are the building blocks of proteins. We utilise about 20. The genetic code operates by specifying the order in which amino acids are strung together

to build proteins. Amino acids also serve other biological functions. For example, the amino acid glycine doubles up as a neurotransmitter, and the amino acid glutamate, itself an excitatory neurotransmitter, is the chemical parent of the inhibitory neurotransmitter gamma-aminobutyric acid (GABA).

Amnesia

Inability to form new memories. In human sufferers the defect is usually selective, for example sparing the ability to acquire new motor skills.

Anatomy

The study of where things are in the body: neuroanatomy is the study of where things are in the brain. Physiology, by contrast, is the study of how the body works.

Anosagnosia

Unawareness of a deficit, quite common in neurological disorders. Patients will sometimes, for example, deny that they have lost their vision or become paralysed following a stroke.

Astrocyte

One of the three varieties of glial cells which support and sustain the brain's neurons. Astrocytes guide developing neurons to their targets and help to regulate exchanges between the bloodstream and the brain.

Atom

Atoms are the building blocks of elements: an atom is the smallest possible quantity of an element, such as oxygen, hydrogen, sodium or gold. Atoms of the same or different elements can combine to form molecules (a water molecule consists of two hydrogen and one oxygen atoms, H_2O).

Attention

Broadly, the ability to focus the mind: but the term is highly ambiguous. Thus attention can be preparatory, selective, sustained, divided, overt or covert and directed towards a wide variety of different processes and tasks.

Autism

A disorder causing difficulties with the development of language and social interaction and impoverishment of imaginative play. It usually becomes apparent in early childhood. Intelligence is often impaired but need not be.

Autonomic

Refers to the part of the nervous system largely outside voluntary control which regulates the smooth muscle in blood vessels, gut, bladder and elsewehere, and modulates the rate and force of the heart. It controls internal bodily functions like blood pressure, sweating and penile erection.

Axon

Transmits signals away from neurons. A single axon leaves the neuron, although it will often branch as it nears its targets, allowing a single neuron to make numerous synaptic connections with other cells.

Basal ganglia

A collective term for an important group of deep nuclei in the brain, including the caudate, putamen, globus pallidus and substantia nigra. In one major signalling loop, signals pass from numerous areas of the cortex to the caudate/putamen (which function as a single unit), thence to the globus pallidus, on to the thalamus, and back to the originating region of cortex. Human diseases resulting from basal ganglia dysfunction include Parkinson's disease and Huntington's chorea. While they are associated particularly with the control of movement they also contribute to the neural control of personality and behaviour.

Behaviourism

Methodological behaviourism is the view that the subject matter of psychology should be restricted to objectively observable behaviour. Philosophical behaviourism is the view that descriptions of mental states can be restated in terms which mention only behaviours or dispositions to behave in certain ways.

Bereitschaftspotential

An electrical potential, also known as the 'readiness potential', recorded from the scalp, which builds during the half-second or so before the performance of a voluntary movement.

Beta rhythm

Rapid rhythms, at 13–25 cycles/second, which can be recorded from the human scalp during mental activity.

Binding

The process by which activity scattered around the brain is harmonised to produce a concerted function: for example, the process by which the activity in the numerous visual areas is harmonised to produce a unified visual image.

Blindsight

Visual abilities surviving damage to the primary visual cortex which leaves sufferers subjectively blind. These abilities are typically demonstrated by asking subjects to *guess* the location, shape, etc. of objects presented to them.

Brainstem

The region of the brain linking the spinal cord below to the cerebral hemispheres above. The brainstem is divided into the medulla (closest to the spinal cord), pons and midbrain. Among other functions, the lower parts of the brainstem control breathing and the heart; the upper parts regulate the sleep–wake cycle by way of widespread connections to the hemispheres. In the United Kingdom 'brain death' is equated with death of the brainstem.

Brodmann's area

One of the areas of cerebral cortex distinguished by the neuroanatomist Korbinian Brodmann (1868–1918) using the light microscope. His areas differ in subtle anatomical features, such as the density of cells in particular layers of the cortex, but the boundaries between them have generally turned out to correspond to differences of function and his map therefore remains in current use.

Cell

Cells are the atoms of biology, the building blocks of complex forms of life, capable of leading an independent existence apart from their owner if they are carefully nurtured . Each cell contains the full complement of genetic material required to build a body, although in bodies like ours the cells in different organs use only the instructions relevant to their particular needs. The neuron is the principal specialist cell in the nervous system. There are around 100,000 million neurons in the brain.

Cell membrane

The semi-fluid boundary of the cell at which it transacts its business with the outside world. It consists of two layers of (water-resistant) fat molecules, containing numerous proteins which communicate with other cells, for example the protein receptor molecules which detect the presence of neurotransmitters released at synapses made by the axons of adjacent neurons.

Central nervous system

The brain and spinal cord (as opposed to the *peripheral* nerves which run to and from muscles and sense organs in the arms, legs, trunk and head).

Cerebellum

A region of the brain tucked in behind the brainstem and beneath the hemispheres, with a highly repetitive neuronal structure, conventionally associated with the smooth coordination of movement (but possibly also involved in the 'coordination' of thought and emotion). Signals pass from the cerebral cortex to the cerebellum, thence to the thalamus and back to the cerebral cortex in a control loop similar to the one involving the basal ganglia.

Cerebral hemispheres

The paired half-circles of the brain, covered by the folded cerebral cortex, each containing deep structures including the basal ganglia.

Cerebrum

Includes the cerebral hemispheres and the 'diencephalon', thalamus and hypothalamus, but not the brainstem or cerebellum.

Channel

The electrical activity of neurons is controlled by proteins situated in the cell membrane containing pores or channels which allow charged particles, like sodium, calcium and potassium, to pass in and out of the cell. Some channels, like those involved in transmitting the action potential, are opened by changes of voltage ('voltage-gated'); others are opened by the arrival of neurotransmitters ('ligand-gated'). A growing band of neurological disorders is turning out to be caused by defects in channels, including some types of epilepsy and migraine.

Chorea

Fidgety involuntary movements which result from disturbance of the function of the basal ganglia.

Chromosome

The genetic material in each cell is condensed into 23 pairs of chromosomes, including the sex chromosomes (this pair comprises two X chromosomes in women, an X and a Y chromosome in men). Thus any given gene is located on a given chromosome, and will be present in each of us in two versions, one originating from our father, one from our mother (genes on the Y chromosome, and the X chromosome in men, are present in only one copy).

Cognition

The sum total of our intellectual activity. The usual list of cognitive functions runs something like: attention, memory, executive function (ability to organise our thought and behaviour), language, praxis (our ability to perform skilled functions), perception (including spatial awareness). Consciousness may or may not be included in this list.

Coma

A state of impaired consciousness associated with a variable degree of depression of brain activity. The eyes are closed. Coma is caused principally by substances or injuries which cause a widespead depression of brain function, or by more focal damage to the areas in the brainstem and thalamus which normally maintain wakefulness.

Cone

The cell type in the retina which detects the presence of coloured light, setting in train the electrical signals which eventually lead to the experience of sight. There are three varieties of cone in the human retina, maximally sensitive to different wavelengths of light: all three are needed for normal colour vision. Cones are packed at the centre of the retina, which we use for scrutinising visual detail. A second type of photoreceptor, the rod, is specialised for grey-tone vision in dim light.

Constancy

The process which allows us to detect the unchanging features of objects despite changing conditions of observation. For example, the brain computes (and we tend to see) the true colour of an object despite variations in the colour of the illuminating light.

Correlation

A predictable relationship between variable quantities: so, for example, our visual experience correlates (up to a point) with activity in visual area 1. But, famously, correlation does not imply cause: the correlation between two variables may be explained as a joint association with a third factor.

Cortex

From the Latin for 'bark', the cortex is the folded outer surface of the cerebral hemispheres, their 'grey matter', rich in layered neurons.

Declarative memory

Memory of the kind we can declare – or articulate. Declarative memory is subdivided into episodic, for one-off events, and semantic, for our database of knowledge about language and the world (what a table is, who is the President of the USA . . .). Declarative memory is contrasted to procedural memory, which comprises acquisition of motor skills, priming and classical conditioning.

Delta rhythm

A slow electrical rhythm at less than 4 cycles/second which can be recorded from the scalp or brain during deep sleep or sometimes in coma.

Dendrite

The branching processes of neurons which receive the majority of signals from other neurons.

Diencephalon

The core of the cerebral hemispheres, comprising the thalamus and hypothalamus.

DNA

Deoxyribonucleic acid is the chemical material which transmits the instructions for building and maintaining our bodies – our genetic make-up.

Dopamine

A neurotransmitter released in the cerebral hemispheres by axons originating in the brainstem, with a role in arousal, motivation and motor control. Parkinson's disease results from loss of dopamine-producing neurons in the brainstem. Schizophrenia is treated with drugs which block the action of dopamine in the basal ganglia.

Dorsal stream

The stream of visual signalling which runs from the occipital to the parietal lobe, principally involved in the processing of information about space and motion. In contrast the ventral stream, running from the occipital to the temporal lobe, is principally involved in object recognition.

Dualism

The philosophical tradition which draws a deep distinction between mental and physical events. Substance dualism distinguishes mental and physical substances; property dualism distinguishes mental and physical properties.

EEG

The electroencephalogram, a recording of the brain's electrical activity, usually recorded from the scalp.

Efference

A collective term for the output to a neuron or region of the nervous system.

Electromagnetic radiation

The energy spectrum which includes high energy gamma rays and X-rays, lower energy micro- and radio waves, and light, in the intermediate energy range of the spectrum.

Eliminativism

The philosophical view that reference to mental states should be or will eventually be eliminated in favour of reference to objective physical states.

Encephalisation (quotient)

See EQ

Encephalitis

An infection of the substance of the brain.

Encephalitis lethargica

A form of brain infection which became epidemic at around the close of the First World War. Disorders of arousal were prominent early in the course of the illness and in its long-drawn-out convalescence. It has all but disappeared.

Endorphin

One of the three families of opioid neurotransmitters important in pain signalling. The 'opiates', like opium and heroin, mimic their action in the brain.

Epilepsy

A disturbance of the brain's electrical activity causing abnormal synchronisation of activity, either locally ('partial epilepsy') or globally ('generalised epilepsy'). It can cause a wide range of disturbances of sensation, memory and thought as well as the more familiar 'grand mal' seizure.

EQ

The 'encephalisation quotient' is a measure of the brain development of a species. It is intended to reflect the ratio between the size of the brain in an average member of the species and the brain size which might be predicted for such a species (given the species' average weight or body surface area and the usual relationship between brain size and body size among the species of interest).

Evoked potential

The electrical response correlated with sensation or a cognitive process recorded from the scalp. Repeated recording with averaging of the recorded signals is usually necessary to demonstrate these tiny electrical events.

Evolution

The process thought to have given rise to and shaped the diversity of living forms. The fundamental characteristics of a living thing are transmitted to its offspring in genetic material (now known to be DNA). Chance alterations (mutations) in this material cause variations in the characteristics of the offspring. Some of these will be advantageous, and enhance the individual's chances of reproduction. They will therefore spread through the population.

Fibre

A term used to refer to the axon.

FMRI

Functional magnetic resonance imaging: one of the two main techniques which can be used to reveal the activity of the living brain as it performs specific tasks.

Frontal lobe

The foremost of the four lobes of the brain. It contains the motor cortex, and, broadly, is the lobe which governs the output of the brain, organising and regulating our behaviour.

Functional imaging

A group of techniques which make it possible to visualise the brain regions activated by specific functions, ranging from seeing a flash of light to mathematical thinking. The two main techniques are PET (positron emission tomography) and fMRI (functional magnetic resonance imaging). The techniques rely on the fact that blood flow and energy consumption increase in active brain areas.

Functionalism

The philosophical view that mental states can be regarded as functions of the nervous system. These functions are often thought of in computational terms.

GABA

Gamma-amino butyric acid, the major inhibitory neurotransmitter in the nervous system.

Gamma rhythm

Fast brain rhythms at 25–100 cycles/second which can be recorded from the surface of the scalp, with a proposed role in maintaining arousal and in unifying the contents of consciousness.

Gene

Our genes are the inherited instructions for building our bodies, written in DNA. Each gene spells out the order of amino acids for a particular protein molecule. The Human Genome Project suggests that 30–50,000 genes are active in the human body.

Gestalt

A gestalt is literally a form or configuration. In psychology, the term refers to the groupings which we tend to perceive even in items which may not have been deliberately patterned. The Gestalt psychologists came up with a set of rules which describe this tendency.

Glia

Three cell types which exist in great abundance in the brain alongside its neurons, playing various supporting roles: astrocytes, oligodendrocytes and microglia.

Global workspace

Bernard Baars' metaphor for the computational function of consciousness: it provides a central source of information which is widely available to specialised psychological subsystems.

Glutamate

A widespread excitatory neurotransmitter, released for example by axons running from thalamus to cortex and vice versa. It is an amino acid.

Glycine

An amino acid neurotransmitter which inhibits neuronal firing.

Grey matter

Areas of the brain rich in neurons as opposed to the 'white matter' which consists mainly of interconnecting fibre bundles.

Gyrus

One of the 'hills' of the folded cerebral cortex, as opposed to its valleys or 'sulci'.

Hebb's law (or rule)

A rule proposed on theoretical grounds by the psychologist Donald Hebb to help explain the neural basis of learning. The rule states that the synaptic connection between neuron *A* and neuron *B* will be strengthened if *A* fires and *B* is successfully excited.

Hippocampus

From the Greek for sea-horse, the hippocampus is a curved structure tucked into the inner surface of the temporal lobes. It is required for the formation of new long-term declarative memories, and to some extent for their retrieval as well.

Histamine

An excitatory neurotransmitter with a role in maintaining wakefulness.

Hominid

Our species' immediate line of descent: we are the only surviving hominids.

Hominoid

A group comprising the gibbons, chimps, gorillas, orang-utans – and man.

Information

An ambiguous term. In colloquial speech information is news *about* something; in computer science the term is used more abstractly to refer to the specification of a particular state from an ensemble of possibilities.

Ion

An atom or molecule carrying net electrical charge. Ions are important for neuronal signalling: the movement of ions, like sodium, potassium or calcium (which carry positive charge) or chloride (which carries negative charge), into and out of neurons shapes the action potential.

Interneuron

A small neuron involved in short-range communication: a component of neuronal circuitry which intervenes between sensory neurons which bring information to and motor neurons which carry it away from the brain.

Lateral geniculate nucleus

The part of the thalamus which receives the major input from the retina, giving a coded description of the visual image.

Lesion

A very general term meaning a discrete area of damage or disease, caused by nature or by man (an 'experimental lesion').

Limbic system

A network of structures at the 'limbus' or border of the brain, with a key role in emotion and memory. It comprises the hippocampus and surrounding cortex in the medial temporal lobe, parts of the thalamus, and (according to taste) other linked areas including the cingulate gyrus in the medial frontal lobe and the amygdala.

'M' cell

A 'magnocell'. In the visual system large magnocellular neurons, found in the retina and beyond, are particularly concerned with rapid signalling about moving stimuli.

Medulla

The part of the brainstem closest to the spinal cord, crucial for life because of its role in maintaining breathing and the activity of the heart.

MEG

Magnetoencephalography: a modern descendant of the EEG, MEG records the magnetic activity set up by the fluctuating electric fields within the brain.

Midbrain

The part of the brainstem closest to the brain proper. Damage here is particularly likely to impair consciousness.

Millisecond

One thousandth of a second.

Mitochondrion

One of the minute chemical machines, or 'organelles, within the cell. Mitochondria are required for energy generation within the cell and contain their own DNA (unlike the other organelles). They are thought to have originated as independent organisms which entered into a symbiotic relationship with the ancestor of our cells about 1,500 years ago.

Molecule

Two or more atoms linked by chemical bonds: water is a simple molecule, proteins are complex ones.

Motor

To do with movement. So the 'motor cortex' is the part of the cortex which most directly influences our choice of movement.

Myelin

The fatty insulating sheath which is wrapped around many axons in the nervous system to increase the speed at which they can conduct signals.

Naturalism

The philosophical view that consciousness can be explained by appealing to basic properties and laws of nature, and without contradicting any of the tenets of science.

NCC

Widely used shorthand for the 'neural correlate of consciousness' (see below).

Nerve

The collective term for a group of neurons which run together. As a rule some will be supplying muscle, others returning from sense organs (although some nerves, like the optic nerve, are purely sensory).

Nervous system

The brain, spinal cord and peripheral nerves: all the nervous tissues of the body.

Neural correlate of consciousness (NCC)

This term is used to refer to the neural basis of conscious experience: the combination of structure (the 'where' of consciousness) and physiology (the 'how' of consciousness) which collectively give rise to our experience (or so one popular view of consciousness holds).

Neurology

The branch of medicine which deals with disorders of the nervous system (closely allied to *neuroscience*, the scientific study of the nervous system).

Neuron

A nerve cell.

Neurotransmitter

A chemical released by a neuron at its junction (or 'synapse') with another cell, which generally has the effect of increasing or reducing the level of excitation in the second cell, thereby influencing the rate at which it transmits signals.

Noradrenaline

This neurotransmitter is called norepinephrine in the USA. Closely related to adrenaline, a hormone released by the adrenal gland to help mobilise the body's resources for 'fight or flight', noradrenaline is one of the neurotransmitters of the brain's 'activating system'. It is synthesised in the brainstem and released widely through the brain.

Nucleus

A term with two entirely separate biological meanings. In cell biology, the nucleus is the part of the cell which contains DNA, the headquarters of chemical operations. In neurology, a 'nucleus' is a cluster of neurons which generally share a function or functions.

Occipital lobe

The hindmost of the four lobes of the brain. It contains the primary visual cortex, right at the back of the brain (the 'occipital pole'), and several of the other visual areas.

Oligodendrocyte

One of the brain's three types of glial cell, oligodendrocytes manufacture the fatty sheaths of 'myelin' which wrap around axons to increase their speed of conduction.

Ontogeny

The development of the individual, as opposed to phylogeny, the development of the species.

Opioids

A family of peptide neurotransmitters with a major role in modulating pain. Their existence in the undoctored brain explains the effects of the opiates, like heroin, which we both prescribe and abuse.

Organelles

The residents of the interior of our cells, including the nucleus and mitochondria.

'P' cell

A parvocellular neuron: a small cell, concerned, in the visual system, with relatively slow resolution of fine detail, colour and form, as opposed to the rapid signalling of information about movement by magnocellular neurons.

P 300

A response which can be recorded from the scalp at around 300 milliseconds after a rare attended event (such as an infrequent target 'beep' in a succession of 'boops'), provided one is paying attention to the sequence.

Parietal lobe

The lobe of the brain bordered by the occipital behind, the temporal below and the frontal ahead. It contains the 'somatosensory cortex' which receives sensory information about touch and joint position, and plays a major role in our appreciation of spatial relationships.

Peptide

A short string of amino acids.

Percept

The current contents of sensory experience – what you can see (or hear or touch . . .). It is useful shorthand, but the term is fraught with scientific and philosophical ambiguity.

Peripheral nervous system

The nerves beyond the brain and spinal cord: the cranial nerves in the head, numbered 1–12, the numerous nerves in the limbs and trunk which run out to muscle and back from sense organs like those in skin and joint.

Persistent vegetative state

See Vegetative state

Photoreceptor

A cell which registers the arrival of light by modulating its neurotransmitter release: in the human eye the photoreceptors are the rods and cones of the retinae.

Phylogeny

The development of the species, as opposed to ontogeny, the development of the individual.

Physicalism

The philosophical view that reality is entirely physical.

Physiology

The study of how the body works, the functioning of its parts.

Plasticity

The capacity of the nervous system to adapt to change. Neural plasticity, the basis of learning and memory, depends mainly on the modifiability of synapses, the connections between neurons: these can multiply, wither and alter their strength according to the play of signals across them.

Pons

The central part of the brainstem, lying above the medulla and below the midbrain ('pons' from Latin for bridge, as the front view of the pons in the intact brain looks like a bridge between the two halves of the cerebellum).

Prefrontal cortex

A region of the frontal lobe which lies beyond the motor and premotor cortex. Activity in motor and premotor cortex is more or less tightly linked to the control of movement; the prefrontal cortex exerts a less direct influence on behaviour, in decision making for example.

Primary visual cortex

Also known as area V1 or the 'striate cortex', the primary visual cortex receives the bulk of input from the retinae via the lateral geniculate nucleus in the thalamus. It contains a 'map' of the visual world. In the Brodmann classification it is area 17.

Procedural memory

Memories which make themselves known by a change in performance rather than by conscious recollection. For example, the best test of whether you can ride a bike is whether you can ride one (rather than whether you can write an essay about how to ride one).

Projection

A bundle of axons conveying signals from one part of the nervous system to another: for example, there are several important projections from the brainstem to the hemispheres which influence our state of arousal.

Prosopagnosia

Loss of the ability to recognise faces (despite otherwise well-preserved visual abilities).

Protein

A molecule formed by a sequence of amino acids, specified by a gene, from the Greek for 'first things'. Proteins build, maintain, support and run the human body (under supervision from the genes which are a step further removed from the immediate business of life).

Psychosis

The group of psychiatric disorders characterised by the occurrence of delusions (fixed false beliefs) and hallucinations.

Pyramidal cells

Large cortical neurons with a pyramidal shape. Their axons leave from the base of the pyramid; their extensive dendritic trees include a major branch from the apex. Most pyramidal cells send their axons out of the immediate vicinity, into the white matter: they are therefore the 'projection' or output cells of the cerebral cortex.

Receptor

A molecule which is designed to lock on to another, with some resulting effect, like the opening of an ion channel. In neuroscience, receptors are usually on the lookout for neurotransmitters (for example the acetylcholine receptor in muscle which picks up the neurotransmitter released by a motor neuron, causing the muscle to contract).

Reductionism

The philosophical view that talk about a complex or mysterious function or entity, like a conscious state, can be reduced to talk about some simpler or better understood function or state, like activity in the brain.

Reflex epilepsy

Epilepsy regularly provoked by a particular trigger: a flashing or flickering light is a common trigger, but a wide range of activities including reading, calculating and summoning up a particular memory have been described as triggers.

REM

Rapid eye movement: one of the characteristic features of dreaming sleep.

Residual vision

Impoverished but conscious vision remaining after damage to visual areas in the brain: as opposed to blindsight which allows visually guided behaviour in the complete absence of experience.

Reticular formation

From the Latin *reticularis*, meaning net, the reticular formation is the region running the length of the brainstem which regulates functions like breathing and the heart in its lower reaches, wakefulness and arousal in its upper parts.

Retina

The region at the back of the eye on which the image formed by the lens is focused. It is made up of the rods and cones which detect the presence of light, and of several types of neurons which process the signals from the rods and cones before relaying the visual news back to the brain along the optic nerve.

Rod

One of the two cell types in the retina which detects the presence of light (the other is the cone). Rods allow grey-tone vision, of the kind we use on a moonlit night. The rods lie away from the centre of the retina.

Second messenger

A chemical generated by the activation of the family of receptors which respond to the arrival of a neurotransmitter by further chemical signalling within the cell, rather than by directly opening or closing an ion channel.

Seizure

A general term for an abrupt disturbance of experience or behaviour, often due to epilepsy.

Sensori-motor integration

The process by which the nervous system transforms sensory signals into motor outputs.

Sensory

To do with sensation: the optic nerve, for example, is a sensory nerve, conveying information about visual sensation from eye to brain.

Serotonin

A neurotransmitter originating mainly in the brainstem with an important role in regulating arousal, appetite and mood.

Sleep stages

Sleep has an internal structure: it is usually divided into four deepening stages of slow wave sleep and a further stage of 'paradoxical' or 'rapid eye movement' sleep, in which we dream.

Slow wave sleep

Sleep characterised electrically by a predominance of 'slow waves' (theta and delta rhythms). Deep slow wave sleep predominates in the early parts of the night, with increasing amounts of lighter slow wave and REM sleep as the night proceeds.

Stimulus

A term now used rather loosely to refer to the item used as the target or trigger in an experiment or of a given type of behaviour.

Striate cortex

Area VI, the primary visual area, is sometimes referred to as striate cortex: 'striate' because it is 'striped', even on close inspection by the naked eye, by the prominence of cortical layer 4 which receives dense input from the retina via the lateral geniculate nucleus.

Stroke

A general term for an episode of neurological impairment caused by death of a part of the brain due to trouble with a blood vessel (usually blockage). Stroke is very common, and much of our established knowledge of the functions of the human brain has come from studies of its effects.

Subcortical

Below the cortex: this term is used to refer to structures and processes which occur below the cortex. For example, the thalamus is an important subcortical nucleus.

Sulcus

One of the depths or valleys of the folded cerebral cortex, as opposed to its summits or 'gyri'.

Synapse

The point at which one neuron makes contact with another, usually chemical contact. This involves the release of chemical neurotransmitter by the presynaptic ('before-synaptic') cell which travels across to receptors on the surface of the post-synaptic ('after-synaptic') cell.

Synchrony

The firing of neurons in time with one another.

Syncope

From the Greek *syncoptein*, to cut, this term describes temporary loss of consciousness due to interruption of the blood supply to the brain, as in a faint.

Temporal lobe

The lowest lying lobe of the brain, above the ear, with a special importance for hearing, smell, visual recognition, language comprehension and memory.

Thalamus

A large nucleus lying at the centre of the cerebral hemispheres around the sides of the third ventricle. The thalamus receives much of the sensory information (relating to vision, hearing and touch) which eventually reaches the cerebral cortex, much of the activating input from the brainstem destined for the cortex, and transmits signals which loop between the cortex and the basal ganglia and the cortex and the cerebellum. It is therefore a microcosm of cortical activity, and damage here is keenly felt by the rest of the brain.

Theta rhythm

A slow electrical rhythm at 4–8 cycles/second which can be recorded from the scalp or brain during sleep or sometimes in coma.

Transduction

To transduce is to convert from one medium to another: the transducers of interest to us convert one form of energy – such as light impinging on the retina – to the electrical-chemical medium of signalling in the nervous system.

Vegetative state

A state of 'wakefulness without awareness' which results from major damage to the cerebral hemispheres or thalamus, with relative sparing of the brainstem. It can follow head injury or loss of the blood or oxygen supply to the brain. When the vegetative state is called 'persistent' it has been present for a while, usually more than a month.

Ventral stream

The stream of visual signalling running from the occipital to the temporal lobe, principally involved in object recognition. In contrast the dorsal stream, which runs from the occipital to the parietal lobe, is principally involved in the processing of information about space and motion.

Ventricle

One of the fluid-filled spaces at the centre of the brain. These spaces enlarge under pressure in 'hydrocephalus' (water on the brain).

Visual cortex

A general term referring to the parts of the cortex concerned with vision, including the primary visual cortex but also the 30 or so further visual areas with more or less specialised roles in visual processing.

White matter

The bundles of fibres interconnecting areas of brain are white because of the concentration of insulating myelin wrapped around axons. White matter contrasts with the 'grey matter' of the cerebral cortex and deep nuclei of the brain, which contain aggregations of neuronal cell bodies.

Notes

Introduction

1 Erwin Schrödinger, *Mind and Matter*, Cambridge: Cambridge University Press, 1977, p. 99.
2 G. K. Chesterton, *Autobiography*, London: Hutchinson, 1937, p. 32.
3 I have borrowed this memorable phrase from Thomas Nagel's book, *The View from Nowhere*, Oxford: Oxford University Press, 1986. The book is a study of the limits of objectivity.
4 Samuel Taylor Coleridge, *Biographia Literaria*, London: Everyman's Library, 1971, Chapter 13.
5 Plato, *The Apology*.
6 S. Langer, *Mind: An Essay on Human Feeling*, Vol. I, Baltimore: Johns Hopkins University Press, 1980, p. 24.

1 As sweet by any other name? Consciousness, self-consciousness and conscience

1 J. Hodges, *Cognitive Testing for Clinicians*, Oxford: Oxford University Press, 1994.
2 N. Humphrey, *Consciousness Regained*, Oxford: Oxford University Press, 1983; J. Searle, *The Rediscovery of the Mind*, Cambridge, Mass.: MIT Press, 1994; O. Flanagan, *Consciousness Reconsidered*, Cambridge, Mass.: MIT Press, 1995; D. Dennett, *Consciousness Explained*, London: The Penguin Press, 1991.
3 http://www.consciousness.arizona.edu
4 http://assc.caltech.edu/
5 See, for example, K. Wilkes, '—, yishi, duh, um and consciousness', in A.J. Marcel and E. Bisiach (eds) *Consciousness in Contemporary Science*, Oxford: Clarendon Press, 1992.
6 C.S. Lewis, *Studies in Words*, Cambridge: Cambridge University Press, 1972.
7 Ibid., Chapter 8: the quotations in this section are either from this chapter or from the *Oxford English Dictionary*.

8 W.L. Davidson, *Logic of Definition*, 1885, cited in the *Oxford English Dictionary* entry on 'consciousness'.

9 See T. Nagel, 'What is it like to be a bat', reprinted in *Mortal Questions*, Cambridge: Cambridge University Press, 1979. As Nagel acknowledges in *The View from Nowhere* (Oxford University Press, 1989), the Edinburgh-based philosopher Timothy Sprigge had previously come up with the same form of words ('an individual is . . . conscious if and only if there is something that it is like to be him or her . . .'): see T.L.S. Sprigge, 'Consciousness', *Synthèse*, 1994: 73–93.

10 G.N. Edelman, *The Remembered Present: A Biological Theory of Consciousness*, New York: Basic Books, 1988.

11 W. James, *The Principles of Psychology*, New York: Holt, 1890. His contemporary descendants include T. Shallice, 'Information-processing models of consciousness', in Marcel and Bisiach (eds) *Consciousness in Contemporary Science*; J. Searle, *The Rediscovery of the Mind*, Cambridge, Mass.: MIT Press, 1994; F. Crick, *The Astonishing Hypothesis*, London: Simon and Schuster, 1994; D. Chalmers, *The Conscious Mind*, New York: Oxford University Press, 1996; S. Greenfield, 'How might the brain generate consciousness?', in S. Rose (ed.) *From Brains to Consciousness*, Princeton, NJ: Princeton University Press, 1998; G. Tononi and G.M. Edelman, 'Consciousness and the integration of information in the brain', in H.H. Jasper, L. Descarries, V.F. Castelucci and S. Rossignol (eds) *Consciousness at the Frontiers of Neuroscience*, Philadelphia: Lipincott-Raven, 1998.

12 Nagel, 'What is it like to be a bat'.

13 G. Ryle, *The Concept of Mind*, Harmondsworth: Penguin University Books, 1978, p. 150.

14 R. Schafer quoted in R.W. Mitchell, 'Multiplicities of self', in S.T. Parker, R.W. Mitchell and M.L. Boccia (eds) *Self-awareness in Animals and Humans*, Cambridge: Cambridge University Press, 1994.

15 Alexander Pope, *The Rape of the Lock* (1714), quoted under the *Oxford English Dictionary* entry for 'conscious'.

16 R.J. Beninger et al., 'The ability of rats to discriminate their own behaviour', *Canadian Journal of Psychology*, 28 (1974): 79–91.

17 M. Merleau-Ponty, *The Child's Relation with Others*, cited in Mitchell, 'Multiplicities of self'.

18 G.G. Gallup, 'Chimpanzees: self-recognition', *Science*, 167 (1970): 86–7.

19 R. Thompson and C. Contie, 'Further lessons on mirror usage by pigeons: lessons from Winnie-the-Pooh and Pinocchio, too', in Parker et al., *Self-awareness in Animals and Humans*.

20 L. Moses, in the Foreword to *Self-awareness in Animals and Humans*.

21 Ibid.

22 M. Lewis, 'Myself and me', ibid.

23 See for example S. Baron-Cohen's *Mindblindness: An Essay on Autism and Theory of Mind*, Cambridge, Mass.: MIT Press, 1995, and C. and U. Frith, 'Interacting minds – a biological basis', *Science*, 286 (1999): 1692–5.

24 Baron-Cohen, *Mindblindness*.

25 O. Sacks, *An Anthropologist on Mars*, London: Picador, 1995.

26 Lewis Carroll, *Alice Through the Looking Glass*, London: Macmillan, 1872, Chapter 6.

27 A. Cowey and P. Stoerig, 'Blindsight in monkeys', *Nature*, 373 (1995): 247–9.

28 Genesis 3:6–7. Revised Standard Version.

29 C. Darwin, *The Descent of Man, and Selection in Relation to Sex*, London: John Murray 1871, p. 472, cited in *Self-awareness in Animals and Humans*.

30 Darwin, *Descent of Man*, p. 72.
31 This state is discussed in Chapter 4. For a brief review of the subject, see A. Zeman, 'Persistent vegetative state', *Lancet*, 350 (1997): 795–9.
32 I am very grateful to several friends and colleagues for linguistic help: Sally Laird, who told me about consciousness words in Danish and Russian, Judit Osman-Sagi who filled me in on Hungarian equivalents, Yin-Bin Ni for help with Chinese and Charles Jedrej for advice on an African language.
33 D. Brown, *Human Universals*, New York and London: McGraw-Hill, 1991.

2 'The nerves in the brain, oh damn 'em': a sketch of the human nervous system

1 Fyodor Dostoevsky, *The Brothers Karamazov*, London: Penguin Books, 1979, p. 691.
2 There are many good introductions to biology, supplying more or less detail. As a brief introduction to biochemistry Steven Rose's *The Chemistry of Life* (London: Penguin, 1991) is very readable. I enjoyed Michael Bliss Vaughan Robert's *Biology: A Functional Approach* (London: Nelson, 1980) during my time in the university museum. If you become seriously addicted, monumental textbooks await your pleasure, such as Bruce Alberts et al., *The Molecular Biology of the Cell* (New York: Garland, 2002).
3 E.R. Kandel, J.H. Schwartz and T.M. Jessell, *Principles of Neural Science* (East Norwalk, Conn.: Prentice-Hall, 1991), is a magnificent encyclopaedic survey of the field: it expands on most of the subjects discussed in this chapter (remember, however, that some of today's organising principles will prove to be tomorrow's bad mistakes).
4 Until recently the orthodox view was that neurons did not reproduce themselves after birth. But times are changing. There is now evidence for continuing generation of neurons (neurogenesis) throughout the life span. See P.S. Erikkson et al., 'Neurogenesis in the adult human hippocampus', *Nature Medicine*, 4 (1998): 1313–17, and E. Gould et al., 'Neurogenesis in the neocortex of adult primates', *Science*, 286 (1999): 548–52.
5 W.R. Wood, 'Introduction to *C. elegans* biology', in *The Nematode Caenorhabditis elegans*, Cold Spring Harbor, N.Y.: Cold Spring Harbor Laboratory, 1988.
6 See Kandel, Schwartz and Jessell, *Principles*, Chapter 65.
7 Thyroid hormones control the body's metabolic rate: an overactive thyroid makes you hot and fidgety; an underactive one makes you feel sluggish and cold.
    Adrenal hormones, 'steroids', are vital in mobilising the body's response to stress: adrenal failure, Addison's disease, renders sufferers vulnerable to collapse under stress unless the adrenal hormones are replaced artificially (they can be swallowed!).
8 Oliver Sacks' *Awakenings* (London: Picador, 1982) is a moving account of the use of L-dopa in the treatment of patients with a condition akin to Parkinson's disease, which followed the outbreak of 'encephalitis lethargica' after the First World War. This is discussed further in Chapter 3.
9 The consequences of severing the corpus callosum, producing a 'split brain', are reviewed by M. S. Gazzaniga in 'Cerebral specialisation and interhemispheric communication: does the corpus callosum enable the human condition?', *Brain*, 123 (2000): 1293–326.
10 For much more detailed discussion of vision, see Chapters 5 and 6. The issue of 'cortical localisation' is discussed further in the following chapter. It remains a

matter of debate: see for example A. Chatterjee and M. Farah, 'Face module, face network', *Neurology*, 57 (2001): 1151–2.

11 'Parallel processing' sounds more technical than it is: it implies that the brain is working on several, relatively independent streams of information at the same time – as it must be, for example, when you competently manoeuvre your car at the same time as holding a lively conversation with the friend sitting beside you.

12 A good account is to be found in Antonio R. Damasio's *Descartes' Error* (London: Picador, 1995).

13 S. Corkin, 'Lasting consequences of temporal lobectomy: clinical course and experimental findings in HM', *Seminars in Neurology*, 4 (1984): 249–59.

14 Other abilities were also spared in HM: in particular the ability to rehearse and process information over short periods ('short term' or 'working memory'), and the ability to acquire new skills ('procedural memory') – despite amnesia for the training sessions. These kinds of memory are less closely tied to the temporal lobes: working memory utilises the areas of the brain concerned with processing the information in question (e.g. language areas for verbal material) and frontal lobe regions which 'organise' working memory; procedural memories form a loose category involving a number of different brain areas (e.g. motor areas for motor memories). They are discussed further in Chapter 8.

15 The predicament of patients who are losing this database of knowledge is described by John Hodges et al., 'Semantic dementia', *Brain*, 115 (1992): 1783–806.

16 See M. Mesulam, 'From sensation to cognition' (review article), *Brain*, 121 (1998): 1013–52.

17 I am also guilty of some concealment here. This section discusses 'transmitter-gated ion channels', and receptors which activate second-messenger systems. The neuronal membrane is also host to a number of other channels which I have skipped over in the interests of (relative) simplicity. They deserve a mention, here. If the influx of charged particles through transmitter-gated channels is sufficiently brisk, another class of ion channel opens – the voltage-gated ion channel – allowing the propagation of a self-regenerating wave of excitation to travel down the cell. This is the 'action potential'. The ion primarily in question is sodium: but the opening and closing of other voltage-gated channels, for potassium, calcium and chloride, also help to shape the action potential. These channels are a favourite target for venomous beasts: puffer fish, scorpions and poisonous frogs all produce poisons which inactivate the sodium channel. They are also a target for disease: a growing family of inherited 'channelopathies' is coming to light, giving rise to disorders as various as intermittent or peristent weakness or unsteadiness, an exaggerated tendency to startle, and epilepsy. Yet other channel types are permanently open, or gated by movement impinging on the channel.

18 See S. Rose, *The Conscious Brain*, London: Penguin, 1976, p. 217.

19 See Chapter 6, p. 201–6ff.

20 In Chapters 8 and 9.

3 The springs of awareness: the structural basis of consciousness (i)

1 Sir Thomas Browne, *Christian Morals* (1716) pt. 1, xxi: 'Annihilate not the mercies of God by the Oblivion of Ingratitude. For Oblivion is a kind of Annihilation, and for things to be as though they had not been is like unto never being'. In *The Prose of Sir Thomas Browne*, New York: New York University Press, 1967.

2 H. Berger, 'Über das Elektroenkephalogramm des Menschen', *Arch Psychiatr Nervenkr*, 87 (1929): 527–70. English translations of Berger's key papers are available in *Hans Berger on the EEG of Man*, ed. and trans. P. Gloor, New York: Elsevier, 1969.

3 Quoted in S. Finger, *Origins of Neuroscience: A History of Explorations into Brain Function*, Oxford: Oxford University Press, 1994, p. 431.

4 Ibid., p. 432.

5 Johann Friedrich Blumenbach, quoted ibid.

6 Quoted in M.A.B. Brazier, *The Electrical Activity of the Nervous System*, London: Pitman Medical, 1960, p. 50.

7 Quoted in Finger, *Origins*, p. 36.

8 See F. Schiller, *Paul Broca*, Oxford: Oxford University Press, 1992, Chapter 10: 'A manner of not speaking'.

9 I have relied heavily in the rest of this section on Mary Brazier's *A History of the Electrical Activity of the Brain: The First Half Century*, London: Pitman, 1961.

10 Their various claims led to a somewhat undignified 'scramble for priority' in the following decade. Ernst Fleischl, an Austrian contender, decided to consign the record of his discovery to the vault of his academy, rather than publish it. This provoked a memorable retort from Adolf Beck, a Polish scientist: 'Nature has held and still holds in her lap innumerable riddles under the seal of secrecy. It makes no difference for science whether these riddles are kept secret under the seal of Nature herself or under that of the Imperial Academy of Sciences in Vienna. Priority for discovery, in my opinion, belongs to the one who breaks the seal . . .': from Brazier, *A History*.

11 Ibid.

12 H. Berger, 'On the electroencephalogram of man, second report', *Journal für Psychologie und Neurologie*, 40 (1930): 160–79, trans. in Gloor (ed.) *Hans Berger*.

13 For an introduction to the EEG, see F.M. Dyro, *The EEG Handbook*, Little, Brown, 1989, or for more detail, B. Fisch, *Spehlman's EEG Primer*, Elsevier, 1991.

14 See E.R. Kandel, J.H. Schwartz and T.M. Jessell, *Principles of Neural Science*, East Norwalk, Conn.: Prentice-Hall, 1991, Chapter 50.

15 M. Steriade, D.A. McCormick and T.J. Sejnowski, 'Thalamocortical oscillations in the sleeping and aroused brain', *Science*, 262 (1993): 679–85.

16 W.B. Matthews, *Practical Neurology*, Oxford: Blackwell Scientific Publications, 1975, p. 54.

17 E. Aserinsky and N. Kleitman, 'Two types of ocular motility occurring during sleep', *Journal of Applied Physiology*, 8 (1995): 1–10.

18 W. Dement and N. Kleitman, 'Cyclic variations in EEG during sleep and their relation to eye movements, body motility and dreaming', *Electroencephalography and Clinical Neurophysiology*, 9 (1957): 673–90.

19 S. Chokroverty, 'An overview of sleep', in S. Chokroverty (ed.) *Sleep Disorders Medicine*, Boston: Butterworth Heinemann, 1999. This book contains several useful

chapters summarising current knowledge of the mechanisms controlling sleep and wakefulness.

20 R. Llinas and U. Ribary, 'Coherent 40-Hz oscillation characterises dream state in humans', *Proceedings of the National Academy of Sciences USA*, 90 (1993): 2078–81.

21 T.S. Kilduff and C.A. Kushida, 'Circadian regulation of sleep', in Chokroverty (ed.) *Sleep Disorders Medicine*.

22 Brazier, *A History*.

23 M. Kutas and A. Dale, 'Electrical and magnetic readings of mental functions', in M.D. Rugg (ed.) *Cognitive Neuroscience*, Hove: Psychology Press, 1997.

24 W.B. Yeats, 'The Circus Animals' Desertion' (1936–39), in *Collected Poems*, London: Macmillan, pp. 391–2.

25 C. von Economo, *Encephalitis Lethargica: Its Sequela and Treatment*, Oxford: Oxford University Press, 1931.

26 O. Sacks, *Awakenings*, London: Picador, 1982.

27 F. Bremer, 'Cerveau "isolé" et physiologie du sommeil', *Comptes rendus de la Société de Biologie*, 102 (1929): 1235–41.

28 G. Moruzzi and H.W. Magoun, 'Brain stem reticular formation and the activation of the EEG', *Electroencephalography and Clinical Neurophysiology*, 1 (1949): 455–73.

29 N. Hofle, T. Paus, D. Reutens, P. Fiset, J. Gotman, A.C. Evans and B.E. Jones, 'Regional cerebral blood flow changes as a function of delta and spindle activity during slow wave sleep in humans', *Journal of Neuroscience*, 17 (1997): 4800–8; P. Macquet, J.M. Peters, J. Aerts, G. Delfiore, C. Degueldre, A. Luxen and G. Franck, 'Functional neuroanatomy of human rapid-eye-movement sleep and dreaming', *Nature*, 383 (1996): 163–6; P. Macquet, C. Degueldre, G. Delfiore, J. Aerts, J.M. Peters, A. Luxen and G. Franck, 'Functional neuroanatomy of human slow wave sleep', *Journal of Neuroscience*, 17 (1997): 2807–12. Interestingly, in REM sleep activity in limbic regions also increases, but activity in the prefrontal cortex declines: this meshes well with the subjective character of dreams, emotionally charged but logic-defying. Functional imaging suggests that the level of arousal during wakefulness also correlates with levels of activity in midbrain and thalamus: S. Kinomura, J. Larsson, B. Gulyas and P.E. Roland, 'Activation by attention of the human reticular formation and thalamic intralaminar nuclei', *Science*, 271 (1996): 512–15; T. Paus, R.J. Zatorre, N. Hofle, Z. Caramanos, J. Gotman, M. Petrides and A.C. Evans, 'Time-related changes in neural systems underlying attention and arousal during the performance of an auditory vigilance task', *Journal of Cognitive Neuroscience*, 9 (1997): 392–408.

30 The title of a chapter by Floyd Bloom in F.G. Worden et al. (eds) *The Neurosciences: Paths of Discovery*, Cambridge, Mass.: MIT Press, 1975.

31 R. McCarley, 'Sleep neurophysiology: basic mechanisms underlying control of wakefulness and sleep', in S. Chokroverty (ed.) *Sleep Disorders Medicine*, Boston: Butterworth Heinemann, 1999.

32 Experiments by Michel Jouvet in the 1960s revealed the role of these nuclei in orchestrating REM sleep.

33 R.K. Zoltoski, R.J. Cabeza and J.C. Gillin, 'Biochemical pharmacology of sleep', in S. Chokroverty (ed.) *Sleep Disorders Medicine*, Boston: Butterworth Heinemann, 1999.

34 T.W. Robbins and B.J. Everitt, 'Arousal systems and attention', in M.S. Gazzaniga (ed.) *The Cognitive Neurosciences*, Cambridge: MIT Press, 1993: this chapter makes the further point that learning more about the individual contributions made by the

chemical subsystems to states of awareness is likely to fractionate our concept of 'arousal' itself into more selective functions, like the ability to maintain or shift attention or the ability to mount a speedy response to a challenge.

35 Cited in A. Brodal, *Neurological Anatomy, in Relation to Clinical Medicine*, 3rd edn, Oxford: Oxford University Press, 1981, p. 447.

36 This is the explanation for the persistent vegetative state, discussed in Chapter 4.

37 M.R. Ralphs et al., 'Transplanted suprachiasmatic nucleus determines circadian period', *Science*, 247 (1990): 975–8.

38 Spindles are distinctive groups of waves occurring 12–14 times per second, which wax and wane in size over half a second or more during the earlier stages of slow wave sleep. They seem to be generated in roughly the following way. The individual cells of the reticular nucleus are equipped with a complement of ionic channels which predisposes them to fire rhythmically at the frequency of spindles, when conditions are right. Conditions are wrong while awake, because input from the activating system, particularly from cholinergic cells, inhibits these neurons. When this input falls quiet at the start of sleep, the rhythmic activities of neurons in the reticular nucleus are released. Because these cells are tightly interconnected – in a 'reticular' net – their rhythmic discharges tend to synchronise. Their output conveys a synchronised signal to the rest of the thalamus, where their axons release GABA, a neurotransmitter which consistently inhibits activity in its targets. This initially lowers the membrane potential of 'thalamocortical' cells which project to the cortex, and they in turn fall silent. Their membrane potential is further reduced by the absence of direct cholinergic input which normally activates them while we are awake. But these thalamocortical cells have their own specialised ionic gates, which eventually open in response to a lowering of the membrane potential, triggering a short burst of signals to the cortex. This gives rise to excitatory postsynaptic potentials in cortical neurons, the source of the spindles recorded in the surface EEG. Computer models which incorporate the known properties of cells in the reticular nucleus, thalamus proper and cortex predict the occurrence of oscillations like these. As sleep proceeds, the membrane potential of thalamocortical cells falls further still. This transforms their behaviour once again, and the electrical phenomena of light sleep, including spindles, are replaced by the monotonous slow waves of deep sleep.

39 James Horne's *Why We Sleep?* (Oxford: Oxford University Press, 1988) is an excellent extended discussion of the functions of sleep.

40 R. Passingham, *The Human Primate*, Oxford: Freeman, 1982, p. 230.

4 The brothers of death: pathologies of consciousness

1 Thomas Browne, *On Dreams*. In Sir Thomas Browne, *Selected Writings*, ed. Sir Geoffrey Keynes, London: Faber and Faber, 1968.

2 I was introduced to this film and to the topic of aviation neurology by my friend and colleague, Dr Colin Mumford.

3 T. Lempert and M. Bauer, 'Mass fainting at rock concerts', *New England Journal of Medicine*, 332 (1955): 1721.

4 T. Lempert, M. Bauer and D. Schmidt, 'Syncope: a videometric analysis of 56 episodes of transient cerebral hypoxia', *Annals of Neurology*, 36 (1994): 233–7. See also D. Schmidt, 'Syncopes and seizures', *Current Opinion in Neurology*, 9(1996): 78–91.

5   J. Whinnery and D. Jones, 'Recurrent +Gz induced loss of consciousness', *Aviation, Space and Environmental Medicine*, 58 (1987): 943–7; J. Whinnery, 'Observations on the neurophysiologic theory of acceleration induced loss of consciousness', *Aviation, Space and Environmental Medicine*, 60 (1989): 589–93; J. Whinnery, 'Acceleration-induced loss of consciousness: a review of 500 episodes', *Archives of Neurology*, 47 (1990): 764–76.

6   The results are summarised in J. Ernsting and P. King, *Aviation Medicine*, London: Butterworths, 1988; R.M. Harding and F.J. Mills, *Aviation Medicine*, London: BMJ Publishing Group, 1993.

7   J. Hughlings-Jackson, 'On a particular variety of epilepsy ("intellectual aura"), one case with symptoms of organic brain disease', *Brain*, 11 (1889): 179–207.

8   J. Duncan et al., *Clinical Epilepsy* (New York and London: Churchill Livingstone, 1995) is a good introduction to the subject.

9   See, for example, M. Critchley, 'Musicogenic epilepsy', *Brain*, 60 (1937): 13–27; F.M. Forster et al., 'Reflex epilepsy induced by decision making', *Archives of Neurology*, 32 (1975): 54–6; V. Ramani, 'Primary reading epilepsy', *Archives of Neurology*, 40 (1983): 39–41; P.B.C. Fenwick and E.S. Brown, 'Evoked and psychogenic epileptic seizures: I precipitation', *Acta Neurologica Scandinavica*, 80 (1989): 535–40; A. Wilkins and J. Lindsay, 'Common forms of reflex epilepsy', Chapter 11 in *Recent Advances in Epilepsy*, Volume 2, Edinburgh: Churchill Livingstone, 1985; O. Martinez, R. Reisin, F. Andermann, B.G. Zifkin and G. Sevlever, 'Evidence for reflex activation of experiential complex partial seizures', *Neurology*, 56 (2001): 121–3.

10 Critchley, 'Musicogenic epilepsy'.

11 D. Antebi and J. Bird, 'The facilitation and evocation of seizures', *British Journal of Psychiatry*, 160 (1992): 154–64.

12 Hughlings-Jackson, 'On a particular variety of epilepsy'.

13 A.Z.J. Zeman, S.J. Boniface and J.R. Hodges, 'Transient epileptic amnesia: a description of the clinical and neuropsychological features in 10 cases and a review of the literature', *Journal of Neurology, Neurosurgery and Psychiatry*, 64 (1998): 435–43.

14 Pierre Gloor has written very thoughtfully on this topic: 'Consciousness as a neurological concept in epileptology: a critical review', *Epilepsia*, 27 (186) (suppl. 2): S14–26.

15 T.M. Cox et al., 'An independent diagnosis', *British Medical Journal*, 300 (1990): 1512–14.

16 Thomas Sydenham, cited in Goodman and Gilman's *Pharmacological Basis of Therapeutics*, 9th edn, ed. J.G. Hardman and L.K. Limebird, New York and London: McGraw-Hill, 1996: Chapter 23, T. Reisine and G. Pasternak, 'Opioid analgesics and antagonists'.

17 I. Welsh, *Trainspotting*, London: Minerva, 1993, p. 177.

18 This story is entertainingly told in Jeff Goldberg's *Anatomy of a Scientific Discovery*, New York: Bantam Books, 1988.

19 Quoted in Roy Porter's *The Greatest Benefit to Mankind: A Medical History of Humanity from Antiquity to the Present*, London: HarperCollins, 1997.

20 From W.E. Henley, 'Before' ('Behold me waiting – waiting for the knife/A little while, and at a leap I storm/The thick, sweet mystery of chloroform,/The drunken dark, the little death-in-life. . . ./Here comes the basket? Thank you. I am ready./But, gentlemen my porters, life is brittle:/You carry Caesar and his fortunes – steady!'). I encountered this poem in Richard Gordon's *Literary Companion to Medicine*, London: Sinclair Stevenson, 1993.

21 For the history of anaesthesia I have relied on Chapter 13, 'History and principles of anaesthesia', by S.K. Kennedy and D.E. Longnecker in Goodman and Gilman's *Pharmacological Basis of Therapeutics*, and Porter, *The Greatest Benefit*.

22 From D.R. Laurence and P.N. Bennett, *Clinical Pharmacology*, Chapter 14, London: Churchill Livingstone, 1980.

23 M.V. Boswell and S.R. Hameroff, 'Theoretic mechanisms of general anaesthesia', Chapter 25, in *The Principles of Anesthesiology: Volume 3, Physiologic and Pharmacologic Basis of Anaesthesia*, ed. V.J. Collins, Philadelphia: Lea and Felbiger, 1996.

24 As mentioned in the previous chapter, these techniques rely on the fact that as neuronal activity increases in an area of the brain, blood flow and metabolic activity also increase. These secondary changes can be imaged using either positron emission tomography (PET), which relies on the use of a radioactive substance that is taken up selectively by active areas of brain, or functional magnetic resonance imaging (fMRI), which does without radioactivity. These methods make it possible to study human brain function in ways which would have possible only in animals 20 years ago. Their limitation is 'temporal': the changes in metabolism and blood flow which the techniques rely on are swift but not immediate, and it is not possible to track the rapid play of activity across the brain without calling on other techniques.

25 A. Fiset, P. Fiset, T. Paus, T. Daloze, P. Gilles, P. Meuret, V. Bonhomme, N. Hajj-Ali, S.B. Backman and A.C. Evans, 'Brain mechanisms of propofol-induced loss of consciousness in humans: a positron-emission tomographic study', *Journal of Neuroscience* 19 (1999): 5506–13; M.T. Alkire, R.J. Haier and J.H. Fallon, 'Toward a unified theory of narcosis: brain imaging evidence for a thalamocortical switch of the neurophysiologic basis of anaesthetic-induced unconsciousness', *Consciousness and Cognition*, 9 (2000): 370–86.

26 Perhaps especially activity in the 40Hz range: see E.R. John et al., 'Invariant reversible QEEG effects of anesthetics', *Consciousness and Cognition*, 10 (2001): 165–83.

27 Editorial: 'On being aware', *British Journal of Anaesthesia*, 51 (1979): 711–12.

28 J.G. Jones, 'Perception and memory during general anaesthesia', *British Journal of Anaesthesia*, 73 (1994): 31–7; 'Memory of intraoperative events', *British Medical Journal*, 309 (1994): 967–8. I am very grateful to Professor Gareth Jones for discussing this subject with me.

29 I.F. Russel, 'Midazolam-alfentanil: an anaesthetic? An investigation using the isolated forearm technique', *British Journal of Anaesthesia*, 70 (1993): 42–6.

30 D. Schwender, A. Kaiser, et al. 'Midlatency auditory evoked potentials and explicit and implicit memory in patients undergoing cardiac surgery', *Anesthesiology*, 80 (1994): 493–501.

31 A. Culebras, 'Neuroanatomic and neurologic correlates of sleep disturbances', *Neurology*, 42 (1992), suppl 6: 24.

32 F. Plum and J.B. Posner, *The Diagnosis of Stupor and Coma*, Philadelphia: F.A. Davis, 1982; F. Plum, 'Coma and related global disturbances of the human conscious state', in A. Peters and E.G. Jones (eds) *Cerebral Cortex*, New York: Plenum, 1991; N.D. Schiff and F. Plum, 'The neurology of impaired consciousness: global disorders and implied models', 2000:http://www.phil.vt.edu/assc/niko.html

33 'The Multi-Society Task Force on PVS I', *New England Journal of Medicine*, 330 (1994): 1499–508; 'The Multi-Society Task Force on PVS II', ibid.: 1572–1579; A. Zeman, 'Persistent vegetative state', *Lancet*, 350 (1997): 795–9.

34 C. Pallis and D.H. Harley, *ABC of Brainstem Death*, 2nd edn, London: BMJ Publications, 1996.

35 T.P. Hung and S.T. Chen, 'Prognosis of deeply comatose patients on ventilators', *Journal of Neurology, Neurosurgery and Psychiatry*, 58 (1995): 75–80.

36 J.-D. Bauby, *The Diving-Bell and the Butterfly*, London: Fourth Estate, 1997.

37 Under current British law.

38 For a recent review of thinking on this subject, see P.W. Halligan and A.S. David, *Conversion Hysteria: Towards a Cognitive Neuropsychological Account*, Hove: Psychology Press, 1999.

39 Quoted by Oliver Zangwill in his entry 'Freud on Hypnosis' in *The Oxford Companion to the Mind*, ed. R. Gregory, Oxford: Oxford University Press, 1987.

40 Virginia Woolf, *Orlando* (1928), London: Granada Publishing, 1983, p. 42.

41 Recent work casts some fascinating light on the lark. Sufferers from familial advanced sleep phase syndrome (fasps) tend to fall asleep at about 7 p.m. and rise between 2 and 4 a.m. The genetic mutation responsible for this predicament is in the hPer2 gene. This gene controls a protein known to regulate the body clock in fruit flies, hamsters, mice – and presumably man (L. Ptacek et al., 'An hPer2 phosphorylation site mutation in familial advanced sleep phase syndrome', *Science*, 291 (2001): 1040–43).

42 See S. Chokroverty (ed.) *Sleep Disorders Medicine*, Boston: Butterworth Heinemann, 1999.

43 Ibid.

44 See R. Medori et al., 'Fatal familial insomnia, a prion disease with a mutation at codon 178 of the prion protein gene', *New England Journal of Medicine*, 326 (1992): 444–9; V. Manetto et al., 'Fatal familial insomnia', *Neurology*, 42 (1992): 312–19. For a recent review of the prion disorders, see S. Prusiner, 'The Shattuck Lecture – neurodegenerative diseases and prions', *New England Journal of Medicine*, 344 (2001): 1516–26.

45 Much has been written on narcolepsy. The Chokroverty textbook already cited contains a useful chapter. Recent guidelines on the treatment of narcolepsy have been published: 'Practice parameters for the treatment of narcolepsy', *Sleep*, 24 (2001): 451–66.

46 Gelineau coined the term in his papers in the *Gazette des hopitaux de Paris* in 1880: pp. 626–8 and 635–7.

47 Documented in a series of recent papers – this is hot news: S. Nishino et al., 'Hypocretin (orexin) deficiency in human narcolepsy', *Lancet*, 355 (2000): 39–40; C. Peyron et al., 'A mutation in a case of early onset narcolepsy and a generalised absence of hypocretin peptides in human narcoleptic brains', *Nature Medicine*, 6 (2000): 991–7.

48 F.J. Zorick et al., 'Narcolepsy and automatic behaviour: a case report', *Journal of Clinical Psychiatry*, 40 (1979): 194–7.

49 Quoted in A. Bonkalo, 'Impulsive acts and confusional states during incomplete arousal from sleep: criminological and forensic implications', *Psychiatric Quarterly*, 48 (1974): 400–9.

50 Cited ibid.

51 J.D. Parkes, *Sleep and its Disorders*, London: W.B. Saunders, 1985, pp. 205–6.

52 This case is described in C. Schenk et al., 'Chronic behavioural disorders of human REM sleep: a new category of parasomnia', *Sleep*, 1986: 293–308. A recent paper describes experience of 93 such cases (E.J. Olson et al., 'REM sleep behaviour disorder: clinical, demographic and laboratory findings in 93 cases', *Brain*, 123 (2000): 331–9).

53 G. Teasdale and B. Jennett, 'Assessment of coma and impaired consciousness', *Lancet*, 2 (1974): 81–4.

54 Schwender et al., 'Midlatency auditory evoked potentials'.

55 R. Munglani et al., 'A measure of consciousness and memory during isoflurane administration: the coherent frequency', *British Journal of Anaesthesia*, 71 (1993): 633–41.

56 H. Schwilden, 'Use of the median EEG frequency and pharmacokinetics in determining depth of anaesthesia', in *Baillière's Clinical Anaesthesiology*, 3 (1989): 603–21.

57 Other EEG indices are under development, for example the 'bispectral index': see *Medical Journal of Australia*, 174 (2001): 212–13.

58 See Plum and Posner, *Diagnosis*.

59 E. Lugaresi et al., 'Endozepine stupor: recurring stupor linked to endozepine-4 accumulation', *Brain*, 121 (1998): 127–33.

60 The question of animal awareness is more fully discussed in Chapters 7 and 9.

61 Ludwig Wittgenstein, *Tractatus Logico-Philosophicus*, 1922.

5 From darkness into light: the structural basis of consciousness (ii)

1 T.S. Eliot, *The Four Quartets*, in *Collected Poems*, London: Faber and Faber, 1970.

2 This sentence is contentious. First, it minimises or ignores the role played by the external world in our experience (when I am looking at a view, the physical elements of the landscape are playing an important part in causing my experience). Second, the idea that the brain 'generates experience' begs some questions. These issues are addressed in Chapter 9.

3 T. Hughes, 'Creation', in *Tales from Ovid: Twenty-four Passages from the 'Metamorphoses'*, London: Faber and Faber, 1997.

4 D. Attenborough, *Life on Earth*, London: Reader's Digest, 1980.

5 J. Locke, *An Essay Concerning Human Understanding* (1690), II, 23, XII.

6 C. Darwin, *The Origin of Species* (1859), London: Everyman's Library, 1971, p. 167.

7 Charles Darwin, writing to Asa Gray, cited in L.V. Salvini-Plawen and E. Mayr, 'On the evolution of photoreceptors and eyes', *Evolutionary Biology*, 10 (1977): 207–63: 'The eye to this day gives me a cold shudder, but when I think of the fine known gradations, my reason tells me I ought to conquer the cold shudder'.

8 Darwin, *Origin of Species*, p. 190.

9 Salvini-Plawen and Mayr, 'On the evolution'.

10 J. Nathans, 'Moelcular biology of visual pigments', *Annual Review of Neuroscience*, 10 (1987): 163–94.

11 C.S. Zucker, 'On the evolution of eyes: would you like it simple or compound?', *Science*, 265 (1994): 742–3; G. Halder et al., 'New perspectives on eye evolution', *Current Opinion in Genetics and Development*, 5 (1995): 602–9; V. van Heyningen, 'The tale of a troublesome gene', *MRC News*, Winter 1995: 24–7. I am grateful to Dr Veronica van Heyningen in Edinburgh for her help in exploring this subject.

12 I. Droscher's *The Magic of the Senses* (London: Panther, 1971) is a wonderful study of the variety of sensory systems in the animal kingdom.

13 Darwin, *Origin of Species*, p. 167.

14 E.R. Kandel, J.H. Schwartz and T.M. Jessell, *Principles of Neural Science* (East Norwalk, Conn.: Prentice Hall, 1991) provides a good account of the basic neurobi-

ology of vision. Richard Gregory's *Eye and Brain* (2nd edn, New York, World University Library, 1973) is an excellent introduction.

15 Semir Zeki's *A Vision of the Brain* (Oxford: Blackwell Scientific Publications, 1993) is a highly readable, partly historical, account of the visual cortices. Other sources for what follows include A. Cowey, 'Cortical visual areas and the neurobiology of higher visual processes', in M. Farah and G. Ratcliff (eds) *The Neuropsychology of High-level Vision*, Hillsdale, NJ: Lawrence Erlbaum, 1994.

16 Alan Cowey's phrase in the paper above. The problems are as follows: first, the distinction between the 'M' and 'P' pathways in the cortex has proved less sharp than initially appeared, M cells providing a substantial input into the stream of signals flowing to V4. Second, the cortical visual areas are highly interconnected, suggesting interdependence: Cowey comments wryly that the diagram of their connections 'yearly grows more like the subway map of a major city without offering the same help in finding our way about'. Dorsal and ventral areas communicate by way of these connections. Finally, the role of each area of visual cortex in processing each feature of the visual scene is far from cut and dried: it may be that the functions of the visual areas often differ in degree rather than kind.

17 B. Julesz, *Foundations of Cyclopean Perception*, Chicago: University of Chicago Press, 1971.

18 Binding is discussed by C. von der Malsburg in 'Binding in models of perception and brain function', *Current Opinion in Neurobiology*, 5 (1995): 520–6; A. Treisman, 'The binding problem', *Current Opinion in Neurobiology*, 55 (1996): 171–8; W. Singer, 'Synchronisation of cortical activity and its putative role in information processing and learning', *Annual Review of Physiology*, 55 (1993): 349–74; W. Singer and C. Gray, 'Visual feature integration and the temporal correlation hypothesis', *Annual Review of Physiology*, 18 (1995): 555–86; and in note 19 below (Engel et al.). For a related approach see P. Brown and C.D. Marsden, 'What do the basal ganglia do?', *Lancet*, 351 (1998): 1801–4.

19 A.K. Engel, P. Fries, P.R. Roelfsema, P. Konig and W. Singer, 'Temporal binding, binocular rivalry, and consciousness', http://www.phil.vt.edu/ASSC/engel/engel.html 2000

20 This is explained clearly in Zeki's *Vision of the Brain*.

21 Virginia Woolf, *Orlando*, London: Granada Publishing, 1983, p. 90.

22 John Donne, 'Air and Angels'.

23 The following chapter gives several examples of ways in which recognition can break down, including the failure of our visual representations to gain access to memory.

24 This is an active area of research. The degree of separation and the explanation for it are in dispute. See for example: E.K. Warrington and T. Shallice, 'Category specific naming impairments', *Brain*, 107 (1984): 829–54; A. Damasio et al., 'A neural basis for lexical retrieval', *Nature*, 380 (1996): 499–505; J.J. Evans et al., 'Progressive prosopagnosia associated with selective right temporal lobe atrophy: a new syndrome?', *Brain*, 118 (1995): 1–13; A. Caramazza, 'The interpretation of semantic category-specific deficits: what do they reveal about the organisation of conceptual knowledge in the brain?' *Neurocase*, 4 (1998): 265–72.

25 For a useful introduction, see S.M. Kosslyn and L.M. Shin, 'Visual mental images in the brain: current issues', in Farah and Ratcliff (eds) *Neuropsychology*.

26 R.N. Shepard, 'The mental image', *American Psychologist*, 1978: 125–37.

27 S.M. Kosslyn, W.L. Thompson, I.J. Kim and N.M. Alpert, 'Topographical representations of mental images in primary visual cortex', *Nature* 378 (1995): 496–8.

28 Nancy Kanwisher has written a recent review article which offers a good introduction to her fascinating work: 'Neural events and perceptual awareness', *Cognition*, 79 (2001): 89–113.

29 A.D. Milner and M.A. Goodale, *The Visual Brain in Action*, Oxford: Oxford University Press, 1995.

30 T.H. Huxley, quoted at the opening of Milner and Goodale, *Visual Brain*.

31 Ibid., p. 52.

32 V. Gallese et al., 'Action recognition in the premotor cortex', *Brain*, 119 (1996): 593–609.

33 W. James, *The Principles of Psychology* (1890), Cambridge, Mass.: Harvard University Press, 1983, Chapter 11, p. 380.

34 G. Eliot, *Middlemarch* (1871–2), Chapter 20.

35 David LaBerge's study, *Attentional Processing* (Cambridge, Mass.: Harvard University Press, 1995), is the source of these distinctions.

36 J. Moran and R. Desimone, 'Selective attention gates visual processing in the extrastriate cortex', *Science*, 229 (1985): 782–4; S. Treue and J.R. Maunsell, 'Attentional modulation of visual motion processing in cortical areas MT and MST', *Nature*, 382 (1996): 539–41.

37 See Kanwisher's 'Neural events' for references.

38 M.I. Posner and M.E. Raichle, *Images of Mind*, New York: Scientific American Library, 1994, Chapter 7, 'Networks of attention'.

39 H. Cairns et al., 'Akinetic mutism with an epidermoid cyst of the third ventricle', *Brain*, 64 (1941): 273–90. For a more up to date account see F. Plum, 'Coma and related global disturbances of the human conscious state', in A. Peters and E.G. Jones (eds) *Cerebral Cortex*. New York: Plenum, 1991; N.D. Schiff and F. Plum, 'The neurology of impaired consciousness: global disorders and implied models', 2000:http://www.phil.vt.edu/assc/niko.html

40 For an account of change blindness, references and an introduction to a theory of vision which flows from it, see J.K. O'Regan and A.A. Noe, 'A sensorimotor account of vision and visual consciousness', *Behavioural and Brain Sciences*, 24 (5), 2001. To see Kevin O'Regan's on-line demonstrations of change blindness and for more precise details of his paper (not yet published in final form), visit http://nivea.psycho.univ-paris5.fr

41 A. Mack and I. Rock, *Inattentional Blindness*, Cambridge, Mass.: MIT Press, 2000.

42 www.wjh.harvard.edu/~viscog/grafs/demos/gorilla.mov

43 S.K. Langer, *Mind: An Essay on Human Feeling*, Baltimore: Johns Hopkins University Press, 1980, p. 24.

44 J.R. Searle, *The Rediscovery of the Mind*, Cambridge, Mass.: MIT Press, 1994, p. 131.

45 A 'bon mot' quoted by Ernst Gombrich in *Art and Illusion*, London: Phaidon Press, 1986, p. 275.

46 See ibid. and Gombrich's chapter in *Illusion in Nature and Art*, ed. R.L. Gregory and E.H. Gombrich, London: Duckworth, 1973.

6 'I cannot see you, Charley, I am blind': clear-sighted blindness and blindsight

1 Charles Dickens, *Bleak House* (1852–3), London: Penguin Books, 1981, Chapter 31, p. 497.

2 I heard, and cannot trace, this quotation from Sir William Herschel, the eighteenth-century astronomer. If anyone can point me to its source, please do!

3 Some recent light has been cast on this phenomenon by functional imaging: A.J. Goldby et al., 'Differential responses in the fusiform region to same-race and other-race faces', *Nature Neuroscience*, 4 (2001): 845–9.

4 B. Magee and M. Milligan, *On Blindness*, Oxford: Oxford University Press, 1995, p. 154.

5 R. Gregory, *Concepts and Mechanisms of Perception*, London: Duckworth, 1974, p. 108.

6 J. Locke, *Essay Concerning Human Understanding* (1960), II.ix.8.

7 Nigel W. Daw, *Visual Development*, New York and London: Plenum Press, 1995, p. 2.

8 O. Sacks, 'To see and not to see', in *An Anthropologist on Mars*, London: Picador, 1995, p. 121.

9 A. Valvo, *Sight Restoration after Long Term Blindness: The Problems and Behavior Patterns of Visual Rehabilitation*, New York: American Foundation for the Blind, 1971.

10 Gregory, *Concepts and Mechanisms*.

11 I have been guided in this section by Nigel Daw's *Visual Development*.

12 A.N. Meltzoff and M.K. Moore, 'Imitation of facial and manual gestures by human neonates', *Science*, 198 (1977): 75–8.

13 In the kitten the comparable figure at birth is 1 per cent: see Daw, *Visual Development*, p. 72.

14 The principle, introduced in Chapter 2, and reiterated a few paragraphs back, that if one neuron successfully excites another, the synaptic connection between them will be strengthened.

15 Valvo, *Sight Restoration*, p. 4.

16 Sacks in *An Anthropologist on Mars*.

17 Magee and Milligan, *On Blindness*.

18 N. Sadato et al., 'Activation of the primary visual cortex by Braille reading in blind subjects', *Nature* 380 (1996): 526–8.

19 J.P. Rauschecker, 'Compensatory plasticity and sensory substitution in the cerebral cortex', *Trends in Neurological Sciences*, 18 (1995): 36–43.

20 P. Heil et al., 'Invasion of visual cortex by the auditory system in the blind mole rat', *NeuroReport*, 2 (1991): 735–8.

21 C.A. Pallis, 'Impaired identification of faces and places with agnosia for colours', *Journal of Neurology, Neurosurgery and Psychiatry*, 18 (1955): 218–24.

22 O. Sacks, 'The case of the color blind painter', in *An Anthropologist on Mars*.

23 For a full discussion, see Semir Zeki in *A Vision of the Brain*, Oxford: Blackwell Scientific Publications, 1993. The loss of colour vision is usually in one half of the visual field only.

24 C.A. Heywood et al., 'Behavioural and electrophysiological chromatic and achromatic contrast sensitivity in an achromatopsic patient', *Journal of Neurology, Neurosurgery and Psychiatry*, 61 (1996): 638–43.

25 Quoted in S. Zeki, 'Cerebral akinetopsia (visual motion blindness)', *Brain*, 114 (1991): 811–24.

26 J. Zihl et al., 'Selective disturbance of movement vision after bilateral brain damage', *Brain*, 106 (1983): 313–40.

27 As an aside, Semir Zeki has pointed to the marked contrast between the histories of work on movement and colour perception. Early accounts of achromatopsia were highly controversial, and on the whole disbelieved, on the grounds that the striate cortex was the single centre for visual sensation. This was the prevailing view in the first part of the twentieth century: if the striate cortex was damaged, all aspects of visual sen-

sation should suffer; if not, all should be well with vision. But the solitary case report of LM, published in 1983, won ready acceptance – from scientists prepared for such a case by the recent discovery of the 'extrastriate' areas and their functional specialisation.

28 Discussed in M.J. Farah, *Visual Agnosia: Disorders of Object Recognition and What They Tell Us about Normal Vision*, Cambridge, Mass.: MIT Press, 1991.

29 See A.D. Milner and M.A. Goodale, *The Visual Brain in Action*, Oxford: Oxford University Press, 1995.

30 Quoted in Farah, *Visual Agnosia*.

31 O. Sacks, *The Man Who Mistook his Wife for a Hat*, London: Duckworth, 1985.

32 See Farah, *Visual Agnosia*.

33 See A. Young, 'Face recognition impairments', *Philosophical Transactions of the Royal Society*, series B, 335 (1992): 47–54.

34 De Renzi, cited in Farah, *Visual Agnosia*, pp. 74–5.

35 J.J. Evans et al., 'Progressive prosopagnosia associated with selective right temporal lobe atrophy', *Brain*, 118 (1995): 1–13.

36 C. Darwin, *The Expression of the Emotions in Man and Animals* (1873), Chicago: University of Chicago Press, 1965, pp. 289–90.

37 D. Brown, *Human Universals*, New York: McGraw-Hill, 1991, p. 23.

38 R. Adolphs et al., 'Impaired recognition of emotion in facial expressions following bilateral damage to the human amygdala', *Nature*, 372 (1994): 669–72; A.W. Young et al., 'Face processing impairments after amygdalotomy', *Brain*, 118 (1995): 15–24; J.S. Morris et al., 'A differential neural response in the human amygdala to fearful and happy facial expressions', *Nature*, 383 (1996): 812–15.

39 Young et al., 'Face processing impairments'.

40 Morris et al., 'Differential neural response'.

41 Andy Young has gone on to produce evidence that the perception of disgust may be dependent on activity in the basal ganglia.

42 R.M. Bauer, 'Autonomic recognition of names and faces in prosopagnosia: a neuropsychological application of the guilty knowledge test', *Neuropsychologia*, 22 (1984): 457–69.

43 J. Sergent and M. Poncet, 'From covert to overt recognition of faces in a prosopagnosic patient', *Brain*, 113 (1990): 989–1004.

44 T. Landis et al., 'Loss of topographic familiarity: an environmental agnosia', *Archives of Neurology*, 43 (1986): 132–6.

45 For more detailed background, see: I.H. Robertson and J.C. Marshall (eds) *Unilateral Neglect: Clinical and Experimental Studies*, Hove: Lawrence Erlbaum, 1993.

46 R. Tegner and M. Levander, 'Through a looking glass. A new technique to demonstrate directional hypokinesia in unilateral neglect', *Brain*, 114 (1991): 1943–51.

47 P.W. Halligan and J.C. Marshall, 'Left neglect for near but not far space in man', *Nature*, 350 (1991): 498–500.

48 J.C. Marshall and P.W. Halligan, 'Blindsight and insight in visuo-spatial neglect', *Nature*, 336 (1988): 766–7.

49 A. Berti and G. Rizzolatti, 'Visual processing without awareness: evidence from unilateral neglect', *Journal of Cognitive Neuroscience*, 4 (1992): 347–51.

50 P. Stoerig and A. Cowey, 'Blindsight in man and monkey (review article)', *Brain*, 120 (1997): 535–59.

51 Larry Weiskrantz, who coined the term blindsight and has studied it in great depth, has written an account of the subject based on his original case: L. Weiskrantz, *Blindsight: A Case Study and Implications*, Oxford: Oxford University Press, 1998. A

thorough review of the subject by Cowey and Stoerig appeared in *Brain*: Stoerig and Cowey, 'Blindsight'.

52 M.D. Sanders, E.K. Warrington, J. Marshall and L. Weiskrantz, '"Blindsight": vision in a field defect', *Lancet* (1974): 707–8.

53 Perenin and Rosetti, 1993, in Milner and Goodale, *Visual Brain*.

54 A. Cowey and P. Stoerig, 'Blindsight in monkeys', *Nature*, 373 (1995): 247–9.

55 W. Richards, 'Visual processing in scotomata', *Experimental Brain Research*, 17 (1973): 333–47.

56 C.S. Pierce and Joseph Jastrow, quoted in J. Kihlstrom et al., 'Implicit perception', in R.F Bornstein and T.S. Pittman (eds) *Perception without Awareness*, New York: Guilford Press, 1992.

57 L. Weiskrantz, 'Varieties of residual experience', *Quarterly Journal of Experimental Psychology*, 32 (1980): 365–86.

58 J. Paillard et al., 'Localisation without content: a tactile analogue of blindsight', *Archives of Neurology*, 40 (1983): 548–51.

59 J.L. Barbur, J.D.G. Watson, R.S.J. Frackowiak and S. Zeki, 'Conscious visual perception without V1', *Brain*, 16 (1993): 1293–302.

60 I have borrowed this title from Alan Cowey. See his chapter, 'Reflections on blindsight', in A.D. Milner and M.D. Rugg, *The Neuropsychology of Consciousness*, London: Academic Press, 1992.

61 Here are some pros and cons, in relation to the anatomical proposals. (1) Blindsight is blind because it depends on subcortical structures. Well, yes, it is virtually certain that the many subspecialised regions of cerebral cortex supply the rich variety of human consciousness. But we should hesitate to dismiss the contribution of subcortical centres entirely. Although subcortical activity may be insufficient for consciousness, it is clearly necessary for it. I have supplied you with plenty of evidence that the cortex is aroused by activating input from the thalamus and brainstem. In its absence, coma ensues. And in any event, the proposed inability of subcortical structures to give rise to visual consciousness cannot entirely account for the 'blindness' of blindsight. For we know that cortical activity *itself* can fail to excite consciousness, for example in prosopagnosia with preserved covert recognition. Indeed, several researchers believe that persisting activity in visual cortical areas outside V1 supplies the basis for blindsight. (2) Blindsight is blind because V1 has been destroyed. A tempting suggestion: as we saw in Chapter 5, V1 orchestrates visual processing in the cortex, receiving the bulk of the input from the LGN and sending it down parallel paths to the numerous visual areas beyond – and as one might expect, vision without V1 is at best impoverished and abnormal. But there is evidence that conscious vision of a kind can survive its destruction. GY's residual awareness of movement, the 'pinpricks' some patients detect within their scotomata, suggest that the *minimum* conditions for visual awareness do not include the integrity of V1 (and see Chapter 8 for discussion of Francis Crick's view that activity in V1 itself is *never* conscious). (3) Blindsight is blind because it involves the wrong set of cortical structures for visual consciousness. Could it be, as Milner and Goodale have argued, that the preserved abilities in blindsight depend on cortical pathways which *never* normally give rise to consciousness, because they are concerned with the automatic regulation of visually guided behaviour? On this account blindsight is blind because the occipito-temporal stream of visual processing, which does normally give rise to awareness, has fallen silent. This distinction has an intuitive appeal. But GY's conscious awareness of motion has been attributed to activity in V5 which would generally be regarded as belonging to the 'dorsal' visual stream.

62 A. Sahraie, L. Weiskrantz, J.L. Barbur, A. Simmons, S.C.R. Williams and M.J. Brammer, 'Pattern of neuronal activity associated with conscious and unconscious processing of visual signals', 94 (1997): 9406–11; J.S. Morris, A. Ohman and R.J. Dolan, 'Conscious and unconscious emotional learning in the human amygdala', *Nature*, 393 (1998): 467–70; S. Dehaene, L. Naccache, H.G. Le Clec, E. Koechlin, M. Mueller, G. Dehaene-Lambertz, P.-F. van de Moortele and D. Le Bihan, 'Imaging unconscious semantic priming', *Nature*, 395 (1998): 595–600; S. Zeki and D.H. ffytche, 'The Riddoch syndrome: insights into the neurobiology of conscious vision', *Brain*, 121 (1998): 25–45.

63 The variety and causes of visual hallucinations are reviewed in M. Manford and F. Andermann, 'Complex visual hallucinations: clinical and neurobiological insights (review article)', *Brain*, 121 (1998): 1819–40.

64 D. Ffytche, R.J. Howard, M.J. Brammer, A. David, P. Woodruff and S. Williams, 'The anatomy of conscious vision: an fMRI study of visual hallucinations', *Nature Neuroscience*, 1 (1998): 738–42.

65 T. Griffiths, 'Musical hallucinosis in acquired deafness', *Brain*, 123 (2000): 2065–76.

66 And, as imagination bodies forth
The forms of things unknown . . .
. . . and gives to airy nothing
A local habitation and a name . . .

Shakespeare, *A Midsummer Night's Dream*, V.i.

67 These might not all underpin the change in experience: some might be *secondary* effects of the neural events which are critical for awareness.

68 N.K. Logothetis and J.D. Schall, 'Neuronal correlates of subjective visual perception', *Science*, 245 (1989): 761–3; D.A. Leopold and N.K. Logothetis, 'Activity changes in early visual cortex reflect monkeys' percepts during binocular rivalry', *Nature*, 379 (1996): 549–53.

69 A.K. Engel, P. Fries, P.R. Roelfsema, P. Konig and W. Singer, 'Temporal binding, binocular rivalry, and consciousness'. http://www.phil.vt.edu/ASSC/engel/engel. html 2000

70 For an excellent review of this and related work, see Geraint Rees, 'Neuroimaging of visual awareness in patients and normal subjects', *Current Opinion in Neurobiology*, 11 (2001): 150–6.

71 J.Z. Young, *Programs of the Brain*, Oxford: Oxford University Press, 1978, p. 57.

72 Bishop Berkeley, *Three Dialogues between Hylas and Philonous*, London: Fontana, 1975. Second dialogue (1725), p. 197.

73 These thought experiments originate with Frank Jackson and Thomas Nagel: they are discussed in more detail in Chapter 9.

74 D. Dennett, *Consciousness Explained*, London: Penguin, 1991, p. 434.

7 The history of everything

1 A. Michaels, *Fugitive Pieces*, London: Bloomsbury, 1996, pp. 176–7.

2 Two very readable books introduced me to these ideas: L.S. Shklovskii and C. Sagan, *Intelligent Life in the Universe*, London: Picador, 1977; S. Weinberg, *The First Three Minutes*, London: Fontana, 1978.

3 Alexander Pope, *An Essay on Man*, 1733–4, Epistle ii, i.1.

4 Gerard Manley Hopkins, 'Pied Beauty', in *Poems*, Oxford University Press, 1930.

5 Stephen Jay Gould, *Wonderful Life*, London: Penguin, 1989, p. 319.

6 Steven Rose, *The Chemistry of Life*, London: Penguin, 1991.

7 Needless to say, the details of this process remain a focus of research and debate. I have relied on elementary sources including M.B.V. Roberts, *Biology: A Functional Approach* (Nelson, 1980) and David Attenborough's *Life on Earth* (Reader's Digest, 1980).

8 Whether the eukaryotes evolved from the prokaryotes is a moot point. I have followed the traditional account of early life. But recent thinking on the 'Last Universal Common Ancestor' (or LUCA) has suggested that the traditional story may have it backwards: that prokaryotic bacteria evolved from eukaryotic cells. A brief survey of the evidence supporting this view is given by M. Ridley in 'The search for LUCA', *Natural History*, 109:9 (2000): 82–5.

9 Absorbingly described in Stephen Jay Gould's *Wonderful Life*.

10 Sylvia Plath, 'The Manor Garden' (1959), in *The Colossus*, London: Faber and Faber, 1972.

11 W.H. Auden, *Collected Shorter Poems 1927–1957*, London: Faber and Faber, 1966, p. 190.

12 Stephen Jay Gould in *Eight Little Piggies*, London: Jonathan Cape, 1993.

13 T.H. Huxley, *Six Lectures to Workingmen*, 1860, cited by H. Jerison, Chapter 12, 'The evolution of biological intelligence', in *Handbook of Human Intelligence*, Cambridge: Cambridge University Press, 1982, p. 723.

14 My sources in this section include E.A. Arbas, 'Evolution in nervous systems', *Annual Review of Neuroscience*, 14 (1991): 9–38; H. Jerison, *Evolution of the Brain and Intelligence*, New York: Academic Press, 1973; Jerison, 'The evolution of human intelligence', in *Handbook of Human Intelligence*; R.G. Northcutt, 'Evolution of the vertebrate brain', in G. Adelman (ed.) *Encyclopaedia of Neuroscience*, Boston, Mass.: Birkhauser, 1987. I am grateful to Dr Matthew Freeman in Cambridge for alerting me to some of these sources.

15 The octopus' eye provides a famous example of convergent evolution: it looks very much like a vertebrate eye, but it differs in telling details, and in fact followed an almost entirely separate evolutionary path, converging on similar design.

16 Arbas, 'Evolution'.

17 See Jerison, 'The evolution of human intelligence'; Northcutt, 'Evolution of the vertebrate brain'; and R. Passingham, *The Human Primate*, Oxford: Freeman, 1982.

18 Jerison, 'The evolution of biological intelligence', p. 723.

19 Passingham, *The Human Primate*, Chapter 5.

20 Jerison, 'The evolution of biological intelligence', p. 742.

21 Passingham, *The Human Primate*, Chapter 4. This view has been questioned. Terence Deacon argues in *The Symbolic Species* (London: Penguin Books, 1997) that the prefrontal cortex is disproportionately enlarged in man. It may prove that more subtle features distinguish human and monkey or hominoid brains – for example the numbers of branches and spines on the dendrites of pyramidal cells in the prefrontal cortex (G.N. Elston et al., 'The pyramidal cell in cognition', *Journal of Neuroscience*, 21 (2001): RC163(1–5).

22 The tree of man was never quiet:
   Then 'twas the Roman, now 'tis I.
   A.E. Housman, *A Shropshire Lad*, XXXI in *Collected Poems*, London: Jonathan Cape, 1982.

23 Aristotle, quoted in Jerison, 'The evolution of biological intelligence', p. 727.

24 *The Cambridge Encyclopaedia of Human Evolution*, Cambridge: Cambridge University Press, 1992. I have relied on this, together with Richard Passingham's *The Human Primate*, in this section. There are a number of excellent popular accounts of the story of human evolution, which is of course liable to change considerably as new fossils are unearthed. Another readable version is given in *Origins Reconsidered* by Richard Leakey and Roger Lewin (London: Little, Brown, 1994).

25 Don Johanson wrote an accessible account of this discovery in *Lucy: The Beginnings of Humankind*, London: Granada, 1981.

26 C. Stringer and C. Gamble, *In Search of the Neanderthals*, London: Thames and Hudson, 1993; E. Trinkaus and P. Shipman, *The Neandertals*, London: Jonathan Cape, 1993.

27 T.H. Huxley quoted in ibid., p. 81.

28 Richard Passingham's *The Human Primate* gives an excellent account.

29 Ibid., p. 233.

30 L. Cavalli-Sforza, 'Genes, peoples and languages', *Scientific American*, November 1991: 72–8.

31 Or indeed the difference between a chimp and an insectivore such as the shrew. See Passingham, *The Human Primate*, pp. 78 and 90.

32 P. Roth, *The Anatomy Lesson*, London: Cape, 1984.

33 E. Schrödinger, *Mind and Matter*, Cambridge: Cambridge University Press, 1977, p. 103.

34 R. Descartes, *Discourse on Method* (1637), London: Penguin Books, 1976, p. 76.

35 J. Searle, *The Rediscovery of the Mind*, Cambridge, Mass.: MIT Press, 1994, pp. 74 and 89.

36 M. Mesulam, 'From sensation to cognition (review article)', *Brain*, 121 (1998): 1013–52.

37 Jerison, 'The evolution of biological intelligence', p. 764.

38 Panpsychists, who believe that every kind of matter has an 'inner' or mental aspect, do not accept that consciousness is restricted to creatures with nervous systems. They take the view that consciousness exists in an 'atomic' form in association with every particle of matter. This view has its attractions: in particular, it is far from clear how or why complex aggregations of matter should come to possess consciousness if their smallest parts do not (unless one accepts a behavioural or functional definition of consciousness). These issues are taken further in Chapters 8 and 9.

39 See Passingham, *The Human Primate*, pp. 136–41.

40 See Jerison, 'The evolution of biological intelligence', p. 778.

8 Scientific theories of consciousness

1 See, for example, L.R. Squire, S. Zola-Morgan, C.B. Cave, F. Haist, G. Musen and W.A. Suzuki, 'Memory: organisation of brain systems and cognition', *Cold Spring Harbor Symposia on Quantitative Biology*, 55 (1990): 1007–23.

2 A psychosis is a psychiatric disorder characterised by the occurrence of delusions (fixed false beliefs) and hallucinations.

3 T.E. Feinberg, R.J. Schindler, N.G. Flanagan and L.D. Haber, 'Two alien hand syndromes', *Neurology*, 42 (1992): 19–24; S. Della Sala, C. Marchetti and H. Spinnler, 'The anarchic hand: a fronto-mesial sign', in F. Boller and J. Grafmann (eds) *Handbook of Neuropsychology*, Vol. 9, Amsterdam: Elsevier Science, 1994.

4 R.E. Clark and L.R. Squire, 'Classical conditioning and brain mechanisms: the role of awareness', *Science*, 280 (1998): 77–81.

5 R.L. Buckner and W. Koutstaal, 'Functional neuroimaging studies of encoding, priming, and explicit memory retrieval', *Proceedings of the National Academy of Sciences USA*, 95 (1998): 891–8.

6 R.J. Haier, B.V. Siegel, A. MacLachlan, E. Soderling, S. Lottenberg and M.S. Buchsbaum, 'Regional glucose metabolic changes after learning a complex visuospatial/motor task: a positron emission tomographic study', *Brain Research*, 57 (1992): 134–43.

7 R. Passingham, 'Functional organisation of the motor system', in R.S.J. Frackowiack, K.J. Friston, C.D. Frith, R.J. Dolan and J.C. Mazziotta (eds) *Human Brain Function*, San Diego: Academic Press, 1997; S.E. Petersen, H. Van Mier, J.A. Fiez and M.A. Raichle, 'The effects of practice on the functional anatomy of task performance', *Proceedings of the National Academy of Sciences USA*, 95 (1998): 853–60; M.E. Raichle, 'The neural correlates of consciousness: an analysis of cognitive skill learning', *Philosophical Transactions of the Royal Society London*, Series B 353 (1998): 1889–901.

8 These analogies are lucidly discussed by C. Frith, R. Perry and E. Lumer, 'The neural correlates of conscious experience: an experimental framework', *Trends in Cognitive Sciences*, 3 (1999): 105–14.

9 John Keats, 'Ode on a Grecian Urn', in *The Poetical Works of John Keats*, Oxford: Oxford University Press, 1962.
   Heard melodies are sweet, but those unheard
      Are sweeter; therefore, ye soft pipes, play on;
   Not to the sensual ear, but, more endear'd,
      Pipe to the spirit ditties of no tone . . .

10 I explored this problem in a talk at Tucson 2000: 'The problem of unreportable consciousness', Abstract 96 in *Toward a Science of Consciousness*, Tucson 2000, *Consciousness Research Abstracts*.

11 Cf. J. Searle: '. . . there is no way I can observe someone else's consciousness as such', *The Rediscovery of the Mind*, Cambridge, Mass.: MIT Press, 1994, p. 97.

12 The underlying problem here has been well defined by Merikle: there is no 'exhaustive measure that exclusively indexes relevant conscious perceptual experiences' (from P.M. Merikle and E.M. Reingold, 'Measuring unconscious perceptual processes', in R.F. Bornstein and T.S. Pittman (eds) *Perception without Awareness*, New York: Guilford Press, 1992). The discussion here focuses on the lack of an *exhaustive* measure. The difficulty of finding an *exclusive* measure is a different one: apparent evidence for consciousness may sometimes be contaminated by the output of unconscious processes. A further problem which I have not raised here is that evidence for consciousness may be ambiguous: what is one to conclude if two different modes of report yield different answers to the question of whether an event has or has not been detected? This problem is discussed by Eduardo Bisiach in 'The (haunted) brain and consciousness', his chapter in *Consciousness in Contemporary Science*, ed. A.J. Marcel and E. Bisiach, Oxford: Oxford Science Publications, 1992.

13 This line of thought raises the possibility of an alternative interpretation of blindsight – rather regrettably, as blindsight seems to provide such promising data for the scientific exploration of consciousness. The alternative possibility is this: might the visual processing which guides accurate 'guessing' in blindsight be conscious,

but so isolated from the mainstream of consciousness that it is unable to make its consciousness known?

14 D. Hebb, *The Organisation of Behaviour: A Neuropsychological Theory*, New York: John Wiley, 1949.

15 Edelman and his group have published prolifically. *Bright Air, Brilliant Fire* (London: Penguin, 1992) is a fairly accessible account of Edelman's views from his own pen; in 'Consciousness and the integration of information in the brain' (in H.H. Jasper, L. Descarries, V.F. Castelucci and S. Rossignol (eds) *Consciousness at the Frontiers of Neuroscience*, Philadelphia: Lippincott-Raven, 1998) Edelman's collaborator Giulio Tononi gives a succinct outline of their theory. An alternative version is to be found in G. Tononi and G.M. Edelman, 'Consciousness and complexity', *Science*, 282 (1998): 1846–51.

16 Like Edelman, Crick has written a popular introduction to the science of consciousness: *The Astonishing Hypothesis* (London: Simon and Schuster, 1994). An updated and slightly more technical version of these views can be found in C. Koch, 'The neuroanatomy of visual consciousness', in Jasper et al., *Consciousness at the Frontiers of Neuroscience*.

17 F.H.C. Crick and C. Koch, 'Are we aware of neural activity in primary visual cortex?', *Nature*, 375 (1995): 121–4.

18 A.D. Milner, 'Cerebral correlates of visual awareness', *Neuropsychologia*, 33 (1995): 1117–30.

19 Larry Weiskrantz's ideas are spelt out most fully in his book, *Consciousness Lost and Found* (Oxford: Oxford University Press, 1997).

20 D.M. Rosenthal, 'Two concepts of consciousness', *Philosophical Studies*, 1986: 329–59.

21 See J. Gray's 'Abnormal contents of consciousness: the transition from automatic to controlled processing', in Jasper et al., *Consciousness at the Frontiers of Neuroscience*.

22 See A. Damasio's 'A neurobiology for consciousness', in T. Metzinger, *Neural Correlates of Consciousness: Empirical and Conceptual Questions*, Cambridge, Mass.: MIT Press, 2000.

23 S. Zeki and A. Bartels, 'The asynchrony of consciousness', *Proceedings of the Royal Society of London*, 265 (1998): 1583–5.

24 See A.K. Engel, P. Fries, P.R. Roelfsema, P. Konig and W. Singer, 'Temporal binding, binocular rivalry, and consciousness', http://www.phil.vt.edu/ASSC/engel/engel.html 2000

25 R. Llinas and U. Ribary, 'Coherent 40-Hz oscillation characterises dream state in humans', *Proceedings of the National Academy of Science, USA*, 90 (1993): 2078–81.

26 E.R. John et al., 'Invariant reversible QEEG effects of anaesthetics', *Consciousness and Cognition*, 10 (2001): 165–83.

27 P. Brown and C.D. Marsden, 'What do the basal ganglia do?', *Lancet*, 351 (1998): 1801–4.

28 E.R. John, 'A field theory of consciousness', *Consciousness and Cognition*, 10 (2001): 184–213.

29 R. Llinas et al. 'The neuronal basis for consciousness', *Philosophical Transactions of the Royal Society of London*, Series B, 353 (1998): 1841–9.

30 J.R. Searle, 'Consciousness', *Annual Review of Neuroscience*, 23 (2000): 557–78.

31 Roger Penrose has developed his ideas in two books, *The Emperor's New Mind* and *Shadows of the Mind*, both Oxford: Oxford University Press, 1994. A succinct

account is given in his chapter in the collection of essays edited by Steven Rose, *From Brains to Consciousness*, Oxford: Oxford University Press, 1998.

32 P.N. Johnson-Laird, 'A computational analysis of consciousness', in Marcel and Bisiach, *Consciousness in Contemporary Science*.

33 B. Baars, *A Cognitive Theory of Consciousness*, Cambridge: Cambridge University Press, 1988. A brief account is given in B. Baars and K. McGovern, 'Cognitive views of consciousness', in M. Velmans (ed.) *The Science of Consciousness*, London: Routledge, 1996.

34 Rose in *From Brains to Consciousness*.

35 N. Humphrey in 'Nature's psychologists', *New Scientist*, 29 June (1978): 900–3.

36 W.H. Auden, 'Heavy date', in *Collected Shorter Poems 1927–1957*, London: Faber and Faber, 1966, p. 154.

37 This point has been developed by Kevin O'Regan as the idea of 'the world as outside memory' in his paper, J.K. O'Regan and A.A. Noe, 'A sensorimotor account of vision and visual consciousness', *Behavioural and Brain Sciences*, 24 (5) (2001); the Introduction to Daniel Dennett's *Consciousness Explained* (London: Penguin, 1991) vividly draws attention to the superiority of vision over imagination.

38 A point made by Wolf Singer, a scientist associated with work on neural synchronisation, in his essay 'Consciousness from a neurobiological perspective', in Rose, *From Brains to Consciousness*.

39 See S. Pinker, *The Language Instinct: The New Science of Language and the Mind*, London: Allen Lane, 1994.

40 Humphrey, 'Nature's psychologists'.

9 The nature of consciousness

1 T. Nagel, 'What is it like to be a bat?', in *Mortal Questions*, Cambridge: Cambridge University Press, 1979, p. 170.

2 D. Dennett, *Consciousness Explained*, London: Penguin, 1991, p. 447.

3 Nagel, 'What is it like to be a bat?'

4 F. Jackson, 'Epiphenomenal qualia', *Philosophical Quarterly*, 32 (1982): 127–36.

5 Dennett, *Consciousness Explained*, p. 401.

6 D. Chalmers, *The Conscious Mind*, Oxford: Oxford University Press, 1996, p. 95.

7 Dennett, *Consciousness Explained*, p. 406.

8 Chalmers, *Conscious Mind*, p. 95.

9 Dennett, *Consciousness Explained*, p. 398.

10 Chalmers, *Conscious Mind*, p. 94.

11 Ibid., p. 95.

12 R. Descartes, *Discourse on Method* (1637), London: Penguin Books, 1976, p. 54.

13 Ibid., p. 52.

14 Ibid., p. 54.

15 Descartes' hidden agenda may have been to open the material world up to science, leaving only the soul to religion (cf. J. Searle, 'Consciousness', *Annual Review of Neuroscience*, 23, 2000: 557–78) : but the study of consciousness fell foul of this division of the intellectual spoils.

16 Chalmers, *Conscious Mind*.

17 Ibid., p. 225. The definition of (awareness*) is reminiscent of the functions of Baars' global workspace.

18 Ibid., p. 222.

19 C. McGinn, 'Can we solve the mind–body problem?', in *The Problem of Consciousness*, Oxford: Blackwell, 1991, p. 1.

20 Ibid.

21 J. Searle, *The Rediscovery of the Mind*, Cambridge, Mass.: MIT Press, 1994, p. 1.

22 Searle: his views are given in full in *The Rediscovery of the Mind*. In his recent article 'Consciousness' he gives a succinct account with interesting reflections on recent scientific theories of consciousness. Searle gives his reasons here for preferring 'field theories' to 'building block theories' of consciousness.

23 Searle, *Rediscovery of the Mind*, p. 95.

24 Ibid., p. 97.

25 Ibid., p. 95.

26 Ibid., pp. 92–3.

27 Ibid., p. 14.

28 Dennett, *Consciousness Explained*, p. 37.

29 Searle, *Rediscovery of the Mind*, p. 30.

30 The psychologists associated with behaviourism include J.B. Watson and B.F. Skinner. Gilbert Ryle's *The Concept of Mind* (London: Penguin University Books, 1973) tries to explain mental states in terms of behaviour and dispositions to behave in certain ways.

31 See P. Churchland, *Matter and Consciousness*, Cambridge, Mass.: MIT Press, 1993, pp. 26–35.

32 Dennett, *Consciousness Explained*, p. 367.

33 Ibid., p. 210.

34 J.K. O'Regan and A. Noe, 'A sensorimotor account of vision and visual consciousness', *Behavioural and Brain Sciences*, 24 (5), 2001.

35 Dennett, *Consciousness Explained*, p. 216.

36 Chalmers, *Conscious Mind*, p. iv.

37 Dennett, *Consciousness Explained*, p. 71.

38 Ibid., p. 434.

39 P. Strawson, 'Self, mind and body', in *Freedom and Resentment*, London: Methuen, 1974.

40 There are two excellent studies of this question: D.R Griffin, *The Question of Animal Awareness*, Los Altos: William Kaufman, 1981; and M. Stamp Dawkins, *Through our Eyes Only? The Search for Animal Consciousness*, Oxford: Oxford University Press, 1998.

41 A. Turing, 'Computing machinery and intelligence', *Mind*, 59 (236) (1950).

42 J.-D. Bauby, *The Diving-Bell and the Butterfly*, London: Fourth Estate, 1997.

43 H. Keller, *The Story of my Life*, New York: Doubleday, 1903.

44 C. Diorio and R.P.N. Rao, 'Computational neuroscience: neural circuits in silicon', *Nature*, 405 (2000): 891–2.

45 See Chapter 8, note 31.

46 An accessible introduction to the debate on whether computers might become conscious was published in *Scientific American* a few years ago: J.R. Searle, 'Is the brain's mind a computer program?' and P.M. Churchland and P. Smith Churchland, 'Could a machine think?', *Scientific American*, January 1990: 20–31.

47 Turing, 'Computing machinery'.

48 L.S. Shklovskii and C. Sagan, *Intelligent Life in the Universe*, London: Picador, 1977. The Drake equation attempts to estimate the number of communicative civilisations,

N, elsewhere in the universe: $N = R^* \times fp \times ne \times fl \times fi \times ft \times L$ where R^* is the rate of formation of suitable sun-like stars, **fp** the fraction of these stars with planets, **ne** the number of suitable planets per planetary system, **fl** the fraction of those planets where life develops, **fi** the fraction of these where intelligent life forms evolve, **ft** the fraction of these where technology develops and **L** the lifetime of communicating civilisations. The result depends on the assumptions made! On plausible assumptions, Jodrell Bank Observatory suggests that the number of communicating civilisations within 200 light years is likely to be between 10 and 10,000 (Jodrell Bank Observatory web site).

49 T. Nagel, *The View from Nowhere*, Oxford: Oxford University Press, 1986, p. 113.
50 Quoted in D. Dennett, *Elbow Room*, Cambridge, Mass.: MIT Press, 1996, p. 50.
51 Giulio Tononi has tried to define the complexity of the brain mathematically. His approach takes account of brain activity as well as brain design. In Tononi's view the essence of the brain's complexity is its combination of markedly segregated local activity with a high degree of global interaction. See: G. Tononi et al., 'A measure for brain complexity: relating functional segregation and integration in the nervous system', *Proceedings of the National Academy of Sciences, USA*, 91 (1994): 5033–7, and G. Tononi and G.M. Edelman, 'Consciousness and complexity', *Science*, 282 (1998): 1846–51.
52 Dennett, *Elbow Room*, p. 77.
53 Thomas Nagel discusses this view in *The View from Nowhere*, Chapter 7.
54 K.R. Popper and J.C. Eccles, *The Self and its Brain*, New York: Springer, 1977. Popper and Eccles make a case for dualism, with interaction of the physical world and the conscious self. This opens the way to claims of 'radical freedom' – at least from the laws which govern the physical world.
55 P.F. Strawson, 'Freedom and resentment', in *Freedom and Resentment and Other Essays*, London: Methuen, 1974.
56 Nagel, *The View from Nowhere*, p. 118.

Epilogue

1 W.H. Auden, 'The Sea and the Mirror', Preface, in *Collected Longer Poems*, London: Faber and Faber, 1968.
2 J. Locke, *An Essay Concerning Human Understanding*, Book Two, Chapter 1: 22, edited by A.D. Woozley, London: Fontana, 1975.

Suggestions for further reading

The literature relevant to consciousness is huge. The detailed references in the Notes should help anyone who wishes to pursue specific points. The suggestions below are some personal favourites.

General and cognitive neuroscience
E.R. Kandel, J.H. Schwartz and T.M. Jessel's *Principles of Neural Science* (East Norwalk, Conn.: Prentice-Hall, 1991) and the long chapter in *Gray's Anatomy*, edited by Peter L. Williams (38th edn, Edinburgh: Churchill Livingstone, 1995), on the nervous system are encyclopaedic summaries of neuroscience. Michael S. Gazzaniga, Richard B. Ivry and George R. Mangun's *Cognitive Neuroscience* (New York: W.W. Norton, 2002) focuses on the neuroscience which is most relevant to consciousness.

Clinical neurology
Although his cases are scarcely the everyday business of neurology, Oliver Sacks' case studies (in *The Man Who Mistook his Wife for a Hat* (London: Duckworth, 1985) and *An Anthropologist on Mars* (London: Picador, 1995)) are wonderfully sympathetic accounts of the strange effects of neurological disorders on experience and behaviour.

Vision
Semir Zeki's *A Vision of the Brain* (Oxford: Blackwell Scientific Publications, 1993) and A. David Milner and Mel A. Goodale's *The Visual Brain in Action* (Oxford: Oxford University Press, 1995) are excellent introductions to the neurology and neuropsychology of vision. Richard Gregory's *Eye and*

Brain (2nd edn, New York: World University Library, 1973) ranges widely over the subject.

Human evolution
The Cambridge Encyclopaedia of Human Evolution (Cambridge: Cambridge University Press, 1992) is a good place to browse. Richard Passingham's *The Human Primate* (Oxford: Freeman, 1982) is a lucid study of the differences between ape and man. *Origins Reconsidered* by Richard Leakey and Roger Lewin (London: Little, Brown, 1994) tells the (constantly changing) story of human evolution well. Robin Dunbar's *Grooming, Gossip and the Evolution of Language* (London: Faber and Faber, 1996) is a thought-provoking and entertaining study of the coevolution of brain and language.

The science of consciousness
Consciousness Lost and Found (Oxford: Oxford University Press, 1997) by Larry Weiskrantz, the leading authority on blindsight, is a highly readable introduction to the neuropsychology of consciousness. Francis Crick's *The Astonishing Hypothesis* (London: Simon and Schuster, 1994) and Gerald Edelman's *Bright Air, Brilliant Fire* (London: Penguin, 1992) are introductions to neuroscience of relevance to consciousness, intended for a general audience. There are numerous collections of essays: H.H. Jasper, L. Descarries, V.F. Castelucci and S. Rossignol (eds) *Consciousness at the Frontiers of Neuroscience* (Philadelphia: Lipincott-Raven, 1998) is a particularly high-quality recent collection.

The philosophy of consciousness
Among recent books, Daniel Dennett's *Consciousness Explained* (London: The Penguin Press, 1991), John Searle's *The Rediscovery of the Mind* (Cambridge, Mass.: MIT Press, 1994) and David Chalmers' *The Conscious Mind* (New York: Oxford University Press, 1996) are good places to start. Erwin Schrödinger's *Mind and Matter* (Cambridge: Cambridge University Press, 1977) is a quirky classic which deserves to be more widely known.

Fiction
David Lodge's *Thinks* (London: Penguin Books, 2002) is a very funny fictional treatment of many of the ideas discussed in this book.

Figures and tables

Index